THE 1998-99
HOCKEY ANNUAL

THE 1998-99
HOCKEY ANNUAL

MURRAY TOWNSEND

Warwick Publishing
Toronto Los Angeles
www.warwickgp.com

Published by Warwick Publishing Inc.
• 388 King Street, Toronto, ON M5V 1H3
• 1300 North Alexandria Avenue, Los Angeles, CA 90027

ISBN: 1-894020-41-3

Front cover photograph: Dan Hamilton, Vantage Point Studios
Design: Heidi L. Gemmill

Distributed in the United States and Canada by:
Firefly Books Ltd.
3680 Victoria Park Avenue
Willowdale, On
M2H 3K1

Printed in Canada.

Contents

Introduction

I've been to hockey hell and I've been to hockey heaven. Both of them last season.

Hockey hell is a season that goes way too long when it doesn't need to. It's poor Olympic performances by both Canadian and American teams, and it's the fact that too many teams now have to build their clubs on the basis of player salary demands rather than the talent they can put together.

Hockey heaven is working in The Hockey Night in Canada studio during the playoffs and being able to watch every single game at the same time, especially in the first round. Hockey heaven is a full slate of regular season games on a given night, and watching all the scores and scorers come in on the internet, while listening to the broadcast of any game I choose. Hockey heaven is around July 15 when I finish this book and can hardly wait for the season to start. Future hockey heaven is October 9 when this year's NHL schedule gets underway.

A couple notes about the content of the book. I rarely mention salaries because the only one that interests me is my own. As to types of injuries, forget it. I don't remember what they are and can rarely pronounce them, much less spell them. I usually just say a player was out with injuries, that's it. For free

agents, I will note them if they're unrestricted. Restricted free agents are anything but free, so I don't add the qualifier.

Thanks to my daughters, Holly and Heather, for putting up with my summer time constraints, which generally means they had to walk a few more places rather than get a drive. Thanks to my ladyfriend, Janis, who was much more helpful and understanding with my time problems this year, although come to think of it, I don't know whether that's good or bad. And to her kids, Laura and Brad.

An extra special thank-you to my father, once again. Without him, I wouldn't be able to wake up every single morning and look forward to working. There's nothing better than that.

Thanks to friend and The Hockey News editor Steve Dryden, the second hardest working person I know, and the single most inspirational factor to me since day one.

And thanks to the Warwick Publishing staff of Nick Pitt, Jim Williamson, Kimberley Young and Heidi Gemmill.

The format of the book is changed slightly from last year, but we're always looking to improve. If you have any comments, suggestions, or questions you can E-Mail me at mtownsend@mailserv.interhop.net.

EASTERN
CONFERENCE

Boston Bruins

The Bruins won the honor of being the NHL's most improved team last season. They managed to earn 30 points more than in 1996-97. Ironically, that's the exact same number of points that they declined by the season before.

Most Improved Teams:

	1996-97 Points	1997-98 Points	Improvement
Boston	61	91	+30
Los Angeles	67	87	+20
Washington	75	92	+17

So, what was so different about the Bruins last year? Why were they able to improve so much?

1. Emergence of Jason Allison - See analysis in the forward section for the most improved players in the league last season.

2. New Coach Pat Burns - He's done this before — join a new team and take them to a considerably higher level. He's also done this before: invoke a defense-first policy that works.

3. Balanced Scoring - The Bruins had seven players with at least 15 goals. That was tied for second most in the league, behind Carolina. The Hurricanes didn't make the playoffs, so you might wonder what's so great about balanced scoring. How about the fact that the team the Bruins were tied with was Detroit.

4. Good Rookie Season by Sergei Samsonov - At the start of the year, the Bruins had all kinds of rookie candidates. Four of them played regularly, and one stood out. Samsonov got off to a slow start, but came on as the season progressed, and he got a spot on the number one line with Dmitri Khristich and Allison.

5. Solid Goaltending - Not Jim Carey, as originally thought, but Byron Dafoe. A team would like to have spectacular goaltending, but solid goaltending is the next best thing.

6. Dmitri Khritich Trade - The Bruins traded Josef Stumpel, Sandy Moger and a fourth round draft pick to Los Angeles for Khristich and Dafoe, just prior to the start of the season. Stumpel led the Kings in scoring, but Dafoe and Khristich were integral parts of the Bruins season, meaning that both teams benefitted from the deal.

7. Stayed Healthier - Two years ago, the Bruins lost 395 man-games due to injury, with only two players playing in more than 72 of the 82 games. Last year, five players played in every single game, and 11 appeared in 77 or more games.

All those improvements, however, did not add up to any playoff success. They lost 4-2 to Washington in the first round, but as it turned out there was no shame in that.

STUFF

* Ray Bourque received the first game misconduct of his career last season, in his 1,341st game. Then, he earned another one later in the season.
* Bourque logged more ice-time than any other player in the league.
* Adam Oates tied Wayne Gretzky for the longest assist streak of the year, eight games. Oates has the second longest assist streak in NHL history, 18 games for Boston in 1992-93. Gretzky has the longest, at 23 games.
* Harry Sinden was named *The Hockey News* Executive of the Year.

TEAM PREVIEW

GOAL: Believe it or not, Byron Dafoe's job at the start of the season was to spell Jim Carey on occasion. The incredible fall from grace for Carey meant that it was Dafoe who was spelled on occasion. And not by Carey.

It's tough to figure just what happened to Carey. Whatever it was, the Bruins gave up on him quickly. This is how the Bruins did in each of Carey's starts last year:

4-1 loss to Montreal
3-0 win at Anaheim
2-0 win at Vancouver
2-1 win at Edmonton
5-4 loss to Florida
3-3 at Dallas
3-3 at Pittsburgh

After earning two shutouts in a row and allowing just one goal to Edmonton, he had a bad game in a 5-4 loss to Florida. He didn't start for 18 days after that one poor outing, and then only got two more starts, both road games against tough teams. In fact, he was undefeated on the road with a 3-0-2 mark. So, after just seven starts and a couple relief appearances for Dafoe, and with just two losses, he was put on waivers and then sent to the minors. He did considerably worse in Providence, with a GAA of 3.97 and a win-loss-tie record of 2-7-1. His nightmare season finally ended with shoulder surgery.

Nobody missed Carey, however, because Dafoe had a goals against average of 2.24 and had six shutouts. Robbie Tallas proved rather exceptional as the backup, which was a bit of a surprise because he was not doing all that well in Providence when called up by the Bruins.

Hockey Annual Rating: 11 of 27

GOALTENDER	GPI	MINS	AVG	W	L	T	EN	SO	GA	SA	SV %
ROBBIE TALLAS	14	788	1.83	6	3	3	0	1	24	326	.926
BYRON DAFOE	65	3693	2.24	30	25	9	8	6	138	1602	.914
JIM CAREY	10	496	2.90	3	2	1	0	2	24	225	.893
BOS TOTALS	82	4995	2.33	39	30	13	8	9	194	2161	.910

DEFENCE: They're young and old, big and small, offensive and defensive.

Somehow that mix seems to work just fine, although it doesn't make your days worry-free.

Hal Gill, the 207th draft pick in 1993, made the team in his first year out of college. He provides size, at 6-7, and the youth. Having Ray Bourque as his playing partner could only be a bonus in his development. Gill played in the team's 15th game of the season, and didn't miss one the rest of the way. Other than him, the only other young players are Kyle McLaren and Darren Van Impe, obtained on waivers from Anaheim.

The older guys, with their ages as of the start of the season, include Ray Bourque (38), Grant Ledyard (36), Dave Ellett (34) and Don Sweeney (32). Clearly, those players have to be replaced within the next couple years, although you wonder if Bourque couldn't just play forever.

Among the future defense candidates within the system are Johnathan Aitkin who is coming off his final junior season, and Ben Clymer, who missed almost all of his first pro season with an injury. Dean Malkoc got into 40 games with the Bruins, and spent the rest of the time in the minors along with Mattias Timander and Dean Chynoweth.

Hockey Annual Rating: 16 of 27

FORWARD: There's no official award for the most improved player or the top emerging star, but if there was, Jason Allison would have won it last year.

Oh, to heck with it, let's give him an award anyway. Jason Allison wins the *Hockey Annual* Most Improved Player of the Year.

There's no trophy and no cash reward, but

Allison, his agent, his family, his team, and anyone else who wants to, can now say that he won. Pretty impressive, huh?

The rules are simple enough. Any player who performs beyond anything he has done previously is eligible. In other words, it's really a breakout player award, or an emerging star. If, for example, a player scores forty goals a season and all of a sudden gets 55, he doesn't qualify. He's already exhibited the abilities in the past that would make a 50-goal season possible. Besides, the winner is the player who exceeds previous performance the most.

Allison had 8 goals and 26 assists in 72 games in 1996-97. Last year, he skyrocketed to 33-50-83. Now, that's improvement.

The contenders include Ray Whitney (Florida), Glen Murray (Los Angeles), Cory Stillman (Calgary), Jamie Langenbrunner (Dallas), Dean McAmmond (Edmonton) and Pavol Demitra (St. Louis). Bruins goalie Byron Dafoe would also merit consideration among the goaltenders, along with Olaf Kolzig.

Allison's linemates by the end of the season were Sergei Samsonov and Dimitri Khristich. Playing with Allison helped Samsonov win the Calder Trophy as rookie of the year. He started out slowly, scoring just 5-8-13 in the first half of the season. In the second half, he ballooned to 17-17-34.

One of these days Steve Heinze is going to get through the season without missing so much time with injuries. The last two seasons, he's played just 91 games. But, he's scored 43 goals in those games which projects to 39 over a full 82 games. He's a good pool sleeper.

A number of the other forwards had up and down seasons. That included Anson Carter. He had a 10-game pointless streak, and a 16-game stretch where he didn't score a goal. All told, however, he had a solid campaign for his first full NHL season.

Ted Donato only scored two goals in the last half of the season. He was 14-14-28 in the first half and 2-9-11 in the second half.

Per Axelsson managed to score just one goal over one 36-goal stretch.

That pretty much accounts for all the forwards. Everyone but Allison and Khristich were inconsistent. The good news about that, however, is that imagine how much better the Bruins will be if they get that consistency.

So, what causes inconsistency? A number of things. One of them is simply a matter of linemates. If you're playing with Allison and Khristich, the points come easier, just ask Samsonov.

Another one is confidence. If you don't have it, it's tough to get it back until you do some scoring. And it's tough to do some scoring if you don't have any confidence. Confidence comes and goes on its own timetable.

Another one is that at times everything bounces your way, for no known reason. And at other times, nothing bounces your way, again for no known reason.

Pressure can be helpful or a problem. It's amazing how many players when first called up from the minors go on a scoring binge. Why? Haven't figured it out, to tell you the truth. How a player performs under pressure is an individual thing.

Finally, there's concentration. You can lose concentration, depending on the type of person you are, and depending on your mental fatigue. You think with all the millions they're earning that they can concentrate every single game, but that's not how it works. I bet if you gave each player a week's vacation during the season, they'd come back refreshed and perform much better.

The Bruins have some young players who have yet to make their mark. Joe Thornton, of course, didn't have a very good rookie year, playing on the fourth line, if he was playing at all. He's still star material.

For youngsters Landon Wilson, Cameron Mann, Shawn Bates and Randy Robitaille, it's only a matter of time and opportunity. But, put your money on Mann making more of a contribution this year.

Hockey Annual Rating: 12 of 27

SPECIAL TEAMS: The Bruins scored the most power play goals of any team after the Olympic Break, and their percentage was third at 19.7%

Allison and Bourque are set-up men on the power play, and Khristich, Heinze and Samsonov are the snipers.

One other curious note about the Bruins special teams is that they had 74 more power play opportunities than shorthanded situations, which was the highest such difference in the league. That could mean trouble if the same thing doesn't happen this year.

POWER PLAY	G	ATT	PCT	
Overall	62	359	17.3%	(8th NHL)
Home	31	197	15.7%	(12th NHL)
Road	31	162	19.1%	(4th NHL)
3 SHORT HANDED GOALS ALLOWED (1st NHL)				

Penalty Killing	G	TSH	PCT	
Overall	44	285	84.6%	(15th NHL)
Home	24	138	82.6%	(22nd NHL)
Road	20	147	86.4%	(9th NHL

5 SHORT HANDED GOALS SCORED (T-23rd NHL)

Penalties	GP	MIN	AVG	
BRUINS	82	1117	13.6	(2nd NHL)

BRUINS SPECIAL TEAMS SCORING

Power play	G	A	PTS
BOURQUE	9	21	30
ALLISON	5	20	25
KHRISTICH	13	10	23
HEINZE	9	7	16
SAMSONOV	7	8	15
CARTER	6	6	12
DONATO	3	7	10
LEDYARD	2	8	10
ELLETT	2	8	10
MCLAREN	2	6	8
VAN IMPE	2	5	7
TAYLOR	1	2	3
DIMAIO	0	3	3
AXELSSON	2	0	2
WILSON	0	2	2
THORNTON	0	1	1
SWEENEY	0	1	1
SULLIVAN	0	1	1
MANN	0	1	1

Short handed	G	A	PTS
TAYLOR	3	0	3
KHRISTICH	2	0	2
BOURQUE	0	2	2
ALLISON	0	2	2
VAN IMPE	0	1	1
LEDYARD	0	1	1
ELLETT	0	1	1
DIMAIO	0	1	1

COACHING AND MANAGEMENT: Pat Burns has been successful everywhere he's gone. The one exception is his final year in Toronto, only because nobody could have coached that team to success. Burns is a reasonable, sane, intelligent guy, which goes a long way in the coaching sweepstakes.

Will this be the year Harry Sinden retires? Probably not, but Mike O'Connell has been getting more responsibilities, and had his hand in a number of deals which helped turn it around for Boston.

The turnaround from last place to a contender is worthy of high praise, both on the management and coaching sides.

Hockey Annual Rating: 9 of 27

DRAFT

Round	Sel.	Player	Pos	Team
2	48	Johnathan Girard	D	Laval (QMJHL)
2	52	Bobby Allen	D	Boston College
3	78	Peter Nordstrom	LW	Sweden
5	135	Andrew Raycroft	G	Sudbury (OHL)
6	165	Ryan Milanovic	LW	Kitchener (OHL)

No first round pick for the Bruins, but they grabbed two offensive-minded defencemen in the second round, perhaps preparing for the day Raymond Bourque is no longer around.

Few first round picks have panned out for the Bruins, anyway. Names like Robert Cimetta, Shayne Stevenson, Dmitri Kvartalnov, Kevyn Adams and Evgeni Ryabchicov are some of the first round disasters since 1988.

PROGNOSIS: There's no reason to think that the Bruins won't build on last year's success and continue to improve. Well, there is one. Often teams that have such a dramatic rise in points, fall back some the next season.

Apart from that they're solid if unspectacular behind the blueline and some of their forwards haven't reached their peak. The defense is aging and needs replacement parts, but they're okay for this year.

Look for more of the same from the Bruins this regular season, perhaps a little better, but probably slightly worse. Once they get into the playoffs, however, they could do some damage and be one of the surprise teams.

PREDICTION
Eastern Conference: 7
Overall: 11

STAT SECTION
Team Scoring Stats

	GP	G	A	PTS	+/-	PIM	SH	CAREER GP	G	A	Pts
JASON ALLISON	81	33	50	83	33	60	158	186	43	81	124
DMITRI KHRISTICH	82	29	37	66	25	42	144	548	196	240	436
RAY BOURQUE	82	13	35	48	2	80	264	1,372	375	1,036	1,411
SERGEI SAMSONOV	81	22	25	47	9	8	159	81	22	25	47
STEVE HEINZE	61	26	20	46	8	54	160	367	97	77	174
ANSON CARTER	78	16	27	43	7	31	179	116	27	34	61
TED DONATO	79	16	23	39	6	54	129	451	112	139	251
TIM TAYLOR	79	20	11	31	16-	57	127	218	35	33	68
ROB DIMAIO	79	10	17	27	13-	82	112	427	58	77	135
PER AXELSSON	82	8	19	27	14-	38	144	82	8	19	27
KYLE MCLAREN	66	5	20	25	13	56	101	198	15	41	56
GRANT LEDYARD	71	4	20	24	4-	20	90	866	81	258	339
DAVE ELLETT	82	3	20	23	3	67	129	1,023	151	401	452
MIKE SULLIVAN	77	5	13	18	1-	34	83	453	41	62	103
DON SWEENEY	59	1	15	16	12	24	55	670	41	157	198
DARREN VAN IMPE	69	3	11	14	6-	40	71	160	8	33	41
JOE THORNTON	55	3	4	7	6-	19	33	55	3	4	7
HAL GILL	68	2	4	6	4	47	56	68	2	4	6
LANDON WILSON	28	1	5	6	3	7	26	84	10	17	27
BYRON DAFOE	65	0	3	3	0	2	0	Goalie			
SHAWN BATES	13	2	0	2	3-	2	12	13	2	0	2
MATTIAS TIMANDER	23	1	1	2	9-	6	17	64	2	9	11
DEAN MALKOC	40	1	0	1	12-	86	15	114	1	2	3
CAMERON MANN	9	0	1	1	1	4	6	9	0	1	1
KEN BAUMGARTNER	82	0	1	1	14-	199	28	627	12	38	50

JOEL PRPIC	1	0	0	0	0	2	0	1	0	0	0
DEAN CHYNOWETH	2	0	0	0	4-	0	1	241	4	18	22
JEAN-YVES ROY	2	0	0	0	0	0	1	61	12	16	28
RANDY ROBITAILLE	4	0	0	0	2-	0	5	5	0	0	0
KIRK NIELSEN	6	0	0	0	1-	0	1	6	0	0	0
JIM CAREY	10	0	0	0	0	0	0	Goalie			
ROBBIE TALLAS	14	0	0	0	0	0	0	Goalie			

PLAYOFFS

Results: Lost 4-2 to Washington in Conference Quarter-finals

Record: 2-4

Home: 0-3

Away: 2-1

Goals For: 13 (2.2/game)

Goals Against: 15 (2.5/game)

Overtime: 1-2

Power play: 15.0% (8th)

Penalty Killing: 85.0% (7th)

	GP	G	A	PTS	+/-	PIM	PP	SH	GW	OT	S
JASON ALLISON	6	2	6	8	0	4	1	0	0	0	13
SERGEI SAMSONOV	6	2	5	7	1	0	0	0	1	0	18
RAY BOURQUE	6	1	4	5	2-	2	1	0	0	0	42
DMITRI KHRISTICH	6	2	2	4	1	2	2	0	0	0	15
DARREN VAN IMPE	6	2	1	3	0	0	1	0	1	1	19
ANSON CARTER	6	1	1	2	3-	0	0	0	0	0	19
ROB DIMAIO	6	1	0	1	3-	8	0	0	0	0	14
KYLE MCLAREN	6	1	0	1	3-	4	1	0	0	0	21
PER AXELSSON	6	1	0	1	3-	0	0	0	0	0	13
DAVE ELLETT	6	0	1	1	1-	6	0	0	0	0	11
MIKE SULLIVAN	6	0	1	1	0	2	0	0	0	0	10
LANDON WILSON	1	0	0	0	0	0	0	0	0	0	1
TED DONATO	5	0	0	0	3-	2	0	0	0	0	3
KEN BAUMGARTNER	6	0	0	0	0	14	0	0	0	0	1
GRANT LEDYARD	6	0	0	0	3-	2	0	0	0	0	8
BYRON DAFOE	6	0	0	0	0	0	0	0	0	0	0

STEVE HEINZE	6	0	0	0	4-	6	0	0	0	0	15
TIM TAYLOR	6	0	0	0	2-	10	0	0	0	0	10
HAL GILL	6	0	0	0	1-	4	0	0	0	0	3
JOE THORNTON	6	0	0	0	0	9	0	0	0	0	3

GOALTENDER	GPI	MINS	AVG	W	LT	EN	SO	GA	SA	SV %
BYRON DAFOE	6	422	1.99	2	4	1	1	14	159	.912
BOS TOTALS	6	423	2.13	2	4	1	1	15	160	.906

*Team Rankings 1997-98 (previous year's ranking in parenthesis)

		Conference Rank	League Rank
Record	39-30-13	5 (13)	9 (26)
Home	19-16-6	6 (13)	12 (25)
Away	20-14-7	2 (12)	3 (24)
VersusOwn Conference	26-19-11	5 (13)	9 (26)
VersusOther Conference	13-11-2	5 (12)	10 (24)
Team Plus\Minus	+9	6 (13)	10 (26)
Goals For	221	5 (7)	12 (15)
Goals Against	194	5 (13)	6 (26)
Average Shots For	27.2	6 (7)	13 (13)
Average Shots Against	26.3	5 (7)	9 (14)
Overtime	3-1-13	3 (6)	4 (12)
One Goal Games	10-9	6 (11)	14 (21)
Times outshooting opponent	48	4 (6)	6 (12)
Versus Teams Over .500	19-14-10	2 (12)	5 (22)
Versus Teams .500 or under	20-16-3	9 (13)	16 (26)

First Half

Record	17-16-8	6 (9)	11 (16)

Second Half

Record	22-14-5	3 (13)	4 (26)

Best Individual Seasons

Goals

Phil Esposito	1970-71	76
Phil Esposito	1973-74	68
Phil Esposito	1971-72	66

Assists

Bobby Orr	1970-71	102
Adam Oates	1992-93	97
Bobby Orr	1973-74	90

Points

Phil Esposito	1970-71	152
Phil Esposito	1973-74	145
Adam Oates	1992-93	142

TEAM

Last 3 years

	GP	W	L	T	Pts	%
1997-98	82	39	30	13	91	.555
1996-97	82	26	47	9	61	.372
1995-96	82	40	31	11	91	.555

Best 3 regular seasons

	GP	W	L	T	Pts	%
1929-30	44	38	5	1	77	.875
1969-70	76	57	14	7	121	.791
1938-39	48	36	10	2	74	.771

Worst 3 regular seasons

	GP	W	L	T	Pts	%
1924-25	30	6	24	0	12	.200
1961-62	70	15	47	8	38	.271
1960-61	70	15	42	13	43	.307

Most Goals (min. 70 game schedule)

1970-71	399
1973-74	349
1974-75	345

Fewest Goals (min. 70 game schedule)

1955-56	147
1952-53	152
1951-52	162

Most Goals Against (min. 70 game schedule)

1961-62	306
1995-96	300
1985-86	288

Fewest Goals Against (min. 70 game schedule)

1952-53	172
1956-57	174
1951-52	176

Buffalo Sabres

It was a special season for the Sabres. They weren't supposed to make it to the conference finals, and making the playoffs was up in the air before the season started.

For a while, the Sabres muddled around near the bottom of the Eastern Conference giving everyone the opportunity to say, "I told you so."

They couldn't win without coach Ted Nolan or general manager John Muckler? Well, they could, it just took them a while.

They broke out of the gate with a 10-16-6 record, and were 15-19-7 at the halfway mark. Then they caught fire. These are the best second-half records in the league:

New Jersey	22-10-9	53 points
Dallas	24-13-4	52 points
BUFFALO	21-10-10	52 points

The Sabres were one point away from being the best team in the second half of the season, and an overtime win or two from being one of the best two teams in the playoffs. They lost three games to Washington in overtime in the conference semi-finals.

Besides Hasek, the Sabres had something else. It's called character. That was evidenced in a lot of ways, but let's look at just one. We don't think of the Sabres as a high scoring team, and they weren't, except for the third period. That's often when you can tell what a team is made of. They were the second highest scoring third period team, after Detroit, but more importantly, they had the best goal differential in the third period, by a large margin.

Best Third Period Goal Differences:

	For	Against	Difference
BUFFALO	86	54	+32
Philadelphia	83	62	+21
Detroit	96	77	+19

Before we get too ga-ga over the Sabres play, it should be remembered that the Sabres had the most shots per game against them, and didn't get that many themselves. That points to one man as the main reason for their success, and it's no surprise that it's Dominik Hasek. If not for him, they could have expected the same results as the other two teams in the chart below.

Biggest Negative Shot Differences Per Game:

	For	Against	Difference
BUFFALO	26.5	31.2	-4.7
Vancouver	25.5	30.2	-4.7
Anaheim	26.6	30.4	-3.8

TEAM PREVIEW

GOAL: Hasek won the Hart Trophy, the Vezina Trophy, the Lester B. Pearson Trophy, *The Hockey News* Player of the Year Award, *The Hockey News* Goalie of the Year Award, finished first in save percentage and first in shutouts. Enough said.

With Steve Shields gone, the Sabres signed free agent Dwayne Roloson from Calgary. Unless Hasek gets hurt, he gets a first hand view of the best goalie in hockey, every game.

Hockey Annual Rating: 1 of 27

DEFENCE: The Sabres lost Bob Boughner in the expansion draft to Nashville, so the remaining top six defencemen are Alexei Zhitnik, Richard Smehlik, Mike Wilson, Darryl Shannon, Jason Wooley and Jay McKee.

It's certainly competent, but not much more than that. There's very little toughness there. In fact, Boughner was the only one of the group to even have a fighting major last season.

The offence comes from Zhitnik, the size from Wilson, the defence from Shannon and

the potential from McKee, who should get more ice-time with Boughner gone.

Look for the Sabres to sign or trade for a veteran free agent to give them some depth, leadership and toughness. Marty McSorley, who was an unrestricted free agent in the summer, might be a good fit.

The Sabres have an outstanding prospect in the wings. Corey Sarich played for Seattle in the WHL last season but probably won't see the Sabres lineup for a year or two. But, you never know if he makes an impression at training camp.

Hockey Annual Rating: 20 of 27

FORWARD: After Mike Peca, and maybe Matthew Barnaby, the Sabres don't have anything special at forward.

Geoff Sanderson used to be special, but needs to rebound from a disastrous season. The same for Derek Plante, who has almost played himself out of a job.

Audette is an oft-injured on-and-off sniper who can fill the net in spurts. Miroslav Satan, who led the team in scoring, can score when he feels like it, which isn't as often as it should be. Michal Grosek is streaky as well and didn't provide the offence he was supposed to.

Brian Holzinger didn't score all that much either, but he looks like he could. Eric Rasmussen is another talented player whose scoring totals don't add up to his talent. He spent

GOALTENDER	GPI	MINS	AVG	W	L	T	EN	SO	GA	SA	SV %
DOMINIK HASEK	72	4220	2.09	33	23	13	3	13	147	2149	.932
STEVE SHIELDS	16	785	2.83	3	6	4	0	0	37	408	.909
BUF TOTALS	82	5019	2.24	36	29	17	3	13	187	2560	.927

most of the season in the minors after a slow start, but is expected to have another go at it.

Vaclav Verada was impressive when called up and should get more work this season.

Randy Burridge was a disappointment, while Paul Kruse is a role-playing tough guy.

Dixon Ward does just about everything, but the Sabres showed their appreciation by leaving him open in the expansion draft. It was expected that Nashville would grab him, but they took Boughner instead. Ward doesn't get any respect, but he's the type of player who can be the difference between winning and losing.

It's time for two players to step up to the next level, and this could be their year. Wayne Primeau and Curtis Brown are two prime breakout candidates.

If those two can do that, along with Rasmussen and Verada, the Sabres will have a good start on the young players they need to replace some of the underachieving and inconsistent dead weight they carry on the forward lines.

Hockey Annual Rating: 21 of 27

SPECIAL TEAMS: Dominik Hasek isn't much of a special teams player, so he can't help out too much on the power play. They do have a power play point specialist in Jason Woolley, and they have Alexei Zhitnik to man the other point. Other than that it's just Audette and whomever among the forwards.

The penalty killing was weak too, but what they were good at was scoring shorthanded goals. Mike Peca tied Pavel Bure for the league shorthanded scoring lead, with nine points. The Sabres have some speed which makes scoring shorthanded goals a better proposition.

Oddly enough, in the playoffs, the Sabres special teams were outstanding. They finished first in penalty killing percentage and second on the power play. Miroslav Satan tied for the playoff lead with eight power play points, with Steve Yzerman and Nicklas Lidstrom, both of whom played six more games.

Power Play	G	ATT	PCT
Overall	51	396	12.9% (T-19th NHL)
Home	30	197	15.2% (13th NHL)
Road	21	199	10.6% (23rd NHL)

12 SHORT HANDED GOALS ALLOWED(T-16th NHL)

Penalty Killing	G	ATT	PCT
Overall	65	413	84.3% (18th NHL)
Home	21	187	88.8% (4th NHL)
Road	44	226	80.5% (26th NHL)

15 SHORT HANDED GOALS SCORED (3rd NHL)

SABRES SPECIAL TEAMS SCORING

Power play	G	A	PTS
WOOLLEY	3	18	21
ZHITNIK	3	2	5
AUDETTE	10	4	14
PLANTE	5	9	14
SATAN	9	4	13
PECA	6	7	13
HOLZINGER	4	7	11
SANDERSON	2	4	6
GROSEK	2	4	6
MCKEE	0	6	6
SHANNON	1	3	4
BROWN	1	3	4
SMEHLIK	0	4	4
PRIMEAU	2	1	3
BARNABY	0	3	3
RAY	1	0	1

	G	A	PTS
BURRIDGE	1	0	1
WARD	0	1	1

Short handed	G	A	PTS
PECA	5	4	9
ZHITNIK	2	15	17
HOLZINGER	2	3	5
WARD	2	1	3
SMEHLIK	1	2	3
BROWN	1	1	2
MCKEE	0	2	2
PLANTE	0	1	1
BURRIDGE	0	1	1

COACHING AND MANAGEMENT: You have to give credit to Lindy Ruff and Darcy Regier for having such an outstanding year, considering the circumstances. Neither was given much chance of success, following in the footsteps of Nolan and Muckler.

And neither one got off to an auspicious debut. The Sabres had problems winning early in the season and Regier was tentative at the start, especially when he offered Nolan an insulting (to a coach) one-year contract.

Both of have earned their stripes, Ruff with his success on the ice, and Regier, whose moves paid off. Getting Jason Wooley was easy and rewarding, and Geoff Sanderson was worth a chance.

Hockey Annual Rating: 17 of 27

DRAFT

Round	Sel.	Player	Pos	Team
1	18	Dimitri Kalinen	D	Russia
2	34	Andrew Peters	LW	Oshawa (OHL)
2	47	Norman Milley	RW	Sudbury (OHL)
2	50	Jaroslav Kristek	RW	Czech
3	77	Mike Pandolfo	LW	St. Sebastien's (USHS)
5	137	Aaron Goldade	C	Brandon (WHL)
6	164	Ales Kotalik	RW	Czech
7	191	Brad Moran	C	Calgary (WHL)

Dimitri Kalinen slipped further down the list than anticipated. He was rated as the top European by Central Scouting, but not many defencemen were picked ahead of him, and the Sabres were able to grab him. He is a defensive defenceman, who scored the grand toal of five assists in the Russian leagues over the past three years.

PROGNOSIS: The Sabres will go as far as Dominik Hasek takes them. Mind you, if he gets them to the dance, they can do some twisting and jiving on their own. The Sabres desperately need to fill in the rest of their game for the rainy day when Hasek doesn't do so much for them. They're coming along, but they have a considerable way to go.

The Sabres play in the last half of the season is encouraging. At the start of the year they had Hasek and didn't win; later they had Hasek and did win.

PREDICTION
Eastern Conference: 4
Overall: 7

STAT SECTION

Team Scoring Stats

	GP	G	A	PTS	+/-	PIM	SH	CAREER GP	G	A	Pts
MIROSLAV SATAN	79	22	24	46	2	34	139	217	65	54	119
ALEXEI ZHITNIK	78	15	30	45	19	102	191	429	56	174	230
DONALD AUDETTE	75	24	20	44	10	59	198	409	164	125	289
MICHAEL PECA	61	18	22	40	12	57	132	245	55	77	132
BRIAN HOLZINGER	69	14	21	35	2-	36	116	212	46	63	109
JASON WOOLLEY	71	9	26	35	8	35	129	254	26	97	123
DEREK PLANTE	72	13	21	34	8	26	150	354	87	134	221
MICHAL GROSEK	67	10	20	30	9	60	114	199	34	47	81
GEOFF SANDERSON	75	11	18	29	1	38	197	514	200	181	381
MATTHEW BARNABY	72	5	20	25	8	289	96	273	43	65	108
CURTIS BROWN	63	12	12	24	11	34	91	96	17	16	33
DIXON WARD	71	10	13	23	9	42	99	317	59	83	142
DARRYL SHANNON	76	3	19	22	26	56	85	390	19	77	96
RICHARD SMEHLIK	72	3	17	20	11	62	90	337	36	97	133
JAY MCKEE	56	1	13	14	1-	42	55	100	2	23	25
WAYNE PRIMEAU	69	6	6	12	9	87	51	117	9	10	19
VACLAV VARADA	27	5	6	11	0	15	27	33	5	6	11
RANDY BURRIDGE	30	4	6	10	0	0	40	696	199	251	450
PAUL KRUSE	74	7	2	9	11-	187	52	368	35	33	68
MIKE WILSON	66	4	4	8	13	48	52	201	10	21	31
ROB RAY	63	2	4	6	2	234	19	569	33	34	67
ERIK RASMUSSEN	21	2	3	5	2	14	28	21	2	3	5
BOB BOUGHNER	69	1	3	4	5	165	26	177	2	11	13
DOMINIK HASEK	72	0	2	2	0	12	0	goalie			
RUMUN NDUR	1	0	0	0	1-	2	0	3	0	0	0
MIKE HURLBUT	3	0	0	0	1-	2	3	27	1	8	9
SCOTT NICHOL	3	0	0	0	0	4	5	5	0	0	0
STEVE SHIELDS	16	0	0	0	0	0	0	goalie			

* Team Rankings 1997-98 (previous year's ranking in parenthesis)

	Conference Rank	League Rank
Record	39-20-13	6 (3)	12 (6)
Home	20-13-8	5 (3)	9 (4)
Away	16-16-9	6 (5)	10 (11)
Versus Own Conference	25-20-11	6 (2)	12 (4)
Versus Other Conference	11-9-6	8 (8)	13 (14)
Team Plus\Minus	+38	1 (2)	4 (13)
Goals For	211	8 (5)	17 (12)
Goals Against	87	2 (3)	3 (6)
Average Shots For	26.5	10 (13)	21 (20)
Average Shots Against	31.2	13 (11)	26 (22)
Overtime	3-1-17	5 (5)	7 (11)
One Goal Games	12-10	5 (3)	12 (5)
Times outshooting opponent	26	12 (13)	22 (26)

Versus Teams Over .500	14-20-10	8 (5)	14 (7)
Versus Teams .500 or under	22-9-7	4 (4)	6 (6)
First Half Record	15-19-7	8 (4)	15 (6
Second Half Record	21-10-10	2 (3)	3 (7)

PLAYOFFS

Results: defeated Philadelphia 4-1 in conference quarter-finals

defeated Montreal 4-0 in conference semi-finals

lost to Washington 4-2 in conference finals

Record: 10-5

Home: 4-3

Away: 6-2

Goals For: 46 (3.1/game)

Goals Against: 32 (2.1/game)

Overtime: 3-3

Power play: 18.0% (2nd)

Penalty Killing: 90.0% (1st)

	GP	G	A	PTS	+/-	PIM	PP	SH	GW	OT	S
MATTHEW BARNABY	15	7	6	13	6	22	3	0	1	0	25
DONALD AUDETTE	15	5	8	13	4-	10	3	0	2	0	31
BRIAN HOLZINGER	15	4	7	11	2-	18	1	1	0	0	24
DIXON WARD	15	3	8	11	8	6	0	0	0	0	29
JASON WOOLLEY	15	2	9	11	8	12	1	0	1	0	32
MICHAL GROSEK	15	6	4	10	5	28	2	0	3	1	40
MIROSLAV SATAN	14	5	4	9	9-	4	4	0	1	0	20
VACLAV VARADA	15	3	4	7	3	18	0	0	0	0	24
DARRYL SHANNON	15	2	4	6	0	8	0	1	0	0	15
MICHAEL PECA	13	3	2	5	4	8	0	0	1	1	24
GEOFF SANDERSON	14	3	1	4	0	4	1	0	1	1	25
WAYNE PRIMEAU	14	1	3	4	1-	6	0	0	0	0	10

BOB BOUGHNER	14	0	4	4	9	15	0	0	0	0	7
CURTIS BROWN	13	1	2	3	6	10	1	0	0	0	23
DEREK PLANTE	11	0	3	3	1	10	0	0	0	0	13
ALEXEI ZHITNIK	15	0	3	3	1	36	0	0	0	0	24
RICHARD SMEHLIK	15	0	2	2	3	6	0	0	0	0	12
PAUL KRUSE	1	1	0	1	1	4	0	0	0	0	2
MIKE WILSON	15	0	1	1	4-	13	0	0	0	0	1
JAY MCKEE	1	0	0	0	1-	0	0	0	0	0	0
ROB RAY	10	0	0	0	2-	24	0	0	0	0	2
DOMINIK HASEK	15	0	0	0	0	4	0	0	0	0	0

GOALTENDER	GPI	MINS	AVG	W	L	EN	SO	GA	SA	SV %
DOMINIK HASEK	15	948	2.03	10	5	0	1	32	514	.938
BUF TOTALS	15	949	2.02	10	5	0	1	32	514	.938

All-Time Leaders
Goals

Gil Perreault	512
Rick Martin	382
Dave Andreychuk	348

Assists

Gil Perreault	814
Dave Andreychuk	423
Craig Ramsay	420

Points

Gil Perreault	1,326
Dave Andreychuk	771
Rick Martin	695

Best Individual Seasons
Goals

Alexander Mogilny	92-93	76
Danny Gare	79-80	56
Pat LaFontaine	92-93	53

Assists

Pat LaFontaine	92-93	95
Dale Hawerchuk	92-93	80
Dale Hawerchuk	91-92	75

Points

Pat LaFontaine	92-93	148
Alexander Mogilny	92-93	127
Gil Perreault	75-76	113

TEAM
Last 3 years

	GP	W	L	T	Pts	%
1997-98	82	36	29	17	89	.598
1996-97	82	40	30	12	92	.561
1995-96	82	33	42	7	72	.445

Best 3 regular seasons

	GP	W	L	T	Pts	%
1974-75	78	49	16	15	113	.724
1979-80	80	47	17	16	110	.688
1975-76	80	46	21	13	105	.656

Worst 3 regular seasons

	GP	W	L	T	Pts	%
1971-72	78	16	43	19	51	.327
1986-87	80	28	44	8	64	.400
1991-92	80	31	37	12	74	.463

Most Goals (min. 70 game schedule)

1974-75	354
1975-76	339
1992-93	335

Fewest Goals (min. 70 game schedule)

1971-72	203
1997-98	211
1996-97	237

Most Goals Against (min. 70 game schedule)

1986-87	308
1987-88	305
1991-92	299

Fewest Goals Against (min. 70 game schedule)

1996-97	187
1979-80	201
1996-97	208

Carolina Hurricanes

The Hurricanes made the move last year from Hartford to...well, the Twilight Zone. It was a bizarre year for the most unwelcome team ever to hit the ice in a new area.

Forget the fact that they couldn't draw any fans to their home games, which in itself is strange enough, and consider some of the statistical weirdness that went on last season.

* Started off the season with a 1-7-2 record in their first 10 games; were 7-2-1 in their next 10 games.

* Allowed 37 fewer goals than they had ever allowed in franchise history; they also scored 26 fewer goals than ever before.

* Did a home-road reversal. They were 4-15-1 in their first 20 road games; were 13-8-0 in their last 21 road games. Were 10-7-4 in their first 21 home games; were 6-11-3 in their second 20 home games.

* Had a road stretch in which they went 13-5. They won just four of their other 23 road games.

* Drew a record high crowd of 19,358 to see the New York Rangers; two days later attendance was 5,516.

* When Carolina outshot its opponents, they were just 10-24-3; when they were outshot, their record was 22-16-5. No other team could even compare to the difference between those two records.

The last item, with the shot record the opposite of what we'd expect, is worth looking into. There is a good reason why a team can get outshot and still win the game. If they score early and build a lead, then it puts the other team on the offensive. If one team is on the offensive and the other is on the defensive, of course the offensive team is likely to get more shots. The fact that the Hurricanes were outscored and outshot in the first period gives credence to that suggestion.

Another reason is that the best defensive teams are the winningest teams in recent years. Defensive teams are likely to be outshot, but are also likely to make the most of their offensive chances because they sit back and wait for the best opportunities.

The fact remains, however, that only two teams won more games than Carolina when they were outshot. One was Buffalo, which shows the contribution of Dominik Hasek, and the other was Los Angeles, which defies explanation.

STUFF

* Kevin Dineen scored the first goal for the Hurricanes, as well as the last goal when the team was still the Whalers. Dino Ciccarelli scored the last goal against the Whalers, and the first against the Hurricanes.
* the team's 1-7-2 start was the worst in franchise history.
* Trevor Kidd set a franchise record with a shutout streak of 219:11. Included in that streak were three consecutive shutouts.

TEAM PREVIEW

GOAL: Sean Burke was the team's MVP for four seasons in a row. It didn't take long for him to become the team's LVP (Least Valuable Player) last year. It was a combination of things: Burke's contract demands, Burke's mediocre play, Burke's off-ice problems, and the emergence of Trevor Kidd.

Enter the new MVP, Trevor Kidd, an unlikely candidate. Booed for his poor play in Calgary, he had a sensational year, recording the lowest GAA and save percentage in franchise history. He even had three shutouts in a row down the stretch when the Hurricanes still had a chance at a playoff spot. Those were his only three shutouts, incidentally.

Kidd is a lock as the number one man, and it appears Mike Fountain, who did a good job in New Haven, will be the backup.

Goaltending hasn't been a problem area for Carolina in recent history, and doesn't look like it will be in the future, either.

Hockey Annual Rating: 13 of 27

DEFENCE: Most teams want to have an quarterback for the power play. The Hurricanes don't have one. Unless free agent signee Al Iafrate stays healthy.

Most teams want some real toughness from their defense corps. The Hurricanes don't have much of that. Unless Iafrate stays healthy.

Most teams want a lot of size behind the blueline. The Hurricanes aren't overly blessed in that area. Unless Iafrate stays healthy.

Most teams would like to have a blue-chip dominant defenseman. The Hurricanes don't have that, either. Unless Iafrate stays healthy and plays like he used to.

What they do have are some all-round defensive types, the kind that can play in both ends of the rink. Steve Chiasson fits that description, as does Glen Wesley, Sean Hill and Kevin Haller. Curtis Leschyshyn and Adam Burt are more stay-at-home types. Nolan Pratt, Steven Halko and Mike Rucinski round out the depth chart. Nikos Tselios, cousin of Chris Chelios, and last year's first round draft choice, is the only prospect.

GOALTENDER	GPI	MINS	AVG	W	L	T	EN	SO	GA	SA	SV %
TREVOR KIDD	47	2685	2.17	21	21	3	6	3	97	1238	.922
SEAN BURKE	25	1415	2.80	7	11	5	2	1	66	655	.899
PAT JABLONSKI	5	279	3.01	1	4	0	1	0	14	115	.878
KIRK MCLEAN	8	401	3.29	4	2	0	1	0	22	180	.878
MICHAEL FOUNTAIN	3	163	3.68	0	3	0	0	0	10	68	.853
CAR TOTALS	82	4973	2.64	33	41	8	10	4	219	2266	.903

All in all, things could be worse. But, they could be better as well. And will be...if Iafrate stays healthy.

Hockey Annual Rating: 8 of 27

FORWARD: All year long we heard about how the Hurricanes needed a centreman, a premier playmaking big guy in the middle. Now they have one in free agent signee Ron Francis.

Now all the the Hurricanes need is Jaromir Jagr on his wing.

Francis isn't going to get the same points he got in Pittsburgh, but he's going to make his wingers better, and he's a character player through and through. Francis, of course, was with the franchise for 10 years and was traded to Pittsburgh in what some suggest was one of the worst trades in NHL history. The Whalers got John Cullen, Jeff Parker and Zarley Zalapski for Francis, Ulf Samuelsson, and Grant Jennings.

Keith Primeau could be considered a number one centre, but now he's a number two centre, unless he moves to the wing where he'd be a number one winger.

Jeff O'Neill came on last year, and is going to get better. Points are going to be more difficult to come by, however, on the third line. Kent Manderville can be the fourth line centre.

The Hurricanes are pretty strong at left wing, as long as they stay healthy. Gary Roberts had a good comeback season, although he only played 61 games, which you have to figure is about as expected with his injury past. Carolina picked up a slumping Martin Gelinas late in the season, who has proven 30-goal

potential. Paul Ranheim is the checker and penalty killer, while Stu Grimson is the enforcer. Bates Battaglia could also get a longer look this season. Geoff Sanderson was an all-star winger before falling off the face of the planet and being traded to Vancouver, which in turn quickly traded him to Buffalo.

The right side has Sami Kapanen, coming off his breakout season, along with Ray Sheppard, Robert Kron, Nelson Emerson, Steven Rice, Kevin Dineen, and Steve Leach. Sheppard is a question mark because he goes into lengthy slumps, and Dineen may just about be finished.

Any time you have a decent forward unit and you add a player as good as Francis to the mix, everybody else on the top lines also becomes a little bit better. Two, maybe three, scoring lines is very unusual in today's NHL.

Hockey Annual Rating: 6 of 27

SPECIAL TEAMS: The collapse of Geoff Sanderson and the trade of Andrew Cassels was all that was needed for the Hurricanes to drop from fourth overall in power play percentage to 18th. And after the Olympic break, the Hurricanes were the worst in the league on the power play.

The addition of Francis will help and Iafrate will be good on the power play, too. Of course, that's if Iafrate can remain healthy. There's no dominant sniper however, it's just who happens to be out there.

The penalty killing was middle of the road and picked up after Ranheim started playing there regularly.

Power Play	G	ATT	PCT
Overall	50	378	13.2% (18th NHL)
Home	26	195	13.3% (20th NHL)
Road	24	183	13.1% (21st NHL)

10 SHORTHANDED GOALS ALLOWED (t-13th)

PENALTY KILLING			
Overall	58	391	85.2% (t-12th NHL)
Home	29	194	85.1% (t-13th NHL)
Road	29	195	85.3% (12th NHL)

8 SHORTHANDED GOALS SCORED (t-18th)

HURRICANES SPECIAL TEAMS SCORING

Power play	G	A	PTS
EMERSON	6	15	21
CHIASSON	6	13	19
PRIMEAU	7	11	18
KAPANEN	4	14	18
SHEPPARD	7	9	16
ROBERTS	4	9	13
O'NEILL	7	4	11
WESLEY	1	7	8
KRON	4	3	7
GELINAS	3	3	6
DINEEN	0	4	4
LESCHYSHYN	1	1	2
LEACH	1	1	2
RICE	0	1	1
HILL	0	1	1
HALLER	0	1	1
BURT	0	1	1

Short handed	G	A	PTS
PRIMEAU	3	1	4
GELINAS	2	2	4
O'NEILL	1	1	2
RANHEIM	1	0	1
LEACH	1	0	1
BURT	1	0	1
WESLEY	0	1	1
ROBERTS	0	1	1
MANDERVILLE	0	1	1
KRON	0	1	1

COACHING AND MANAGEMENT: Management of this team tries awfully hard, you have to give them that. GM Jim Rutherford is always busy trying to make improvements. You know they're working within budgetary constraints, but you also know that they're not afraid to spend money if they think it's worthwhile. They're just not going to throw it away. They don't want players who are going to whine about being there, and they do their best to dispose of them. Those type players do nothing for a team's winning attitude and that's what the Hurricanes are building.

The offer sheet for Sergei Fedorov was intelligently put together. Everybody knows that the team holding the restricted free agents' rights are always going to match, so the Hurricanes structured it so that there was a possibility the Wings would not match the offer. There was the 12 million dollar bonus that was spread over four years as long as the team didn't make it to the conference finals. If they did make it to the conference finals, the whole amount had to be paid this year. The liklihood of that happening in Detroit was much higher than in Carolina.

Paul Maurice was the youngest coach in professional sports last year, at age 31, and shockingly enough, was the coach who had been with his current team the longest in the Eastern Conference.

Management here is smart enough to know that you have to have the horses to win the race, and they didn't have them. If Maurice can't get the Hurricanes to the playoffs this year, however, he'll be the youngest coach fired in professional sports.

Management here likes stability. They're loyal to the players as much as any other organization in the league. The players in turn, seem to recognize that, and want to stay with the team. Although there's no evidence to suggest that that quality translates to winning hockey, it's still a nice thing to have.

The Hurricanes are making every effort possible to ensure that they don't become the next team on the list below. They currently have missed the playoffs for six years in a row.

Longest Playoff Droughts in NHL History:

Team	Years	
New Jersey	9	1978 - 1987
Washington	8	1975 - 1982
Boston	8	1960 - 1967
Detroit	7	1971 - 1977

Hockey Annual Rating: 13 of 27

DRAFT

Round	Sel.	Player	Pos	Team
1	11	Jeff Heerema	RW	Sarnia (OHL)
3	71	Erik Cole	RW	Clarkson (ECAC)
5	91	Josef Vasicek	C	Czech
5	93	Tommy Westlund	LW	Sweden
5	97	Chris Madden	G	Guelph (OHL)
7	184	Donald Smith	C	Clarkson (ECAC)
8	208	Jaroslav Svoboda	LW	Czech
9	217	Mark Kosick	C	Michigan (CCHA)
9	239	Brent McDonald	C	Red Deer (WHL)

The Whalers wanted speed in the draft and they got it with Jeff Heerema. He still has to fill out physically to be the finished product, but he has the raw materials to be a good scoring winger in the NHL eventually.

PROGNOSIS: The Hurricanes are finally going to make it to the playoffs. Finally.

Normally, we just think of this team in terms of will they or will they not make the post-season. Now we have to consider how well they'll do in the playoffs.

That remains to be seen, but the Hurricanes are building a team that has players with character, with winning attitudes and whose players aren't as one-dimensional as those many teams build with.

They're definitely a team on the way up.

PREDICTION
Eastern Conference: 6
Overall: 9

STAT SECTION
Team Scoring Stats

	GP	G	A	PTS	+/-	PIM	SH	CAREER GP	G	A	Pts
KEITH PRIMEAU	81	26	37	63	19	110	180	519	149	195	344
SAMI KAPANEN	81	26	37	63	9	16	190	161	44	53	97
GARY ROBERTS	61	20	29	49	3	103	106	646	277	277	554
NELSON EMERSON	81	21	24	45	17-	50	203	524	151	236	387
JEFF O'NEILL	74	19	20	39	8-	67	114	211	41	55	97
RAY SHEPPARD	71	18	19	37	11-	23	169	696	322	257	579
ROBERT KRON	81	16	20	36	8-	12	175	497	110	129	239
MARTIN GELINAS	64	16	18	34	5-	40	147	587	168	161	329
STEVE CHIASSON	66	7	27	34	2-	65	173	723	92	297	389
GLEN WESLEY	82	6	19	25	7	36	121	803	99	305	404
KEVIN DINEEN	54	7	16	23	7-	105	96	925	330	372	702
PAUL RANHEIM	73	5	9	14	11-	28	77	629	125	157	282
CURTIS LESCHYSHYN	73	2	10	12	2-	45	53	661	40	130	170
ADAM BURT	76	1	11	12	6-	106	51	575	36	103	139
STEPHEN LEACH	45	4	5	9	19-	42	60	615	127	147	274
KENT MANDERVILLE	77	4	4	8	6-	31	80	294	21	29	50
KEVIN HALLER	65	3	5	8	5-	94	67	462	36	81	117
STU GRIMSON	82	3	4	7	0	204	17	504	9	17	26
SEAN HILL	55	1	6	7	5-	54	53	284	18	60	78
JON BATTAGLIA	33	2	4	6	1-	10	21	33	2	4	6
STEVEN RICE	47	2	4	6	16-	38	39	329	64	61	125
STEVEN HALKO	18	0	2	2	1-	10	7	18	0	2	2
NOLAN PRATT	23	0	2	2	2-	44	11	32	0	4	4
MIKE RUCINSKI	9	0	1	1	0	2	3	9	0	1	1
JEFF DANIELS	2	0	0	0	0	0	1	156	8	13	21
MICHAEL FOUNTAIN	3	0	0	0	0	2	0	goalie			
STEVE MARTINS	3	0	0	0	0	0	0	28	1	4	5
KEVIN BROWN	4	0	0	0	2-	0	0	45	3	7	10
PAT JABLONSKI	5	0	0	0	0	0	0	goalie			
TREVOR KIDD	47	0	0	0	0	2	0	goalie			

* Team Rankings 1997-98 (previous year's ranking in parenthesis)

		Conference Rank	League Rank
Record	33-41-8	9 (10)	17 (19)
Home	16-18-7	8 (6)	17 (9)
Away	17-23-1	9 (13)	17 (25)
Versus Own Conference	20-32-4	11 (5)	19 (9)
Versus Other Conference	13-9-4	2 (13)	5 (25)
Team Plus\Minus	2-2-8	7 (12)	13 (23)
Goals For	200	10 (9)	21 (18)
Goals Against	219	9 (10)	15 (19)
Average Shots For	26.5	8 (6)	19 (13)
Average Shots Against	27.6	7 (9)	13 (19)
Overtime	2-2-8	8 (9)	13 (18)
One Goal Games	12-18	10 (9)	20 (19)
Times outshooting opponent	37	7 (9)	15 (17)
Versus Teams Over .500	17-29-5	9 (7)	17 (15)
Versus Teams .500 or under	16-12-3	8 (9)	15 (19)
First Half Record	15-21-5	11 (7)	18 (17)
Second Half Record	18-20-3	9 (12)	17 (23)

PLAYOFFS
- did not make playoffs

All-Time Leaders
Goals
Ron Francis	264
Kevin Dineen	242
Blaine Stoughton	219

Assists
Ron Francis	557
Kevin Dineen	286
Andrew Cassels	253

Points
Ron Francis	821
Kevin Dineen	526
Pat Verbeek	403

Best Individual Seasons
Goals
Blaine Stoughton	1979-80	56
Blaine Stoughton	1981-82	52
Geoff Sanderson	1992-93	46

Assists
Ron Francis	1989-90	69
Mike Rogers	1980-81	65
Andrew Cassels	1992-93	65

Points
Mike Rogers	1979-80	105
Mike Rogers	1980-81	105
Ron Francis	1989-90	101

TEAM
Last 3 years

	GP	W	L	T	Pts	%
1997-98	82	33	41	8	74	.451
1996-97	82	32	39	11	75	.457
1995-96	82	34	39	9	77	.470

Best 3 regular seasons

	GP	W	L	T	Pts	%
1986-87	80	43	30	7	93	.600
1989-90	80	38	33	9	85	.531
1985-86	80	40	36	4	84	.525

Worst 3 regular seasons

	GP	W	L	T	Pts	%
1982-83	80	19	54	7	45	.281
1992-93	84	26	52	6	58	.345
1993-94	84	27	48	9	63	.375

Most Goals (min. 70 game schedule)
1985-86	332
1979-89	303
1988-89	299

Fewest Goals (min. 70 game schedule)
1997-98	200
1996-97	226
1993-94	227

Most Goals Against (min. 70 game schedule)
1982-83	403
1980-81	372
1992-93	369

Fewest Goals Against (min. 70 game schedule)
1997-98	219
1996-97	256
1995-96	259

Florida Panthers

Blame it on El Nino. It was a disasterous year for Florida. The state, that is. Storms, floods, tornados, fires, and their two hockey teams had the two worst records in the league.

In last year's Hockey Annual, it was suggested that the Panthers could be the "disaster team" of last year. That wasn't the consensus at the time because they were coming off an 89-point season and were just a year removed from the Stanley Cup finals. Guess what? They were.

Biggest Point Drops:

	97-98 Points	96-97 Points	Difference
Tampa Bay	74	34	-40
Florida	89	63	-26
Anaheim	85	65	-20

Now, isn't that a coincidence — three of the four newest expansion franchises with the biggest point drops. Maybe not so much a coincidence.

All three of those teams were successful early in their franchise history. Far more successful than anyone would have thought. The Panthers made it to the Stanley Cup finals in just their third year, while the Lightning and Ducks have both made the playoffs in their short history, and both were surprisingly competitive in their initial years.

Here's the oddity. The fourth team in this group is Ottawa, a franchise that was horrendous at the start and has improved gradually. This year, they were the best of the four and now might have the best future.

It could be that success is the root of the problem. Teams that experience success too quickly don't think in the same terms as a gradually improving expansion team should. Expectations became higher, so instead of looking to be a good team three years down the road, they feel they're in a position to make improvements immediately. That means making moves that they might not make otherwise, such as getting a player to help down the stretch and giving up a prospect for that immediate help. Maybe, for example, they need someone for the power play, and as teams do when they're headed for the playoffs, give up more than they would have otherwise.

Another problem is that expansion teams don't have a lot of depth. The prospects have been built up, but the potential winners are being drawn from a smaller pool. In other words, they usually have the numbers by this time, but not the talent.

Another factor is that teams can build a little quicker now through free agency. Unrestricted free agents, however, are older players, so while they may help in the short run, they may be retarding the progress of younger prospects who aren't getting the chance to play.

STUFF

* the Panthers set a team record for most goals in a game when they beat Boston 10-5. It was the first game after Doug MacLean was fired.
* John Vanbiesbrouck earned his 300th win, the 15th goalie in NHL history to do so.
* Kirk Muller played in his 1,000th game.
* Dino Ciccarelli became the ninth player to score 600 NHL goals.
* The 32-goals Ray Whitney scored while with Florida tied a team record for most goals in a season.

TEAM PREVIEW

GOAL: It looks like Kirk McLean and Kevin Weekes will take care of the Florida goaltending this year. Looks can be deceiving, however. Another goalie must be on the way.

Vanbiesbrouck had a great run as the Panthers goalie, and was a big part of their early success. His stay had run its course, and he wasn't going to do anything to turn the

Panthers around last season, or this season.
Hockey Annual Rating: 26 of 27

DEFENCE: Everybody was all over Ed Jovanovski for poor play last year, but there's not a team in the league that wouldn't fall all over themselves to get him. Big deal, he had a bad season. He'll be back, and a Norris Trophy as the league's best defenseman isn't out of his range within the next couple years. He's got toughness, size, and can contribute offensively.

Robert Svehla is a premier offensive defenseman and power play quarterback, although he faded some later in the year. Most teams in the league would love to have him, too.

Paul Laus is a premier tough guy defensemen, who also played the wing last year. Ditto on most teams wanting him.

Gord Murphy is an all-round defensman, Rhett Warrener is reliable stay-at-home defensemen.

Terry Carkner looks like he could be a pressbox regular and Jeff Norton isn't assured of regular work, either.

GM Bryan Murray apparently is interested in another offensive defensman, but Jovanovski hasn't shown all he can do yet, and other teams are a lot weaker offensively than they are.

At the draft, Murray used a fifth round pick to draft Jaroslav Spacek who Murray says was the best defenceman in the Swedish league last

GOALTENDER	GPI	MINS	AVG	W	L	T	EN	SO	GA	SA	SV %
J. VANBIESBROUCK	60	3451	2.87	18	29	11	4	4	165	1638	.899
MARK FITZPATRICK	12	640	3.00	2	7	2	0	1	32	265	.879
KIRK MCLEAN	7	406	3.25	4	2	1	0	0	22	207	.894
KEVIN WEEKES	11	485	3.96	0	5	1	1	0	32	247	.870
FLA TOTALS	82	5009	3.07	24	43	15	5	5	256	2362	.892

season. Spacek is 24-years-old, and with Murray singing his praises so loud, it's a good bet he'll be in the Florida lineup next year.

The prize may be junior Chris Allen, who was 38-56-94 in 66 games with Kingston in the OHL last year. He's got a booming shot, and although the other parts of his game may not be up to scratch, it may be good enough.

Hockey Annual Rating: 21 of 27

FORWARD: Considering there were so many players who didn't meet expectations last year, you have to figure this group has a chance of doing something. Something more than last year, at any rate.

Ray Whitney may have exceeded expectations more than any player in the league. A waiver wire pickup from Edmonton after spending a year in the minors, and he scores 33 goals.

Viktor Kozlov looks like he may be ready to show why he was taken sixth overall in the 1993 draft.

Rob Niedermayer is coming off an injury-plagued season and could reclaim his status as the team's top forward.

There are also a lot of guys who are at about an eight or nine count. They may or may not be able to pick themselves up off the mat for another year or two. Kirk Muller, Dave Gagner, Dino Ciccarelli, Johan Garpenlov and Scott Mellanby all fit into that category.

Among the younger players, Radek Dvorak is a walking question mark, while David Nemirovsky and Steve Washburn showed some scoring ability and could do even better with increased ice time. Chris Wells doesn't look like like scoring will be his bag.

Bill Lindsay continues to fill the role of checker, while Peter Worrell can handle the enforcer role. Worrell had 153 penalty minutes in just 19 games. Projected over 82 games that works out to an incredible 660 penalty minutes.

The Panthers are high on prospect winger Mark Parrish who scored 54 goals in 54 games for Seattle in the WHL. He could step into the lineup this year. Olag Kvasha is another prospect who played in the AHL last year, as is Ryan Johnson.

Overall, there's certainly nothing very special about the Florida forwards that you'd want to hang your hat on. They should do better, however, if only because they couldn't have been any worse.

Hockey Annual Rating: 25 of 27

SPECIAL TEAMS: The Panthers had the snipers who were going to do the job on the power play. They just failed to show up. That's a list that includes everyone but Ray Whitney, who showed up almost uninvited.

The Panthers really lost it after the Olympic Break. In those 25 games, they managed to score just 16 while giving up a whopping 37, the most in the league.

Most Power Play Goals Allowed After Olympic Break:

Florida	37
Anaheim	32
Chicago	29
League Ave.	20

A new coach has a way of making special teams a priority, especially when they've been so

bad.Power Play	G	ATT	PCT	
Overall	55	409	13.4%	(17th NHL)
Home	28	207	13.5%	(19th NHL)
Road	27	202	13.4%	(20th NHL)

16 SHORT HANDED GOALS ALLOWED (T-23rd NHL)

PENALTY KILLING

Overall	82	403	79.7%	(26th NHL)
Home	41	181	77.3%	(26th NHL)
Road	41	222	81.5%	(25th NHL)

12 SHORT HANDED GOALS SCORED (T-7th NHL)

PANTHERS SPECIAL TEAMS SCORING

Power play	G	A	PTS
WHITNEY	12	17	29
SVEHLA	3	23	26
GAGNER	5	12	17
MELLANBY	6	6	12
CICCARELLI	5	5	10
NORTON	4	3	7
NEMIROVSKY	2	5	7
JOVANOVSKI	2	5	7
NIEDERMAYER	5	1	6
KOZLOV	5	1	6
WASHBURN	4	2	6
MURPHY	3	1	4
DVORAK	2	2	4
MULLER	1	3	4
LAUS	0	2	2
WELLS	0	1	1

Short handed	G	A	PTS
DVORAK	3	2	5
WELLS	1	3	4
LINDSAY	2	1	3
KOZLOV	2	0	2
MURPHY	0	2	2
JOVANOVSKI	1	0	1
GAGNER	1	0	1

WASHBURN	0	1	1
SVEHLA	0	1	1
MULLER	0	1	1
LAUS	0	1	1

COACHING AND MANAGEMENT: The Florida management is very patient. They waited a full 23 games into the season to fire Doug MacLean, a man who had guided them to the Stanley Cup finals and two winning seasons. It didn't take long for MacLean to find another job anyway, as he was named GM of the expansion Columbus Blue Jackets.

GM Bryan Murray stepped behind the bench and the Panthers promptly set a team record in his first game when they scored 10 goals in a 10-5 win over Boston. Of course, that was before the 14-game losing streak and the rest of the disastrous season.

So, Murray could probably conclude afer that, that coaching wasn't the problem. It won't be his problem in any event, after hiring his brother Terry to coach the team this season.

Management doesn't sit quiet in Florida. They try a lot of different things and lots of trades in order to improve the team. Some of them work, some don't. What they can be faulted for, however, is paying out too much money for too long to veterans. Geez, it wasn't all that difficult to see that Muller and Garpenlov were just about finished as NHL'ers. So, a three year contract at big bucks for Muller? That's just lousy judgement.

Sometimes people don't understand that as players get older their skills diminish. That's because they're not looking at birthdates. Of course, players are going longer these days, but they're not yet going forever. When they lose it, it goes fast. Good management should be able to anticipate that a player isn't going to last three more years when they're already a couple seasons past their 30th birthday.

There are exceptions, of course. Goalies tend to play longer into their thirties, and extremely fast skaters tend to last longer. Paul Coffey and Mike Gartner are two good examples of that.

It will be a interesting news day when Murray fires Murray, and without a doubt it's going to happen eventually. Presumably, Murray will give Murray longer than 23 games to prove himself.

Hockey Annual Rating: 21 of 27

DRAFT

Round	Sel.	Player	Pos	Team
2	30	Kyle Rossiter	D	Spokane (WHL)
3	61	Joe Dipenta	D	Boston U. (HE)
3	63	Lance Ward	D	Red Deer (WHL)
4	89	Ryan Jardine	LW	S.S. Marie (OHL)
5	117	Jaroslav Spacek	D	Sweden
6	148	Chris Ovington	D	Red Deer (OHL)
7	176	B.J. Ketcheson	D	Peterborough (OHL)
8	203	Ian Jacobs	RW	Ottawa (OHL)
9	231	Adrian Wichser	C	Sweden

No first round pick for the Panthers but they think they got their prize in the fifth round when they selected 24-year-old Jaroslav Spacek from Sweden. An offensive defenceman, they like him to make the lineup this year and quarterback the power play. Easier said than done.

PROGNOSIS

It's pretty iffy with the Panthers. We can pretty much rule out them being as bad as last year, but challenging for a playoff spot seems a stretch. It's going to take a while for them to get back in the game. Questionable goaltending, ancient forwards and unproven youngsters don't guarantee anything.

PREDICTION

Eastern Conference: 11th
Overall: 21st

STAT SECTION

Team Scoring Stats

| | GP | G | A | PTS | +/- | PIM | SH | CAREER | | | |
								GP	G	A	Pts
RAY WHITNEY	77	33	32	65	9	28	175	277	81	105	186
DAVE GAGNER	78	20	28	48	21-	55	165	877	312	379	691
ROBERT SVEHLA	79	9	34	43	3-	113	144	247	31	116	147
SCOTT MELLANBY	79	15	24	39	14-	127	188	872	238	291	529
RADEK DVORAK	64	12	24	36	1-	33	112	219	43	59	102
DINO CICCARELLI	62	16	17	33	16-	70	161	1,218	602	591	1,193

VIKTOR KOZLOV	64	17	13	30	3-	16	165	220	41	51	92
KIRK MULLER	70	8	21	29	14-	54	115	1,032	510	582	1,092
BILL LINDSAY	82	12	16	28	2-	80	150	435	57	89	146
ED JOVANOVSKI	81	9	14	23	12-	158	142	212	26	41	67
DAVID NEMIROVSKY	41	9	12	21	3-	8	62	89	16	21	37
STEVE WASHBURN	58	11	8	19	6-	32	61	77	14	15	29
GORD MURPHY	79	6	11	17	3-	46	123	711	81	208	289
JEFF NORTON	56	4	13	17	32-	44	61	591	46	278	324
ROB NIEDERMAYER	33	8	7	15	9-	41	64	288	61	89	150
CHRIS WELLS	61	5	10	15	4	47	57	162	9	18	27
PAUL LAUS	77	0	11	11	5-	293	64	808	5	36	41
TERRY CARKNER	74	1	7	8	6	63	34	796	40	179	219
JOHAN GARPENLOV	39	2	3	5	6-	8	43	472	103	174	277
RHETT WARRENER	79	0	4	4	16-	99	66	169	4	16	20
J. VANBIESBROUCK	60	0	3	3	0	6	0	goalie			
RYAN JOHNSON	10	0	2	2	4-	0	6	10	0	2	2
DALLAS EAKINS	23	0	1	1	1	44	16	80	0	4	4
KIRK MCLEAN	44	0	1	1	0	0	0	goalie			
CHRIS ALLEN	1	0	0	0	0	2	1	1	0	0	0
JOHN JAKOPIN	2	0	0	0	3-	4	1	2	0	0	0
KEVIN WEEKES	11	0	0	0	0	0	0	goalie			
PETER WORRELL	19	0	0	0	4-	153	15	19	0	0	0

* Team Rankings 1997-98 (previous year's ranking in parenthesis)

		Conference Rank	League Rank
Record	24-43-15	12 (4)	25 (8)
Home	11-24-6	13 (5)	26 (8)
Away	13-19-9	10 (3)	20 (9)
Versus Own Conference	22-26-8	8 (4)	16 (15)
Versus Other Conference	2-17-7	13 (5)	26 (10)
Team Plus\Minus	-26	11 (5)	22 (9)
Goals For	203	9 (11)	20 (21)
Goals Against	256	12 (2)	23 (4)
Average Shots For	27.8	5 (10)	7 (19)
Average Shots Against	28.8	10 (5)	19 (9)
Overtime	3-2-15	6 (8)	10 (17)
One Goal Games	12-13	8 (5)	18 (8)
Times outshooting opponent	35	9 (7)	17 (14)
Versus Teams Over .500	15-27-5	11 (3)	19 (5)
Versus Teams Under .500	9-16-10	12 (7)	25 (14)
First Half Record	15-20-6	10 (2)	18 (3)
Second Half Record	9-23-9	12 (7)	25 (16)

PLAYOFFS

- did not make the playoffs.

Goals

Scott Mellanby	117
Rob Niedermayer	61
Jody Hull	56

Assists

Scott Mellanby	133
Robert Svehla	116
Gord Murphy	93

Points

Scott Mellanby	250
Rob Niedermayer	150
Robert Svehla	147

Best Individual Seasons
Goals

Ray Whitney	1997-98	32
Scott Mellanby	1995-96	32
Scott Mellanby	1993-94	30

Assists

Robert Svelha	1995-96	49
Scott Mellanby	1995-96	38
Rob Niedermayer	1995-96	35

Points

Scott Mellanby	1995-96	70
Ray Whitney	1997-98	61
Rob Niedermayer	1995-96	61

TEAM
Last 3 years

	GP	W	L	T	Pts	%
1997-98	82	24	43	15	63	.384
1996-97	82	35	28	19	89	.549
1995-96	82	41	31	10	92	.561
1994-95	48	20	22	6	46	.479

Best 3 regular seasons

	GP	W	L	T	Pts	%
1995-96	82	41	31	10	92	.561
1996-97	82	35	28	19	89	.549
1993-94	84	33	34	17	83	.494

Worst 3 regular seasons

	GP	W	L	T	Pts	%
1997-98	82	24	43	15	63	.384
1994-95	48	20	22	6	46	.479
1993-94	84	33	34	17	83	.494

Most Goals (min. 70 game schedule)
1995-96   254
1993-94   233
1996-97   221

Fewest Goals (min. 70 game schedule)
1997-98   203
1996-97   221
1993-94   233

Most Goals Against (min. 70 game schedule)
1997-98   256
1995-96   234
1993-94   233

Fewest Goals Against (min. 70 game schedule)
1996-97   201
1993-94   233
1995-96   234

Montreal Canadiens

It was a year of improvement in Montreal. They only gained 10 points from their previous season, but a record of 37-32-13 is a lot more impressive than one of 31-36-15. And they were just a much better team.

New coach Alain Vigneault has to take credit for a lot of it, and assistant coach Dave King also deserves some for helping turn the team around defensively.

Consider the biggest improvements in goals against last season.

Biggest Drops in Goals Against:

Boston   106
Pittsburgh   92
MONTREAL   68

Something we should point out, however, is that almost every team in the league dropped their goals against. There was a drop of more than half a goal a game scored in the league from the previous season.

A better indication of a team's goal scoring and defensive improvement would be to consider their net goals improvement — goals scored for difference plus goals against difference.

Only three of the 26 teams showed an increase in goals against, and only three teams scored better than they had the previous season.

	Goals For Increase	Goals Against Reduction	Net Difference
Boston	-13	+104	+90
San Jose	-1	+62	+61
Los Angeles	+13	-43	+58
St. Louis	+20	-35	+55
MONTREAL	-14	+68	+54

Montreal was a good scoring team before, so what the stats show is that they were able to improve defensively, without giving up hardly anything offensively, and that's impressive and difficult to do. The teams listed above Montreal on the latter chart were not good scoring teams prior to last season, except for St. Louis.

What it comes down to is that Montreal were able to do something that few teams could but all would like to do, keep their offence while improving their defence.

So, guess how many votes Vigneault got in the Adams voting for coach of the year. The answer is zero. If it was because voters thought King had too much to do with it, fine. It's generally an award for the most improved team, anyway, and there was a lot of that going around, especially in Boston, where Pat Burns turned around a last place team and in Los Angeles where Larry Robinson also turned things around. Robinson didn't do it overnight, though, and Burns had a different team to work with.

The Hockey News didn't even list Vigneault among its honorable mentions, but what Vigneault did last season was very impressive and he deserves more recognition for it.

STUFF

* Andy Moog retired with 372 wins, fifth on the all-time list.
* Montreal's losing home record was their first since the 1939-40 season.
* It was the first time in Canadiens history that they had a winning record on the road and a losing record at home.

TEAM PREVIEW

GOAL: If you were watching the playoffs last season you might have retained the image of Andy Moog being pulled from his last ever NHL game. He still had a year left on his contract, but it looked as if he knew it was the end, which it was.

So many players hang on well past their effectiveness. Moog didn't want to do that, giving up the final year of his contract. That's an honorable thing to do that is so rare in professional sports nowadays.

Jocelyn Thibault and Jose Theodore take over the duties, and this time they'll be more ready than the last time.

The bottom line, however, is that Montreal fans won't be happy with them unless they play like Patrick Roy in his prime.

Hockey Annual Rating: 21 of 27

DEFENCE: The Canadiens worked hard to go from a weak defence to a good one. They've got all the things they need: mobility, toughness, experience, and now some youth.

Of course, every team has that to some degree, but the Canadiens didn't, and that wasn't long ago.

There is a problem, however, and his name is Vladimir Malakhov. He had a good offensive season and he can quarterback the power play, but the Canadiens aren't sure they even want him around. They've made thinly veiled comments to the effect that they'll have to see whether he fits into their team concept. He sat out the last game of the playoffs because he had a sore neck, when players with far more serious injuries were still playing. The Canadiens might just think he's a pain in the butt, and move him out. Mind you, they could just forget about it, too.

Patrice Brisebois has taken a lot of heat in Montreal in previous years, but he had a good season. Dave Manson, too, although his PIM

GOALTENDER	GPI	MINS	AVG	W	L	T	EN	SO	GA	SA	SV %
JOCELYN THIBAULT	47	2652	2.47	19	15	8	1	2	109	1109	.902
ANDY MOOG	42	2337	2.49	18	17	5	1	3	97	1024	.905
MTL TOTALS	82	5009	2.49	37	32	13	2	5	208	2135	.903

dropped to the lowest in his career. Sometimes, all it takes is the threat of lunacy to keep opposing players from taking liberties. Stephane Quintal, Igor Ulanov and Craig Rivet round out the veterans on defence.

Brett Clark should get more work this year, and the Canadiens like Miroslav Guren, and want to get him into the lineup. Brad Brown, who was upset that the Canadiens didn't call him up last year, is a toughnik, who somebody will want if Montreal doesn't.

Hockey Annual Rating: 11 of 27

FORWARD: Not many teams can score more goals than Montreal. Last year, less than a handful could do it, and only Philadelphia in the Eastern Conference, with just seven more than the Canadiens.

When you consider that Saku Koivu and Vincent Damphousse didn't have good years, and that Brian Savage missed 18 games and Shayne Corson 20 games, then you have to figure it can only get better.

Mark Recchi never has a bad year, and never misses any games. He played in all his teams' games for the seventh year in a row. The last time he missed any was in the 1990-91 season, and that was because of a short contract holdout.

Among the supporting cast, Martin Rucinsky has been much more consistent that previously thought, although he did make a faux pas in the playoffs by saying the Buffalo Sabres were just average after Dominik Hasek. Everybody knows that to be true, but you don't say it when there's any chance you could motivate the opposing team at the wrong time.

Jonas Hoglund should score more or he's out. Benoit Brunet added some surprising

offence to his game last year. Turner Stevenson and Scott Thornton are role players who aren't expected to score.

Patrick Poulin had seven points in his first seven games with Montreal, which isn't unusual when a player is traded during the season. But, he had just three points in the other 27 Montreal games he played. He's a lost cause.

Gone is Marc Bureau, who had an outstanding season as a defensive forward with a little unexpected punch in his offence. He signed with Philadelphia as an unrestricted free agent. He can be replaced though, and maybe it wouldn't be such a bad idea. Bureau was quoted as saying something bothersome. He said his motivation was that he was to become a free agent at the end of the year. Oh? What about the team winning? Isn't that motivation enough? And what about if he has a three-year contract, does that mean he won't be motivated anymore?

A prospect who could get a long look is Terry Ryan, a tough forward who had 242 minutes and 19 goals in 61 games for Fredericton last year.

Hockey Annual Rating: 8 of 27

SPECIAL TEAMS: The Canadiens should have and did do well on the power play. They've got good offensive players, including a power play sniper in Corson and quarterback in Malakhov.

Power Play	G	ATT	PCT	
Overall	68	372	18.3%	(3rd NHL)
Home	31	186	16.7%	(9th NHL)
Road	37	186	19.9%	(3rd NHL)

8 SHORT HANDED GOALS ALLOWED (8th NHL)

PENALTY KILLING

Overall	62	401	84.5%	(T-16th NHL)
Home	25	194	87.1%	(T-6th NHL)
Road	37	207	82.1%	(T-23rd NHL)

13 SHORT HANDED GOALS SCORED (T-5th NHL)

CANADIENS SPECIAL TEAMS SCORING

Power play	G	A	PTS
RECCHI	9	20	29
MALAKHOV	8	17	25
CORSON	14	9	23
KOIVU	2	19	21
BRISEBOIS	5	12	17
DAMPHOUSSE	2	13	15
RUCINSKY	5	9	14
SAVAGE	8	3	11
MANSON	2	8	10
HOGLUND	4	2	6
ZALAPSKI	2	4	6
BORDELEAU	2	4	6
BRUNET	1	3	4
THORNTON	1	1	2
POULIN	0	2	2
ULANOV	1	0	1
STEVENSON	1	0	1

Short handed	G	A	PTS
RUCINSKY	3	2	5
BRUNET	2	2	4
KOIVU	2	1	3
POULIN	1	2	3
DAMPHOUSSE	1	2	3
CORSON	1	2	3
BUREAU	0	2	2
ZALAPSKI	1	0	1
RECCHI	1	0	1
BORDELEAU	1	0	1
MALAKHOV	0	1	1
BRISEBOIS	0	1	1

COACHING AND MANAGEMENT: Alain Vigneault and Rejean Houle did a tremendous job turning this team around. Assistant coach Dave King, too. The organized Vigneault was the opposite of Tremblay right from the start, and that was just what the team needed.

Hockey Annual Rating: 14 of 27

DRAFT

Round	Sel.	Player	Pos	Team
1	16	Eric Chouinard	C	Quebec (QMJHL)
2	45	Mike Ribeiro	C	Rouyn-Noranda (QMJHL)
3	75	F. Beauchemin	D	Laval (QMJHL)
5	132	Andrei Bashkirov	LW	Fort Wayne (IHL)
6	152	Gordie Dwyer	LW	Quebec (QMJHL)
6	162	Andrei Markov	C	Russia
7	189	Andrei Kruchinin	D	Russia
8	201	Chris Murray	C	Penticton (BCJHL)
8	216	Michael Ryder	C	Hull (QMJHL)
9	247	Darcy Harris	RW	Kitchener (OHL)

Eric Chouinard is a smooth centreman who posted numbers of 41-42-83 in his first season in the QMJHL. Chouinard was born in Atlanta, Georgia, not a hockey hotbed unless your father (Guy) happened to have been playing with the Flames at the time. Chouinard's father also happened to be his coach last year in Quebec.

PROGNOSIS: The Canadiens might be worried about their goaltending, but they can score goals and their defence can stop the opposition. With a number of forwards coming off injury-plagued or off-seasons, it wouldn't be a surprise if the Canadiens were one of the top three scoring teams in the league.

If they can stay healthy their win total is going to rise as well.

PREDICTION
Eastern Conference: 5th
Overall: 8th

STAT SECTION
Team Scoring Stats

	GP	G	A	PTS	+/-	PIM	SH	CAREER GP	G	A	Pts
MARK RECCHI	82	32	42	74	11	51	216	710	317	472	789
VINCENT DAMPHOUSSE	76	18	41	59	14	58	164	928	328	552	880
SAKU KOIVU	69	14	43	57	8	48	145	201	51	107	158
SHAYNE CORSON	62	21	34	55	2	108	142	809	221	328	549
MARTIN RUCINSKY	78	21	32	53	13	84	192	389	109	165	274
VLADIMIR MALAKHOV	74	13	31	44	16	70	166	380	56	176	232
BRIAN SAVAGE	64	26	17	43	11	36	152	260	87	69	156
PATRICE BRISEBOIS	79	10	27	37	16	67	125	391	39	127	166
DAVE MANSON	81	4	30	34	22	122	148	844	91	253	344
BENOIT BRUNET	68	12	20	32	11	61	87	333	61	104	165
JONAS HOGLUND	78	12	13	25	7-	22	186	146	31	29	60
MARC BUREAU	74	13	6	19	0	12	82	433	48	72	120
PATRICK POULIN	78	6	13	19	4-	27	88	391	74	96	170
STEPHANE QUINTAL	71	6	10	16	13	97	88	593	38	109	147
SCOTT THORNTON	67	6	9	15	0	158	51	382	40	52	92
ZARLEY ZALAPSKI	63	3	12	15	13-	63	73	625	99	283	382
SEBASTIEN BORDELEAU	53	6	8	14	5	36	55	85	8	17	25
TURNER STEVENSON	63	4	6	10	8-	110	43	252	27	36	63
IGOR ULANOV	49	2	8	10	7-	97	36	351	11	68	79
PETER POPOVIC	69	2	6	8	6-	38	40	3	7	48	55
JOCELYN THIBAULT	47	0	2	2	0	0	0	goalie			
CRAIG RIVET	61	0	2	2	3-	93	26	120	1	11	12
ERIC HOUDE	9	1	0	1	3-	0	4	22	1	2	3
BRETT CLARK	41	1	0	1	3-	20	26	41	1	0	1
MICK VUKOTA	64	1	0	1	4-	192	23	574	17	29	46
FRANCOIS GROLEAU	1	0	0	0	1	0	3	8	0	1	1
DAVID LING	1	0	0	0	1-	0	1	3	0	0	0
MATT HIGGINS	1	0	0	0	1-	0	1	1	0	0	0
TERRY RYAN	4	0	0	0	0	31	0	7	0	0	0
ANDY MOOG	42	0	0	0	0	4	0	goalie			

*Team Rankings 1997-98
(previous year's ranking in parenthesis)

		Conference Rank	League Rank
Record	37-31-13	7 (7)	12 (16)
Home	15-17-9	9 (10)	18 (18)
Away	22-15-4	1 (8)	2 (14)
Versus Own Conference	22-26-8	8 (11)	16 (22)
Versus Other Conference	15-6-5	1 (6)	3 (10)
Team Plus\Minus	+21	4 (8)	7 (15)
Goals For	235	2 (4)	5 (9)
Goals Against	208	8 (11)	13 (23)
Average Shots For	27.8	4 (5)	8 (10)
Average Shots Against	26.0	4 (12)	8 (23)
Overtime	3-4-13	8 (11)	17 (21)
One Goal Games	10-17	11 (6)	21 (10)
Times outshooting opponent	43	5 (10)	11 (20)
Versus Teams Over .500	17-22-6	7 (11)	12 (20)
Versus Teams .500 or under	20-10-7	6 (6)	9 (12)
First Half Record	20-15-6	4 (10)	8 (17)
Second Half Record	17-17-7	7 (6)	14 (15)

PLAYOFFS

Results: defeated Pittsburgh 4-2

lost to Buffalo 4-0

Record: 4-6

Home: 2-3

Away: 2-3

Goals For: 28 (2.8/game)

Goals Against: 32 (3.2/game)

Overtime: 1-2

Power play: 12.0% (12th)

Penalty Killing: 84.5%(9th)

	GP	G	A	PTS	+/-	PIM	PP	SH	GW	OT	S
MARK RECCHI	10	4	8	12	2	6	0	0	2	0	22
SHAYNE CORSON	10	3	6	9	3	26	1	0	1	0	33
VINCENT DAMPHOUSSE	10	3	6	9	4-	22	1	0	0	0	42
VLADIMIR MALAKHOV	9	3	4	7	3-	10	2	0	0	0	19
TURNER STEVENSON	10	3	4	7	1	12	0	0	0	0	21
SAKU KOIVU	6	2	3	5	4	2	1	0	0	0	14
IGOR ULANOV	10	1	4	5	3	12	0	0	0	0	6

MARTIN RUCINSKY	10	3	0	3	2-	4	1	0	0	0	35
MARC BUREAU	10	1	2	3	1-	6	0	0	0	0	16
JONAS HOGLUND	10	2	0	2	1-	0	0	0	0	0	7
PETER POPOVIC	10	1	1	2	2	2	0	0	0	0	3
STEPHANE QUINTAL	9	0	2	2	2	4	0	0	0	0	12
SCOTT THORNTON	9	0	2	2	0	10	0	0	0	0	13
BRIAN SAVAGE	9	0	2	2	2-	6	0	0	0	0	24
BENOIT BRUNET	8	1	0	1	1	4	0	0	1	1	5
PATRICE BRISEBOIS	10	1	0	1	5-	0	0	0	0	0	26
JOCELYN THIBAULT	2	0	1	1	0	0	0	0	0	0	0
ZARLEY ZALAPSKI	6	0	1	1	3-	4	0	0	0	0	0
DAVE MANSON	10	0	1	1	0	14	0	0	0	0	25
MICK VUKOTA	1	0	0	0	0	0	0	0	0	0	0
PATRICK POULIN	3	0	0	0	1-	0	0	0	0	0	1
JOSE THEODORE	3	0	0	0	0	0	0	0	0	0	0
CRAIG RIVET	5	0	0	0	2-	2	0	0	0	0	5
SEBASTIEN BORDELEAU	5	0	0	0	1-	2	0	0	0	0	1
ANDY MOOG	9	0	0	0	0	0	0	0	0	0	0

GOALTENDER	GPI	MINS	AVG	W	L	T	EN	SO	GA	SA	SV %
JOSE THEODORE	3	120	.50	0	1		1	0	1	35	.971
ANDY MOOG	9	474	3.04	4	5		1	1	24	204	.882
JOCELYN THIBAULT	2	43	5.58	0	0		1	0	4	16	.750
MTL TOTALS	10	643	2.99	4	6		3	1	32	258	.876

All-Time Leaders

Goals

Maurice Richard	544
Guy Lafleur	518
Jean Beliveau	507

Assists

Guy Lafleur	728
Jean Beliveau	712
Henri Richard	688

Points

Guy Lafleur	1,246
Jean Beliveau	1,219
Henri Richard	1,046

Best Individual Seasons

Goals

Steve Shutt	1976-77	60
Guy Lafleur	1977-78	60
Guy Lafleur	1976-77	56
Guy Lafleur	1975-76	56

Assists

Peter Mahovlich	1974-75	82
Guy Lafleur	1976-77	80
Guy Lafleur	1978-79	77

Points

Guy Lafleur	1976-77	136
Guy Lafleur	1977-78	132
Guy Lafleur	1978-79	129

TEAM

Last 3 years

	GP	W	L	T	Pts	%
1997-98	82	37	32	13	87	.530
1996-97	82	31	36	15	77	.470
1995-96	82	40	32	10	90	.549

Best 3 regular seasons

	GP	W	L	T	Pts	%
1976-77	80	60	8	12	132	.825
1977-78	80	59	10	11	129	.806
1975-76	80	58	11	11	127	.794

Worst 3 regular seasons

	GP	W	L	T	Pts	%
1939-40	48	10	33	5	25	.260
1925-26	36	11	24	1	23	.319
1935-36	48	11	26	11	33	.344

Most Goals (min. 70 game schedule)

1976-77	387
1981-82	360
1977-78	359

Fewest Goals (min. 70 game schedule)

1952-55	155
1949-50	172
1950-51	173

Most Goals Against (min. 70 game schedule)

1983-84	295
1982-83	286
1992-93	280
1985-86	280

Fewest Goals Against (min. 70 game schedule)

1955-56	131
1953-54	141
1952-53	148

New Jersey Devils

Pay no attention to the Devils early playoff loss last season. Anything can happen in a short series, especially one where hardly any goals are scored.

There's little to worry about in New Jersey because it is such a well run organization in terms of moving up talent.

Each year, somebody new is moved up to the new club, and maybe are brought along slowly so that by the following year they're even more valuable. It's not as if other teams don't try to bring someone new into the lineup when they can, it's just that the quality of that individual rarely can match the consistency with which the Devils manage to do it.

We don't need to be told how important that is, but we should be aware of how rare it happens outside of the Devils.

Consider the rookie additions to their line-up in previous years:

1997-98
*Patrik Elias (2nd round, 1994) - third in Calder Trophy voting for rookie of the year.
*Sheldon Souray (3rd round, 1994) - after getting in the lineup the defenceman played the entire season, although he was a scratch for half the playoff games.

*Brad Bombadir (3rd round, 1990) - another defenceman was in and out of the lineup after serving a three year apprenticeship in the minors.
*Krzysztof Oliwa (4th round, 1993) - after lengthy apprenticeship, Oliwa now beats up NHLers rather than minor-leaguers.

1996-97
*Denis Pederson (1st round, 1993) - played a year in the minors after junior and is a regular in second NHL season.

1995-96
*Petr Sykora (1st round, 1995) - didn't follow the traditional Devils way, and ended up paying for it later, with a stint to the minors. He had a good rookie season, however, and is still a big part of New Jersey's plans.

1994-95
*Brian Rolston (1st round, 1991) - made steady progress until becoming a regular.
*Sergei Brylin (2nd round, 1992) - has shown potential and has played in bunches, but has not yet caught on as a regular.

1993-94

*Martin Brodeur (1st round, 1990) - played a season in the minors, the rest is history.

STUFF

* were 13-5-4 following a loss.

* did not register a tie until their 33rd game. The Rangers had already tied 11 by that time and every other team in the league had at least four.

* the most shots the Devils allowed in any game was just 34.

* Ken Daneyko has played in all 101 franchise playoff games.

* leading scorer, Bobby Holik, did not play in the Devils final playoff game against Ottawa because of reported case of food poisoning.

* had the longest winning streak of the season, eight games in November.

* tied with Buffalo for the longest undefeated streak, 13 games from January 31 to March 12.

* John Maclean left the Devils (traded to San Jose) as their all-time leading goal, assist and point-earner.

TEAM PREVIEW

GOAL: The Devils might like a veteran backup to Brodeur, but it can't matter that much. If Brodeur gets hurt, they can play rent-a-goalie until he's better.

Otherwise, they have at least the second or third best goalie in the league and he hasn't even reached his 27th birthday.

Brodeur has had 10 shutouts in each of the last two seasons and while we could list a lot more impressive stats, another that stands out is that in the playoffs (except for 1992 when he played part of one game) his goals against average has always been under 2.00.

Hockey Annual Rating: 2 of 27

DEFENCE: If they're not the best, they're pretty close. They have a premier offensive defenceman (Scott Niedermayer), a premier leader (Scott Stevens), a premier enforcer (Lyle Odelein), another good enforcer and defensive defenceman (Ken Daneyko), and some youth in Sheldon Souray, Brad Bombadir, who were both rookies worked slowly into the lineup. Throw in extras, Kevin Dean and Vlastimil Kroupa, and when they mess up they still have a premier goaltender behind them.

Some teams change their defence yearly, or even monthly it seems, but the Devils keep their core together. It's more important for defencemen to know what each other is going to do because if they don't it costs the team goals. Forwards can get away with it and might even benefit from having different linemates, but mistakes aren't as likely to cost them.

GOALTENDER	GPI	MINS	AVG	W	L	T	EN	SO	GA	SA	SV %
MARTIN BRODEUR	70	4128	1.89	43	17	8	4	10	130	1569	.917
RICH SHULMISTRA	1	62	1.94	0	1	0	0	0	2	30	.933
MIKE DUNHAM	15	773	2.25	5	5	3	0	1	29	332	.913
PETER SIDORKIEWICZ	1	20	3.00	0	0	0	0	0	1	8	.875
N.J TOTALS	82	4991	2.00	48	23	11	4	11	166	1943	.915

Daneyko is a rarity, because he has played so long with one team. He played his first game with New Jersey in the 1983-84 season. Stevens is entering his eighth year with the Devils, same as Niedermayer, and Odelein his third.

Hockey Annual Rating: 2 of 27

FORWARD: Just how good is Brendan Morrison? He's so good that the Devils didn't bat an eye when Doug Gilmour became an unrestricted free agent and signed with Chicago. So good that he could be the team's number one centre. So good that he could be the team's leading scorer. So good that he is a likely candidate for rookie of the year. So good that he earned nine points in 11 games after joining the team late in the year.

Bobby Holik may have something to say about Morrison taking over the number one centre job, but he plays best when he has something to prove anyway, and they'll both play together on the power play.

Most of the Devils forwards are players on the way up, with just a few on the way down. That's the New Jersey way.
On the way up:
* Patrik Elias had a good rookie year, and finished third in Calder Trophy voting, but he was also inconsistent. During one 19-game stretch his scoring totals were just 2-1-3. More consistency will equal more points.

* Jason Arnott had a stinkin' lousy year. He's all of 24-years-old, and already has a 33-goal season and a 28-goal season. He will be back.
* Denis Pederson. Still young, still improving.
* Brian Rolston. Same as Pederson.
* Petr Sykora. Has had his problems, but still

scored 16 goals in 58 games and is line for full-time duty this year.

Oliwa is likely to remain the same, while the Devils allowed Doug Gilmour and Steve Thomas to go to free agency. If they had wanted to keep them, chances are good that they would have.

On the way down are Dave Andreychuk and Bobby Carpenter, veterans who have some value, but not enough to be signed again when their contracts are up.

One player who isn't likely to reproduce last year's stats is Randy McKay. Not that it wasn't an outstanding season. He set a career high with 24 goals, after scoring just nine the season before, and only 17 in his previous best season, way back in 1991-92. He had a six-game goal-scoring streak, a four-gamer, and a hat-trick. He also went without a goal for 17- and 15-game stretches, which is more in character. Usually, players who have big seasons out of his ordinary, at his age and stage of his career, return to normal the next season.

Hockey Annual Rating: 7 of 27

SPECIAL TEAMS: No problems here. And if somebody isn't working out too well, there are more than enough Devils to jump in and take over.

Power Play	G	ATT	PCT	
Overall	63	333	18.9%	(2nd NHL)
Home	38	158	24.1%	(1st NHL)
Road	25	175	14.3%	(16th NHL)

9 SHORT HANDED GOALS ALLOWED (T-9th NHL)

PENALTY KILLING				
Overall	41	309	86.7%	(4th NHL)

| Home | 19 | 142 | 86.6% | (T-9th NHL) |
| Road | 22 | 167 | 86.8% | (7th NHL) |

4 SHORT HANDED GOALS SCORED (25th NHL)

DEVILS SPECIAL TEAMS SCORING

Power play	G	A	PTS
NIEDERMAYER	11	18	29
HOLIK	8	18	26
GILMOUR	3	20	23
ANDREYCHUK	4	12	16
ARNOTT	4	10	14
SYKORA	3	10	13
MCKAY	8	3	11
PEDERSON	7	4	11
ELIAS	5	6	11
BODGER	3	7	10
ODELEIN	1	6	7
THOMAS	3	1	4
ROLSTON	0	3	3
STEVENS	1	1	2
DEAN	1	1	2
MORRISON	0	1	1
CARPENTER	0	1	1

Short handed	G	A	PTS
CARPENTER	1	2	3
ROLSTON	2	0	2
SYKORA	1	0	1
STEVENS	0	1	1
ODELEIN	0	1	
GILMOUR	0	1	
DEAN	0	1	1

COACHING AND MANAGEMENT: If you take the best of Jacques Lemaire, and change the worst, that's what new coach Robbie Ftorek has in mind when he takes over the Devils this year. He's an admirer of Lemaire's game plan, but would like to have a little more offence.

Ftorek has coached previously in the Devils system and with Los Angeles in the late eighties when he made the ridiculous mistake of playing hardball with Wayne Gretzky. A little older, a little wiser, a lot more experienced, he's unlikely to repeat former mistakes.

GM Lou Lamoriello is close to being the best GM in the NHL, if he isn't already. He has a gameplan that he sticks to, he puts the organization above individuals, he develops outstanding prospects without rushing them, he doesn't pay ridiculous salaries just because players and their agents want them, and he wins.

Hockey Annual Rating: 7 of 27

DRAFT

Round	Sel.	Player	Pos	Team
1	26	Mike Van Ryn	D	Michigan (CCHA)
1	20	Scott Gomez	D	Tri-City (WHL)
2	37	Christian Berglund	W	Sweden
4	96	Mikko Jokela	D	Finland
4	105	Pierre Dagenais	LW	Rouyn-Noranda (QMJHL)
5	119	Anton But	W	Russia
5	143	Ryan Flinn	LW	Laval (QMJHL)
6	172	Jacques Lariviere	LW	Moncton (QMJHL)
7	199	Erik Jensen	RW	Des Moines, Iowa (Jr.A)
8	227	Marko Ahositta	C	Finland
9	257	Ryan Held	C	Kitchener (OHL)

Van Ryn will be playing again for the University of Michigan this year, the same school as Brendan Morrison. He's considered an all-round defenceman, and the Devils can afford to wait for him to develop.

The other first round pick was Alaskan born Scott Gomez, a smallish centre who is coming off a disappointing rookie season in the WHL, which was hampered by injuries. Watch his stats soar this year.

PROGNOSIS: Maybe 107 points is too high a goal. Or maybe it isn't high enough. They've only lost a couple things of significance — coach Lemaire, and Doug Gilmour. Both have been replaced, so it remains to be seen how effective they are. Chances are things won't change much, and the Devils will be back up on top.

They have most everything it takes to be winners, and except in goal, they don't have any big stars, which probably goes a lot further in the team concept of winning.

Besides that, they have fewer worries than most teams. Their defence and goaltending is top of the line, and there are just a few problems at forward that aren't too significant to matter.

The Devils were knocked out early last year by Ottawa, but they know how to win in the playoffs, so it shouldn't be considered too big a deal. They're only a couple years removed from a Stanley Cup.

PREDICTION
Eastern Conference: 2nd
Overall: 4th

STAT SECTION
Team Scoring Stats

	GP	G	A	PTS	+/-	PIM	SH	CAREER GP	G	A	Pts
BOBBY HOLIK	82	29	36	65	23	100	238	560	150	187	337
SCOTT NIEDERMAYER	81	14	43	57	5	27	175	454	52	179	231
DOUG GILMOUR	63	13	40	53	10	68	94	1,125	381	795	1,176
RANDY MCKAY	74	24	24	48	30	86	141	574	93	114	207
DAVE ANDREYCHUK	75	14	34	48	19	26	180	1,158	578	595	1,173
PATRIK ELIAS	74	18	19	37	18	28	147	92	20	22	42
PETR SYKORA	58	16	20	36	0	22	130	140	35	46	81
JASON ARNOTT	70	10	23	33	24-	99	199	321	105	149	254
BRIAN ROLSTON	76	16	14	30	7	16	185	255	54	63	117
DENIS PEDERSON	80	15	13	28	6-	97	135	160	30	34	64
SCOTT STEVENS	80	4	22	26	19	80	94	1,200	166	606	772
STEVE THOMAS	55	14	10	24	4	32	111	860	324	372	696
LYLE ODELEIN	79	4	19	23	11	171	76	578	27	107	134
DOUG BODGER	77	9	11	20	1-	57	96	993	103	410	513
BOB CARPENTER	66	9	9	18	4-	22	81	1,122	318	400	718
SHELDON SOURAY	60	3	7	10	18	85	74	60	3	7	10
BRENDAN MORRISON	11	5	4	9	3	0	19	11	5	4	9

KEVIN DEAN	50	1	8	9	12	12	28	136	3	19	22
BRAD BOMBARDIR	43	1	5	6	11	8	16	43	1	5	6
SERGEI BRYLIN	18	2	3	5	4	0	20	123	14	18	32
KRZYSZTOF OLIWA	73	2	3	5	3	295	53	74	2	3	5
JAY PANDOLFO	23	1	3	4	4-	4	23	69	7	11	18
SCOTT DANIELS	26	0	3	3	1	102	17	148	8	12	20
MARTIN BRODEUR	70	0	3	3	0	10	0	goalie			
VLASTIMIL KROUPA	2	0	1	1	1	0	1	105	4	19	23
MIKE DUNHAM	15	0	1	1	0	0	0	goalie			
KEN DANEYKO	37	0	1	1	3	57	18	910	32	110	142
PETER SIDORKIEWICZ	1	0	0	0	0	0	0	goalie			
RICH SHULMISTRA	1	0	0	0	0	0	0	goalie			
SASHA LAKOVIC	2	0	0	0	0	5	2	21	0	1	1

* Team Rankings 1997-98 (previous year's ranking in parenthesis)

		Conference Rank	League Rank
Record	48-23-11	1 (1)	2 (3)
Home	29-10-2	1 (2)	1 (3)
Away	19-13-9	3 (2)	4 (4)
Versus Own Conference	36-13-7	1 (1)	1 (3)
Versus Other Conference	12-10-4	6 (2)	11 (3)
Team Plus\Minus	+37	2 (3)	5 (4)
Goals For	225	4 (8)	9 (16)
Goals Against	166	1 (1)	1 (1)
Average Shots For	29.3	1 (2)	2 (4)
Average Shots Against	23.7	1 (3)	2 (5)
Overtime	2-3-11	10 (10)	19 (19)
One Goal Games	18-10	1 (2)	2 (3)
Times outshooting opponent	60	1 (2)	1 (3)

Versus Teams Over .500	22-12-5	1 (4)	1 (6)
Versus Teams .500 or under	26-11-6	3 (1)	4 (2)
First Half Record	26-13-2	3 (5)	4 (7)
Second Half Record	22-10-9	1 (1)	1 (1)

PLAYOFFS

Results: lost to Ottawa in the conference quarter-finals 4-2

Record: 2-4
Home: 2-1
Away: 0-3
Goals For: 12 (2.0/game)
Goals Against: 13 (2.2/game)
Overtime: 0-2
Power play: 13.0% (10th)
Penalty Killing: 82.1% (12th)

	GP	G	A	PTS	+/-	PIM	PP	SH	GW	OT	S
DOUG GILMOUR	6	5	2	7	4	4	1	0	1	0	12
STEVE THOMAS	6	0	3	3	1	2	0	0	0	0	12
LYLE ODELEIN	6	1	1	2	2	21	1	0	1	0	7
DENIS PEDERSON	6	1	1	2	0	2	0	1	0	0	8
JAY PANDOLFO	3	0	2	2	0	0	0	0	0	0	1
JASON ARNOTT	5	0	2	2	1	0	0	0	0	0	6
SCOTT NIEDERMAYER	6	0	2	2	0	4	0	0	0	0	15
KEVIN DEAN	5	1	0	1	1-	2	0	0	0	0	4
DAVE ANDREYCHUK	6	1	0	1	2-	4	1	0	0	0	17
BOB CARPENTER	6	1	0	1	0	0	0	0	0	0	3
SCOTT STEVENS	6	1	0	1	4	8	0	0	0	0	11
BRIAN ROLSTON	6	1	0	1	2	2	0	1	0	0	14
BRENDAN MORRISON	3	0	1	1	1-	0	0	0	0	0	4
SHELDON SOURAY	3	0	1	1	0	2	0	0	0	0	1
PATRIK ELIAS	4	0	1	1	2-	0	0	0	0	0	9
KEN DANEYKO	6	0	1	1	0	10	0	0	0	0	7
RANDY MCKAY	6	0	1	1	1-	0	0	0	0	0	7
MARTIN BRODEUR	6	0	1	1	0	0	0	0	0	0	0
SCOTT DANIELS	1	0	0	0	0	0	0	0	0	0	0
PETR SYKORA	2	0	0	0	0	0	0	0	0	0	5
DOUG BODGER	5	0	0	0	5-	0	0	0	0	0	8
BOBBY HOLIK	5	0	0	0	4-	8	0	0	0	0	18
KRZYSZTOF OLIWA	6	0	0	0	0	23	0	0	0	0	5

GOALTENDER	GPI	MINS	AVG	W	L	EN	SO	GA	SA	SV %
MARTIN BRODEUR	6	366	1.97	2	4	1	0	12	164	.927
N.J TOTALS	6	369	2.11	2	4	1	0	13	165	.921

All-Time Leaders
Goals
John MacLean	347
Kirk Muller	185
Pat Verbeek	170

Assists
John MacLean	354
Kirk Muller	335
Bruce Driver	328

Points
John MacLean	701
Kirk Muller	520
Aaron Broten	469

Best Individual Seasons
Goals
Pat Verbeek	1987-88	46
John MacLean	1990-91	45
John MacLean	1988-89	42

Assists
Scott Stevens	1993-94	60
Aaron Broten	1987-88	57
Kirk Muller	1987-88	57

Points
Kirk Muller	1987-88	94
John MacLean	1988-89	87
Kirk Muller	1989-90	86

TEAM
Last 3 years
	GP	W	L	T	Pts	%
1997-98	82	48	23	11	107	.652
1996-97	82	45	23	14	104	.634
1995-96	82	37	33	12	86	.524

Best 3 regular seasons
	GP	W	L	T	Pts	%
1997-98	82	48	23	11	107	.652
1996-97	82	45	23	14	104	.634
1993-95	84	47	25	12	106	.631

Worst 3 regular seasons
	GP	W	L	T	Pts	%
1975-76	80	12	56	12	36	.225
1983-84	80	17	56	7	41	.256
1974-75	80	15	54	11	41	.256

Most Goals (min. 70 game schedule)
1992-93	308
1993-94	306
1985-86	300

Fewest Goals (min. 70 game schedule)
1974-75	184
1975-76	190
1978-79	210

Most Goals Against (min. 70 game schedule)
1985-86	374
1986-87	368
1981-82	362

Fewest Goals Against (min. 70 game schedule)
1997-98	166
1996-97	182
1995-96	202

New York Islanders

So, is this the year?

Is this the year the Islanders finally get over the hump?

They've missed the playoffs for four years in a row, and this past season they just spun their wheels, recording one more point than the previous year.

On paper, the Islanders look like they're ready to move up. Good teams have a lot of similar components to what they have.

Game Breaker - Ziggy Palffy isn't a question mark, he's a proven and consistent commodity. In each of the last three seasons he's had both goals and assists in the forties.

Two Scoring Lines - Some teams have trouble coming up with one, but the Islanders can put together two legitimate scoring lines, or close to it. If you have Trevor Linden and Robert Reichel at centre, that's like having two number one centres. And if you have Palffy and Smolinski on the right side, along with Jason Dawe on the left wing and Mariusz Czerkawksi when he's on, that's not too bad. Sergi Nabokov, obtained from Chicago in the off-season for junior J-P Dumont, could also contribute on the scoresheet. It's not too bad, but it's not too great, either.

Good Checking - Claude Lapointe, Joe Sacco, Tom Chorske and Sergei Nemchinov are all defense-first type players.

Enforcers - If you're going to have an enforcer, you can't do much better than Gino Odjick. Ken Belanger and Richard Pilon also know how to take care of things when the going gets rough.

Power Play Quarterback - Bryan Berard had slump periods last year, but he also piled in the points at times. He had 16 points in the team's first 15 games, but during another stretch, had just one point in 12 games. As a player gets older and more used to life in the NHL, you would expect them to become more consistent.

Franchise Goalie Coming - So far, Roberto Luongo is the best goalie to never play in the NHL. That could change soon.

Decent Defence - Nobody said great, but they're decent and young and improving.

Character players - Trevor Linden, who was named captain almost immediately after being obtained from Vancouver, heads up a list that includes some hard-working checkers.

New Coaching Staff - The Islanders are going football-style in the coaching department. With more coaches concentrating on smaller areas, maybe it will be a help. Sometimes too many heads aren't better than one, but it doesn't appear as if it could hurt them.

One-Goal Games - The Islanders had the worst one-goal winning percentage in the league last season, again, at 6-14. The year before they were also dead-last with a record of 7-15. That's a two-year total of 13-29. Theoretically, teams that lose a lot of close games are closer to turning it around.

Despite how well the Islanders stack up on paper, they still have to win on the ice. That means intangibles, such as attitude, cohesiveness, committment and the ability of the coach to get the most out of his players.

One other thing is that the Islanders were plagued with inconsistent scorers last season. Not just short little slumps, but long lengthy ones. Maybe a sports psychologist among their coaches would be a good idea.

So, the final word on whether the Islanders can do it this year?

Maybe.

STUFF
* The Lightning earned shutouts in four of their last nine games, three of them were against Tampa Bay.
* Wade Flaherty had a shutout string of 169:12, which was 10:17 short of the team record, held by Glenn Resch in the 1975-76 season.

* Zigmund Palffy's 13 game point streak, in February and March, was the longest of the season in the league.
* When the Islanders beat New Jersey April 8 it was the first time since December 26, 1996 that they had trailed after two periods and came back for the win.

TEAM PREVIEW
GOAL: The Islanders hope their goaltending problems will soon be solved. Roberto Luongo is close, at the very most a year away.

Even without Luongo, the Islanders looked as if they were going to make a play for a free agent goaltender.

Milbury wasn't very happy with Salo, and despite words to the effect, he was never a number one goalie. He'd be fine as a number two goalie, however, or else his days are numbered.

Eric Fichaud was shipped out last season, and Wade Flaherty was a blast in a late-season callup. He was involved in three shutouts in a row, earning two himself and sharing another after being kicked out of a fight-filled game. Mind you, all three of Flaherty's full shutouts were over Tampa Bay.

Every GM's dream is to not have to worry about their goaltending. That hasn't been a luxury for Milbury in recent years, but it could happen within a year or two.

Hockey Annual Rating: 25 of 27

GOALTENDER	GPI	MINS	AVG	W	L	T	EN	SO	GA	SA	SV %
WADE FLAHERTY	16	694	1.99	4	4	3	0	3	23	309	.926
TOMMY SALO	62	3461	2.64	23	29	5	9	4	152	1617	.906
ERIC FICHAUD	17	807	2.97	3	8	3	1	0	40	422	.905
NYI TOTALS	82	4982	2.71	30	41	11	10	8	225	2358	.905

WADE FLAHERTY and TOMMY SALO shared a shutout vs NYR on Apr 4, 1998

DEFENCE: The "Fab Four" of Bryan Berard, Kenny Jonsson, Scott Lachance and Scott McCabe was broken up last year when McCabe was traded, but the Islanders have more talent on the way.

Eric Brewer has been an outstanding junior defenseman with Prince George in the WHL, but missed almost half of last season with a shoulder injury. He's not far away, however, and could be in the lineup this season.

Bryan Berard was a dreadful -32 for the Islanders, twice as bad as any other player. That's just something the team will have to live with, considering his outstanding offensive skills. He was up and down in his sophomore jinx season.

Jonsson has rounded into an excellent two-way defensman, and had more ice-time than any other Islander last year.

Scott Lachance and Richard Pilon round out the regulars, while Zdeno Chara and Ray Shultz played a lot at the end of last season when injuries were a problem.

Often, the plus-minus stat is meaningless, but when one player stands out from the rest of the team, then coaches say it's more worthy of their attention.

Anybody who played regularly on Tampa Bay was going to be a big minus, because the team was a big minus. The list of worst plus-minus players shows that. After a couple Lightning players, comes Brian Leetch and Berard. Ironically, Berard is often compared to Leetch in terms of offensive-first style.

Worst Plus-Minus Players

-43	Paul Ysebeart	Tampa Bay
-38	Alexander Selivanov	Tampa Bay
-37	Mikael Renberg	Tampa Bay
-36	Brian Leetch	NY Rangers
-32	BRYAN BERARD	NY Islanders
-32	Jeff Norton	Florida

Hockey Annual Rating: 19 of 27

FORWARD: What is it with the Islanders? How come so much inconsistency? Zigmund Palffy rarely went longer than a game between points, but look at some of the other key players.
* Reichel went 14 games without a goal.
* Czercawski scores one goal in 35 games, then has eight in nine games.
* Jonsson has just one assist in a 20-game stretch.
* Berard goes 23 games without a goal.
* Lapointe plays 20 games without a single point.
* Nemchinov doesn't get an assist after January 30, in 23 games.
* Smolinski has a 16-game goal-less streak and another of 14 games. And for good measure, throws in an 18-game stretch in which he couldn't earn an assist.

What causes inconsistency? Europeans are often inconsistent, but it didn't affect Palffy at all. Young players are often inconsistent, but most of the players in the above list are veterans. Players who aren't motivated are inconsistent. Players who are unhappy are inconsistent. Players who aren't worried about next year's contract can be inconsistent.

When it comes right down to it, there's no reason to worry about Palffy, but there is about almost every single other forward in their line-up. Not their talent, mind you, but their consistency. It just isn't there.

Linden may be able to provide the necessary leadership to shake this team, although the Vancouver Canucks haven't been all that successful and if there ever was a team that needed leadership, that was it.

Linden has been playing centre so long that he is a centreman, despite the fact his "natural position" is considered right wing. Reichel is a centreman, too and then there are role players Nemchinov and Lapointe. But, the Islanders keep making waves about acquiring a big-time playmaking centre, which means they're considering moving Linden back to the wing, and that they're unhappy with Reichel's inconsistency.

Palffy is the premier winger, but then it gets iffy after that. Smolinski should be up there. He's coming off a bad year, and is a likely candidate to rebound. Jason Dawe can score goals from the left side. Czercawski scores when he's in the mood, but that only lasts for a short time and then he gets traded. That's it for scoring. The Islanders think Sergei Nabokov, obtained from Chicago for top draft pick J-P Dumont, can put the puck in the net, which he did in Czercawski-like fashion on occasion with the Blackhawks.

That leaves role playing winger Joe Sacco, Tom Chorske and maybe Mike Hough, along with tough guys Gino Odjick and Ken Belanger.

Maybe they'll score and maybe Milbury will make some big changes. The latter seems more likely.

Hockey Annual Rating: 10 of 27

SPECIAL TEAMS: Decent power play and decent penalty killing. With Berard minding the points and Palffy popping them in up front, the man advantage is good enough. Both special teams are mediocre, but sometimes, as in this case, that's enough.

Power Play	G	ATT	PCT
Overall	61	364	16.8% (T-9th NHL)
Home	38	197	19.3% (2nd NHL)
Road	23	167	13.8% (18th NHL)

16 SHORT HANDED GOALS ALLOWED (T-23rd NHL)

Penalty Killing	G	ATT	PCT
Overall	54	384	85.9% (10th NHL)
Home	24	186	87.1% (T-6th NHL)
Road	30	198	84.8% (15th NHL)

11 SHORT HANDED GOALS SCORED (T-9th NHL)

ISLANDERS SPECIAL TEAMS SCORING

Power play	G	A	PTS
PALFFY	17	18	35
REICHEL	8	24	32
BERARD	8	21	29
JONSSON	6	12	18
LINDEN	5	9	14
DAIGNEAULT	1	10	11
DAWE	4	6	10
SMOLINSKI	3	7	10
CHORSKE	1	3	4
NEMCHINOV	2	1	3
CZERKAWSKI	2	1	3
LACHANCE	1	2	3
NAMESTNIKOV	0	1	1
MILLER	0	1	1

Short handed	G	A	PTS
CHORSKE	4	1	5
PALFFY	2	2	4
LINDEN	2	2	4
SACCO	2	0	2

LAPOINTE	1	1	2
JONSSON	0	2	2
NEMCHINOV	1	0	1
DAWE	1	0	1
BERARD	1	0	1
SMOLINSKI	0	1	1

COACHING AND MANAGEMENT: Give Mike Milbury credit. He's not afraid to make changes. In fact, he may be impatient, but then who said patience was a virtue.

You can only rebuild for so long, especially today when tickets are big bucks.

Milbury isn't one of those GM's who fall in love with his players and thinks they're more valuable then they really are.

Milbury shipped out Bryan McCabe, a premier defenseman, and Todd Bertuzzi, a promising prospect who hasn't hit his stride, and Travis Green, a good all-round player.

The team wasn't winning with those guys, so he made changes that he felt would strengthen the team.

He'll make more moves if the team needs it. He does some experimenting, too. Team needs scorers, let's give these guys a try. Team needs character, how about we bring in Trevor Linden. Team needs a coach, how about I do it myself.

Milbury is a hardliner, but he makes as much sense as anyone in hockey besides Sather. Some general managers stupidly give out big long-term contracts to older players, thinking they're going to play forever. Getting your money out of Milbury isn't that easy. He's not going to give out an unreasonable contract just so a player will be happy. Plus, he plays it smart. He doesn't talk up a player and say how good he is unless he has him under contract.

That way, the agent can't come back and say he said such and such. It just makes sense to undervalue an asset until its yours.

Apparently, Milbury won't be handling contract negotiations anymore anyway, with the new owners in place. He will have a lot of help, which may or may not be good.

So, at least to start the year, Milbury will be both coach and general manager. You get the feeling he'd like to give up the coaching part, but the new owners want him behind the bench. When he took over from Rick Bowness late last year, he put together an 8-9-2 mark.

At least one traded player said that the other players didn't respect Milbury. Whether that's sour grapes or whether it's true, it doesn't much matter. They just have to win, and that's all Milbury cares about.

Hockey Annual Rating: 20 of 27

DRAFT

Round	Sel.	Player	Pos	Team
1	9	Mike Rupp	LW	Erie (OHL)
2	36	Chris Nielsen	C	Calgary (WHL)
4	95	Andy Burnham	RW	Windsor (OHL)
5	122	Jiri Dopata	C	Czech
6	155	Kevin Clauson	D	Western Michigan (CCHA)
7	182	Evgeny Korolev	D	London (OHL)
8	209	F. Brind'Amour	G	Sherbrooke (QMJHL)
9	237	Ben Glais	D	Walpole (USHS)

| 9 | 242 | Jason Doyle | RW | Owen Sound (OHL) |
| 9 | 250 | Radek Matejovsky | RW | Czech |

Mike Rupp came as a surprise selection in the number nine slot. The Hockey News had him rated 24th and Central Scouting had him at 23rd among North Americans. He doesn't have a lot of experience, or goals or points for that matter (16-11-27 for Erie in OHL) but he's got size at 6-5, 220, and is projected as a future power forward.

PROGNOSIS: It's difficult to be too optimistic about the Islanders season, but it's also difficult to be too pessimistic. Not exactly going out on a limb.

This team has a chemical imbalance. If it's fixed, then maybe. If people play as advertised, then maybe. If they get a legitimate number one goalie, then maybe.

Maybe, maybe, maybe. That's how it stacks up for the Islanders.

PREDICTION
Eastern Conference: 12th
Overall: 23rd

STAT SECTION
Team Scoring Stats

	GP	G	A	PTS	+/-	PIM	SH	CAREER GP	G	A	Pts
ZIGMUND PALFFY	82	45	42	87	2-	34	277	281	146	135	281
ROBERT REICHEL	82	25	40	65	11-	32	201	519	183	255	438
BRYAN BERARD	75	14	32	46	32-	59	192	157	22	72	94
BRYAN SMOLINSKI	81	13	30	43	16-	34	203	362	115	134	249
KENNY JONSSON	81	14	26	40	2-	58	108	267	23	52	75
JASON DAWE	81	20	19	39	8	42	134	303	80	81	161
TREVOR LINDEN	67	17	21	38	14-	82	133	727	257	329	586
TOM CHORSKE	82	12	23	35	7	39	132	537	114	114	228
SERGEI NEMCHINOV	74	10	19	29	3	24	94	498	117	141	258
M. CZERKAWSKI	68	12	13	25	11	23	136	265	69	72	141
JOE SACCO	80	11	14	25	0	34	122	418	76	84	160
J.J. DAIGNEAULT	71	2	21	23	9-	49	92	775	50	182	233
CLAUDE LAPOINTE	78	10	10	20	9-	47	82	439	67	93	160
SCOTT LACHANCE	63	2	11	13	11-	45	62	391	25	71	96
MIKE HOUGH	74	5	7	12	4-	27	44	696	100	156	256
RICHARD PILON	76	0	7	7	1	291	37	448	6	48	54
GINO ODJICK	48	3	2	5	2-	212	52	457	46	52	98
KEN BELANGER	37	3	1	4	1	101	10	65	3	3	6
KIP MILLER	9	1	3	4	2-	2	11	90	14	25	39
DENNIS VASKE	19	0	3	3	2	12	16	232	5	41	46

DANE JACKSON	8	1	1	2	1	4	5	45	12	6	18
VLAD CHEBATURKIN	2	0	2	2	1-	0	0	22	0	2	2
Y. NAMESTNIKOV	6	0	1	1	1-	4	2	41	0	9	9
DAN PLANTE	7	0	1	1	1-	6	7	159	9	14	23
VLADIMIR ORSAGH	11	0	1	1	3-	2	9	11	0	1	1
RAY SCHULTZ	13	0	1	1	3	45	4	13	0	1	1
WADE FLAHERTY	16	0	1	1	0	0	0	goalie			
ZDENO CHARA	25	0	1	1	1	50	10	25	0	1	1
TOMMY SALO	62	0	1	1	0	31	0	goalie			
JEFF LIBBY	1	0	0	0	0	0	0	1	0	0	0
MARK LAWRENCE	2	0	0	0	0	2	4	17	0	1	1
SEAN HAGGERTY	5	0	0	0	3-	0	2	6	0	0	0
WARREN LUHNING	8	0	0	0	4-	0	6	8	0	0	0
JASON HOLLAND	8	0	0	0	4-	4	6	12	1	0	1
ERIC FICHAUD	17	0	0	0	0	0	0	goalie			
STEVE WEBB	20	0	0	0	2-	35	6	61	1	4	5

* Team Rankings 1997-98 (previous year's ranking in parenthesis)

		Conference Rank	League Rank
Record	30-41-11	10 (12)	19 (22)
Home	17-20-4	10 (9)	18 (17)
Away	13-21-7	11 (11)	21 (23)
Versus Own Conference	22-26-8	8 (10)	16 (18)
Versus Other Conference	8-15-3	11 (11)	22 (23)
Team Plus\Minus	-20	10 (7)	19 (14)
Goals For	212	7 (6)	15 (12)
Goals Against	225	10 (9)	17 (18)
Average Shots For	25.8	11 (12)	23 (25)
Average Shots Against	28.8	10 (8)	19 (16)
Overtime	0-2-11	12 (4)	22 (9)
One Goal Games	6-14	13 (13)	25 (26)

Times outshooting opponent	29	11 (11)	21 (21)
Versus Teams Over .500	14-26-7	10 (9)	18 (18)
Versus Teams Under .500	16-15-4	11 (12)	19 (24)
First Half Record	15-21-5	11 (12)	18 (25)
Second Half Record	15-20-6	10 (7)	20 (16)

PLAYOFFS

- did not make the playoffs

All-Time Leaders
Goals

Mike Bossy	573
Bryan Trottier	500
Denis Potvin	310

Assists

Bryan Trottier	853
Denis Potvin	742
Mike Bossy	553

Points

Bryan Trottier	1,153
Mike Bossy	1,126
Denis Potvin	1,052

Best Individual Seasons
Goals

Mike Bossy	1978-79	69
Mike Bossy	1980-81	68
Mike Bossy	1981-82	64

Assists

Bryan Trottier	1978-79	87
Mike Bossy	1981-82	83
Bryan Trottier	1981-82	79

Points

Mike Bossy	1981-82	147
Bryan Trottier	1978-79	134
Pierre Turgeon	1992-93	132

TEAM
Last 3 years

	GP	W	L	T	Pts	%
1997-98	82	30	41	11	71	.433
1996-97	82	29	41	12	70	.427
1995-96	82	22	50	10	54	.329

Best 3 regular seasons

	GP	W	L	T	Pts	%
1981-82	80	54	16	10	118	.738
1978-79	80	51	15	14	116	.725
1977-78	80	48	17	5	111	.694

Worst 3 regular seasons

	GP	W	L	T	Pts	%
1972-73	78	12	60	6	30	.192
1995-96	82	22	50	10	54	.329
1973-74	78	19	41	18	56	.359

Most Goals (min. 70 game schedule)

1981-82	385
1978-79	358
1983-84	357

Fewest Goals (min. 70 game schedule)

1972-73	170
1973-74	185
1997-98	212

Most Goals Against (min. 70 game schedule)

1972-73	347
1988-89	325
1995-96	315

Fewest Goals Against (min. 70 game schedule)

1975-76	190
1976-77	193
1977-78	210

New York Rangers

The Rangers had high hopes before last season, and they signed on the veteran free agents to prove it. Coming off their final four appearance in the playoffs, they were going to make a run for it, thinking the old guys would be hungry for one last chance at winning it all.

Then Mark Messier signed with Vancouver instead of the Rangers, and it was all downhill from there. It was a disastrous season, and they had some odd stats to prove it.

* The Rangers didn't have a single month in which they had a winning record. They shared that dubious honor with just Florida and Tampa Bay.

* The Rangers didn't have any shutouts. That put them 13 behind Dominik Hasek. Calgary was the only other team that didn't earn one.

* The Rangers had less than 20 shots in 21 games, which is better than one-quarter of their season, and not even close to anyone else. If you add in the games in which they fired exactly 20 on the opposing net that number jumps to 24. The Rangers were able to keep opponents under 20 shots just five times.

* The Rangers had a league-low 25.3 shots on net per game. The whole league dropped in shots in net, but they dropped six shots a game.

* The Rangers were a team -41, second worst to Tampa Bay. The season before they were +33, sixth best. They dropped 74 even strength goals in one season.

* The Rangers were 10-26-1 against teams with records over .500. The season before they were 19-11-7, which was first in the Eastern Conference and second overall.

* The Rangers had exactly the same number of goals scored against them last year (231) as they did the season before. However, they scored 61 fewer.

* The Rangers scored exactly zero shorthanded goals. Not one. The second fewest any other team had was four, and the Canucks led the way with 19. New York had 13 shorthanded goals scored against them.

* The Rangers tied their first four games of the season. Another time they tied four out of five, and a different time they tied three in a row. They ended up tied for the league lead with 18.

* Brian Leetch was -36, which was almost the worst in the league. The thing was, he was on the ice for more time than any other player in the league except for Ray Bourque and Chris Chelios, with an average of 29:48 per game. Not that he can be completely absolved from

blame, but with his team stinking out the joint, and him on the ice half the time, compared to every third or fourth shift for forwards, well, that's why he had such a high minus.

STUFF
* Brian Leetch is 30 points away from taking over third place on the all-time Rangers point list, ahead of Andy Bathgate, who has 729.
* Gretzky tied for the longest assist streak of the season, eight games, with Adam Oates. It was well short of Gretzky's all-time record 23-game streak, in 1990-91 with Los Angeles.
* The Rangers were the first team in NHL history to tie their first four games of the season.
* Tied a franchise record when they went unbeaten in their first five games of the season (1-0-4).
* When Gretzky earned assist number 1,851 last season it gave him more assists than any other player has total points.

TEAM PREVIEW
GOAL: After all the speculation, unrestricted free agent Mike Richter is right back where he started.

Too bad for Dan Cloutier. He was supposed to be their goaltender of the future. He was a first rounder in 1994. An impressive junior career was followed by an unimpressive first season in the AHL, followed by an impressive one in which he was called up to the Rangers, where once again he was impressive.

The worst that can happen to Cloutier is that he'll be a back up again this year. The best that can happen to him is that he won't.

It's getting tougher for young goaltenders to get a chance to play. It's not so much a glut of great goaltending, but with scoring down so much around the league it takes less to make teams happy. They'd rather go with old reliable than young up-and-coming.

Hockey Annual Rating: 10 of 26

DEFENCE: First things first. Brian Leetch had a bad year. He won't have two in a row. And by the way, that lousy -36 is mostly because he was on the ice so often.

The Rangers want to be more mobile, more offensive, and don't think they have to be so physical anymore.

One thing for sure, they had to do something about the oldtimers club they had back on defence. Doug Lidster, who is 38, and Bruce Driver, who is 36, won't be invited back. That still leaves them with Ulf Samuelsson (35), Jeff Beukeboom (34), Jeff Finley (31), Brian Leetch (30) and Geoff Smith (29).

They also have Alexander Karpovtsev, big-guy Eric Cairns, and newly-acquired Peter Popovic.

Expect changes there, and expect Maxim Galanov to get a look and maybe Burke Henry, who was supposed to be a defensive defenceman, but who ended up leading the WHL in defence scoring with 18-65-83. Henry still has

GOALTENDER	GPI	MINS	AVG	W	L	T	EN	SO	GA	SA	SV %
DAN CLOUTIER	12	551	2.50	4	5	1	0	0	23	248	.907
MIKE RICHTER	72	4143	2.66	21	31	15	6	0	184	1888	.903
JASON MUZZATTI	6	313	3.26	0	3	2	1	0	17	156	.891
NYR TOTALS	82	5028	2.76	25	39	18	7	0	231	2299	.900

another year of eligibility.

Hockey Annual Rating: 24 of 27

FORWARD: It's out with the old, and in with the new. The Rangers dumped off some of the players who were going to carry them to the Stanley Cup finals, when it became clear they weren't going to even make the playoffs. Brian Skrudland, Mike Keane, and Mike Eastwood were shipped out, and the Rangers started going with the younger guys.

Wayne Gretzky isn't a young guy, but he was the best player on the Rangers last year, and finished tied for third in the scoring race, with a heck of a lot of young guys behind him.

This is how weak the Rangers forwards are: after Gretzky and Niklas Sundstrom there isn't one guy they can depend on. Not one.

Alexei Kovalev - He came through in the long run, especially after John Muckler took over as coach, but he had no goals in his first 18 games of the season. Is that a slump or what?

Pat LaFontaine - Still suffering from post-concussion sydrome, we don't even know if he can play this year, or ever again.

Kevin Stevens - His best days are so far behind him, he can't even see them.

Adam Graves - The former 50-goal scorer had 23, but even worse, had just 12 assists. He has to come back from injuries.

Scott Fraser - The Rangers gave big bucks to a free agent career minor leaguer who had some success in a two month stint with the Oilers. It's not the least bit unusual for new-comers to catch on fire when they first make the NHL before realizing that it's not that easy.

Todd Harvey - He's been underachieving too long. He could break out. It's not that far

beyond his grasp, but it's not that close, either.

Darren Langdon, Bill Berg, Harry York, Bob Errey - Maybe you can depend on those guys to do their job, but one of their jobs isn't scoring.

Youngsters Marc Savard, P.J. Stock, Daniel Goneau, and Johan Lindbom — They will all get a look, and some will make the team, but none have proven a thing at the NHL level.

The Rangers signed free agent John MacLean, a player in the Kevin Stevens mold. In other words, his best years are long behind him.

Manny Maholta, the character player of the draft, is being given a shot at making the team. One of the reasons being, it won't be that hard.

Hockey Annual Rating: 22 of 27

SPECIAL TEAMS: Some teams don't score many shorthanded goals because they concentrate on defence when short a man. The Devils were a team like that. But, whatever way you're playing, nobody gets 0 shorthanded markers, except of course, the Rangers.

The power play was pretty good, which you would expect when you have Wayne Gretzky and Brian Leetch, but they'll miss LaFontaine there if he doesn't return.

Power Play	G	ATT	PCT	
Overall	62	351	17.7%	(5th NHL)
Home	33	175	18.9%	(T-3rd NHL)
Road	29	176	16.5%	(8th NHL)

13 SHORT HANDED GOALS ALLOWED (T-20th NHL)

PENALTY KILLING				
Overall	55	376	85.4%	(11th NHL)
Home	24	170	85.9%	(12th NHL)
Road	31	206	85.0%	(T-13th NHL)

0 SHORT HANDED GOALS SCORED (26th NHL)

RANGERS SPECIAL TEAMS SCORING

Power Play	G	A	PTS
LEETCH	11	23	34
GRETZKY	6	24	30
LAFONTAINE	11	18	29
KOVALEV	8	14	22
GRAVES	10	5	15
STEVENS	5	7	12
SUNDSTROM	4	3	7
SWEENEY	2	5	7
DRIVER	1	4	5
KARPOVTSEV	1	2	3
SAVARD	0	3	3
VOROBIEV	0	2	2
SMYTH	0	2	2
Smith	1	0	1
SAMUELSSON	0	1	1
FINLEY	0	1	1

Short handed	G	A	PTS
ERREY	0	3	3

COACHING AND MANAGEMENT: Neil Smith had a bad season, just like players do, but you can expect him to do something about turning it around quickly. There isn't much on board yet to suggest that, but there will be, it's guaranteed.

John Muckler has had success as a coach. Not last year when he joined the Rangers, mind you, but give him the start of a season and we'll see what he can do.

Hockey Annual Rating: 12 of 27

DRAFT

Round	Sel.	Player	Pos	Team
1	7	Manny Mahotra	C	Guelph
				(OHL)
2	40	Randy Copley	RW	Cape Breton (QMJHL)
3	66	Jason Labarbera	G	Portland (WHL)
4	114	Boyd Kane	LW	Regina (WHL)
5	122	Pat Leahy	RW	Miami-OHIO (CCHA)
5	131	Tomas Kloucek	D	Czech
7	180	Stefan Lundqvist	F	Sweden
8	207	Johan Witehall	F	Sweden
9	235	Jan Mertzig	D	Sweden

Manny Maholtra is considered an excellent two-way player whose biggest assets are his determination and character. The Rangers need a player like him, and he could crack the lineup right away, despite the fact his scoring totals are relatively low for junior at 16-35-51.

PROGNOSIS: The Rangers have too much ground to make up to do it all in one year. Two years at best. Too much depends on guys having comeback seasons or doing something they've never done before.

The playoffs are not a good bet for the Rangers.

PREDICTION
Eastern Conference: 10th
Overall: 20th

STAT SECTION
Team Scoring Stats

	GP	G	A	PTS	+/-	PIM	SH	CAREER GP	G	A	Pts
WAYNE GRETZKY	82	23	67	90	11-	28	201	1,417	885	1,910	2,795
PAT LAFONTAINE	67	23	39	62	16-	36	160	865	468	545	1,013
ALEXEI KOVALEV	73	23	30	53	22-	44	173	388	116	152	268
BRIAN LEETCH	76	17	33	50	36-	32	230	725	164	536	700
NIKLAS SUNDSTROM	70	19	28	47	0	24	115	234	52	68	120
KEVIN STEVENS	80	14	27	41	7-	130	144	668	292	346	638
ADAM GRAVES	72	23	12	35	30-	41	226	748	232	216	448
TIM SWEENEY	56	11	18	29	7	26	75	291	55	83	138
BRUCE DRIVER	75	5	15	20	3-	46	116	922	96	390	486
ULF SAMUELSSON	73	3	9	12	1	122	59	960	52	265	317
BOB ERREY	71	2	9	11	2	53	45	895	170	212	382
HARRY YORK	60	4	6	10	1-	31	44	134	18	24	42
A. KARPOVTSEV	47	3	7	10	1-	38	46	278	21	75	96
BILL BERG	67	1	9	10	15-	55	74	502	53	65	118
PETER FERRARO	30	3	4	7	4-	14	37	37	3	5	8
JEFF FINLEY	63	1	6	7	3-	55	32	335	7	42	49
DARREN LANGDON	70	3	3	6	0	197	15	212	14	14	28
MARC SAVARD	28	1	5	6	4-	4	32	28	1	5	6
P.J. STOCK	38	2	3	5	4	114	9	38	2	3	5
JEFF BEUKEBOOM	63	0	5	5	25-	195	23	759	30	120	150
VLADIMIR VOROBIEV	15	2	2	4	10-	6	27	31	7	7	14
BRAD SMYTH	10	1	3	4	1-	4	13	69	11	12	23
JOHAN LINDBOM	38	1	3	4	4	28	38	38	1	3	4
DOUG LIDSTER	36	0	4	4	2	24	25	880	75	268	343
ERIC CAIRNS	39	0	3	3	3-	92	17	79	0	4	4
DANIEL GONEAU	11	2	0	2	4-	4	13	52	12	3	15
Geoff Smith	15	1	1	2	4-	6	11	458	18	73	91
MAXIM GALANOV	6	0	1	1	1	2	5	6	0	1	1
MIKE RICHTER	72	0	1	1	0	2	0	goalie			
SYLVAIN BLOUIN	1	0	0	0	0	5	0	7	0	0	0
RONNIE SUNDIN	1	0	0	0	0	0	0	1	0	0	0
PIERRE SEVIGNY	3	0	0	0	0	2	1	78	4	5	9
DAN CLOUTIER	12	0	0	0	0	19	0	goalie			

* Team Rankings 1997-98 (previous year's ranking in parenthesis)

		Conference Rank	League Rank
Record	25-39-18	11 (5)	21 (8)
Home	14-18-9	11 (7)	22 (11)
Away	11-21-9	12 (4)	22 (10)
Versus Own Conference	15-30-11	12 (7)	24 (14)
Versus Other Conference	10-9-7	9 (4)	14 (8)
Team Plus\Minus	+41	12 (4)	25 (6)
Goals For	197	11 (3)	22 (4)
Goals Against	231	11 (5)	20 (9)
Average Shots For	25.3	13 (4)	26 (7)
Average Shots Against	28.0	9 (10)	16 (20)
Overtime	2-4-18	11 (1)	20 (1)
One Goal Games	11-15	9 (8)	19 (14)
Times outshooting opponent	32	10 (8)	20 (15)
Versus Teams Over .500	10-26-10	12 (1)	23 (2)
Versus Teams .500 or Under	15-13-8	10 (10)	17 (21)
First Half Record	12-17-12	10 (6)	17 (9)
Second Half Record	13-22-6	11 (5)	23 (12)

PLAYOFFS

- did not make the playoffs

All-Time Leaders

Goals

Rod Gilbert	406
Jean Ratelle	336
Andy Bathgate	272

Assists

Rod Gilbert	615
Brian Leetch	536
Jean Ratelle	481

Points

Rod Gilbert	1,021
Jean Ratelle	817
Andy Bathgate	729

Best Individual Seasons

Goals

Adam Graves	1993-94	52
Vic Hadfield	1971-72	50
Mike Gartner	1990-91	49

Assists

Brian Leetch	1991-92	80
Sergei Zubov	1993-94	77
Wayne Gretzky	1996-97	72
Brian Leetch	1990-91	72

Points

Jean Ratelle	1971-72	109
Mark Messier	1991-92	107
Vic Hadfield	1971-72	106

TEAM

Last 3 years

	GP	W	L	T	Pts	%
1997-98	82	30	41	18	68	.415
1996-97	82	38	34	10	86	.524
1995-96	82	41	27	14	96	.585

Best 3 regular seasons

	GP	W	L	T	Pts	%
1970-71	78	49	18	11	109	.699
1971-72	78	48	17	13	109	.699
1993-94	84	52	24	8	112	.667
1939-40	48	27	11	10	64	.667

Worst 3 regular seasons

	GP	W	L	T	Pts	%
1943-44	50	6	39	5	17	.170
1942-43	50	11	31	8	30	.300
1944-45	50	11	29	10	32	.320

Most Goals (min. 70 game schedule)

1991-92	321
1974-75	319
1971-72	317

Fewest Goals (min. 70 game schedule)

1954-55	150
1952-53	152
1953-54	161

Most Goals Against (min. 70 game schedule)

1984-85	345
1975-76	333
1986-87	323

Fewest Goals Against (min. 70 game schedule)

1970-71	177
1953-54	182
1967-68	183

Ottawa Senators

What are the distinguishing characteristics of an Ottawa Senator?

It used to be that an Ottawa Senator was a loser. Not any more.

So again, what is an Ottawa Senator?

If we go by last year, there are a lot of distinguishing characteristics.

* Ottawa European

The top scorer on the Senators was European. Same with the third, fourth, fifth, sixth, seventh and eighth placed players. An American was second, a Canadian defenceman ninth, and a European 10th. The top Canadian forward was Denny Lambert, and he was 11th. More than half the defencemen were European, and the top prospect is, you guessed it, European.

For the record, no team has been successful longer than the short term when they load up on Europeans.

* Ottawa Sissy Boys

Ouch! Ooh, that hurts. Stop it.

It's a wonder teams don't pound on the Senators until they give up. It should be even easier this year, with Denny Lambert lost in the expansion draft. He had 250 penalty minutes. Chris Murray had 118, and then you go all the way down to 64 minutes for that well known goon, Janne Laukkanen.

The Senators were the least penalized team in the league and Lambert had almost a quarter of the team's total. It's worth noting, however, that the four least penalized teams all made the playoffs while the four most penalized teams didn't.

* Ottawa Streakers

The Senators were 8-3-3 in October, one of the best starts in the league. In November, they were 2-10-1, worst in the league for that month.

They had two four-game winning streaks, a six-game undefeated road streak which included five straight wins, a nine-game winless streak and a five-game winless streak. During one 11-game road streak, they won just one game.

* Ottawa Kids

The Senators are a young team and have something which is unusual. Most of their best talent is also their young talent. Alexei Yashin, Daniel Alfredsson, Wade Redden and Chris Phillips head up a cast, with yet more youngsters among their secondary players.

* Ottawa Low Scorers

Ottawa scored the third fewest goals in the league. They're stingy at giving them up too, so an Ottawa-New Jersey playoff series isn't going to make it on the Excitement Channel, unless you live in one of those two markets.

STUFF

* the Senators had the league's worst record for November at 2-10-1.

TEAM PREVIEW

GOAL: Damian Rhodes and Ron Tugnutt may look like two different goalies, but they're not. They're the same person. Honest. Just check out their stats, this year and last year. Almost identical.

The Senators started out the season on a strict rotation basis, but then started giving two or three games at a time to one or the other. It's better for goalies to alternate games rather than play hot and cold. They both want to play, of course, and being able to prepare in advance for your game is a help. It also means that they can cheer each other on and that there's nobody sulking when they don't get to play. That's not to say that either of these two are sulkers, but in general it works better.

If a goalie's not playing, what he will say to the press is this: "It doesn't matter as long as the team is winning." That's just a big load of crap. What he's doing is privately hoping that the other goalie messes up so he can get in the lineup. And the goalie who messes up starts looking over his shoulder instead of concentrating on the task at hand.

Of course, that only happens on teams where they have two goalies that are equal. When there's a clear number one, then the backup knows his role and accepts it.

For the record, if the Senators had to pick, Rhodes would be number one. They left Tugnutt exposed in the expansion draft.

Hockey Annual Rating: 16 of 27

DEFENCE: The Senators have two of the best young defencemen in the league, in Phillips and Redden. Igor Kravchuk is a decent blueliner, and then there's a drop to Jason York, Stanislav Neckar, Janne Laukannen, and Lance Pitlick.

All of them are Lady Byng candidates except for Pitlick, and he's not that far off either. The Senators are one of the few teams without any kind of enforcer type on the blue-line. A tough guy back there tends to make everyone else a little bit tougher themselves.

The only offence of note is provided by Kravchuk, and that won't win any prizes, because it comes and goes. They would have been better keeping Steve Duchesne.

A quarterback and a tough guy should be high on their defence shopping list.

Hockey Annual Rating: 12 of 27

FORWARD: Not much depth and hardly enough for four lines. But the top two players

GOALTENDER	GPI	MINS	AVG	W	L	T	EN	SO	GA	SA	SV %
RON TUGNUTT	42	2236	2.25	15	14	8	6	3	84	882	.905
DAMIAN RHODES	50	2743	2.34	19	19	7	3	5	107	1148	.907
OTT TOTALS	82	5002	2.40	34	33	15	9	8	200	2039	.902

are worth the price of admission.

Alexei Yashin had an outstanding season, with 72 points, which would be worth a 100 points in a free scoring season of not long ago. Alfredsson is injured a lot, but when he plays, he scores. He missed 28 games, in which the Sens compiled a 9-15-4 record, including a 7-game winless streak.

Shawn McEachern can score if he's on the top line, but after that turn out the lights, nobody's home. Just one other player had more than 11 goals.

The Senators will not have Sergei Zholtok (not offered a contract) Denny Lambert (drafted by Nashville) captain Randy Cunneyworth (not offered a contract) and Pat Falloon (not offered a contract) in the lineup.

Falloon was a bust, Cunneyworth was sitting out games and wasn't happy about it, Zholtok is a minor leaguer, and Lambert was one of the few players who was willing to stick up for anyone.

Bruce Gardiner, Shaun Van Allen, Andreas Dackell, Magnus Arvedson, Vaclav Prospal, Radek Bonk and Chris Murray make out the rest of the forwards. Take away Yashin and Alfredsson and this lineup would make an expansion team proud.

It would be nice for the Senators if Bonk did something. It almost looked like he was going to last season, when he had three goals and four assists in the first eight games. But then he returned to form by going pointless in his next 16 games, making people wonder just exactly what was the point.

They're small and they're fast, but it isn't enough. Only a couple of them can score goals and most of them can be pushed around. They need to add some players and they better be physical types or goal scorers.

The one major prospect they have is Marian Hossa, but what a prospect he is. *The Hockey News* named him the number one prospect in the NHL. But, Radek Bonk might have held that distinction at one time, as well.

Hossa started out with the Senators last year, but was returned to junior where he had another outstanding season. He was 40-45-85 in 53 games for Portland in the WHL.

Hockey Annual Rating: 11 of 27

SPECIAL TEAMS: The Senators were lousy at special teams, but would improve greatly with Alfredsson in the lineup every game. He's a wizard on the power play, and was only three points away from leading the team in power play points, despite missing 28 games.

There is no second unit after the first unit goes out, because all their scoring eggs are in one basket.

The Sens draw a lot of penalties because of their speed, and don't take many, but it doesn't do them much good. Despite 72 more power play advantages than shorthanded situations, they scored just one more goal than they allowed.

Power Play	G	ATT	PCT	
Overall	48	375	12.8%	(22nd NHL)
Home	30	199	15.1%	(14th NHL)
Road	18	176	10.2%	(24th NHL)

9 SHORT HANDED GOALS ALLOWED (T-9th NHL)

PENALTY KILLING				
Overall	47	303	84.5%	(T-16th NHL)
Home	21	141	85.1%	(T-13th NHL)
Road	26	162	84.0%	(18th NHL)

6 SHORT HANDED GOALS SCORED (22nd NHL)

SENATORS SPECIAL TEAMS SCORING

Power play	G	A	PTS
YASHIN	5	14	19
ALFREDSSON	7	9	16
KRAVTCHOUK	3	13	16
MCEACHERN	8	6	14
ZHOLTOK	7	7	14
PROSPAL	4	8	12
DACKELL	3	5	8
PHILLIPS	2	6	8
LAUKKANEN	2	6	8
FALLOON	3	4	7
REDDEN	3	3	6
YORK	0	5	5
BONK	1	3	4
CUNNEYWORTH	1	2	3
GUSTAFSSON	0	3	3
VAN ALLEN	0	1	1
HOSSA	0	1	1
ARVEDSSON	0	1	1

Short handed	G	A	PTS
MCEACHERN	2	2	4
DACKELL	2	1	3
KRAVTCHOUK	1	0	1
ARVEDSSON	1	0	1
VAN ALLEN	0	1	1
LAUKKANEN	0	1	1

COACHING AND MANAGEMENT: Rick Dudley is the new general manager, replacing Pierre Gauthier, who put his family ahead of his job and resigned. It's a good thing everybody doesn't do that or there wouldn't be anybody left to run the teams.

Gauthier brought the team to where it is now, and Dudley will try and take them up to the next level. It won't be an easy job.

Jacques Martin deserves all the credit he gets as coach. One way to judge a coach's value is by how well a team does in the playoffs. The Senators have overachieved each time they've been in the post-season, upsetting the Devils this year and losing to Washington, the eventual Stanley Cup finalists.

Hockey Annual Rating: 22 of 27

DRAFT

Round	Sel.	Player	Pos	Team
1	15	Mathieu Chouinard	G	
				Shawinigan (QMJHL)
2	44	Mike Fisher	C	Sudbury
				(OHL)
2	58	Chris Bala	LW	Harvard
				(ECAC)
3	74	Julien Vauclair	D	Switzerland
4	101	Petr Schastivy	LW	Russia
5	130	Gavin McLeod	D	Kelowna
				(WHL)
6	161	Christopher Neil	RW	North Bay
				(OHL)
7	188	Michael Periard	D	
				Shawinigan (QMJHL)
8	223	Sergei Verenikin	RW	Russia
9	246	R. Pavlikovsky	RW	Las Vegas
				(IHL)

The Senators need a lot of other things before they need goaltending, but the organization was thin in this area. Mathieu Chouinard led the QMJHL in goals against average and says he patterns his style after Patrick Roy, which makes him exactly the same as every other goalie coming out of Quebec.

PROGNOSIS: The Senators have some young talent, but they're still not a very good team.

They came within a hot streak of not even making the playoffs, and that hot streak might not be there next time they need it.

At best they're a .500 team, at worst they're, well, worse than .500.

They've got speed, they've got defence, but they're don't have much resembling toughness.

And despite the dedication to defence around the league in recent years, teams still have to be able to put the puck in the net once in a while.

PREDICTION
Eastern Conference: 8th
Overall: 13th

STAT SECTION
Team Scoring Stats

	GP	G	A	PTS	+/-	PIM	SH	CAREER GP	G	A	PTS
ALEXEI YASHIN	82	33	39	72	6	24	291	340	134	175	309
SHAWN MCEACHERN	81	24	24	48	1	42	229	447	120	145	265
DANIEL ALFREDSSON	55	17	28	45	7	18	149	213	57	110	167
IGOR KRAVCHUK	81	8	27	35	19-	8	191	419	49	141	190
ANDREAS DACKELL	82	15	18	33	11-	24	130	161	27	37	64
MAGNUS ARVEDSON	61	11	15	26	2	36	90	61	11	15	26
VACLAV PROSPAL	56	6	19	25	11-	21	88	74	11	29	30
SERGEI ZHOLTOK	78	10	13	23	7-	16	127	160	24	31	55
WADE REDDEN	80	8	14	22	17	27	103	162	14	38	52
JANNE LAUKKANEN	60	4	17	21	15-	64	69	170	8	40	48
DENNY LAMBERT	72	9	10	19	4	250	76	198	14	37	51
SHAUN VAN ALLEN	80	4	15	19	4	48	104	357	40	96	136
PAT FALLOON	58	8	10	18	8-	16	136	430	117	134	252
BRUCE GARDINER	55	7	11	18	2	50	64	122	18	21	39
RADEK BONK	65	7	9	16	13-	16	93	236	41	49	90
CHRIS PHILLIPS	72	5	11	16	2	38	107	72	5	11	16
JASON YORK	73	3	13	16	8	62	109	261	12	63	75
R. CUNNEYWORTH	71	2	11	13	14-	63	81	852	187	223	410
CHRIS MURRAY	53	5	4	9	3	118	51	168	13	11	24
LANCE PITLICK	69	2	7	9	8	50	66	178	8	19	27
PER GUSTAFSSON	31	1	5	6	2-	16	36	89	8	27	35
S. NECKAR	60	2	2	4	14-	31	43	195	6	14	20
PHILIP CROWE	9	3	0	3	3	24	6	82	4	4	8
D. ARMSTRONG	9	2	0	2	1	9	8	79	9	10	19
MARIAN HOSSA	7	0	1	1	1-	0	10	7	0	1	1
DAMIAN RHODES	50	0	1	1	0	0	0	goalie			

RADIM BICANEK	1	0	0	0	0	0	0	28	0	1	1
IVAN CIERNIK	2	0	0	0	0	0	0	2	0	0	0
JASON ZENT	3	0	0	0	0	4	1	25	3	3	6
DENNIS VIAL	19	0	0	0	0	45	9	242	4	15	19
RON TUGNUTT	42	0	0	0	0	0	0	goalie			

* Team Rankings 1997-98 (previous year's ranking in parenthesis)

		Conference Rank	League Rank
Record	34-33-15	8 (7)	13 (16)
Home	18-16-7	7 (11)	14 (19)
Away	16-17-8	8 (6)	12 (12)
Versus Own Conference	24-22-10	7 (6)	14 (11)
Versus Other Conference	10-11-5	10 (10)	15 (21)
Team Plus\Minus	-8	8 (10)	16 (18)
Goals For	193	12 (9)	24 (18)
Goals Against	200	6 (7)	9 (12)
Average Shots For	29.3	1 (9)	2 (18)
Average Shots Against	24.9	2 (1)	5 (3)
Overtime	2-0-15	4 (12)	5 (22)
One Goal Games	16-10	3 (7)	5 (13)
Times outshooting opponent	51	2 (3)	4 (5)

Versus Teams Over .500	16-20-8	4 (12)	8 (25)
Versus Teams .500 or under	18-13-7	7 (3)	14 (7)
First Half Record	18-18-5	7 (13)	12 (26)
Second Half Record	16-15-10	6 (4)	12 (10)

PLAYOFFS

Results: defeated New Jersey 4-2 in conference quarter-finals

lost to Washington 4-1 in conference semi-finals

Record: 5-6

Goals Against: 30 (2.7/game)

Home: 4-1

Overtime: 2-0

Away: 1-5

Power play: 18.2% (1st)

Goals For: 20 (1.8/game)

Penalty Killing: 82.1% (12th)

	GP	G	A	PTS	+/-	PIM	PP	SH	GW	OT	S
DANIEL ALFREDSSON	11	7	2	9	4-	20	2	1	1	0	36
ALEXEI YASHIN	11	5	3	8	6-	8	3	0	2	1	42
IGOR KRAVCHUK	11	2	3	5	2-	4	0	0	0	0	24
JANNE LAUKKANEN	11	2	2	4	3-	8	1	0	1	0	14
BRUCE GARDINER	11	1	3	4	2-	2	0	0	1	1	21
SHAWN MCEACHERN	11	0	4	4	6-	8	0	0	0	0	27
JASON YORK	7	1	1	2	2-	7	1	0	0	0	13
ANDREAS DACKELL	11	1	1	2	4-	2	1	0	0	0	14
WADE REDDEN	9	0	2	2	5-	2	0	0	0	0	11
SERGEI ZHOLTOK	11	0	2	2	1-	0	0	0	0	0	23
CHRIS PHILLIPS	11	0	2	2	2-	2	0	0	0	0	24
CHRIS MURRAY	11	1	0	1	2-	8	0	0	0	0	12
RANDY CUNNEYWORTH	6	0	1	1	0	6	0	0	0	0	2
SHAUN VAN ALLEN	11	0	1	1	3-	10	0	0	0	0	16
LANCE PITLICK	11	0	1	1	3-	17	0	0	0	0	6
MAGNUS ARVEDSON	11	0	1	1	6-	6	0	0	0	0	21
PAT FALLOON	1	0	0	0	0	0	0	0	0	0	2
PER GUSTAFSSON	1	0	0	0	2-	0	0	0	0	0	3
RON TUGNUTT	2	0	0	0	0	0	0	0	0	0	0
RADEK BONK	5	0	0	0	3-	2	0	0	0	0	6
VACLAV PROSPAL	6	0	0	0	2-	0	0	0	0	0	7
STANISLAV NECKAR	9	0	0	0	4-	2	0	0	0	0	4
DAMIAN RHODES	10	0	0	0	0	0	0	0	0	0	0
DENNY LAMBERT	11	0	0	0	2	19	0	0	0	0	5

GOALTENDER	GPI	MINS	AVG	W	L	EN	SO	GA	SA	SV %
DAMIAN RHODES	10	590	2.14	5	5	3	0	21	236	.911
RON TUGNUTT	2	74	4.86	0	1	0	0	6	25	.760
OTT TOTALS	11	669	2.69	5	6	3	0	30	264	.886

All-Time Leaders
Goals
Alexei Yashin	134
Alexandre Daigle	74
Daniel Alfredsson	67

Assists
Alexei Yashin	175
Daniel Alfredsson	110
Alexandre Daigle	98

Points
Alexei Yashin	309
Alexandre Daigle	182
Daniel Alfredsson	177

Best Individual Seasons
Goals
Alexei Yashin	1996-97	35
Alexei Yashin	1997-98	33
Alexei Yashin	1993-94	30

Assists
Alexei Yashin	1993-94	49
Daniel Alfredsson	1996-97	47
Norm MacIver	1992-93	46

Points
Alexei Yashin	1993-94	79
Alexei Yashin	1996-97	75
Alexei Yashin	1977-78	72

TEAM
Last 3 years
	GP	W	L	T	Pts	%
1997-98	82	34	33	15	83	.506
1996-97	82	31	36	15	77	.470
1995-96	82	18	59	5	41	.250

Best 3 regular seasons
	GP	W	L	T	Pts	%
1997-98	82	34	33	15	83	.506
1996-97	82	31	36	15	77	.470
1995-96	82	18	59	5	41	.250

Worst 3 regular seasons
	GP	W	L	T	Pts	%
1992-93	84	10	70	4	24	.143
1993-94	84	14	61	9	37	.220
1994-95	48	9	34	5	23	.240

Most Goals (min. 70 game schedule)
1996-97	226
1992-93	202
1993-94	201

Fewest Goals (min. 70 game schedule)
1995-96	191
1997-98	193
1993-94	201

Most Goals Against (min. 70 game schedule)
1993-94	397
1992-93	394
1995-96	291

Fewest Goals Against (min. 70 game schedule)
1997-98	200
1996-97	234
1995-96	291

Philadelphia Flyers

The Flyers seem to be a team around which there are always a lot of questions. Here's some of them, and the answers.

Question: Will John Vanbiesbrouck solve the Flyers goaltending woes.

Answer: Yes and no. First of all, there wasn't a goaltending problem during the regular season. Ron Hextall was fifth in goals against average. In the playoffs, it's an attitude thing among a team that has little confidence in their netminding, and Vanbiesbrouck should change that. At 35-years-old, however, Vanbiesbrouck's playoff stamina is a factor.

Question: Did the Flyers sign Vanbiesbrouck instead of Mike Richter or Curtis Joseph because he came cheaper?

Answer: Not that there's anything wrong with that, but it looks that way. Joseph said when he signed with Toronto that his main consideration for picking a team was winning, and that once Philadelphia signed Vanbiesbrouck, Toronto was the next winningest team pursuing him. Joseph would have been a much better addition to the Flyers than Vanbiesbrouck.

Question: What happens to Hextall in the playoffs all the time?

Answer: He lets in bad goals, but so do most goalies at times. But, when Hextall lets in a softee, it's, "See, I told you so," all over again. That said, he didn't come up big when the Flyers needed him.

Question: Why hasn't Lindros become the dominant player expected of him?

Answer: He has. He is a dominant player. The question won't stop, however, until the Flyers win the Stanley Cup.

Question: Was the Janne Niinimaa for Dan McGillis trade a bad one for the Flyers?

Answer: The generally accepted answer is yes. But, not so fast. People saw more of Niinimaa because of the previous playoffs, but McGillis is a better player. Niinimaa was a great passer and an offensive force, with 4-39-43 scoring stats last season. But, McGillis isn't far behind in scoring (11-20-31) and as an extra big added bonus, he was one of the top physical players in the league, the opposite of Niinimaa. The following are the top hitters in the league as recorded by the new NHL statistical process. It seems kind of strange, however, because the Oilers said he was too passive, and the number is so far ahead of everyone else.

Top Hitters:

Daniel McGillis	Phi	308
Darren McCarty	Det	231
Darius Kasparaitis	NYI	225
Richard Matvichuk	Dal	222
Richard Pilon	NYI	214
Lance Pitlick	Ott	200

Question: Was trading Vaclav Prospal and Pat Falloon to Ottawa for Alexandre Daigle a good trade?

Answer: Yes, Bobby Clarke knew Prospal's initial scoring prowess was a fluke and that he's a career minor leaguer. Falloon was a bust in Ottawa and they didn't even offer him a contract. Daigle was impressive at times, and has an opportunity to be impressive all the time.

Question: When the Flyers needed offence in the playoffs why didn't they play Paul Coffey.

Answer: Good question. Coffey's defensive skills aren't good, but they never were. He could have made a contribution offensively.

Question: Do the Flyers have what it takes to make it over the hump?

Answer: They've had what it took for a couple years now. Vanbiesbrouck in net may make them think they have what it takes, and that may be enough.

STUFF

* Eric Lindros became the fifth fastest player in NHL history to score 200 goals when he notched the milestone in his 307th game. Only Wayne Gretzky (242), Mike Bossy (255), Mario Lemieux (277) and Brett Hull (280) were faster.

TEAM PREVIEW

GOAL: John Vanbiesbrouck has seen better days, but that's what they thought when he went to the expansion Florida team and dazzled everyone for a couple years. But, he is 35-years-old and is coming off a poor season in Florida, although everybody on that team had a lousy year.

Vanbiesbrouck is in the danger zone, but a trade may revitalize him just as it did five years ago. Then again, maybe it won't.

Hockey Annual Rating: 7 of 27

DEFENCE: They're big, they're bad, and they're outdated. Punishing, bruising hitting may not cut it these days, with speed theoretically taking over the game. They have some mobility there, but it's not a strength.

Eric Desjardins, Dan McGillis, Luke Richardson, and Chris Therien are the nucleus, the latter three premier physical types. Petr Svoboda is in a class by himself, and that class is usually on the injured list. Funny how he always makes it back in time for the playoffs. If he plays 60 games in a season he's doing well.

Dave Babych is an old-timer, but the Flyers have one less with Kjell Samuelsson gone. Chris Joseph has to pick up his game, and the Flyers would like to see Jeff Lank get a chance to play more this year.

Hockey Annual Rating: 3 of 27

GOALTENDER	GPI	MINS	AVG	W	L	T	EN	SO	GA	SA	SV %
RON HEXTALL	46	2688	2.17	21	17	7	2	4	97	1089	.911
GARTH SNOW	29	1651	2.43	14	9	4	0	1	67	682	.902
SEAN BURKE	11	632	2.56	7	3	0	0	1	27	311	.913
PHI TOTALS	82	4988	2.32	42	29	11	2	6	193	2084	.907

FORWARD: The Flyers have good left wing-centre duos: LeClair-Lindros, and Gratton-Brind'Amour. Actually, we can keep going to the third and fourth lines with Forbes-Sillinger and Podein-Bureau.

The right side is mix-and match. Daigle, Trent Klatt, Danius Zubrus and maybe Paul Healey this year. Daigle did well, with 26 points in 37 games after being traded from Ottawa, and gives the Flyers some speed. Zubrus was once touted as the right winger on the big line, but he had a disappointing season. Klatt sometimes played on the top line, but ideally that's not where he belongs.

Paul Healey has impressed the Flyer brass and should get some more playing time, while the extras include tough guy Dan Kordic, Daniel Lacroix and even John Druce on occasion.

Gratton took some heat because people think he didn't have a good year, especially in relation to all the cash he was getting. But, 62 points last year is the equivalent of about 80 points a couple seasons ago, so it was hardly disappointing.

The Flyers had three 30-goal scorers last year, an extreme rarity. Most teams didn't even have one, and only a few had two. Nobody but the Flyers had three 30-goal scorers.

Hockey Annual Rating: 4 of 27

SPECIAL TEAMS: When you have Lindros, LeClair, and Brind'Amour on the power play you'd have a hard time finding a better forward unit. Desjardins and McGillis can play the points, but Brind'Amour also plays back there, so Gratton or Daigle can play up front.

The Flyers lose a good penalty killer in Otto, who wasn't offered a contract, but pick up another good defensive centre in Marc Bureau.

Power Play	G	ATT	PCT	
Overall	71	399	17.8%	(4th NHL)
Home	33	209	15.8%	(11th NHL)
Road	38	190	20.0%	(2nd NHL)

9 SHORT HANDED GOALS ALLOWED (T-9th NHL)

PENALTY KILLING				
Overall	51	382	86.6%	(T-5th NHL)
Home	15	171	91.2%	(1st NHL)
Road	36	211	82.9%	(T-20th NHL)

7 SHORT HANDED GOALS SCORED (21st NHL)

FLYERS SPECIAL TEAMS SCORING

Power play	G	A	PTS
LECLAIR	16	11	27
LINDROS	10	14	24
BRIND'AMOUR	10	14	24
COFFEY	1	19	20
DESJARDINS	2	14	16
DAIGLE	8	7	15
MCGILLIS	6	9	15
GRATTON	5	8	13
KLATT	5	6	11
SVOBODA	2	6	8
SILLINGER	2	5	7
ZUBRUS	1	3	4
THERIEN	1	2	3
PODEIN	1	2	3
RICHARDSON	2	0	2
FORBES	2	0	2
BABYCH	0	2	2

Short handed	G	A	PTS
SILLINGER	4	1	5
BRIND'AMOUR	2	2	4
PODEIN	1	0	1
LINDROS	1	0	1
DESJARDINS	1	0	1
THERIEN	0	1	1

OTTO	0	1	1
MCGILLIS	0	1	1
KLATT	0	1	1
FORBES	0	1	1

COACHING AND MANAGEMENT: Bob Clarke is one of the best general managers in the game. He has a grasp on things that others don't. For example, he knows inflated point totals are sometimes the result of circumstance than merit and has traded accordingly. He's a good judge of talent and character and a good wheeler-dealer. He's always been a little stubborn on the goaltending issue, but he might have been proven right if circumstances were slightly altered. Of course, Clarke makes mistakes, but he probably makes fewer than most. And he fixes them sooner or later.

You don't want to call Roger Nielson a dinosaur because he's been one of the most innovative coaches in modern hockey, and one of the most travelled. He had his team playing defence before it came in vogue, and won that way. Now, he's smart enough to figure out something else. If everybody else is playing defence, he'll adjust and come up with something different that works.

Hockey Annual Rating: 5 of 27

DRAFT

Round	Sel.	Player	Pos	Team
1	22	Simon Gagne	C	Quebec (QMJHL)
2	42	Jason Beckett	D	Seattle (WHL)
2	51	Ian Forbes	D	Guelph (OHL)
4	109	J-P Morin	D	Drummondville (QMJHL)
5	124	Francis Belanger	LW	Rimouski (QMJHL)
6	168	Antero Nittymaki	G	Finland
7	175	Cam Ondrik	G	Medicine Hat (WHL)
7	195	Tomas Divisek	LW	Czech
8	222	Luomir Pistek	LW	Czech
9	243	Petr Hubacek	C	Czech
9	253	Bruno St. Jacques	D	Baie-Comeau (QMJHL)
9	258	Sergei Skrobat	D	Russia

Simon Gagne is a speedy centre whose numbers (30-39-69) will improve this season in the QMJHL. He missed part of last season with a broken finger.

PROGNOSIS: The Flyers are going to be one of the top teams in the regular season, and come the playoffs they have a lot to prove. Vanbiesbrouck on board may take away the excuses. Don't be the least bit surprised to see the Flyers back in the Stanley Cup finals this year.

PREDICTION
Eastern Conference: 1st
Overall: 2nd

STAT SECTION
Team Scoring Stats

	GP	G	A	PTS	+/-	PIM	SH	CAREER GP	G	A	Pts
JOHN LECLAIR	82	51	36	87	30	32	303	507	226	222	448
ROD BRIND'AMOUR	82	36	38	74	2-	54	205	696	249	380	629
ERIC LINDROS	63	30	41	71	14	134	202	360	223	284	507
CHRIS GRATTON	82	22	40	62	11	159	182	376	89	142	231
ALEXANDRE DAIGLE	75	16	26	42	8-	14	146	338	83	115	198
TRENT KLATT	82	14	28	42	2	16	143	385	75	114	189
MIKE SILLINGER	75	21	20	41	11-	50	96	371	68	114	182
DAINIUS ZUBRUS	69	8	25	33	29	42	101	137	16	38	54
ERIC DESJARDINS	77	6	27	33	11	36	150	678	73	255	328
DANIEL MCGILLIS	80	11	20	31	21-	109	137	153	17	36	53
PAUL COFFEY	57	2	27	29	3	30	107	1,268	383	1,090	1,473
SHJON PODEIN	82	11	13	24	8	53	126	355	59	59	118
COLIN FORBES	63	12	7	19	2	59	93	66	13	7	20
CHRIS THERIEN	78	3	16	19	5	80	102	279	14	65	79
PETR SVOBODA	56	3	15	18	19	83	44	880	50	297	347
DAVE BABYCH	53	0	9	9	9-	49	46	1154	140	575	715
JOEL OTTO	68	3	4	7	2-	78	53	943	195	313	508
LUKE RICHARDSON	81	2	3	5	7	139	57	795	26	104	130
DANIEL LACROIX	56	1	4	5	0	135	28	183	11	7	18
JOHN DRUCE	23	1	2	3	0	2	18	531	113	126	239
KJELL SAMUELSSON	49	0	3	3	9	28	23	767	47	134	181
DAN KORDIC	61	1	1	2	4-	210	12	195	4	8	12
SEAN BURKE	52	0	2	2	0	20	0	goalie			
CRAIG DARBY	3	1	0	1	0	0	3	35	2	8	10
CHRIS JOSEPH	15	1	0	1	1	19	20	418	36	99	135
PAUL HEALEY	4	0	0	0	0	12	0	6	0	0	0
BRANTT MYHRES	23	0	0	0	1-	169	0	85	5	1	6
RON HEXTALL	46	0	0	0	0	10	0	goalie			

* Team Rankings 1997-98 (previous year's ranking in parenthesis)

		Conference Rank	League Rank
Record	42-29-11	3 (2)	6 (4)
Home	24-11-6	2 (4)	5 (6)
Away	18-18-5	5 (1)	9 (2)
Versus Own Conference	29-19-8	3 (3)	4 (5)
Versus Other Conference	13-10-3	4 (1)	9 (2)
Team Plus\Minus	+29	3 (1)	6 (2)
Goals For	242	1 (2)	3 (3)
Goals Against	193	4 (4)	5 (8)
Average Shots For	28.7	3 (1)	4 (2)
Average Shots Against	25.4	3 (1)	6 (1)
Overtime	3-1-11	2 (4)	3 (10)
One Goal Games	14-15	7 (1)	17 (1)
Times outshooting opponent	51	2 (1)	4 (1)
Versus Teams Over .500	15-19-6	5 (2)	9 (3)
Versus Teams Under .500	27-10-5	1 (2)	1 (5)
First Half Record	24-10-7	1 (1)	3 (1)
Second Half Record	18-19-4	8 (2)	15 (5)

PLAYOFFS

Results: lost to Buffalo in the conference quarter-finals

Record: 1-4

Home: 1-2

Away: 0-2

Goals For: 9 (1.8/game)

Goals Against: 18 (3.6/game)

Overtime: 0-1

Power play: 8.3% (15th)

Penalty Killing: 71% (16th)

	GP	G	A	PTS	+/-	PIM	PP	SH	GW	OT	S
R. BRIND'AMOUR	5	2	2	4	2	7	0	0	0	0	15
ERIC LINDROS	5	1	2	3	3-	17	0	0	0	0	13
DANIEL MCGILLIS	5	1	2	3	0	10	1	0	0	0	14
CHRIS GRATTON	5	2	0	2	1-	10	0	0	0	0	16
JOHN LECLAIR	5	1	1	2	4-	8	1	0	1	0	19
A. DAIGLE	5	0	2	2	0	0	0	0	0	0	6
MIKE SILLINGER	3	1	0	1	1	0	0	0	0	0	7
DAVE BABYCH	5	1	0	1	2	4	1	0	0	0	12
PETR SVOBODA	3	0	1	1	1-	4	0	0	0	0	1
ERIC DESJARDINS	5	0	1	1	3-	0	0	0	0	0	17
CHRIS THERIEN	5	0	1	1	1-	4	0	0	0	0	15
DAINIUS ZUBRUS	5	0	1	1	2	2	0	0	0	0	6
RON HEXTALL	1	0	0	0	0	0	0	0	0	0	0

CHRIS JOSEPH	1	0	0	0	0	2	0	0	0	0	2
K. SAMUELSSON	1	0	0	0	1	0	0	0	0	0	0
JOHN DRUCE	2	0	0	0	1-	2	0	0	0	0	3
DANIEL LACROIX	4	0	0	0	0	4	0	0	0	0	0
SEAN BURKE	5	0	0	0	0	0	0	0	0	0	0
JOEL OTTO	5	0	0	0	1-	0	0	0	0	0	8
L. RICHARDSON	5	0	0	0	3-	0	0	0	0	0	2
TRENT KLATT	5	0	0	0	6-	0	0	0	0	0	6
SHJON PODEIN	5	0	0	0	1-	10	0	0	0	0	5
COLIN FORBES	5	0	0	0	2	2	0	0	0	0	9

GOALTENDER	GPI	MINS	AVG	W	L	T	EN	SO	GA	SA	SV %
RON HEXTALL	1	20	3.00	0	0		0	0	1	8	.875
SEAN BURKE	5	283	3.60	1	4		0	0	17	121	.860
PHI TOTALS	5	306	3.53	1	4		0	0	18	129	.860

All-Time Leaders
Goals

Bill Barber	420
Brian Propp	369
Tim Kerr	363

Assists

Bobby Clarke	852
Brian Propp	480
Bill Barber	463

Points

Bobby Clarke	1,210
Bill Barber	883
Brian Propp	849

Best Individual Seasons
Goals

Reg Leach	1975-76	61
Tim Kerr	1986-87	58
Tim Kerr	1985-86	58

Assists

Bobby Clarke	1975-76	89
Bobby Clarke	1974-75	89
Mark Recchi	1992-93	70

Points

Mark Recchi	1992-93	123
Bobby Clarke	1975-76	119
Bobby Clarke	1974-75	116

TEAM
Last 3 years

	GP	W	L	T	Pts	%
1997-98	82	42	29	11	95	.579
1996-97	82	45	24	13	103	.628
1995-96	82	45	24	13	103	.628

Best 3 regular seasons

	GP	W	L	T	Pts	%
1975-76	80	51	13	16	118	.738
1979-80	80	48	12	20	116	.725
1973-74	76	51	18	11	113	.718

Worst 3 regular seasons

	GP	W	L	T	Pts	%
1969-70	76	17	35	24	58	.382
1968-69	76	20	35	21	61	.401
1971-72	78	26	38	14	66	.423

Most Goals (min. 70 game schedule)
1983-84   350
1984-85   348
1975-76   348

Fewest Goals (min. 70 game schedule)
1967-68   173
1968-69   174
1969-70   197

Most Goals Against (min. 70 game schedule)
1992-93   319
1993-94   314
1981-82   313

Fewest Goals Against (min. 70 game schedule)
1973-74   164
1967-68   179
1974-75   181

Pittsburgh Penguins

The Penguins weren't supposed to win last year, but they did.

Guess what? They're not supposed to win this year, either.

*Couldn't win (before last year started) because: No scoring balance.
*Won (last year) because: They had mediocre second and third line scoring, but one scoring line was enough.
*Won't win (this year) because: They have less balance than last year, with Francis gone.

*Couldn't win because: No reliable goaltending.
*Won because: Barrasso had a sensational comeback season.
*Won't win because: Barrasso is sure to get injured again.

*Couldn't win because: Poor team attitude and character.
*Won because: New coach Kevin Constantine demanded it, anyway.
*Won't win because: Don't have character players and it will be too difficult for Constantine to continue getting the most out of these guys.

*Couldn't win because: They couldn't sign free agent Petr Nedved.
*Won because: They didn't have Petr Nedved.
*Won't win because: They'll probably sign Petr Nedved.

*Couldn't win because: Defence was weak.
*Won because: Don't know.
*Won't win because: Defence is still weak.

*Couldn't win because: They didn't have Mario Lemieux anymore.
*Won because: Jaromir Jagr is a superstar in his own right.
*Won't win because: Jagr can't do everything, all the time.

*Couldn't win because: They drafted lousy players in the first round.
*Won because: Finally, first rounders Alexei Morozov and Robert Dome made contributions.
*Won't win because: They're still drafting lousy first rounders.

*Couldn't win because: They had too many holes.
*Won because: GM Craig Patrick somehow always manages to get the players they need.

*Won't win because: Patrick has just too many more holes to fill this year.

STUFF
* The Penguins only had one losing month, and that was 1-2-3 in February, the month shortened by the Olympic break.
* The Pens were 19-14-8 on the road, their second best road winning percentage in team history.
* Tom Barrasso became the first American goaltender to win 300 NHL games.
* Jaromir Jagr was second in Hart Trophy voting, behind Dominik Hasek.

TEAM PREVIEW
GOAL: That was some comeback season for Tom Barrasso. The year before, he played five games, and lost them all, with a 5.78 goals against average. A couple years before that, he played two games. So many injury problems that the Penguins couldn't depend on him to play at all.

Then, all of a sudden, he posts his lowest goals against average by about half a goal, he ties his season high in games played, has more shutouts than any other season, and is second in the league in save percentage. Go figure.

Ken Wregget was traded to Calgary, leaving Peter Skudra to back up Barrasso. He did an outstanding job in the games he played last year. In the future, the Penguins are looking toward Craig Hillier, their first round pick in

1996, who has had an outstanding junior career for Ottawa in the OHL.

Hockey Annual Rating: 12 of 27

DEFENCE: The Penguins rarely have had a good defence on paper in recent years, and this year is no different.

Darius Kasparaitis and Chris Tamer provide the little toughness they have.

Kevin Hatcher, who used to be a tougher player, is the only offensive defenceman of note.

Everything else is filling in the blanks. Fredrik Olausson filled in a blank for a while last year as an offensive help, but he became an unrestricted free agent, so that will require a blank fill-in. Brad Werenka, Jiri Slegr, Neil Wilkinson, newly acquired Bobby Dollas, and Tomas Gronman are all blank-fillers.

Blankety-blank-blank-blank. A whole new set of blanks is on the way.

Hockey Annual Rating: 15 of 27

FORWARD: One line, if they're lucky. Without Francis, it might be Jaromir Jagr, Stu Barnes and German Titov. Titov, incidentally, sat in the press box on occasion in Calgary and went through incredibly long scoring slumps.

Martin Straka is coming off a pretty good season with 19 goals, but he has a history of disappearing without giving notice. In other words, he might score five goals this year.

Alexei Morozov had a pretty good rookie

GOALTENDER	GPI	MINS	AVG	W	L	T	EN	SO	GA	SA	SV %
PETER SKUDRA	17	851	1.83	6	4	3	2	0	26	341	.924
TOM BARRASSO	63	3542	2.07	31	14	13	8	7	122	1556	.922
KEN WREGGET	15	611	2.75	3	6	2	2	0	28	293	.904
PIT TOTALS	82	5022	2.25	40	24	18	12	7	188	2202	.915

season and you'd expect him to improve. Robert Lang was good at times, but not many times.

Before we go any further, just in case it isn't evident. You take away Jagr from this group and they have a tough time winning in the IHL. Stu Barnes never even scored 20 goals before he was united with Jagr.

Rob Brown had an excellent comeback season, but he's gone to free agency. Ed Olczyk went the same route.

The Penguins have some fourth line checkers such as Tyler Wright, Alex Hicks and Sean Pronger, but after that they have to depend on Robert Dome, Todd Hlushko and Andreas Johansson.

There's a chance that Petr Nedved could return. He sat out the season because he didn't get the contract he wanted. Squabbling over millions. Good for the Penguins that they didn't give in to him. He's a greedy selfish player who obviously doesn't want to play hockey. Any character-type team just wouldn't want him, nor should they. Pittsburgh might, though.

There's almost nothing here. It's scary. If Jagr gets hurt, they're the worst forwards in the NHL.

Hockey Annual Rating: 17 of 27

SPECIAL TEAMS: What do Zigmund Palffy, John LeClair, Brendan Shanahan and Stu Barnes have in common?

They were the top power play goal scorers in the league last year. Pretty heady company for Barnes, who never even had a 20-goal season before.

The power play with suffer without Francis, but then again they weren't all that great last year, anyway.

Power Play	G	ATT	PCT	
Overall	67	407	16.5%	(11th NHL)
Home	37	209	17.7%	(8th NHL)
Road	30	198	15.2%	(13th NHL)

16 SHORT HANDED GOALS ALLOWED (T-23rd NHL)

Penalty Killing	G	ATT	PCT	
Overall	46	338	86.4%	(T-8th NHL)
Home	25	165	84.8%	(15th NHL)
Road	21	173	87.9%	(3rd NHL)

11 SHORT HANDED GOALS SCORED (T-9th NHL)

PENGUINS SPECIAL TEAMS SCORING

Power play	G	A	PTS
JAGR	7	31	38
FRANCIS	7	25	32
BARNES	15	12	27
HATCHER	13	12	25
OLAUSSON	2	14	16
BROWN	4	11	15
STRAKA	4	6	10
OLCZYK	5	2	7
WERENKA	2	4	6
PRONGER	1	5	6
SLEGR	1	4	5
LANG	1	3	4
GRONMAN	1	2	3
MOROZOV	2	0	2
WILKINSON	1	1	2
KASPARAITIS	0	2	2
WRIGHT	1	0	1
DOME	1	0	1
TAMER	0	1	1
JOHANSSON	0	1	1
HICKS	0	1	1
FERRARO	0	1	1
Short handed	G	A	PTS
STRAKA	3	3	6

OLCZYK	1	2	3
HATCHER	1	2	3
KASPARAITIS	2	0	2
SLEGR	1	1	2
JOHANSSON	1	1	2
BARNES	1	1	2
WERENKA	0	2	2
LANG	1	0	1
WILKINSON	0	1	1
VALK	0	1	1
OLAUSSON	0	1	1
HICKS	0	1	1

COACHING AND MANAGEMENT: Kevin Constantine was exactly what the Penguins needed last year to remind the players they were going to the arena instead of the beach. That said, he's reportedly at odds with Jagr. If you don't have the superstar in your corner, it often spells doom.

GM Patrick is a master at making something out of nothing. He makes a ton of changes every year and most of the time it works out. Most of the time.

Hockey Annual Rating: 3 of 27

DRAFT

Round	Sel.	Player	Pos	Team
1	23	Milan Kraft	C	Czech
2	54	Alexander Zevakhin	W	Russia
3	80	David Cameron	C	Prince Albert (WHL)
4	110	Scott Myers	G	Prince George (WHL)
5	134	Rob Scuderi	D	Boston College (HE)
6	169	Jan Fadrny	C	Czech
7	196	Joel Scherban	C	London (OHL)
8	224	Toby Petersen	C	Colorado Col. (WCHA)
9	254	Matt Hussey	C	Avon Old Farms (USHS)

The Penguins keep picking Europeans in the first round and keep coming up empty. At least since they got Jagr in 1990. Milan Kraft isn't a great skater and isn't a great physical specimen, but he can put the puck in the net.

PROGNOSIS: They're not going anywhere. It's very likely they will be the team that drops the most in the standings. They're a one-player team, and one-player teams don't win.

The only thing that could change things is if Patrick works his magic and somehow makes the transactions that change things. He's done it before.

PREDICTION
Eastern Conference: 9th
Overall: 18th

STAT SECTION
Team Scoring Stats   CAREER

	GP	G	A	PTS	+/-	PIM	SH	GP	G	A	Pts
JAROMIR JAGR	77	35	67	102	17	64	262	581	301	434	735
RON FRANCIS	81	25	62	87	12	20	189	1,247	428	1,006	1,434
STU BARNES	78	30	35	65	15	30	196	433	121	152	273
KEVIN HATCHER	74	19	29	48	3-	66	169	960	208	390	598
MARTIN STRAKA	75	19	23	42	1-	28	117	370	77	135	212
ROB BROWN	82	15	25	40	1-	59	172	435	167	224	391
F. OLAUSSON	76	6	27	33	13	42	89	787	112	356	468
ALEXEI MOROZOV	76	13	13	26	4-	8	80	76	13	13	26
ED OLCZYK	56	11	11	22	9-	35	123	937	330	435	765
ROBERT LANG	54	9	13	22	7	16	66	201	28	52	80
SEAN PRONGER	67	6	15	21	10-	32	73	113	13	23	36
ALEX HICKS	58	7	13	20	4	54	78	195	24	45	69
BRAD WERENKA	71	3	15	18	15	46	50	133	8	30	38
JIRI SLEGR	73	5	12	17	10	109	131	280	20	90	110
A. JOHANSSON	50	5	10	15	4	20	49	95	9	20	29
D. KASPARAITIS	81	4	8	12	3	127	71	370	12	64	76
ROBERT DOME	30	5	2	7	1-	12	29	30	5	2	7
CHRIS FERRARO	46	3	4	7	2-	43	42	60	5	5	10
TYLER WRIGHT	82	3	4	7	3-	112	46	168	8	7	15
IAN MORAN	37	1	6	7	0	19	33	124	6	12	18
CHRIS TAMER	79	0	7	7	4	181	55	242	8	21	29
NEIL WILKINSON	34	2	4	6	0	24	19	436	16	67	83
GARRY VALK	39	2	1	3	3-	33	32	474	69	92	161
T. GRONMAN	22	1	2	3	3	25	33	38	1	3	4
TOM BARRASSO	63	0	2	2	0	14	0	goalie			
PETER SKUDRA	17	0	1	1	0	2	0	goalie			
S. BUTENSCHON	8	0	0	0	1-	6	4	8	0	0	0
KEN WREGGET	15	0	0	0	0	6	0	goalie			

* Team Rankings 1997-98 (previous year's ranking in parenthesis)

		Conference Rank	League Rank
Record	40-24-18	2 (6)	5 (10)
Home	21-10-10	4 (1)	7 (2)
Away	19-14-8	4 (10)	5 (20)
Versus Own Conference	28-16-12	2 (9)	4 (16)
Versus Other Conference	12-8-6	3 (3)	7 (7)
Team Plus\Minus	+19	5 (6)	8 (13)
Goals For	228	3 (1)	7 (1)
Goals Against	188	3 (12)	4 (25)
Average Shots For	26.5	8 (8)	19
Average Shots Against	26.9	6 (13)	11
Overtime	3-2-18	7 (13)	12
One Goal Games	12-7	2 (12)	4
Times outshooting opponent	37	7 (12)	15
Versus Teams Over .500	16-15-12	3 (10)	6
Versus Teams .500 or under	24-9-6	2	3
First Half Record	21-12-8	3	7
Second Half Record	19-12-10	5	8

PLAYOFFS

Results: lost 4-2 to Montreal in conference quarter-finals
Record: 2-4
Home: 1-2
Away: 1-2
Goals For: 15 (2.5/game)
Goals Against: 18 (3.0/game)
Overtime: 0-1
Power play: 12.1% (11th)
Penalty Killing: 81.5% (14th)

	GP	G	A	PTS	+/-	PIM	PP	SH	GW	OT	S
JAROMIR JAGR	6	4	5	9	5	2	1	0	0	0	23
STU BARNES	6	3	3	6	2	2	0	0	1	0	12
RON FRANCIS	6	1	5	6	5	2	0	0	0	0	19
JIRI SLEGR	6	0	4	4	3	2	0	0	0	0	10
FREDRIK OLAUSSON	6	0	3	3	0	2	0	0	0	0	17
ROBERT LANG	6	0	3	3	4-	2	0	0	0	0	6
ED OLCZYK	6	2	0	2	3-	4	1	1	1	0	6
MARTIN STRAKA	6	2	0	2	3-	2	0	1	0	0	10
ROB BROWN	6	1	0	1	4-	4	1	0	0	0	10
KEVIN HATCHER	6	1	0	1	1	12	1	0	0	0	15
BRAD WERENKA	6	1	0	1	3-	8	0	1	0	0	3
CHRIS TAMER	6	0	1	1	1-	4	0	0	0	0	2

TYLER WRIGHT	6	0	1	1	0	4	0	0	0	0	3
ALEXEI MOROZOV	6	0	1	1	3-	2	0	0	0	0	10
ANDREAS JOHANSSON	1	0	0	0	0	0	0	0	0	0	0
TUOMAS GRONMAN	1	0	0	0	0	0	0	0	0	0	0
SEAN PRONGER	5	0	0	0	1-	4	0	0	0	0	4
DARIUS KASPARAITIS	5	0	0	0	2-	8	0	0	0	0	3
TOM BARRASSO	6	0	0	0	0	2	0	0	0	0	0
IAN MORAN	6	0	0	0	1-	2	0	0	0	0	0
ALEX HICKS	6	0	0	0	5-	2	0	0	0	0	6

GOALTENDER	GPI	MINS	AVG	W	L	EN	SO	GA	SA	SV %
TOM BARRASSO	6	376	2.71	2	4	1	0	17	171	.901
PIT TOTALS	6	379	2.85	2	4	1	0	18	172	.895

All-Time Leaders
Goals
Mario Lemieux	613
Jean Pronovost	316
Rick Kehoe	312

Assists
Mario Lemieux	881
Ron Francis	449
Jaromir Jagr	434

Points
Mario Lemieux	1,494
Jaromir Jagr	735
Rick Kehoe	636

Best Individual Seasons
Goals
Mario Lemieux	1988-89	85
Mario Lemieux	1987-88	70
Mario Lemieux	1992-93	69
Mario Lemieux	1995-96	69

Assists
Mario Lemieux	1988-89	114
Mario Lemieux	1987-88	98
Mario Lemieux	1985-86	93

Points
Mario Lemieux	1988-89	199
Mario Lemieux	1987-88	168
Mario Lemieux	1995-96	161

TEAM
Last 3 years
	GP	W	L	T	Pts	%
1997-98	82	40	24	18	98	.598
1996-97	82	38	36	8	84	.561
1995-96	82	49	29	4	102	.622

Best 3 regular seasons
	GP	W	L	T	Pts	%
1993-94	84	56	21	7	119	.708
1994-95	48	29	16	3	61	.635
1995-96	82	49	29	4	102	.622

Worst 3 regular seasons

1983-84	80	16	58	6	38	.238
1982-83	80	18	53	9	45	.281
1984-85	80	24	51	5	53	.331

Most Goals (min. 70 game schedule)

1992-93	367
1995-96	362
1988-89	347

Fewest Goals (min. 70 game schedule)

1969-70	182
1968-69	189
1967-68	195

Most Goals Against (min. 70 game schedule)

1982-83	394
1983-84	390
1984-85	385

Fewest Goals Against (min. 70 game schedule)

1997-98	188
1967-68	216
1969-70	238

Tampa Bay Lightning

We could spend a lot of time here going over just how bad the Tampa Bay Lightning were last season. A lot of time.

But, there are also a lot of reasons to be excited about the upcoming season if you're one of their fans. And not just because it couldn't be any worse than last year. Consider.

* Top draft pick Vincent Lecavalier. No, he's not the next Michael Jordan, as new owner, Art Williams overstated, but he is the first Lecavalier, and he's already pretty close to being their best player before he even steps on the ice.
* New goalie Bill Ranford. He's got something to prove, just as John Vanbiesbrouck did in the early years of the Florida Panthers.
* Youthful potential. On some teams, what you see is what you get. On the Lightning, they haven't seen much yet from some of their prospects. There's Darcy Tucker, Jason Bonsignore, Steve Kelly, Daymond Langkow, Alexander Selivanov, and offensive defenceman hopeful, David Wilkie. There may not be room this year for Kelly or Bonsignore, and Langkow may be traded, but everybody mentioned has yet to reach their potential.

* Tough Guys. Enrico Ciccone and Sandy McCarthy aren't just two tough guys, they're two of the toughest in the league. Andrei Nazarov fits right in there, too, and he's a European, to boot.
* A premier defensive forward. Rob Zamuner is one of the best in the game. Mind you, you can't stop a flood with an umbrella, but he's still worth watching, especially if he's in the right situation.

STUFF
* the Lightning were winless in two months of the season: in January they were 0-12-1, and in April they were 0-9-1.

TEAM PREVIEW
GOAL: It looks like the Lightning have given up on Daren Puppa and his injury problems. They just can't keep waiting until he's healthy while filling in the blanks in the meantime. They left him open in the expansion draft, along with Corey Schwab and Mark Fitzpatrick. And none of them were selected.

The Lightning obtained Bill Ranford from Washington for some draft picks. Ranford is a season away from being one of the premier goalies in the NHL. Last year, he wasted away on the end of the bench, with injury problems and one slightly bigger problem in the name of Olaf Kolzig, who took over the number one role and carried the Capitals to the finals.

It's not that goaltending was the major problem with this team last year, but it's a handy excuse. If the Lightning had used two goalies at the same time it wouldn't have made much difference.

But, Ranford has something to prove, and the Lightning are accomodating. Somebody might be interested in the three incumbents, but there's a glut of goaltending in the NHL right now, so one of them will have to win the backup role to Ranford.

Hockey Annual Rating: 17 of 27

DEFENCE: The Lightning are going to need some help here. Maybe lots of it. Karl Dykuis is the best of the bunch, while Cory Cross and Enrico Ciccone have experience. Jassen Cullimore, Mike McBain and David Wilkie are the opposite of experienced. They played a total of 89 games in the NHL last season.

With Ciccone, you take away the need for a nutty guy that opposing forwards will want to stay away from. He had 175 penalty minutes in just 39 games.

They've got lots of size, but that really isn't a major consideration anymore because most NHL defencemen have size by definition.

Mobility wouldn't appear to be a strong suit, and they don't have an offensive threat unless Wilkie or McBain develop into that role. Wilkie was well-known for his big shot before he made it to the NHL, although he doesn't shoot much yet, and McBain had some offensive success as a junior. As it stands now, the Lightning pretty much have to put forwards on defence on the power play.

The Lightning had Jeff Norton and Yves Racine around some last year as experienced veterans, but tossed them away. Experienced but limited NHL defencemen are a phone call and an eighth round draft pick away, so it's not a big worry.

The top prospect is Paul Mara, the 7th pick overall in the 1997 draft. He was 16-33-49 in 50 games for Plymouth in the OHL last season, and was rated the 15th best NHL prospect by *The Hockey News*. Mario Larocque, who played for Sherbrooke in the QMJHL and Pavel Kubina, who was with Adirondack in the AHL last season, are next on the prospect depth chart.

Most of the Tampa Bay defencemen wouldn't be playing on a lot of teams, so an upgrade or quick development is essential.

GOALTENDER	GPI	MINS	AVG	W	L	T	EN	SO	GA	SA	SV %
DAREN PUPPA	26	1456	2.72	5	14	6	6	0	66	660	.900
COREY SCHWAB	16	821	2.92	2	9	1	2	1	40	370	.892
MARK FITZPATRICK	34	1938	3.16	7	24	1	5	1	102	975	.895
DEREK WILKINSON	8	311	3.28	2	4	1	1	0	17	148	.885
ZAC BIERK	13	433	4.16	1	4	1	0	0	30	210	.857
T.B TOTALS	82	4978	3.24	17	55	10	14	3	269	2377	.887

COREY SCHWAB and DEREK WILKINSON shared a shutout vs NYR on Dec 31, 1997

Hockey Annual Rating: 25 of 27

FORWARD: The Lightning were the lowest scoring team in 44 years. The last time a club scored fewer than Tampa Bay's 151 goals was 1955-56 when Boston scored 147. They were also the first team since that year not to have at least one 20-goal scorer. Selivanov and Mikael Renberg led the way with 16. GM Phil Esposito used to get that many in a couple weeks when he played with the Bruins.

The addition of Craig Janney is going to help. He's a good playmaking centre, who will make his wingers better. Top draft pick, Lecavalier will help out there eventually as well.

Other than that, not much else has changed, so Janney better be one hell of a play-maker. In fact, he'd better be Shakespeare.

It's not that a lot of forwards couldn't have and shouldn't have done much better. Selivanov is a former 31-goal scorer. Renberg should have more, Langkow should have had more, heck they all should have had more.

The addition of Stephane Richer late last season is expected to help, but that means he'd have to stay healthy, and that's fairly unlikely.

Forget about Brian Bradley. He thinks everybody's out to get him and that some of his teammates think he was faking last year when he was out with headaches and wrist surgery. Medical reports showed at first that there was nothing wrong with him, but subsequent tests showed there was some swelling in his head. He's vowed never to play for Tampa Bay again. It's unlikely the team will think of that as a punishment.

John Cullen will attempt a comeback after a year off of being treated with non-Hodgkins nymphoma. He is technically an unrestricted free agent.

The Lightning is loaded with centres anyway. There's Janney, Lecavalier, Darcy Tucker, Langkow, and prospects Jason Bonsignore and Steve Kelly. Nazarov can also play there.

Paul Ysebeart led the team in scoring, but wasn't protected in the expansion draft. That's probably because he only had 40 points. Getting 40 points on this team, however was akin to getting 70 somewhere else.

Zamuner does his job, so there's no worry there, as do tough guys McCarthy and Nazarov. Mikael Andersson never goes away, so he must be doing his job, too.

The Lightning will score more goals this season, if only because they couldn't score fewer, but how many more is an interesting question.

Hockey Annual Rating: 26 of 27

SPECIAL TEAMS: Tim Kerr holds the NHL record for most power play goals in a season, which he did for Philadelphia in the 1985-86 season. He had 34, one more than the Lightning scored all last year. At least the Lightning would have been second, because the Dave Andreychuk only scored 32 for Buffalo and Toronto in the 1992-93 season.

The Lightning allowed 16 shorthanded goals, so their net on the power play was 17, in 83 games. The good news is that it can't possibly get any worse.

Craig Janney is a decent playmaker and will probably lead the team in power play points. Brian Bradley, back and healthy, could help out there, as should Stephane Richer, who joined the team late last year. Lecavalier is likely to see a lot of time on the ice with the extra man.

Other than that, it's whatever falls into place.

Power Play	G	ATT	PCT	
Overall	33	353	9.3%	(26th NHL)
Home	19	182	10.4%	(25th NHL)
Road	14	171	8.2%	(25th NHL)

16 SHORT HANDED GOALS ALLOWED (T-23rd NHL)

Penalty Killing	G	TSH	PCT	
Overall	72	410	82.4%	(23rd NHL)
Home	43	212	79.7%	(25th NHL)
Road	29	198	85.4%	(11th NHL)

11 SHORT HANDED GOALS SCORED (T-9th NHL)

LIGHTNING SPECIAL TEAMS SCORING

Power play	G	A	PTS
YSEBAERT	2	13	15
RENBERG	6	8	14
SELIVANOV	4	8	12
RICHER	5	3	8
MCCARTHY	1	4	5
RACINE	0	5	5
LANGKOW	2	2	4
BRADLEY	2	2	4
WILKIE	0	3	3
CULLIMORE	1	1	2
ZAMUNER	0	2	2
TUCKER	1	0	1
KELLY	1	0	1
DYKHUIS	0	1	1
CROSS	0	1	1
CICCONE	0	1	1
BONSIGNORE	0	1	1

Short handed	G	A	PTS
ZAMUNER	3	2	5
RENBERG	3	0	3
YSEBAERT	1	2	3
ANDERSSON	1	2	3
RICHER	0	3	3
TUCKER	1	1	2
HULL	1	1	2
DYKHUIS	1	0	1
CROSS	1	0	1
CULLIMORE	0	1	1

COACHING AND MANAGEMENT: New team owner, Art Williams, has vowed that the Lightning will win the Stanley Cup this year. Not really, but keep an ear out. He brings enthusiasm, if nothing else to the franchise, after declaring their number one draft pick, Vincent Lecavalier, would be the Michael Jordan of hockey.

General Manager, Phil Esposito, who manages to keep his job no matter what happens, is used to ownership that's a little out of the norm. And he's used to being slapped around some, which is what the new owner Art Williams did in effect when he named coach Jacques Demers director of player personnel and said he and Esposito would have equal say in player matters.

Jacques Demers is a positive, upbeat guy who has been known to make good teams play up to their potential. It remains to be seen if there's anything he can do with this team.

Hockey Annual Rating: 26 of 27

DRAFT

Round	Sel.	PlayerPos		Amateur Team
1	1	Vincent Lecavalier	C	Rimouski (QMJHL)
2	64	Brad Richards	LW	Rimouski (QMJHL)
2	72	Dimitri Afansenkov	W	Russia
4	92	Eric Beaudoin	LW	Guelph (OHL)

5	121	Curtis Rich	D	Calgary (WHL)
6	146	Sergei Kuznetsov	C	Russia
7	174	Brett Allen	C	Swift Current (WHL)
7	194	Oak Hewer	C	S.S. Marie (OHL)
8	221	Daniel Hulak	D	Swift Current (WHL)
9	229	Chris Lyness	D	Rouyn-Noranda (QMJHL)
9	252	Martin Cibak	D	Slovakia

It's tough these days to figure how well a rookie will do. You'd think Lecavalier would have a great season because he has all the opportunity in the world, but last year's top pick, Joe Thornton, couldn't do much at all with Boston.

PROGNOSIS: At least the Tampa Bay Lightning won't be the worst team in the league this year. That honor should go to the Nashville Predators. Tampa Bay is an improved team, anyway. Not a winning team, but an improving team and quite possibly an entertaining team.

PREDICTION
Eastern Conference: 14th
Overall: 26th

STAT SECTION
Team Scoring Stats

	GP	G	A	PTS	+/-	PIM	SH	CAREER GP	G	A	Pts
PAUL YSEBAERT	82	13	27	40	43-	32	145	522	149	186	335
MIKAEL RENBERG	68	16	22	38	37-	34	175	326	125	154	279
A. SELIVANOV	70	16	19	35	38-	85	206	261	72	64	136
STEPHANE RICHER	40	14	15	29	6-	41	95	866	380	341	721
ROB ZAMUNER	77	14	12	26	31-	41	126	426	75	107	182
D. LANGKOW	68	8	14	22	9-	62	156	151	23	28	51
DARCY TUCKER	74	7	13	20	14-	146	63	150	14	26	40
SANDY MCCARTHY	66	8	10	18	19-	241	94	290	30	30	60
M. ANDERSSON	72	6	11	17	4-	29	105	659	91	159	250
KARL DYKHUIS	78	5	9	14	8-	110	91	273	17	53	70
J. BONSIGNORE	35	2	8	10	11-	22	29	56	3	10	13
CORY CROSS	74	3	6	9	24-	77	72	269	10	30	40
JODY HULL	49	4	4	8	3	8	51	526	99	105	204
YVES RACINE	60	0	8	8	23-	41	76	508	37	194	231
BRIAN BRADLEY	14	2	5	7	9-	6	24	651	182	321	503
DAVID WILKIE	34	2	5	7	22-	21	48	120	9	19	28
VLADIMIR VUJTEK	30	2	4	6	2-	16	44	102	7	29	36
BRENT PETERSON	19	5	0	5	2-	2	15	36	7	0	7
STEVE KELLY	43	2	3	5	13-	23	22	51	3	3	6

ANDREI NAZAROV	54	2	2	4	13-	170	50	183	24	29	53
ENRICO CICCONE	39	0	4	4	2-	175	22	312	7	17	24
PAVEL KUBINA	10	1	2	3	1-	22	8	10	1	2	3
JASSEN CULLIMORE	28	1	2	3	4-	26	18	141	5	11	16
LOUIE DEBRUSK	54	1	2	3	2-	166	14	282	20	14	34
PAUL BROUSSEAU	11	0	2	2	0	27	6	11	0	2	2
DAVID SHAW	14	0	2	2	2-	12	12	769	41	153	194
COREY SPRING	8	1	0	1	1-	10	12	8	1	0	1
MIKE MCBAIN	27	0	1	1	10-	8	17	27	0	1	1
MARK FITZPATRICK	46	0	1	1	0	16	0	goalie			
TROY MALLETTE	3	0	0	0	0	7	0	456	51	69	120
DEREK WILKINSON	8	0	0	0	0	0	0	goalie			
ALAN EGELAND	8	0	0	0	0	9	4	17	0	0	0
ZAC BIERK	13	0	0	0	0	0	0	goalie			
COREY SCHWAB	16	0	0	0	0	2	0	goalie			
DAREN PUPPA	26	0	0	0	0	6	0	goalie			

* Team Rankings 1997-98 (previous year's ranking in parenthesis)

		Conference Rank	League Rank
Record	17-55-10	13 (11)	26 (20)
Home	11-23-7	12 (12)	25 (22)
Away	6-32-3	13 (7)	26 (13)
Versus Own Conference	10-38-8	13 (12)	26 (24)
Versus Other Conference	7-17-2	12 (7)	25 (12)
Team Plus\Minus	-79	13 (11)	26 (20)
Goals For	151	13 (12)	26 (22)
Goals Against	269	13 (8)	25 (16)
Average Shots For	25.6	12 (3)	24 (5)
Average Shots Against	29.0	12 (6)	21 (10)
Overtime	0-3-10	13 (3)	26 (6)
One Goal Games	7-13	12 (3)	22 (5)

Times outshooting opponent	25	13 (4)	25 (8)
Versus Teams Over .500	6-33-6	13 (6)	26 (8)
Versus Teams .500 or Under	11-22-4	13 (11)	26 (23)
First Half Record	9-24-8	13 (11)	26 (18)
Second Half Record	8-31-2	13 (10)	26 (19)

PLAYOFFS

- did not make the playoffs

All-Time Leaders
Goals

Brian Bradley	102
Rob Zamuner	76
Petr Klima	63

Assists

Brian Bradley	184
Roman Hamrlik	132
Rob Zamuner	105

Points

Brian Bradley	269
Petr Klima	133
Roman Hamrlik	130

Best Individual Seasons
Goals

Brian Bradley	1992-93	43
Dino Ciccarelli	1996-97	35
Alexander Selivanov	1995-96	31

Assists

Brian Bradley	1995-96	56
Roman Hamrlik	1995-96	49
Brian Bradley	1992-93	44

Points

Brian Bradley	1992-93	86
Brian Bradley	1995-96	79
Roman Hamrlik	1995-96	65

TEAM
Last 3 years

	GP	W	L	T	Pts	%
1997-98	82	17	55	10	44	.268
1996-97	82	32	40	10	74	.451
1995-96	82	38	32	12	88	.543
1994-95	48	17	28	3	37	.385

Best 3 regular seasons

	GP	W	L	T	Pts	%
1995-96	82	38	32	12	88	.543
1996-97	82	32	40	10	74	.451
1993-94	84	30	43	11	71	.423

Worst 3 regular seasons

	GP	W	L	T	Pts	%
1997-98	82	17	55	10	44	.268
1992-93	84	23	54	7	53	.315
1994-95	48	17	28	3	37	.385

Most Goals (min. 70 game schedule)

1992-93	245
1995-96	238
1993-94	224

Fewest Goals (min. 70 game schedule)

1997-98	151
1996-97	217
1993-94	224

Most Goals Against (min. 70 game schedule)

1992-93	332
1993-94	251
1995-96	248

Fewest Goals Against (min. 70 game schedule)

1996-97	247
1995-96	248
1993-94	251

Toronto Maple Leafs

Nothing escapes the attention of the media and fans in Toronto. Nothing. Every little thing that happens to the Toronto Maple Leafs is analyzed to death.

What happens after that is kind of odd. Eventually, there are few dissenting opinions on a particular issue. Most of the time it involves some form of management decision, or more to the point, indecision. A strange way to unite a group of people, but as they say, misery loves company.

Here's a different take on a lot of the issues that have been surrounding this team.

Mike Murphy Firing

Oh, the outrage. The whole city was up in arms over the way management was treating Mike Murphy. How could they do this to him, keeping him hanging into the summer so that he didn't know whether or not he'd be back. My, my, just the worst possible way to treat a human being.

Big, stinking deal. In fact, it was one of the few things management had done right at the time. Why fire Murphy until they're sure the guy they really want (probably Marc Crawford before compensation became an issue) is available.

Murphy was going to be paid for this season no matter what happened, and people in this business, or any business, get fired all the time, rarely with any advance notice. Those who called for his dismissal during the season weren't worried about him or his family's feelings then.

To his credit, Murphy didn't play the wounded warrior outwardly.

Ken Dryden's job isn't to worry about feelings being hurt, it's to make the team better. If he thought this would make the team better then that's the way it goes.

Dryden just doesn't know how to play the game properly. He should have done what smart management people do all the time. Say Murphy's job was not in jeopardy to keep the media off his back, and then lower the hammer when he's ready.

Steve Stavro

Every so often, people say Steve Stavro should speak up and be accounted for. Why is that? Because media people want him to?

He's a private person who prefers not to speak to the media. What exactly is wrong with that? He can do whatever the heck he wants.

And to those who think he's cheap and is just in it for the money. Well, he's got lots of money as it is. Why do people assume he has no pride and no desire to win?

Although it hasn't worked out too well, he did make an effort by hiring Ken Dryden to turn the franchise around and the Curtis Joseph signing was a blockbuster.

Fan Support

About seven times a night on the sports talk shows, fans call in and say the reason the team doesn't do more to win is because fans go to the games no matter how well the team is playing. They should stay away, suggest the callers.

The fans go to the games to see NHL hockey, the Toronto Maple Leafs and the stars of their opponent on any given night. Whether or not Toronto is going to win has no bearing on that fact. Staying away from the games, in other words, is a lot less enjoyable than going to them.

Maple Leaf Gardens

Maple Leaf Gardens is the last of the hockey shrines. Just walking into the building is enough to make your heart beat a little faster.

The only thing wrong with the place, as far as the fans were concerned, is that the seats were too close together. For the rich history lesson the building gave every time you entered it, it was probably worth it.

Revelations that some of the staff used the lure of the building to abuse boys overshadows its heritage and fewer tears will be shed when the Maple Leafs move out later this season.

Changing Conferences

Everybody loves this idea. Renewing rival-ries with Montreal and playing in the East. Hard to argue that it makes sense, but I asked as many young hockey fans as I could which teams they'd rather see play: Detroit, Colorado and Vancouver, or Montreal, Buffalo and Ottawa. None hesitated. Detroit is Toronto's biggest and most fun rival to many young fans, not Montreal. Those days are long dead.

They will probably be renewed eventually, but the Western Conference plays more exciting hockey, and the Leafs are going to have a tougher time in the East, for at least a while.

Won't Spend the Money

All season long, the fans cried that the Leafs were cheap and wouldn't spend the money to make the team better.

At that point in the season, just what was it they were going to spend their money on? You can't just pick out a player and say, okay I've got money, hand him over. That's just stupid.

Once free agency starts, then they can spend the money, but there are a lot of teams vying for the over-priced services of a few, and not everybody gets what they want.

The Leafs did pick up Curtis Joseph in the summer which should make the cheap accusations disappear for a while.

Ken Dryden

Sure he's a slow-talker and a long-talker and slow-to-get-to-the-point talker and a sounds-like-you're-reading-a-book-talker, but that's all besides the point. And he could rationalize anything that happens on the planet if he wanted. That just makes it easier to criticize him. Criticism should be based on his performance. There's more than enough ammunition there.

Mike Smith

This publication has been most uncomplimentary toward Mike Smith in the past, perhaps unfairly, but who doesn't deserve a second chance? When does he start work.

TEAM PREVIEW
GOAL: As popular as Felix Potvin was with the Toronto fans, Curtis Joseph will be even more so. If they kept records for this sort of thing, Joseph jerseys are going to set record sales.

Potvin was inconsistent at times during his career. When he was on, he was great, but when he wasn't, he let in a lot of weak goals.

And, it's not as if goaltending was the major weakness in Toronto anyway. They had much bigger problems.

The free agent signing happened right at press time so the Leafs hadn't dealt Potvin away. There's no way they would keep both of them.

Glen Healy didn't have a particularly good year, and the Leafs were reluctant to use him. It's kind of tough to be sharp when you don't get to play very often, but the Leafs didn't play him very often because he wasn't sharp. You figure it out.

He will probably play even less this year, backing up Joseph.

Hockey Annual Rating: 4 of 27

DEFENCE: You almost get the impression that progress is being made in this area, at least more so than at the other positions.

In fact, it's pretty close to an actual NHL defence. The way to tell is that some of them could play for good teams.

We're not talking about the Bob Rouse's and Jamie Macoun's and Larry Murphy's, here. Unless the Leafs trade for Nicklas Lidstrom, then those guys couldn't be effective here.

It's a little tiresome for guys like Larry Murphy and Jamie Macoun to be so proud that they're able to "stick-it" to their old team by holding up their Stanley Cup winning rings. If they had made more of a contribution here then they wouldn't have been let go in the first place. In Murphy's case, his contribution was usually to opposing teams. He should shut up and express remorse that he wasn't able to help the Maple Leafs, rather than be so happy he can "stick it" to them.

Jason Smith is a solid defensive-defenceman, who also plays the physical game. Mathieu Schneider is an offensive force, who is great when he's on, but also makes way too many boneheaded plays. Yushkevich wasn't as noticably bad last season, which you could probably consider a good thing. Sylvain Cote was a nice addition and a help to the power play, although there was probably good reason

GOALTENDER	GPI	MINS	AVG	W	L	T	EN	SO	GA	SA	SV %
MARCEL COUSINEAU	2	17	.00	0	0	0	0	0	0	9	1.000
FELIX POTVIN	67	3864	2.73	26	33	7	4	5	176	1882	.906
GLENN HEALY	21	1068	2.98	4	10	2	4	0	53	453	.883
TOR TOTALS	82	4970	2.86	30	43	9	8	6	237	2352	.899

GLENN HEALY and MARCEL COUSINEAU shared a shutout vs S.J on Nov 4, 1997

he was sitting in the press box while he was with Washington. Craig Wolanin missed most of last season with injuries.

Among the rookies last year, Yannick Tremblay looked pretty good at times, but the most impressive was Daniil Markov. He looks like a player.

As at all their positions, the Leafs have no prospects, other than those who already played some last year.

Hockey Annual Rating: 23 of 27

FORWARD: Here's an indication of how far away the Leafs are from winning. Say you're the Colorado Avalanche and you can have any or all of the Leaf forwards.

You grab Mats Sundin immediately, and probably Tie Domi to be your enforcer. The rest of the team you say thanks, but no thanks.

There is so little here, it's scary. Very scary. So scary that the Nashville Predators might be better if you take away Sundin.

The Leafs have a savior, however. During the summer they forked over big bucks for a 35-year-old 14-goal scorer. Parade to follow. Steve Thomas is a likeable guy and was a good scorer in his day. He'll get more than 14 goals playing with Sundin than playing on a checking line in New Jersey, but that's how ridiculous it is. Thomas jumps to the head of the class and the first line. And another thing. All those players who think they're going to pile up the points after leaving the Devils, well it doesn't seem to work out that way.

Mike Johnson had a good rookie year, finishing second on the team in scoring. He has speed and savvy, and appears to be a good prospect. He's a first-liner, too, when he should

be a third liner until he learns the game more.

Darby Hendrickson showed a lot of value as a checker, and was one of the Leafs most consistent players.

Alyn McCauley has a chance to do well, and for a month last year, Fredrik Modin looked like the second coming. He stopped firing it over the net or twenty feet wide, and scored 11 goals in that month. Eventually, he went back to normal with five goals in the other six months of the season.

Sergei Berezin doesn't have a clue and doesn't seem to care; the team has no confidence in Steve Sullivan; Martin Prochazka can't play in the NHL; Kris King is a dinosaur, although a dinosaur with "character"; Derek King deserves credit for playing years beyond his usefulness; Todd Warriner is something, but what that is isn't clear; Lonny Bohonos should request a trade to St. Louis where they make stars out of career minor-leaguers; and someone made a big gaff with Igor Korolev by forgetting to tell him that the season was 82 games, not 32.

That pretty much sums it up, except for the fact that there are no real prospects. That's in terms of players coming up through the system, and in overall hope.

At press time, however, the Leafs hadn't yet dealt Potvin, so you can figure on some real forwards being obtained in a trade.

Hockey Annual Rating: 24 of 27

SPECIAL TEAMS: There was one thing the Leafs did better than most teams last year: kill penalties. There was one thing the Leafs did better than only one team last year: score on the power play.

Toronto was 14-173 on the road on the

power play last year, amazingly poor production. They allowed 13 shorthanded goals, so their net power play goals on the season was 28.

If Sundin could figure out a way to pass it to himself, then they would be in much better shape.

Power Play	G	ATT	PCT	
Overall	41	359	11.4%	(25th NHL)
Home	27	186	14.5%	(15th NHL)
Road	14	173	8.1%	(26th NHL)

13 SHORT HANDED GOALS ALLOWED (T-20th NHL)

Penalty Killing	G	ATT	PCT	
Overall	50	372	86.6%	(T-5th NHL)
Home	29	181	84.0%	(16th NHL)
Road	21	191	89.0%	(2nd NHL)

5 SHORT HANDED GOALS SCORED (T-23rd NHL)

MAPLE LEAFS SPECIAL TEAMS SCORING

Power play	G	A	PTS
SUNDIN	9	12	21
SCHNEIDER	4	14	18
KING	4	10	14
JOHNSON	5	8	13
KOROLEV	6	6	12
CLARK	4	3	7
COTE	1	3	4
YUSHKEVICH	0	4	4
BEREZIN	3	0	3
TREMBLAY	1	2	3
SULLIVAN	1	1	2
MODIN	1	1	2
MARKOV	1	1	2
ZETTLER	0	2	2
MCCAULEY	0	2	2
PROCHAZKA	0	1	1

Short handed	G	A	PTS
SUNDIN	1	3	4
KOROLEV	3	0	3
SCHNEIDER	1	0	1
COTE	0	1	1

COACHING AND MANAGEMENT: Mike Murphy did a remarkable job with the Leafs last year. He probably should even have received votes for coach of the year. To be able to win with this rag-tag group is a credit to his hard work, motivational skills, and intensity. Toronto could just have easily been battling Tampa Bay and Florida for the worst team in the league, but they were still in the playoff race late into the season.

It's hard to see how Pat Quinn could get more out of the Leaf talent than Murphy, but we'll see. He used to make a habit out of coming out of the GM chair to take over the coaching reigns in Vancouver, and he almost always made the team play better.

The general manager team of Ken Dryden and Mike Smith is trying very hard not to embarrass themselves. There's a lot of inactivity or indecision, and they had done nothing of consequence until signing free agent goalie, Curtis Joseph.

The best thing that can be said about Dryden is that he appears to be an honorable man. That's not a bad thing to be. He doesn't pass along the responsibility or blame when he could take it on himself. As for hockey genius, we'll have to wait for his next book to find out about that.

Hockey Annual Rating: 25 of 27

DRAFT

Round	Sel.	Player	Pos	Team
1	10	Nikolai Antropov	C	Kazakhstan
2	35	Petr Svoboda	D	Czech
3	69	Jamie Hodson	G	Brandon

				(WHL)
4	87	Alexei Ponikarvsky	W	Russia
5	126	Morgan Warren	RW	Moncton (QMJHL)
6	154	Allan Rourke	D	Kitchener (OHL)
7	181	Jonathan Gagnon	C	Val D'or (QMJHL)
8	215	Dwight Wolfe	D	Halifax (QMJHL)
8	228	Michal Travnicek	W	Czech
9	236	Sergei Rostov	D	Russia

First there was Mario Lemieux, and now...Nikolai Antropov. At least that's the impression you might have gotten at the draft. Apparently, a lot of teams drafting late in the first round had him pegged as a sleeper and wanted him. Even so, Antropov is considered a risky picky. Since when were the Leafs in a position to take risks at the draft table?

A lot of talk about Antropov was about the big game he had where he scored 11 goals and 15 assists in a 63-0 romp over Iceland. Cool, huh? Yeah, unless you happened to be playing for Iceland. What kind of guy keeps punching an opponent who is already obviously knocked out?

PROGNOSIS: The Eastern Conference will be cruel to the Maple Leafs. Playing all those teams once, as in previous years, they could surprise them and maybe get a win. Now, teams in both conferences will know how to beat them. It won't be pretty and hard work and discipline won't be nearly enough.

PREDICTION
Eastern Conference: 13th
Overall: 25th

STAT SECTION
Team Scoring Stats

	GP	G	A	PTS	+/-	PIM	SH	CAREER GP	G	A	Pts
MATS SUNDIN	82	33	41	74	3-	49	219	611	265	367	632
MIKE JOHNSON	82	15	32	47	4-	24	143	95	17	34	41
DEREK KING	77	21	25	46	7-	43	166	727	235	316	551
IGOR KOROLEV	78	17	22	39	18-	22	97	384	60	113	173
MATHIEU SCHNEIDER	76	11	26	37	12-	44	181	553	95	216	311
FREDRIK MODIN	74	16	16	32	5-	32	137	150	22	23	45
SERGEI BEREZIN	68	16	15	31	3-	10	167	141	41	31	72
STEVE SULLIVAN	63	10	18	28	8-	40	112	439	46	77	123
SYLVAIN COTE	71	4	21	25	3-	42	103	877	99	440	539
WENDEL CLARK	47	12	7	19	21-	80	140	683	294	216	510
ALYN MCCAULEY	60	6	10	16	7-	6	77	60	6	10	16
JASON SMITH	81	3	13	16	5-	100	97	266	6	16	22
TIE DOMI	80	4	10	14	5-	365	72	486	42	27	69

TODD WARRINER	45	5	8	13	5	20	73	182	24	37	61
DARBY HENDRICKSON	80	8	4	12	20-	67	115	214	26	21	47
DIMITRI YUSHKEVICH	72	0	12	12	13-	78	92	412	20	93	113
LONNY BOHONOS	37	5	4	9	8-	8	50	76	16	16	32
DANIIL MARKOV	25	2	5	7	0	28	15	15	25	2	57
ROB ZETTLER	59	0	7	7	8-	108	28	477	4	55	59
KRIS KING	82	3	3	6	13-	199	53	730	61	79	140
MARTIN PROCHAZKA	29	2	4	6	1-	8	40	40	29	2	46
YANNICK TREMBLAY	38	2	4	6	6-	6	45	45	43	2	46
JAMIE BAKER	13	0	5	5	1	10	16	403	71	78	149
DAVID COOPER	9	0	4	4	2	8	13	28	3	7	10
MARCEL COUSINEAU	2	0	0	0	0	0	0	goalie			
JEFF WARE	2	0	0	0	1	0	0	15	0	0	0
KEVYN ADAMS	5	0	0	0	0	7	3	5	0	0	0
CRAIG WOLANIN	10	0	0	0	9-	6	5	695	40	133	173
GLENN HEALY	21	0	0	0	0	0	0	goalie			
FELIX POTVIN	67	0	0	0	0	8	0	goalie			

* Team Rankings 1997-98 (previous year's ranking in parenthesis)

		Conference Rank	League Rank
Record	30-43-9	10 (11)	21 (23)
Home	16-20-5	10 (9)	20 (20)
Away	14-23-4	11 (11)	22 (21)
Versus Own Conference	22-27-7	9 (9)	19 (19)
Versus Other Conference	8-16-2	13 (12)	23 (22)
Team Plus\Minus	-34	13 (11)	24 (22)
Goals For	194	12 (9)	23 (17)
Goals Against	237	10 (11)	21 (21)
Average Shots For	27.7	5 (9)	10 (17)
Average Shots Against	28.7	9 (13)	18 (26)
Overtime	1-0-9	2 (9)	6 (16)

One Goal Games	15-12	4 (10)	8 (18)
Times outshooting opponent	33	10 (11)	19 (22)
Versus Teams Over .500	9-29-3	13 (12)	25 (24)
Versus Teams .500 or under	21-14-6	7 (9)	13 (16)
First Half Record	13-21-7	9 (10)	21 (21)
Second Half Record	17-22-4	10 (12)	19 (23)

PLAYOFFS

- did not make the playoffs

All-Time Leaders
Goals
Darryl Sittler	389
Dave Keon	365
Ron Ellis	332

Assists
Borje Salming	620
Darryl Sittler	527
Dave Keon	493

Points
Darryl Sittler	916
Dave Keon	858
Borje Salming	768

Best Individual Seasons
Goals
Rick Vaive	1981-82	54
Dave Andreychuk	1993-94	53
Rick Vaive	1983-84	52

Assists
Doug Gilmour	1992-93	95
Doug Gilmour	1993-94	84
Darryl Sittler	1977-78	72

Points
Doug Gilmour	1992-93	127
Darryl Sittler	1977-78	117
Doug Gilmour	1993-94	111

TEAM
Last 3 years
	GP	W	L	T	Pts	%
1997-98	82	30	43	9	69	.421
1996-97	82	30	44	8	68	.415
1995-96	82	34	36	12	80	.488

Best 3 regular seasons
	GP	W	L	T	Pts	%
1950-51	70	41	16	13	95	.679
1934-35	48	30	14	4	64	.667
1940-41	48	28	14	6	62	.646

Worst 3 regular seasons
	GP	W	L	T	Pts	%
1918-19	18	5	13	0	10	.278
1984-85	80	20	52	8	48	.300
1987-88	80	21	49	10	52	.325

Most Goals (min. 70 game schedule)
1989-90	337
1980-81	322
1985-86	311

Fewest Goals (min. 70 game schedule)
1954-55	147
1953-54	152
1955-56	153

Most Goals Against (min. 70 game schedule)
1983-84	387
1985-86	386
1981-82	380

Fewest Goals Against (min. 70 game schedule)
1953-54	131
1954-55	135
1950-51	130

Washington Capitals

In the latter half of last season, the Capitals went into a tailspin that saw them go winless in eight games. Seven of those games were losses and incredibly they played the same team three times in a row and lost to them each time. That team was Tampa Bay.

Nobody was predicting much of anything for the Caps at that time, except maybe a hard time getting into the playoffs.

That might have been the end of the line for last year's Caps, but after those disastrous eight games, the Caps went an amazing 16-4-1 the rest of the season and all the way to the finals.

There weren't a lot of personnel changes at the time. Phil Housley didn't play much anymore, and Esa Tikkanen was acquired right when they started to get hot.

You could probably make an argument that those eight games turned the season around. Sometimes, it takes hitting rock bottom to know how far you have to go to the top.

The Capitals have a rich history of outstanding regular seasons followed by poor playoff performances. This is an encouraging reversal of trend.

You don't want to rain on anybody's parade, but the Caps didn't make it to the finals simply because they're the best team in the Eastern Conference. More goes into it than that.

In fact, they almost didn't make it out of the first round. They won two games against Boston in overtime, including the sixth game. If Boston wins that one it goes to seven games and anything could happen. Overtime goals are generally a matter of good fortune or bad fortune. One wrong or right move and it's all over. In the conference finals against Buffalo, three of the four Washington wins were in overtime.

In the playoffs, one of the major determining factors of who wins what is who happens to have the hot goalie at the time. Olaf Kolzig was the hottest of the hot in the playoffs. If Olie the Goalie wasn't phenomenal, the Caps don't make it to the finals.

Last year, it was him, the year before it was someone else, the year before someone else again. And next year, it will be somebody different. That's not to say Kolzig hasn't earned the right to be recognized as a premier goalie in the league, it's just that that's the way it works.

So, while the Capitals are sitting pretty at the moment, wallowing in their final appearance, history suggests it's not going to get any better than that this year. It's called the Stanley

Cup Finals Jinx. I just made that name up, but consider what has happened to the finals loser over an extended period of time.

Stanley Cup Finalist Loser the following year (since Conference setup in 1982)

	Final Loser	Next Year
1997	Philadelphia	Lost First Round
1996	Florida	Lost First Round
1995	Detroit	Lost Conference Finals
1994	Vancouver	Lost Conference Semi-Finals
1993	Los Angeles	Missed Playoffs
1992	Chicago	Lost first round
1991	Minnesota	Lost first round
1990	Boston	Lost Conference Finals
1989	Montreal	Lost Division Finals
1988	Boston	Lost Division Finals
1987	Philadelphia	Lost First Round
1986	Calgary	Lost First Round
1985	Philadelphia	Lost First Round
1984	NY Islanders	Lost Division Finals
1983	Edmonton	WON STANLEY CUP
1982	Vancouver	Lost first round

Summary

* of the 16 finalist losers since the conference setup in 1982, eight of them were knocked out in the first round the next year, and one of them didn't even make the playoffs.
* only three of the 16 made it as far as the conference finals the next year, and only one won the Stanley Cup (Edmonton in 1983).
* only one team has made it back to the finals (Edmonton) and nobody has done it in the last 14 years.

TEAM PREVIEW

GOAL: Bill Ranford found out last season that backing up Olaf Kolzig is an unrewarding job. Because of his status, however, he got into more games than, say, this year's backup will get. In fact, they didn't even have a backup as of this writing. Heck, maybe they won't even need one.

Hockey Annual Rating: 3 of 27

DEFENCE: The Capitals defence managed to mix and match their talents just right last year. They had defensive-minded Mark Tinordi with offensive-minded Calle Johansson, and defensive-minded Joe Reekie with offensive-minded Sergei Gonchar.

The problem was that they had to play too much, and that all of them except Gonchar have passed the 30-year-old mark. Phil Housely isn't someone you want on the ice much except on the power play, and Brendan Witt was the odd man out.

The Caps figure Dmitri Mironov, signed as a free agent over the summer, can take care of their quarterbacking problems for the power play. They tried out Jeff Brown after getting him

GOALTENDER	GPI	MINS	AVG	W	L	T	EN	SO	GA	SA	SV %
OLAF KOLZIG	64	3788	2.20	33	18	10	5	5	139	1729	.920
BILL RANFORD	22	1183	2.79	7	12	2	3	0	55	555	.901
WSH TOTALS	82	4997	2.43	40	30	12	8	5	202	2292	.912

in a trade for Sylvain Cote, but he became an unrestricted free agent and is injured too much anyway, and Housley can't do the job anymore. Mironov was traded to Detroit last season, but didn't get to play much during the playoffs. He has the skills, but not the hockey sense.

The Caps are aging on defence, but along with Witt and Gonchar, they have some excellent young prospects on the way. Nolan Baumgartner will make a run at a job and Nick Boynton will be there sooner than later. Defencemen get labels. They're offensive or defensive. It's relatively rare to find an all-round defenceman who can play both ends of the rink, can skate well, and doesn't shy away from physical contact. That's what Boynton will bring to the show.

Hockey Annual Rating: 4 of 27

FORWARD: Peter Bondra didn't have to do it all himself this year. Check that. He didn't have to do it all himself in the playoffs, the regular season was the same old story. He had 52 goals, while the second top goal scorer, Adam Oates, got 18. That's one of the reasons why the Caps were supposed to be easy to stop in the playoffs. Just stop him and they couldn't score.

Bondra was far from a dominant factor in the playoffs. He led the team in goals, but he was tied with three other players, and two others were just a goal behind. Bondra was just fifth in points in the playoffs on Washington.

Balanced scoring was the key in the playoffs, but there's no reason to suggest it will continue on during this regular season. A bunch of guys played way over their heads.

Joe Juneau had seven playoff goals after just nine in the regular season. He was on the

left side of Oates and Brian Bellows to form a number one scoring line. Bondra was with Andrei Nikolishin and Richard Zednik on another scoring line.

Bellows became a free agent at the end of the season, but it doesn't matter. He had a good run, but his days of putting up big numbers over the course of a full year are long behind him. His days of even playing at all got a jump start when the Caps signed him late in the season.

There's more hope for the likes of Nikolishin and Zednik, both of whom came up big in the playoffs. If they can continue that momentum into the regular season, it will be a major spark for the team.

Chris Simon is a key contributor who will be even more effective if he can get through an entire season without being injured. Dale Hunter doesn't have to contribute anything on the scoreboard to have an effect on the team.

The rest of the forwards are checkers, fill-ins and prospects. Tikkanen was lost to free agency, so the Caps can see if he signs with someone else and then pick him up in a trade at the trading deadline for the playoff run. That way they don't have to pay his salary for most of the season. Not likely, but it would make sense.

Andrew Brunette was lost to Nashville in the expansion draft. He had a spectacular scoring run when called up from the minors, but a couple games with no points and it was so long, back to the minors. He was the hottest scorer in the league over a time. He had a six-game goal streak and had nine over nine games. Following that he had 13 points in an eight-game stretch. In his first 19 games after being called up he had points in 17 of them. Talk about having high standards to meet. He had three games with no points and then he wasn't even in the lineup.

Steve Konowalchuk, enforcer Craig Berube, checker Jeff Toms, and whatever Michal Pivonka is, fill out the lineup.

The top prospects are Yogi Svejkovsky and Jan Bulis, who could give the Caps more scoring balance.

Hockey Annual Rating: 9 of 27

SPECIAL TEAMS: The Caps ranked first in penalty killing, despite the fact that Bondra and Oates were out there trying to score goals. Often that means more goals against. The Caps defence is to be applauded for making sure that didn't happen.

Despite the fact that Bondra is a premier scorer in the league, the power play doesn't seem to be a place for him to pad his goal scoring stats. He led the team with 11, but defenceman Johansson was only one behind him. Most of the other top goal scorers around the league get a big chunk of goals on the power play.

The Caps think their power play problems are on the blueline. They've tried out a couple would-be quarterbacks, and now will try Mironov.

Power Play	G	ATT	PCT	
Overall	55	350	15.7%	(13th NHL)
Home	31	174	17.8%	(7th NHL)
Road	24	176	13.6%	(19th NHL)

4 SHORT HANDED GOALS ALLOWED (T-2nd NHL)

Penalty Killing	G	ATT	PCT	
Overall	39	361	89.2%	(1st NHL)
Home	18	169	89.3%	(2nd NHL)
Road	21	192	89.1%	(1st NHL)

14 SHORT HANDED GOALS SCORED (4th NHL)

CAPITALS SPECIAL TEAMS SCORING

Power play	G	A	PTS
OATES	3	23	26
BONDRA	11	10	21
JOHANSSON	10	10	20
HOUSLEY	4	15	19
BROWN	4	15	19
JUNEAU	4	8	12
SIMON	4	5	9
GONCHAR	2	7	9
TIKKANEN	1	8	9
BRUNETTE	4	4	8
BELLOWS	5	0	5
SVEJKOVSKY	2	1	3
KONOWALCHUK	2	1	3
NIKOLISHIN	1	2	3
KRYGIER	0	3	3
ZEDNIK	2	0	2
WITT	0	1	1
PIVONKA	0	1	1
HUNTER	0	1	1
BULIS	0	1	1
BAUMGARTNER	0	1	1

Short handed	G	A	PTS
OATES	2	4	6
BONDRA	5	0	5
HUNTER	0	4	4
MILLER	3	0	3
TINORDI	1	1	2
JUNEAU	1	1	2
JOHANSSON	1	1	2
HOUSLEY	1	0	1
WITT	0	1	1
TOMS	0	1	1
REEKIE	0	1	1

COACHING AND MANAGEMENT: Great rookie seasons for coach Ron Wilson and GM George McPhee. Wilson, of course, coached in Anaheim, but he didn't have the horses to actually coach, other than putting Teemu Selanne and Paul Kariya on the ice as often as possible. Usually, you can judge a coach by how successful they are in the playoffs because that's where it counts.

McPhee made some key moves in his first season, ones that took imagination. One was getting Tikkanen in a trade, and the other was signing Brian Bellows after he returned from Europe. Often, it's those little touches that mean the difference between winning and losing. McPhee is a go-getter so if the Caps see themselves lacking somewhere, he'll, uh, go get it.

Hockey Annual Rating: 4 of 27

DRAFT

Round	Sel.	Player	Pos	Team
2	49	Jomar Cruz	G	Brandon (WHL)
2	59	Todd Hornung	C	Portland (WHL)
4	106	Krys Barch	LW	London (OHL)
4	107	Chris Corrinet	RW	Princeton (ECAC)
5	118	Mike Siklenka	D	Olds (AJHL)
5	124	Erik Wendell	C	Maple Grove HS (USHS)
7	179	Nathan Forster	D	Seattle (WHL)
7	193	Ratislav Stana	G	Slovakia
8	220	Michael Farrell	D	Providence (ECAC)
9	251	Blake Evans	C	Tri-City (WHL)

The Caps didn't have a draft pick until the second round when they grabbed goalie Jomar Cruz. Cruz will step directly into the Caps net and replace Kolzig. Just kidding. Goalies take a long time to develop, and the Caps have a long time to wait.

PROGNOSIS: Just because the Caps made it into the Stanley Cup finals there's no reason to think they'll be a dominating regular season team. They should be a good one because they have such a solid defence, and great goaltending, but Bondra still scores all the goals. If their prospects start putting the puck in the net, like they think they will, then they'll be that much better. None of their prospects have yet to live up to advance billing yet, so upper tier success isn't guaranteed.

PREDICTION

Eastern Conference: 3rd
Overall: 6th

STAT SECTION

Team Scoring Stats

	GP	G	A	PTS	+/-	PIM	SH	CAREER GP	G	A	Pts
PETER BONDRA	76	52	26	78	14	44	284	544	285	205	490
ADAM OATES	82	18	58	76	6	36	121	908	276	796	1,072
CALLE JOHANSSON	73	15	20	35	11-	30	163	783	92	323	415
S. KONOWALCHUK	80	10	24	34	9	80	131	373	77	106	183
JOE JUNEAU	56	9	22	31	8-	26	87	410	99	277	376
PHIL HOUSLEY	64	6	25	31	10-	24	116	1,131	291	730	1,021
JEFF BROWN	60	4	24	28	5	32	102	747	154	430	584
RICHARD ZEDNIK	65	17	9	26	2-	28	148	77	19	10	29
DALE HUNTER	82	8	18	26	1	103	82	1,345	321	688	1,009
ANDREW BRUNETTE	28	11	12	23	2	12	42	62	18	22	40
SERGEI GONCHAR	72	5	16	21	2	66	134	238	35	64	99
ESA TIKKANEN	48	3	18	21	11-	18	67	845	244	383	627
MARK TINORDI	47	8	9	17	9	39	57	615	52	142	194
CHRIS SIMON	28	7	10	17	1-	38	71	216	40	55	95
ANDREI NIKOLISHIN	38	6	10	16	1	14	40	209	37	76	113
JAN BULIS	48	5	11	16	5-	18	37	48	5	11	16
CRAIG BERUBE	74	6	9	15	3-	189	68	719	47	78	125
KELLY MILLER	76	7	7	14	2-	41	68	995	179	277	456
TODD KRYGIER	45	2	12	14	3-	30	71	543	100	143	24
JEFF TOMS	46	4	6	10	17-	15	69	81	6	14	20
JOE REEKIE	68	2	8	10	15	70	59	641	21	107	128
BRIAN BELLOWS	11	6	3	9	3-	6	26	1,112	468	518	986
MICHAL PIVONKA	33	3	6	9	5	20	38	789	176	412	588
BRENDAN WITT	64	1	7	8	11-	112	68	156	6	12	18
KEN KLEE	51	4	2	6	3-	46	44	220	18	14	32
J. SVEJKOVSKY	17	4	1	5	5-	10	29	36	11	4	15
MIKE EAGLES	36	1	3	4	2-	16	25	776	68	120	188
JAN BENDA	9	0	3	3	1	6	8	9	0	3	3
N. BAUMGARTNER	4	0	1	1	0	0	4	5	0	1	1
BENOIT GRATTON	6	0	1	1	1	6	5	6	0	1	1
BILL RANFORD	22	0	1	1	0	0	0	goalie			
OLAF KOLZIG	64	0	1	1	0	12	0	goalie			
PAT PEAKE	1	0	0	0	0	4	0	134	28	41	69
BRAD CHURCH	2	0	0	0	0	0	4	2	0	0	0
DWAYNE HAY	2	0	0	0	0	2	1	2	0	0	0

RYAN MULHERN	3	0	0	0	0	0	1	3	0	0	0
DAVID HARLOCK	6	0	0	0	2	4	2	14	0	0	0
STEWART MALGUNAS	8	0	0	0	1	12	5	115	1	4	5

* Team Rankings 1997-98 (previous year's ranking in parenthesis)

		Conference Rank	League Rank
Record	40-30-12	4 (9)	8 (18)
Home	23-12-6	3 (8)	6 (15)
Away	17-18-6	7 (9)	11 (18)
Versus Own Conference	28-20-8	4 (8)	8 (15)
Versus Other Conference	12-10-4	6 (9)	11 (18)
Team Plus\Minus	+1	7 (9)	14 (17)
Goals For	219	6 (13)	12 (23)
Goals Against	202	7 (5)	10 (9)
Average Shots For	27.1	7 (11)	14 (21)
Average Shots Against	28.0	8 (4)	15 (6)
Overtime	4-1-12	1 (7)	2 (14)
One Goal Games	19-13	4 (10)	6 (20)
Times outshooting opponent	38	6 (5)	14 (10)

Versus Teams Over .500	14-18-8	6 (8)	10 (18)
Versus Teams .500 or Under	26-12-4	5 (8)	6 (18)
First Half Record	18-15-8	5 (10)	9 (17)
Second Half Record	22-15-4	5 (9)	8 (18)

PLAYOFFS

Results: defeated Boston 4-2 in conference quarter-finals
defeated Ottawa 4-1 in conference semi-finals
defeated Buffalo 4-2 in conference finals
lost to Detroit 4-0 in finals
Record: 12-9
Home: 5-6
Away: 7-3
Goals For: 53 (2.5/game)
Power play: 16.7% (5th)
Penalty Killing: 87% (6th)
Overtime: 5-2
Goals Against: 44 (2.1/game)

	GP	G	A	PTS	+/-	PIM	PP	SH	GW	OT	S
JOE JUNEAU	21	7	10	17	6	8	1	1	4	2	54
ADAM OATES	21	6	11	17	8	8	1	1	1	0	31
ANDREI NIKOLISHIN	21	1	13	14	4	12	1	0	0	0	29
BRIAN BELLOWS	21	6	7	13	6	6	2	0	1	1	62
PETER BONDRA	17	7	5	12	4	12	3	0	2	1	48

SERGEI GONCHAR	21	7	4	11	2	30	3	1	2	0	37
RICHARD ZEDNIK	17	7	3	10	0	16	2	0	0	0	40
CALLE JOHANSSON	21	2	8	10	9	16	0	0	0	0	42
ESA TIKKANEN	21	3	3	6	2-	20	1	0	0	0	23
PHIL HOUSLEY	18	0	4	4	2-	4	0	0	0	0	27
DALE HUNTER	21	0	4	4	1-	30	0	0	0	0	14
TODD KRYGIER	13	1	2	3	2-	6	0	0	1	1	12
JOE REEKIE	21	1	2	3	4	20	0	0	0	0	16
MARK TINORDI	21	1	2	3	6	42	0	0	0	0	14
MICHAL PIVONKA	13	0	3	3	5	0	0	0	0	0	16
JEFF BROWN	2	0	2	2	1	0	0	0	0	0	2
MIKE EAGLES	12	0	2	2	1	2	0	0	0	0	7
KEN KLEE	9	1	0	1	2	10	0	0	0	0	6
BRENDAN WITT	16	1	0	1	1-	14	0	0	0	0	9
CHRIS SIMON	18	1	0	1	3-	26	0	0	0	0	17
CRAIG BERUBE	21	1	0	1	0	21	0	0	1	0	15
KELLY MILLER	10	0	1	1	2	4	0	0	0	0	8
JEFF TOMS	1	0	0	0	1-	0	0	0	0	0	0
JAROSLAV SVEJKOVSKY	1	0	0	0	0	2	0	0	0	0	0
OLAF KOLZIG	21	0	0	0	0	4	0	0	0	0	0

GOALTENDER	GPI	MINS	AVG	W	L	T	EN	SO	GA	SA	SV %
OLAF KOLZIG	21	1351	1.95	12	9		0	4	44	740	.941
WSH TOTALS	21	1357	1.95	12	9		0	4	44	740	.941

All-time Leaders
Goals

Mike Gartner	397
Peter Bondra	285
Mike Ridley	218

Assists

Michal Pivonka	406
Mike Gartner	392
Dale Hunter	370

Points

Mike Gartner	789
Michal Pivonka	579
Bengt Gustafsson	555

Best Individual Seasons
Goals

Dennis Maruk	1981-82	60
Bob Carpenter	1984-85	53
Peter Bondra	1995-96	52
Peter Bondra	1997-98	52

Assists

Dennis Maruk	1981-82	76
Michal Pivonka	1995-96	65
Scott Stevens	1988-89	61

Points

Dennis Maruk	1981-82	136
Mike Gartner	1984-85	102
Dennis Maruk	1980-81	97

TEAM

Last 3 years

	GP	W	L	T	Pts	%
1997-98	82	40	30	12	92	.561
1996-97	82	33	40	9	75	.457
1995-96	82	39	32	11	89	.543

Best 3 regular seasons

	GP	W	L	T	Pts	%
1985-86	80	50	23	7	107	.669
1983-84	80	48	27	5	101	.631
1984-85	80	46	25	9	101	.631

Worst 3 regular seasons

	GP	W	L	T	Pts	%
1974-75	80	8	67	5	21	.131
1975-76	80	11	59	10	32	.200
1977-78	80	17	49	14	48	.333

Most Goals (min. 70 game schedule)

1991-92	330
1992-93	325
1984-85	322

Fewest Goals (min. 70 game schedule)

1974-75	181
1977-78	195
1996-97	214

Most Goals Against (min. 70 game schedule)

1974-75	446
1975-76	394
1981-82	338

Fewest Goals Against (min. 70 game schedule)

1997-98	202
1995-96	204
1983-84	226

WESTERN CONFERENCE

Anaheim Mighty Ducks

Two years ago, the Ducks were a two-man team: Paul Kariya and Teemu Selanne. Last year, they became a one-man team, and the one man wasn't Kariya.

Selanne had a remarkable season, his 52 goals tying him with Peter Bondra for the league lead. The amazing part is what those 52 goals represented in a season where goal scoring was at its lowest since before Hull was in his prime. That's Bobby Hull, not Brett.

Something I developed years ago for *Inside Hockey* and revamped for a feature in *The Hockey News* last season was a method of comparing different eras of hockey.

The process is fairly simple. We take the league overall goals per game and compare it to the goals per game of a different season. Then we project the same overall rate of scoring change down to the individuals. Last year, there were 5.3 goals per game, the lowest since the 1955-56 season. In 1981-82, there were 8.3 goals per game. If you scored 20 goals last season, all things being equal, it would equate to 31 goals in 1981-82 (20/5.3 x 8.3).

The following shows the top 10 scorers from this season and their equivalent scoring to 1981-82.

	Team	1997-98			1981-81 Equivalent		
		G	A	P	G	A	P
Jagr	Pit	35	67	102	55	105	160
Forsberg	Col	25	66	91	39	103	142
Bure	Van	51	39	90	80	61	141
Gretzky	NYR	23	67	90	36	105	141
LeClair	Phi	51	36	87	80	56	136
Palffy	NYI	45	42	87	70	66	136
Francis	Pit	25	62	87	39	97	136
Selanne	Ana	52	34	86	81	53	134
Allison	Bos	33	50	83	52	78	130
Stumpel	LA	21	58	79	33	91	124

In 1981-82, Wayne Gretzky set an NHL record with 92 goals. Working in reverse, his 1997-98 equivalent would be 59 goals.

Getting back to Selanne, his 52 goals are equivalent to 81 goals in 1981-82. But, he missed nine games last year, so his projected total for the full season would be 58 goals. Now, 58 goals last year is equivalent to 91 goals in 1981-82, or just one short of Gretzky's all-time NHL record.

A lot of assumptions go into that, but the fact remains, Selanne had one of the best goal-scoring seasons in NHL history. And he did it mostly on his own.

We'd have to assume too much to include Kariya in the above scoring comparison. He only played 22 games because of a holdout and then an injury. But, if we project the 17 goals he scored in 22 games over the entire season, it works out to 63 goals. Those 63 goals would be the equivalent of 99 goals in 1981-82, an NHL record.

STUFF

* Tomas Sandstrom became the all-time highest scoring Swede last season, with 817 points, passing Thomas Steen.
* Teemu Selanne had an 11-game goal streak, longest of the year in the league.
* Selanne was third in Hart Trophy voting, and second in Lady Byng Trophy voting, behind Ron Francis.

TEAM PREVIEW

GOAL: It wouldn't have mattered if Dominik Hasek had been playing net for the Ducks last season. Or Terry Sawchuk, Ken Dryden or Jacques Plante in their prime.

Goaltending wasn't the problem with the Ducks, and while a soft goal or shaky outing wasn't a rarity, that wasn't the difference. With the inexperienced defence the Ducks are icing, it's not easy for any goalie to look good.

Guy Hebert is a capable goalie if he's on a capable team. He was the third goalie for the U.S. Olympic team, which isn't to say that team proved very capable, but to be chosen says something. Because of injuries, he didn't play in any of the final 20 games of the season for the Ducks.

Mikail Shtalenkov did well in a backup role, but isn't a number one man. When playing sporadically to spell Hebert, he started off the season with a 4-1-3 record. Sometimes he would get two starts in a row, having earned it from good play in the first start, but almost invariably did not perform nearly as well in the second game.

Shtalenkov wasn't protected in the expansion draft, but that's because of regulations that required each team to leave one goalie available who had played at least 10 NHL games last season. Nashville grabbed him, and he looks like he could be the backup there.

GOALTENDER	GPI	MINS	AVG	W	L	T	EN	SO	GA	SA	SV %
TOM ASKEY	7	273	2.64	0	1	2	2	0	12	113	.894
GUY HEBERT	46	2660	2.93	13	24	6	4	3	130	1339	.903
M. SHTALENKOV	40	2049	3.22	13	18	5	3	1	110	1031	.893
ANA TOTALS	82	5007	3.13	26	43	13	9	4	261	2492	.895

The Ducks picked up the rights to Patrick Lalime, who made a big initial splash with Pittsburgh, before sinking back to the minors. He set an NHL record by going undefeated in his first sixteen games.

Tom Askey was called up from Cincinnati last season and played fine as a backup to Shtalenkov when Hebert was injured.

Hockey Annual Rating: 19 of 27

DEFENCE: Yikes, call them the Duckling Defense. As in young, and, uh, ugly.

Go ahead, try to find the veterans. I dare you.

There's journeyman Doug Houda, who came over in a trade, but the 32-year-old has been around, and around, and around. David Karpa has been around for awhile too, but he's more of an enforcer.

Check out the ages and experience of the Duck hopefuls for this season:

Pavel Trnka	22	(48 games)
Mike Crowley	23	(8 games)
Ruslan Salei	23	(96 games)
Drew Bannister	24	(139 games)
Jamie Pushor	25	(144 games)
Jason Marshall	27	(172 games)
David Karpa	28	(323 games)
Doug Houda	32	(556 games)

The Ducks are likely to add a veteran to the mix at some time, but they'll also need an offensive defenseman to replace Dmitri Mironov and J.J. Daigneault, two guys who handled that for most of last year before being shipped out.

Mike Crowley has the inside track for that role. He was the leading scorer in the WCHA for

the University of Minnesota two years ago, and scored well for Cincinnati in the AHL last season before getting in eight games with the Ducks. He's no physical presence, however, so he'll have to show a lot offensively to compensate. Mind you, there's no competition at the moment.

Among the defencemen remaining with the Ducks at the end of last season, Salei was the leading scorer with 15 points. Yes, that's just 15 points.

The top prospect is Maxim Balmochnykh, who played in Russia last season and made an impression while on the Russian junior team.

Free agent signings are a very real possibility. In fact, they're a necessity.

Hockey Annual Rating: 26 of 27

FORWARD: It used to be that a team needed balanced scoring to be successful in the NHL. It seems in more recent years that only one or two players are scoring the bulk of the goals on each team. If that's the case, then Kariya and Selanne are about as good as it gets.

It's like having a big jigsaw puzzle and not knowing what the picture is. But, then you get two giant pieces and the rest is easy to figure out.

The problem is that if one of those two big pieces get injured, it throws everything else out of whack.

With Selanne scoring almost every goal, and with Kariya holding out and then injured, the Ducks still had a respectable start to last season, going 8-5-4 before tailing off to 3-10-2. In other words, one of the two guys can carry the team on his shoulders for a while, but not forever.

The Ducks are trying to fill out the picture, and it looks to be coming along. Travis Green was a great addition last year in a trade. Matt Cullen looks like he could become a good playmaking centre, and Frank Banham and Josef Marha scored when they were late season additions. That shows some promise, but with the exception of Green, it's still just promise.

Scott Young and Tomas Sandstrom won't be back, but it doesn't much matter because neither one was burning up the scoring charts.

Bob Wren was a big scorer in the minors for Cincinnati, so he may get a shot at making the team. Mike LeClerc may get an opportunity at a power forward spot.

Other than that, you fill in even more with the grinders such as Ted Drury, and hope youngsters such as Jeff Nielsen, Jeremy Stevenson, or Peter Reichert can make the grade.

One player who won't be getting another shot is Norwegian Espen Knutsen, who started out the season on the top line. He had more points in the exhibition season than the three he had during the regular season. He went down to Cincinnati in the AHL and showed little interest in making a go of it.

The Ducks are also signed 1994 second round draft pick Swede Johan Davidson, a centreman, who will probably start out in the minors.

As for enforcers, the Ducks don't have one because Brent Severyn and Shawn Antoski became unrestricted free agents. They're not hard to find, but they better get one with guys like Kariya and Selanne to protect.

There is some hope here, besides Kariya and Selanne, but the only real key to success is that Kariya and Selanne stay healthy.

Hockey Annual Rating: 5 of 27

SPECIAL TEAMS: The Anaheim special teams weren't very special at all last season. They couldn't score on the power play and they couldn't stop the other teams from scoring. Only Tampa Bay had worse special teams.

That's not a big problem because the answer to turning it around is simple, and the same problem with everything on the Ducks last year. If Kariya plays 82 games instead of 22 games, all will be well.

There are no pointmen for the power play, however, and for certain there's not a quarterback. That means forwards on the point until they rectify the situation.

Power Play	G	ATT	PCT
Overall	46	392	11.7% (24th NHL)
Home	18	190	9.5% (26th NHL)
Road	28	202	13.9% (17th NHL)
10 SHORT HANDED GOALS ALLOWED (T-13th NHL)			

Penalty Killing	G	TSH	PCT
Overall	72	396	81.8% (25th NHL)
Home	33	176	81.3% (24th NHL)
Road	39	220	82.3% (22nd NHL)
9 SHORT HANDED GOALS SCORED (17th NHL)			

Penalties	GP	MIN	AVG
MIGHTY DUCKS	82	1843	22.5 (24th NHL)

MIGHTY DUCKS SPECIAL TEAMS SCORING

Power play	G	A	PTS
GREEN	9	11	20
SELANNE	10	7	17
RUCCHIN	8	8	16
YOUNG	4	9	13
TODD	3	4	7
MARHA	3	4	7
CULLEN	2	4	6
KARIYA	3	2	5

SALEI	1	4	5
SANDSTROM	2	2	4
TRNKA	1	3	4
MARSHALL	1	3	4
BANHAM	1	1	2
KNUTSEN	1	0	1
KARPA	0	1	1
HOUDA	0	1	1
BANNISTER	0	1	1

Short handed	G	A	PTS
RUCCHIN	1	4	5
YOUNG	2	1	3
SELANNE	1	1	2
SANDSTROM	1	0	1
HOUDA	1	0	1
DRURY	1	0	1
KARPA	0	1	1

COACHING AND MANAGEMENT: A lot of people were ready to jump on Jack Ferreira and Pierre Page for last season's disaster. That would be like blaming the captain of the Titanic because there was an iceberg where it shouldn't have been.

Okay, so maybe he should have been ready for the iceberg, but you catch the drift.

Paul Kariya is arguably the best player in the NHL, and he only played 22 games. What that means is last season doesn't count.

You want to blame Ferreira for not having more depth to pick up the slack for Kariya? I don't think so. It was only their fifth season in the league. The fact that they had done so well previously was a testament to Ferreira's ability to find talent that others had overlooked, while waiting for the draft picks to develop.

You want to blame Ferreira for not signing Kariya earlier? If you're a Mighty Duck fan, you have to understand what it means when Kariya gets all the dough. Less money for other free agents, and higher ticket prices. You can't have it every way.

Ferreira has made some of the best trades in the game in recent years, most notably getting Selanne in the first place.

Very slowly, you can see the rest of the Ducks team starting to take shape. Younger players are getting the opportunity, and some of them will become bona fide NHL players.

The process can't be rushed too much. Ferreira will likely continue to find free agent talent at a reasonable price, and then one day we'll look up and he won't need it any more. There are talentless teams in the NHL who do very little and then ask what do the fans expect them to do? Not the Ducks.

Pierre Page's season didn't count, either, and Ferreira should have realized that more than anybody. Page was fired, anyway.

No coach had been hired as of press time, but speculation was centring around Craig Hartsburg, who was fired from Chicago last season.

Hockey Annual Rating: 24 of 27

DRAFT

Round	Sel.	Player	Pos	Team
1	5	Vitaly Vishnevsky	D	Russia
2	30	Stephen Peat	D	Red Deer (WHL)
4	112	Viktor Wallin	D	Sweden
6	150	Trent Hunter	RW	Prince George (WHL)
7	178	Jesse Fibiger	D	Minn-Duluth (WCHA)
8	205	David Bernier	RW	Quebec (QMJHL)

| 9 | 233 | Pelle Prestburg | LW | Sweden |
| 9 | 245 | Andreas Andersson | G | Sweden |

The Ducks took defencemen with their first three picks, because that's obviously where they need the most help. Vitaly Vishnevsky is described as a Darius Kasparaitis type defenceman, which in some books means dirty, but in other books means aggressive. Vishnevsky has the added element of being an offensive force for the power play, another component lacking on the Ducks.

PROGNOSIS: The Ducks will be a better team this year, and not only because they couldn't be any worse. In fact, if Selanne and Kariya are on the ice every game, they will probably make the playoffs.

The defense is young and inexperienced, but that can be fixed easily with a journeyman dime-a-dozen defenceman, which Anaheim has proven very adept at obtaining. The goaltending is capable, but will only be as good as the defence.

The forward lines are starting to fill in with quality as opposed to quantity and if the youngsters can do more than stand around and admire Kariya and Selanne, they could do better than expected.

PREDICTION
Western Conference: 11
Overall: 21

STAT SECTION
Team Scoring Stats

	GP	G	A	PTS	+/-	PIM	SH	CAREER Gm	G	A	Pts
TEEMU SELANNE	73	52	34	86	12	30	268	410	256	271	527
STEVE RUCCHIN	72	17	36	53	8	13	131	258	61	120	181
TRAVIS GREEN	76	19	23	42	29-	82	141	410	97	156	253
SCOTT YOUNG	73	13	20	33	13-	22	187	672	186	259	445
PAUL KARIYA	22	17	14	31	12	23	103	220	129	148	277
MATT CULLEN	61	6	21	27	4-	23	75	61	6	21	27
JOSEF MARHA	23	9	9	18	4	4	31	31	9	11	20
T. SANDSTROM	77	9	8	17	25-	64	136	925	379	445	824
TED DRURY	73	6	10	16	10-	82	110	272	33	44	77
RUSLAN SALEI	66	5	10	15	7	70	104	96	5	11	16
DAVE KARPA	78	1	11	12	3-	217	64	323	12	56	68
FRANK BANHAM	21	9	2	11	6-	12	43	24	9	2	11
KEVIN TODD	27	4	7	11	5-	12	30	383	70	133	203
JEFF NIELSEN	32	4	5	9	1-	16	36	34	4	5	9
JASON MARSHALL	72	3	6	9	8-	189	68	172	5	16	21
JAMIE PUSHOR	64	2	7	9	3	81	51	144	6	15	21

J. STEVENSON	45	3	5	8	4-	101	43	53	3	6	9
DREW BANNISTER	61	0	8	8	9-	89	50	139	4	23	27
PAVEL TRNKA	48	3	4	7	4-	40	46	48	3	4	7
DOUG HOUDA	55	2	4	6	11-	99	24	556	19	62	81
MIKE CROWLEY	8	2	2	4	0	8	17	8	2	2	4
J-F. JOMPHE	9	1	3	4	1	8	8	104	10	29	39
BRENT SEVERYN	37	1	3	4	3-	133	27	298	9	28	37
ESPEN KNUTSEN	19	3	0	3	10-	6	21	19	3	0	3
P. LEBOUTILLIER	12	1	1	2	1-	0	6	35	2	1	3
RICHARD PARK	15	0	2	2	3-	0	14	84	5	10	15
SHAWN ANTOSKI	9	1	0	1	1	0	6	183	3	5	8
DANIEL TREBIL	21	0	1	1	8-	0	11	50	3	4	7
M. SHTALENKOV	40	0	1	1	0	0	0	goalie			
GUY HEBERT	46	0	1	1	0	0	0	goalie			
BARRY NIECKAR	1	0	0	0	0	0	0	8	0	0	0
TONY TUZZOLINO	1	0	0	0	2-	0	0	1	0	0	0
MARC MORO	1	0	0	0	0	0	0	1	0	0	0
BOB WREN	3	0	0	0	0	0	4	3	0	0	0
ANTTI AALTO	3	0	0	0	1-	0	1	3	0	0	0
TOM ASKEY	7	0	0	0	0	0	0	goalie			
MIKE LECLERC	7	0	0	0	6-	0	11	12	1	1	2

* Team Rankings 1997-98 (previous year's ranking in parenthesis)

		Conference Rank	League Rank
Record	26-43-13	12 (4)	23 (9)
Home	12-23-6	13 (3)	24 (6)
Away	14-20-7	10 (9)	19 (17)
Versus Own Conference	16-32-8	13 (5)	25 (10)
Versus Other Conference	10-11-5	6 (6)	15 (12)
Team Plus\Minus	-30	13 (5)	23 (10)
Goals For	205	11 (6)	19 (10)
Goals Against	261	12 (5)	24 (11)
Average Shots For	26.6	11 (12)	18 (23)
Average Shots Against	30.3	13 (11)	25 (21)
Overtime	3-4-13	9 (20)	17 (3)
One Goal Games	11-9	7 (6)	11 (10)
Times outshooting opponent	26	11 (12)	22 (24)
Versus Teams Over .500	10-21-7	10 (6)	21 (11)
Versus Teams .500 or under	15-23-6	13 (9)	24 (20)
First Half Record	13-21-7	9 (9)	21 (20)
Second Half Record	13-22-6	13 (3)	24 (4)

PLAYOFFS
- did not make the playoffs

All-Time Leaders
Goals
Paul Kariya	129
Teemu Selanne	118
Joe Sacco	62

Assists
Paul Kariya	148
Steve Rucchin	119
Teemu Selanne	113

Points
Paul Kariya	277
Teemu Selanne	231
Steve Rucchin	181

Best Individual Seasons
Goals
Teemu Selanne	1997-98	52
Teemu Selanne	1996-97	51
Paul Kariya	1996-97	44

Assists
Teemu Selanne	1996-97	58
Paul Kariya	1995-96	58
Paul Kariya	1996-97	55

Points
Teemu Selanne	1996-97	109
Paul Kariya	1995-96	108
Paul Kariya	1996-97	99

TEAM
Last 3 years
	GP	W	L	T	Pts	%
1997-98	82	26	43	13	65	.396
1996-97	82	36	33	13	85	.518
1995-96	82	35	39	8	78	.476

Best 3 regular seasons
	GP	W	L	T	Pts	%
1996-97	82	36	33	13	85	.518
1995-96	82	35	39	8	78	.476
1993-94	84	33	46	5	71	.423

Worst 3 regular seasons
	GP	W	L	T	Pts	%
1994-95	48	16	27	5	37	.385
1997-98	82	26	43	13	65	.396
1993-94	84	33	46	5	71	.423

Most Goals (min. 70 game schedule)
1996-97	245
1995-96	234
1993-94	229

Fewest Goals (min. 70 game schedule)
1997-98	205
1993-94	229
1995-96	234

Most Goals Against (min. 70 game schedule)
1997-98	261
1995-96	247
1993-94	251

Fewest Goals Against (min. 70 game schedule)
1996-97	233
1993-94	251
1995-96	247

Calgary Flames

The Flames are coming off the worst season in their 26-year history. Worse than their expansion year, worse than any year. And for the first time they failed to make the playoffs for two consecutive seasons.

The Flames will be better this year, for a number of reasons, not including the fact that they couldn't have been much worse:

* One-Goal Games. The Flames were 8-17 in one-goal games. Only the Blackhawks lost more games by one goal. What it means is that they're not too far from turning it around. If you figure they had a chance to win or tie those 17 losses, something close to .500 in one-goal games would make a big difference.

* Slow Starters. The Flames were horrendous in the first period of games last season. They were outscored by 31 goals, second worst to Tampa Bay. The 83 goals Calgary allowed in the first period were the most in the league. In the second and third periods combined, they were just -5 in goal scoring. Now, part of the reason they scored better in the second and third periods was because they were usually behind and had to play more offensive. But the

fact remains that if they can get out of the first period leading or tied, they'll win a lot more often. They trailed 41 times after the first period, and led only 20 times. And get this, the Flames were the second lowest scoring team in the first period, and tied for the highest scoring team in the second. This is how their goals for and against broke down:

Period	1	2	3	OT
For	52	87	74	4
Against	83	79	87	3

* Slow Start to Season. The Flames burst out of the box with a mark of 1-8-2.

Their record the rest of the season was 25-33-13, still not good, but better. The Flames record after the Olympic break was 10-11-4, and from February 1 they were a .500 team.

* Underachieving Forwards. Most everyone except Theoren Fleury, Cory Stillman and maybe Marty McInnis could and should have done more scoring. That means this year they could and should do more scoring. A number of other forwards, including Jason Wiemer, have a chance at a breakout season.

* Youth is getting less Youthful. That's less youthful, not less useful. We're talking specifically about the defense. The bad news is that they made a lot of mistakes; the good news is that they should learn from them and make fewer of them.

* Injuries. Many of the key players missed significant time. You would expect that to be less of a factor this season.

* Special teams - The Flames were lousy on the power play and lousy at killing penalties. Often, this is an area that can be improved through coaching or with a minor adjustment, such as a power play quarterback. Besides that, power play and penalty killing percentages tend to fluctuate from year to year, anyway. One thing that could help is not taking so many penalties. They were -74 in power play opportunities, worst in the league, which is a big contributor in the fact that they were -26 in special team goals.

* Identifiable Weaknesses. One thing about losing so often is that it provides a lot more opportunity to see what's going wrong. The Flames know they need help on the power play, veteran help on defense, more scoring, and think they need help in net, as well as a front-line centre. They will try to shore up those weaknesses.

STUFF
* Theoren Fleury became the Flames all-time leading goal scorer last season, passing Joe Nieuwendyk.
* The Flames were winless in their first 11 road games last season, and were the last team to record a road win.
* Calgary was one of just two teams (NY Rangers) that did not earn a shutout last season. Every other team had at least three.

TEAM PREVIEW
GOAL: Goaltending has been a sore spot with the Flames for....well, forever. Mike Vernon has been the team's most successful goalie, and even he wasn't exactly revered as a hero.

Trevor Kidd was supposed to change all that, but he didn't, and mercifully was traded. He was more successful with Carolina, showing that he needed the change in scenery.

The Flames will now try to stop the puck through shear numbers. After obtaining Ken Wregget in an off-season trade, they had Rick Tabaracci, Dwayne Roloson, Tyler Moss, Tyrone Garner and J.S. Giguere.

Roloson and Tabaracci were left available in the franchise draft, while Wregget was protected. The others did not need protecting. Neither was chosen, however, and Roloson was not offered a contract, although Buffalo signed him to back up Dominik Hasek.

Tabaracci is the best of the bunch, whether

GOALTENDER	GPI	MINS	AVG	W	L	T	EN	SO	GA	SA	SV %
RICK TABARACCI	42	2,419	2.88	13	22	6	2	0	116	1,087	.893
DWAYNE ROLOSON	39	2,205	2.99	11	16	8	4	0	110	997	.890
TYLER MOSS	6	367	3.27	2	3	1	0	0	20	186	.892
CGY TOTALS	82	5,016	3.01	26	41	15	6	0	252	2,276	.889

his record reflects it or not, and whether the Flames think so or not. He started off last season with a 1-9-2 record. In seven of those 12 games, the Flames scored one or zero goals. Actually, his record did reflect that he was the best, earning the lowest goals against average and the highest save percentage. When a team is as porous defensively as the Flames were last season, blaming the goalies doesn't make a lot of sense.

Roloson proved to be spectacular at times and the opposite of spectacular at other times. Moss made a bit of a splash because he started off with two victories and a tie before losing his final three starts, all by the same 4-3 score.

Giguere is supposed to be the goalie of the future. He put up fine numbers in Saint John, but so did almost all their netminders. Seven goalies played for Saint John, and the five who played at least four games all had goals against averages under 2.50. The AHL team was outstanding and it had nothing at all to do with the goalies.

So, anyway, here is what's going to happen. Wregget will probably be the starting goalie, with Tabaracci or Moss as the backup. Incidentally, if Tabaracci is the backup, it won't be long before he's number one again. And, you can figure on Giguere and Garner getting a full season under their belts in the AHL.

Hockey Annual Rating: 22 of 27

DEFENCE: When a team gives up as many goals as the Flames did last year, you need three hands to do all the finger-pointing. One of those fingers can be directed at the defence.

Youth and inexperience is the main problem. Todd Simpson was named team captain in just his second full NHL season. Derek Morris was a rookie who played all 82 games. Cale Hulse played 79 games in his second full NHL season. Joel Bouchard was in and out of the lineup in his second season, while Jason Allison did the same in his first year in the bigs.

That left the defense experience to veterans Tommy Albelin and James Patrick, neither of whom played 70 games, and neither of whom resembles an impact defenceman. Zarley Zalapski was a veteran, but watched a lot of games from the press box until he was traded.

With all that inexperience and youth, you can expect another rookie in the lineup this year, Denis Gauthier, a crushing bodychecker who is still learning how to play all facets of the game.

The Flames would like to have a legitimate power play quarterback, but if given more opportunity Morris could fill that role. He was off and on the power play, but offensive defencemen usually take a few years to get comfortable with their game to the point of providing more points. Hulse was a surprise contributor offensively, but that's about it for offensive production.

A youthful defense has one thing in its favor: it's not getting any younger.

Hockey Annual Rating: 22 of 27

FORWARD: It's a lot better to start the season with a group of underachieving forwards than it is with overachievers because there's more potential for improvement. Only one forward exceeded expectations last season, and only one met expectations.

Cory Stillman was the one who performed better than was expected. He tied for the team lead with 27 goals, after getting just six the previous season. Theoren Fleury was the one who did what was expected, having a comeback year of sorts, and leading the team with 78 points.

German Titov was traded during the off-season to Pittsburgh after an inconsistent season. He scored just one goal in the Flames first 20 games and then scored in bunches the rest of the season. When a player is supposed to be the team's top goal scorer, you don't expect him to be munching on popcorn in the press box.

The rest of the forwards have room to move up as well:

Marty McInnis - his point total wasn't great, with 44, but it's just slightly below his average.

Andrew Cassels - the centre was supposed to be the playmaker the team needed, but wasn't. He had averaged 68 points a season in his previous four full seasons, so 44 points is a huge disappointment.

Valeri Bure - did his underachieving in Montreal before coming to Calgary in a trade.

Michael Nylander - his season was cut short because of injuries, but with respect to scoring, it made little difference.

Jarome Iginla - was way off in production from his rookie year.

Jason Wiemer - was the definition of underachieving when in Tampa Bay.

Chris Dingman - couldn't score, but was a physical presence on the ice.

Aaron Gavey - got off to a slow start, got injured, never came around.

Aside from Fleury, the whole forward situation revolves around all of the above performing better than they did last season, except Gavey who was traded to Dallas for Bob Bassen. Not all of them will, of course, but you have to

figure that some of them can. Still, that's not what you'd like to pin your hopes upon.

Hnat Domenichelli made an impression in 31 games, but made more of one in the minors. He may or may not be ready for prime time, although if he is, he could post a high amount of points. Daniel Tkachuk is the top prospect, but did not have a very good final junior season, and will probably spend some time in the minors.

There's no front-line centre and very few wingers that can be counted on. A bleak situation for the Flames.

Hockey Annual Rating: 23 of 27

SPECIAL TEAMS: The only thing the Flames were good at on special teams was scoring goals while shorthanded. They scored 18 when down a man, second best in the league. Heck, they only scored 43 on the power play.

With a lack of offensive defensemen, the Flames actually used two forwards on the points at times.

Power Play	G	ATT	PCT
Overall	43	356	12.1% (23rd NHL)
Home	22	180	12.2% (21st NHL)
Road	21	176	11.9% (22nd NHL)
13 SHORT HANDED GOALS ALLOWED (T-20th NHL)			

Penalty Killing	G	TSH	PCT
Overall	69	430	84.0% (20th NHL)
Home	28	201	86.1% (11th NHL)
Road	41	229	82.1% (T-23rd NHL)
18 SHORT HANDED GOALS SCORED (2nd NHL)			

Penalties	GP	MIN	AVG
FLAMES	82	1859	22.7 (25th NHL)

FLAMES SPECIAL TEAMS SCORING

Power play	G	A	PTS
FLEURY	3	19	22
STILLMAN	9	6	15
CASSELS	6	6	12
MORRIS	5	7	12
BURE	2	10	12
MCINNIS	5	5	10
TITOV	6	3	9
HULSE	1	6	7
NYLANDER	0	6	6
IGINLA	0	5	5
PATRICK	1	3	4
ALBELIN	1	3	4
WIEMER	3	0	3
DOMENICHELLI	1	0	1
DINGMAN	1	0	1
O'SULLIVAN	0	1	1
DOWD	0	1	1
BOUCHARD	0	1	1

Short handed	G	A	PTS
FLEURY	2	5	7
STILLMAN	4	1	5
MCINNIS	4	1	5
CASSELS	1	4	5
IGINLA	2	1	3
MORRIS	1	2	3
ALBELIN	0	3	3
TITOV	1	1	2
BOUCHARD	1	1	2
PATRICK	0	2	2
ALLISON	0	2	2
HULSE	1	0	1
DOWD	1	0	1
SIMPSON	0	1	1

COACHING AND MANAGEMENT: Brian

Sutter didn't perform any miracles in his first year back on the job. But, he didn't get fired, which is sort of a miracle in today's NHL.

That's probably because GM Al Coates was too busy making deals to improve the team rather than blaming its failure on the coach, as do so many general managers. When management is being patient in bringing the young players along, especially the defence, firing the coach shows that you're more desperate than patient.

Coates and Sutter seem intent on getting rid of freeloaders and whiners. Titov was traded in the off-season, and Nylander is probably not far behind. Zalapski, who wasn't happy in Calgary, was traded, and so was Sandy McCarthy. No point keeping guys who aren't interested in playing there.

Patience is a word that is quickly becoming obsolete in the NHL. Ticket prices are too high, salaries are too high, and everybody sees that some teams accomplish quick success after showing no patience whatsoever.

But, patience could just pay off for the Flames. *Hockey Annual* Rating: 23 of 27

DRAFT

Round	Sel.	Player	Pos	Team
1	6	Rico Fata	C	London (OHL)
2	33	Blair Betts	C	Prince George (WHL)
3	62	Paul Manning	D	Colorado Col. (WCHA)
4	102	Shaun Sutter	C	Lethbridge (WHL)
4	108	Dany Sabourin	G	Sherbrooke (QMJHL)
5	120	Brent Gauvreau	RW	Oshawa (OHL)

7	192	Radek Duda	RW	Czech
8	206	Jonas Frogren	D	Sweden
9	234	Kevin Mitchell	D	Guelph (OHL)

Rico Fata is supposed to be the fastest player in the draft. The knock on him is his hockey sense. Here's the thing with that. Sometimes fast players take longer for their head to catch up to the game. Happens in the NHL all the time. It makes sense that a fast player would have less time to decide on the correct play to make. Sometimes they overcome that problem, and sometimes they don't. Some NHL players have actually shown more hockey sense when they got older and slower.

The Sutter taken in the fourth round is indeed coach Brian Sutter's son. If they had want-ed to pick him for just that reason they would have saved him for the ninth round. A Sutter is a Sutter, even if they're the son of a Sutter.

PROGNOSIS

Okay, so we've already established that the Flames will be better this season. How much better? Well, they won't be winning the Stanley Cup, but if things come together and players score like they can, this is a playoff team. It won't be easy, however. If Cassels isn't their answer to a number one centre, then they need to get one. If they get a power play quarterback they'll be in better shape as well.

PREDICTION
Western Conference: 12
Overall: 24

STAT SECTION
Team Scoring Stats

	GP	G	A	PTS	+/-	PIM	SH	CAREER Gm	G	A	Pts
THEOREN FLEURY	82	27	51	78	0	197	282	731	334	427	761
CORY STILLMAN	72	27	22	49	9-	40	178	214	49	63	112
MARTY MCINNIS	75	19	25	44	1	34	128	422	101	230	331
ANDREW CASSELS	81	17	27	44	7-	32	138	579	122	299	421
GERMAN TITOV	68	18	22	40	1-	38	133	345	107	121	228
VALERI BURE	66	12	26	38	5-	35	179	231	51	68	119
M. NYLANDER	65	13	23	36	10	24	117	276	54	126	180
JAROME IGINLA	70	13	19	32	10-	29	154	152	34	48	82
DEREK MORRIS	82	9	20	29	1	88	120	82	9	20	29
CALE HULSE	79	5	22	27	1	169	117	163	6	28	34
JASON WIEMER	79	12	10	22	10-	160	122	244	31	28	59
TOMMY ALBELIN	69	2	17	19	9	32	88	614	35	163	198
JAMES PATRICK	60	6	11	17	2-	26	57	935	126	439	565
H. DOMENICHELLI	31	9	7	16	4	6	70	54	12	10	22
JIM DOWD	48	6	8	14	10	12	58	144	17	37	54
JOEL BOUCHARD	44	5	7	12	0	57	51	126	9	12	21

JAMIE ALLISON	43	3	8	11	3	104	27	64	3	8	11
ED WARD	64	4	5	9	1-	122	52	154	14	19	33
CHRIS DINGMAN	70	3	3	6	11-	149	47	70	3	3	6
TODD SIMPSON	53	1	5	6	10-	109	51	147	2	18	20
AARON GAVEY	26	2	3	5	5-	24	27	156	18	18	36
D. ROLOSON	39	0	4	4	0	10	0	goalie			
ERIK ANDERSSON	12	2	1	3	4-	8	11	12	2	1	3
CHRIS O'SULLIVAN	12	0	2	2	4	10	12	39	2	10	12
ERIC LANDRY	12	1	0	1	2-	4	7	12	1	0	1
LADISLAV KOHN	4	0	1	1	2	0	2	9	1	1	2
TODD HLUSHKO	13	0	1	1	0	27	7	79	8	13	21
KEVIN DAHL	19	0	1	1	3-	6	17	181	7	22	29
RICK TABARACCI	42	0	1	1	0	14	0	goalie			
S. VARLAMOV	1	0	0	0	0	0	0	1	0	0	0
ERIC CHARRON	2	0	0	0	0	4	1	97	2	6	8
MARTY MURRAY	2	0	0	0	1	2	2	19	3	3	6
TRAVIS BRIGLEY	2	0	0	0	0	2	1	2	0	0	0
STEVE BEGIN	5	0	0	0	0	23	2	5	0	0	0
TYLER MOSS	6	0	0	0	0	0	0	goalie			
DENIS GAUTHIER	10	0	0	0	5-	16	3	10	0	0	0
R. THOMPSON	12	0	0	0	0	61	3	12	0	0	0
MIKE PELUSO	23	0	0	0	6-	113	8	458	38	52	90

* Team Rankings 1997-98 (previous year's ranking in parenthesis)

		Conference Rank	League Rank
Record	26-41-15	11 (10)	22 (21)
Home	18-17-6	8 (6)	15 (13)
Away	8-24-9	13 (12)	25 (22)
Versus Own Conference	16-30-10	12 (9)	22 (19)
Versus Other Conference	10-11-5	6 (7)	15 (15)
Team Plus\Minus	-9	9 (11)	17 (22)
Goals For	217	8 (11)	14 (23)
Goals Against	252	11 (6)	21 (13)
Average Shots For	27.7	6 (3)	11 (6)
Average Shots Against	27.8	7 (4)	14 (8)
Overtime	4-3-15	5 (10)	11 (20)
One Goal Games	8-17	12 (9)	24 (17)
Times outshooting opponent	45	5 (3)	9 (6)
Versus Teams Over .500	11-23-4	11 (5)	22 (11)
Versus Teams .500 or under	15-18-11	11 (12)	22 (22)
First Half Record	11-22-8	12 (12)	24 (24)
Second Half Record	15-19-7	9 (9)	18 (14)

PLAYOFFS
- did not make the playoffs

All-Time Leaders
Goals
Theoren Fleury	334
Joe Nieuwendyk	314
Gary Roberts	257

Assists
Al MacInnis	609
Gary Suter	437
Theoren Fleury	427

Points
Al MacInnis	822
Theoren Fleury	761
Joe Nieuwendyk	616

Best Individual Seasons
Goals
Lanny McDonald	1982-83	66
Gary Roberts	1991-92	53
Joe Nieuwendyk	1987-88	51
Joe Mullen	1988-89	51
Joe Nieuwendyk	1988-89	51
Theoren Fleury	1990-91	51

Assists
Kent Nilsson	1980-81	82
Al MacInnis	1990-91	75
Bob MacMillen	1978-79	71

Points
Kent Nilsson	1980-81	131
Joe Mullen	1988-89	110
Joe Mullen	1978-79	108

TEAM

Last 3 years

	GP	W	L	T	Pts	%
1997-98	82	26	41	15	67	.409
1996-97	82	32	41	9	73	.445
1995-96	82	34	37	11	79	.482

Best 3 regular seasons

	GP	W	L	T	Pts	%
1988-89	80	54	17	9	117	.731
1987-88	80	48	23	9	105	.656
1990-91	80	46	26	8	100	.625

Worst 3 regular seasons

	GP	W	L	T	Pts	%
1997-98	82	26	41	15	67	.409
1972-73	78	25	38	15	65	.416
1996-97	82	32	41	9	73	.445

Most Goals (min. 70 game schedule)

1987-88	397
1984-85	363
1988-89	354
1985-86	354

Fewest Goals (min. 70 game schedule)

1972-73	191
1996-97	214
1973-74	214

Most Goals Against (min. 70 game schedule)

1981-82	345
1982-83	317
1985-86	315

Fewest Goals Against (min. 70 game schedule)

1988-89	226
1974-75	233
1975-76	237

Chicago Blackhawks

The problem with the Chicago Blackhawks last season is extremely simple: they couldn't put the puck in the net.

They had a decent chance to make the playoffs near the end, but down the stretch they couldn't score. In their last 12 games, they didn't get more than two goals in any game. They went 2-9-1 in those games. In their last 10 home games, they scored zero goals once, popped in one goal in five games, and poured it on with two big goals in the other four.

That's why they didn't make the playoffs.

Here's another reason, which sort of ties in to not scoring goals: they had a lousy start and a lousy finish:

First seven games: 0-7-0 (6 goals scored)
Last seven games: 0-6-1 (10 goals scored)
Middle 68 games: 30-26-12

The Blackhawks had made the playoffs for 28 straight seasons before last year, which was the longest consecutive streak at the time. That honor now belongs to St. Louis, which has not missed the playoffs in the last 19 years.

The longest consecutive playoff streaks in NHL history are as follows:

Boston	29	1968-1996
CHICAGO	28	1970-1997
Montreal	24	1971-1994

An odd Chicago stat is that they lost 21 games by one goal, more than half of their losses. They've lost the most games by one goal for two years in a row. Last year, I suggested that a team that lost a lot of games by one goal was closer to turning it around than other teams. Now, I think that it could just be that they were good at holding the opposition away from the scoresheet, but they were worse at getting on it themselves. That means low-scoring games, which follows that more of them will be decided by one goal.

The score in seven of their one-goal losses was 2-1, and in two others it was 1-0. Goal scoring will be a major priority this season for the Hawks, and in the process they could turn around a lot of those 2-1 and 1-0 losses.

STUFF
* Chris Chelios played in his 1,000th game
* a 0-0 tie with Edmonton in December was the first for Chicago since 1979.
* the Hawks had five 1-0 games, winning three and losing two.

* Denis Savard's number 18 was retired last season.

* Chris Chelios had the second largest amount of ice-time last season in the league, with only Ray Bourque logging more minutes.

TEAM PREVIEW

GOAL: Goalies aren't counted on to score goals, so the Hawks don't have a problem in net. Jeff Hackett is going to get the majority of playing time, but Chris Terreri is as good a backup as there is the NHL. He could actually be playing more without hurting the team.

The Hawks are concerned about bringing along another goalie to replace Hackett eventually. Jeff Daubenspeck spent some time on the end of the Blackhawks bench, but it was Mark Lamothe who shone in Indianapolis with a 2.44 goals against average. Andrei Trefilov is still around, too.

Hockey Annual Rating: 8 of 27

DEFENCE: This position isn't as strong as it has been in recent years.

Chris Chelios is starting to show his age (36) which doesn't mean he still isn't one of the best defensemen in the game, but rather that he doesn't dominate all the time. There's still not a team in the league that wouldn't take him.

Gary Suter is gone to free agency, a player who is consistently on and off depending on the season. Last year, he was on, so he'll be missed. He was signed by San Jose. Suter's biggest claim to fame last year was knocking Paul Kariya out of the Olympics and the play-off race. He received a three-game suspension, which depending on who you're talking to, was too little or too much.

Eric Weinrich could probably pick up the slack offensively, although he's not a kid, either, turning 33-years-old this year.

Cam Russell, Michal Sykora and Trent Yawney were bit players last season, and won't be counted on to be among the top four. Jason More has gone to Nashville.

Rookie Christian Laflamme had a very solid rookie year and eventually was not playing like a rookie at all. He rounds out the top four.

The top prospect is Remi Royer, who has toughness and offensive ability, two things the Hawks could use. He had 68 points in 66 games for Rouyn-Noranda in the Quebec Junior League and 205 penalty minutes.

GM Bob Murray, however, says he doesn't want to rush prospects along, so Royer could get some time in the minors.

Murray also says he wants to get some more muscle on defense, so any trades or acquisitions would likely be along those lines.

The Chicago defense isn't as good as it was last year, and if you take into account that the Hawks are likely going to play a more offensive game this

GOALTENDER	GPI	MINS	AVG	W	L	T	EN	SO	GA	SA	SV %
JEFF HACKETT	58	3441	2.20	21	25	11	3	8	126	1520	.917
CHRIS TERRERI	21	1222	2.41	8	10	2	4	2	49	519	.906
ANDREI TREFILOV	6	299	3.41	1	4	0	0	0	17	145	.883
CHI TOTALS	82	4999	2.39	30	39	13	7	10	199	2191	.909

season, then the boys on the blueline are likely to be busier than they might have hoped.

Hockey Annual Rating: 17 of 27

FORWARD: Tony Amonte can score goals, Eric Daze can score goals, and if he's in the right mood, Alexei Zhamnov can score goals.

That's it. At least as far as proven goal scoring.

And of the above three, Daze doesn't get assists, and Zhamnov gets his points in bunches after prolonged slumps. That leaves Amonte...and a sorry state of affairs.

The Hawks had eight players with at least 10 goals last season. Of those, James Black (10) was released and Gary Suter (14) became an unrestricted free agent. Another, Greg Johnson (12) was left unprotected in the waiver draft.

It was thought that the Blackhawks might sign Brett Hull, who was an unrestricted free agent in the summer. Instead, he went to Dallas, and the Blackhawks picked up Doug Gilmour.

Gilmour is an outstanding playmaker, although he's 35 years old and his best years are behind him. Something about him, however, is that he rises to the occasion when he joins a new team. He may get stuck in neutral after a year or two, but his best season is always his first with a new club.

So where are the goals going to come from? Logically, from a trade or a free agent signing. Otherwise, they'll have to come from the following.

Chad Kilger - scored three goals last year in 32 games. He has potential to be a decent scoring centre, but will have to do it from the third line.

Ethan Moreau - He had 15 goals in his rookie

season, and his nine goals in 54 games projects to 14 over 82 games. But, this is his third year, so he could be ready to break out. That could mean 20 goals from him.

J-P Dumont - Acquired in a trade from the Islanders for Dmitri Nabokov, he's a highly touted junior who could step right into the lineup on right wing. He scored 57 goals in the Quebec League last season, and was selected third overall in the 1996 draft. Either Mike Milbury and the Islanders didn't think he was all that, or they didn't want to pay his salary. Let's say if he has a good season, he'll score 15 goals.

Jeff Shantz - Scored 11 goals in 61 games, which projects to 15 goals. That would be good enough.

Along with Amonte, Zhamnov and Daze, the above players had better produce offensively, or Chicago is again in big trouble. Too many ifs.

Down the middle, the Hawks have Gilmour, Zhamnov, Kilger, Steve Dubinsky, and Jeff Shantz. Zhamnov and his 49 points just don't cut it. He's like a daily disappointment. That's not to say he won't live up to expectations, anything is possible. The others are third and fourth line centres, although not bad for third and fourth line centres.

The Hawks signed free agent Mark Janssens, also a centre, and still have Dan Cleary who will try to make another go of it this year.

There's plenty of toughness on the wings, with Bob Probert, Ryan Vandenbussche and Reid Simpson.

Among those not already mentioned is sophomore Jean-Yves Leroux, who should see regular duty, and Kevin Miller, who isn't likely to see much playing time anymore.

The top prospect is Ty Jones, a tough guy

who can also score. He was 35-47-82 with Spokane in the WHL last season.

Hockey Annual Rating: 16 of 27

SPECIAL TEAMS: The power play shouldn't be this bad. They've got snipers in Amonte and Daze, and now a better playmaker in Gilmour. Chelios is still great on the point. It wouldn't be a surprise, with a new coach and new systems, if the power play picks up a lot. That alone would make a big difference in the amount of games this team wins.

Power Play	G	ATT	PCT
Overall	47	364	12.9% (T-19th NHL)
Home	20	189	10.6% (T-23rd NHL)
Road	27	175	15.4% (T-11th NHL)

5 SHORT HANDED GOALS ALLOWED (T-4th NHL)

Penalty Killing	G	TSH	PCT
Overall	58	381	84.8% (14th NHL)
Home	30	184	83.7% (17th NHL)
Road	28	197	85.8% (10th NHL)

13 SHORT HANDED GOALS SCORED (T-5th NHL)

BLACKHAWKS SPECIAL TEAMS SCORING

Power play	G	A	PTS
SUTER	5	18	23
CHELIOS	1	22	23
AMONTE	7	12	19
ZHAMNOV	6	8	14
DAZE	10	2	12
JOHNSON	4	3	7
WEINRICH	0	7	7
NABOKOV	3	2	5
SHANTZ	1	4	5
KILGER	2	2	4
BLACK	2	2	4
PROBERT	2	0	2
MOREAU	2	0	2
SYKORA	0	2	2
SIMPSON	1	0	1
KRIVOKRASOV	1	0	1
SUTTER	0	1	1
SKALDE	0	1	1
MORE	0	1	1
LAFLAMME	0	1	1

Short handed	G	A	PTS
AMONTE	3	3	6
SHANTZ	2	2	4
DUBINSKY	1	3	4
ZHAMNOV	2	1	3
SUTER	2	0	2
SUTTER	1	1	2
BLACK	1	1	2
MORE	1	0	1
WEINRICH	0	1	1
LAFLAMME	0	1	1

COACHING AND MANAGEMENT: It wasn't the kind of year Bob Murray would have liked for his first as Chicago GM, missing the playoffs for the first time in 28 years. But at least he made somebody else pay for it when he fired coach Craig Hartsburg. That's just sound management — pin the tail on a different donkey.

Murray didn't do much to help Hartsburg, but he's been a little more active since the end of the season, signing Doug Gilmour and Paul Coffey, and trading for junior scoring start J-P Dumont. In other words, he's addressing the Blackhawks biggest problem, which is scoring goals.

Dirk Graham is the new coach, a job it appeared he earned by default, when the other candidates were dropped one by one, perhaps by the salary they commanded. Still, we're made to believe Graham was the number one choice all along. Graham was a scout for the Blackhawks last season, and has no head coaching experience. None.

Who knows, maybe that's better because he's starting from scratch and don't have any pre-conceived notions about coaching that may be wrong. That's called rationalization.

Probably another good move by Murray because if the team doesn't win he can just pin the tail on another donkey, one who's too new to know it's the general manager's fault.

Murray failed to get Brett Hull, despite the fact that he signed for less than Chicago paid Gilmour. People are going to hold that against him, whether it's his fault of not.

Hockey Annual Rating: 27 of 27

DRAFT

Round	Sel.	Player	Pos	Team
1	8	Mark Bell	C	Ottawa (OHL)
4	94	Matthais Trattnig	C	Maine (HE)
6	156	Kent Huskins	D	Clarkson (ECAC)
6	158	Jari Viuhkola	C	Finland
6	166	Jonathan Pelletier	G	Drummondville (QMJHL)
7	183	Tyler Amason	C	Fargo-Moorehead (USHL)
8	210	Sean Griffin	D	Kingston (OHL)
9	238	Alexandre Couture	LW	Sherbrooke (QMJHL)
9	240	Andrei Yershov	D	Russia

The Blackhawks traded up in order to get Mark Bell, a player who became a wanted man when it got down to the eighth spot in the draft. A number of teams were apparently interested in trying to get the draft pick. Bell is a big centre whose scoring totals in junior are probably going to increase dramatically from the 34-26-60 he earned for Ottawa in the OHL last year.

PROGNOSIS: It doesn't look particularly good for the Blackhawks. Maybe they can make the playoffs, but they're an iffy group. If so and so does this then we'll win.

A lot of their key players are oldtimers, such as Gilmour, Coffey and Chelios, and they have and will lose more of their effectiveness.

It's not out of the question that the Hawks could make the playoffs, but with an inexperienced coach, resentment over the fact that the team didn't sign Hull, and all the question marks surrounding scoring and depth, it's just too much to hope for.

PREDICTION
Western Conference: 9
Overall: 15

STAT SECTION
Team Scoring Stats

	GP	G	A	PTS	+/-	PIM	SH	Gm	G	A	Pts
TONY AMONTE	82	31	42	73	21	66	296	533	203	232	435
ALEXEI ZHAMNOV	70	21	28	49	16	61	193	379	144	234	378
ERIC DAZE	80	31	11	42	4	22	216	235	84	54	138
GARY SUTER	73	14	28	42	1	74	199	918	181	565	744
CHRIS CHELIOS	81	3	39	42	7-	151	205	1,001	158	606	765
GREG JOHNSON	74	12	22	34	2-	40	89	283	52	79	131
JEFF SHANTZ	61	11	20	31	0	36	69	305	35	80	115
S. KRIVOKRASOV	58	10	13	23	1-	33	127	225	42	41	83
ERIC WEINRICH	82	2	21	23	10	106	85	602	41	185	226
ETHAN MOREAU	54	9	9	18	0	73	87	144	24	26	50
STEVE DUBINSKY	82	5	13	18	6-	57	112	173	9	22	31
JAMES BLACK	52	10	5	15	8-	8	90	186	33	28	61
J-Y. LEROUX	66	6	7	13	2-	55	57	67	7	7	14
JAY MORE	58	5	7	12	7	61	57	388	18	52	70
CHAD KILGER	32	3	9	12	0	10	32	130	14	22	36
DMITRI NABOKOV	25	7	4	11	1-	10	34	25	7	4	11
JARROD SKALDE	30	4	7	11	2-	18	34	78	11	22	33
KEVIN MILLER	37	4	7	11	4-	8	37	574	146	176	322
C. LAFLAMME	72	0	11	11	14	59	75	76	0	12	12
BRENT SUTTER	52	2	6	8	6-	28	43	1,111	363	466	809
REID SIMPSON	44	3	2	5	3-	118	24	105	4	11	15
BRIAN FELSNER	12	1	3	4	0	12	14	12	1	3	4
MICHAL SYKORA	28	1	3	4	10-	12	35	208	9	41	50
BOB PROBERT	14	2	1	3	7-	48	18	648	144	181	325
CRAIG MILLS	20	0	3	3	1	34	5	24	0	5	5
R. VANDENBUSSCHE	20	1	1	2	2-	43	2	31	2	1	3
CAM RUSSELL	41	1	1	2	3	79	18	354	8	19	27
TODD WHITE	7	1	0	1	0	2	3	7	1	0	1
TRENT YAWNEY	45	1	0	1	5-	76	19	573	27	102	129
CHRIS TERRERI	21	0	1	1	0	2	0	goalie			
RYAN HUSKA	1	0	0	0	0	0	0	1	0	0	0
PERI VARIS	1	0	0	0	0	0	0	1	0	0	0
M. GENDRON	2	0	0	0	1-	0	3	30	4	2	6
A. TREFILOV	6	0	0	0	0	0	0	goalie			
DANIEL CLEARY	6	0	0	0	2-	0	4	6	0	0	0
JEFF HACKETT	58	0	0	0	0	8	0	goalie			

* Team Rankings 1997-98 (previous year's ranking in parenthesis)

		Conference Rank	League Rank
Record	30-39-13	9 (8)	18 (14)
Home	14-19-8	11 (12)	22 (21)
Away	16-20-5	8 (5)	16 (7)
Versus Own Conference	16-29-11	10 (8)	21 (17)
Versus Other Conference	14-10-2	3 (5)	4 (11)
Team Plus\Minus	+4	7 (4)	13 (8)
Goals For	192	13 (10)	25 (20)
Goals Against	199	3 (4)	8 (7)
Average Shots For	27.8	4 (5)	7 (9)
Average Shots Against	26.7	5 (6)	10 (12)
Overtime	1-4-13	11 (11)	23 (23)
One Goal Games	12-21	11 (12)	22 (23)
Times outshooting opponent	43	6 (6)	10 (11)
Versus Teams Over .500	15-20-5	6 (3)	13 (9)
Versus Teams .500 or under	15-19-8	12 (8)	23 (15)
First Half Record	15-18-8	7 (8)	14 (19)
Second Half Record	15-21-5	12 (5)	22 (8)

PLAYOFFS

- did not make playoffs

All-Time Leaders
Goals

Bobby Hull	604
Stan Mikita	541
Steve Larmer	406

Assists

Stan Mikita	926
Denis Savard	719
Doug Wilson	554

Points

Stan Mikita	1,467
Bobby Hull	1,153
Denis Savard	1,096

Best Individual Seasons
Goals

Bobby Hull	1968-69	58
Al Secord	1982-83	54
Bobby Hull	1965-66	54

Assists

Denis Savard	1987-88	87
Denis Savard	1981-82	87
Denis Savard	1982-83	86

Points

Denis Savard	1987-88	131
Denis Savard	1982-83	121
Denis Savard	1981-82	119

TEAM

Last 3 years

	GP	W	L	T	Pts	%
1997-98	82	30	39	13	73	.445
1996-97	82	34	35	13	81	.494
1995-96	82	40	28	14	94	.573
1994-95	48	24	19	5	53	.552

Best 3 regular seasons

	GP	W	L	T	Pts	%
1970-71	78	49	20	6	107	.686
1971-72	78	46	17	5	107	.686
1973-74	78	41	14	23	105	.673

Worst 3 regular seasons

	GP	W	L	T	Pts	%
1927-28	44	7	34	3	17	.193
1953-54	70	12	51	7	31	.221
1928-29	44	7	29	8	22	.250

Most Goals (min. 70 game schedule)

1985-86	351
1982-83	338
1981-82	332

Fewest Goals (min. 70 game schedule)

1953-54	133
1955-56	155
1951-52	158

Most Goals Against (min. 70 game schedule)

1981-82	363
1985-86	349
1988-89	335

Fewest Goals Against (min. 70 game schedule)

1973-74	164
1971-72	166
1963-64	169

Colorado Avalanche

What, me worry?

Worry: The Avalanche were knocked out in the first round of the playoffs by Edmonton.
Don't Worry: It may be good for the talent-laden team. It could shake them up a bit. They've already proven they can win in the playoffs and this will help them remember how to do it.

Worry: They had a 3-1 lead over Edmonton in that series.
Don't Worry: They would have lost to Detroit eventually, anyway.

Worry: Team getting older.
Don't Worry: Most of the core players are still in their prime years, and the ones who aren't aren't as affected by age. Goalies have a longer shelf life, as do defensive defencemen.
Don't Worry: The Avs had four first-round picks this year.

Worry: Coach Marc Crawford is gone.
Don't Worry: The team is talented enough to win for any coach.

Worry: New coach Bob Hartley has no NHL experience.
Don't worry: Neither did Crawford before Colorado got him, and Hartley has some strong admirers among those who have played for him in the minors.

Worry: Crawford knew which buttons to press to make this team winners, most of the time.

Worry: Hartley is supposed to be tough with the players, which can upset some veterans and make them resentful because the coach is new to the scene.

Worry: Colorado was lousy down the stretch, with a 2-6-1 record in their last nine games.
Don't Worry: A lot of good teams play poorly at the end of the regular season, especially when they have nothing to play for and are gearing up for the playoffs.

Worry: Colorado was just a .500 team in the second half of the season, with a record of 18-18-5, after being 21-8-12 in the first half.

Worry: Dissension in the dressing room.

Don't Worry: There's always some dissension in the dressing room, it just gets overblown in certain quarters and circumstances.

Don't Worry: Usually, dressing room dissension doesn't have any effect on whether a team wins or not.

Worry: Anonymous press reports about players (Claude Lemieux) can mean division rather than dissension, and that's more serious.

Worry: Team chemistry

Don't Worry: Chemistry can be fixed by changing a few ingredients.

Worry: GM Pierre Lacroix might not have a handle on it, considering the Mike Ricci trade, who by all accounts was a chemist on ice. That, and a few other changes that upset the mix.

Worry: This team needs leaders on the ice and off it. Every time they seem to have a good one (i.e. Chris Simon, Mike Keane) they lose him somehow.

Worry: Many of the players, and ex-coach Crawford, apparently didn't like Claude Lemieux much.

Don't Worry: Nobody's ever like him much wherever he's played, until the playoffs when he becomes one of the best post-season performers, maybe in the history of the game.

Worry: Sometimes the team has to defend Lemieux, on the ice, when they probably wished they didn't have to. That can be a negative factor for team unity as opposed to the positive one it could be sometimes.

Worry: There's seems to be a lot to worry about with the Avs, and we haven't even touched much on the team's actual play.

Don't Worry: No matter what happens off the ice, Colorado is still one of the most talented teams on it.

STUFF
* were outshot 50-19 by Edmonton in a regular season game and won 6-2.
* were outshot 53-19 by Toronto and tied 2-2.
* The Avs scored the fewest goals in franchise history and tied for the fewest allowed.
* Joe Sakic scored a goal in seven consecutive games, two short of the team record of nine, held by Michel Goulet in the 1983-84 season.

TEAM PREVIEW
GOAL: Patrick Roy had a Patrick Roy type season, but he didn't have a Patrick Roy type playoffs. He'll get over it and so will the Avs.

The only concern Colorado has at the moment is grooming his future replacement. His name is Marc Denis, but he's not quite ready. *The Hockey News* had him pegged in 1997 as the top prospect in the NHL, but a

GOALTENDER	GPI	MINS	AVG	W	L	T	EN	SO	GA	SA	SV %
CRAIG BILLINGTON	23	1162	2.32	8	7	4	2	1	45	588	.923
PATRICK ROY	65	3835	2.39	31	19	13	5	4	153	1825	.916
COL TOTALS	82	5017	2.45	39	26	17	7	5	205	2420	.915

mediocre rookie season in the AHL dropped him to number seven.

Craig Billington was re-signed over the summer to continue on as a backup.
Hockey Annual Rating: 6 of 27

DEFENCE: Adam Foote, Sandis Ozolinsh, and Sylvain Lefebvre are three defencemen better than most teams have. The Avs will miss Krupp, but they have some young players they want to get playing more on a regular basis, such as Eric Messier and tough guy Wade Belak.

Toughness is one of the few things that has been in short supply on the Colorado defence. Maybe not toughness as much as roughness.

Alexei Gusarov, Jon Klemm, Francoixe Leroux and Aaron Miller fill out the roster. It's worth noting that Miller was impressive late in the season and played every playoff game, and Klemm didn't. Klemm sometimes plays forward as well.

Miller became Ozolinsh's partner, which is not an easy job because often it means you're the only defenceman actually playing defence. Ozolinsh would move to the net if the team was down two men if he thought he could get a chance to score.

Ozolinsh is the only point-threat among the defencemen, with Krupp gone, but on the power play the Avs often use a forward for the point, anyway. And with the team having more than enough offence elsewhere, they don't need it from their defencemen, which gives them a chance to concentrate on defence, which is better for the team as a whole.
Hockey Annual Rating: 6 of 27

FORWARD: Two scoring lines that rank as the best in the league, plus an award winning supporting cast.

At left wing are Valeri Kamensky and Keith Jones, coming back after missing most of last season with an injury.

At centre are Peter Forsberg and Joe Sakic. Enough said.

At right wing are Claude Lemieux and Adam Deadmarsh, both tough, both snipers, both good on the power play.

That's the scoring lines, and then you have your third and fourth liners which include Eric Lacroix, Rene Corbet and Stephane Yelle, all of whom can add offence. The enforcers are Jeff Odgers and Warren Rychel, although the trading of Chris Simon a couple years ago, never seems to go away as a major loss.

Jari Kurri has retired, Tom Fitzgerald was lost to free agency, and Shean Donovan didn't play well or at all in the playoffs.

That means the Avs will need to add some checkers or fourth liners. Since they have just about everything else, they better make sure they make these character guys whose contribution is more than the sum of their ice-time.
Hockey Annual Rating: 2 of 27

SPECIAL TEAMS: If you could pick anybody in the NHL to be on your power play, chances are Peter Forsberg, Joe Sakic, Claude Lemieux, Sandis Ozolinsh, and Valeri Kamensky would all be in the running.

They're so good they ought to be ranked number one. Maybe this year.

Penalty killing ranked third, thanks to some outstanding defensive defencemen, who know how to do their job.

Power Play	G	ATT	PCT
Overall	74	425	17.4% (7th NHL)
Home	36	218	16.5% (10th NHL)
Road	38	207	18.4% (5th NHL)

12 SHORT HANDED GOALS ALLOWED (T-16th NHL)

Penalty Killing	G	TSH	PCT
Overall	53	410	87.1% (3rd NHL)
Home	27	201	86.6% (T-9th NHL)
Road	26	209	87.6% (4th NHL)

8 SHORT HANDED GOALS SCORED (T-18th NHL)

AVALANCHE SPECIAL TEAMS SCORING

Power play	G	A	PTS
FORSBERG	7	30	37
OZOLINSH	9	26	35
SAKIC	12	16	28
KAMENSKY	8	19	27
LEMIEUX	11	7	18
DEADMARSH	10	6	16
KRUPP	5	8	13
CORBET	4	5	9
LACROIX	5	3	8
KURRI	2	5	7
MESSIER	0	6	6
JONES	1	3	4
RYCHEL	1	1	2
LEFEBVRE	0	2	2
GUSAROV	0	1	1
FOOTE	0	1	1

Short handed	G	A	PTS
FORSBERG	3	0	3
FITZGERALD	2	0	2
GUSAROV	1	1	2
DEADMARSH	0	2	2
YELLE	1	0	1
SAKIC	1	0	1
LEMIEUX	1	0	1
LEFEBVRE	0	1	1
KURRI	0	1	1
KRUPP	0	1	1
FOOTE	0	1	1

COACHING AND MANAGEMENT: Pierre Lacroix is getting his detractors after receiving so much credit for turning the team into winners. Questionable trades, questionable personnel decisions, and his seemingly stubborn refusal to make team cohesiveness and character a major priority.

He gets knocked for being slow to correct weaknesses, but if people can get over the Chris Simon trade they would see how hard he's tried to correct the enforcer problem. Last year, he had both Warren Rychel and Jeff Odgers, one more than most teams can afford to have on the ice.

The fact of the matter is that Lacroix seems to learn from mistakes and plans his strategy well in advance. For example, four first round draft picks this year were meant to give the team a shot a Vincent Lecavalier as the number one pick. It could have worked, in which case he would have been revered as a genius for all the manipulations it required. It didn't, but that's a matter of circumstance and bad luck more than anything else.

Bob Hartley is the new coach. He's paid his dues in the minors and is said to be tough but fair. This team needs tough but fair, but they're also likely to resent the tough part from a rookie coach.

Hockey Annual Rating: 16 of 27

DRAFT

Round	Sel.	Player	Pos	Team
1	12	Alex Tanguay	C	Halifax (QMJHL)
1	17	Martin Skoula	D	Barrie (OHL)
1	19	Robyn Regehr	D	Kamloops (WHL)
1	20	Scott Parker	D	Kelowna (WHL)
2	28	Ramzi Abid	LW	Chicoutimi (QMJHL)
2	38	Philippe Sauve	G	Rimouski (QMJHL)
2	53	Steve Moore	C	Harvard (ECAC)
3	79	Evgeny Lazarev	LW	Kitchener (OHL)
5	141	Kristinn Timons	LW	Tri-City (WHL)
6	167	A. Ryazantsev	D	Russia

Four first rounders and a second rounder projected to go in the first round. As great as that is, the Avalanche would have given them all up for Vincent Lecavalier.

Alex Tanguay was 47-38-85 for Halifax Mooseheads in the QMJHL. His speed is said to be lacking, but not much else.

Martin Skoula was rated a lot higher than he was chosen, but he's also been called a blue-chipper. He was 8-36-44 for Barrie in the OHL, but only had 36 PIM.

Robyn Regehr is a defensive defenceman.

Scott Parker re-entered the draft when New Jersey didn't sign him. He is older than the other prospects, and more likely to be able to step into the Colorado lineup quicker. He was 41-81-122 for Kelowna in the WHL.

Ramzi Abid was the first choice in the second round, so he's almost a first-rounder. That's where he was projected to go. He was rated 12th by *The Hockey News* and 11th by Central Scouting among North Americans. The knock against him is his skating, but he led the QMJHL in scoring with 50-85-135, and had 266 penalty minutes. Enforcers don't exist with that kind of scoring, so it was a surprise that he didn't go earlier in the draft.

PROGNOSIS: The Avalanche are arguably the most talented team in the league. That's almost all the battle. The rest of it requires them to play like it. They have to add the "bit" players that are going to contribute more than a bit. They have to somehow all get together on the same page and focus all their on-ice efforts on winning. They can do that because they've done it before. It's the intangibles that can hurt this team, and it's the intangibles that can carry them over the top.

PREDICTION
Western Conference: 3
Overall: 5

STAT SECTION
Team Scoring Stats

	GP	G	A	PTS	+/-	PIM	SH	CAREER Gm	G	A	Pts
PETER FORSBERG	72	25	66	91	6	94	202	266	98	245	343
V. KAMENSKY	75	26	40	66	2-	60	173	395	152	218	370
JOE SAKIC	64	27	36	63	0	50	254	719	334	549	883
C. LEMIEUX	78	26	27	53	7-	115	261	836	298	302	600
SANDIS OZOLINSH	66	13	38	51	12-	65	135	379	92	193	285
A. DEADMARSH	73	22	21	43	0	125	187	277	85	83	168
ERIC LACROIX	82	16	15	31	0	84	126	283	59	56	115
UWE KRUPP	78	9	22	31	21	38	149	695	66	199	265
RENE CORBET	68	16	12	28	8	133	117	194	32	37	69
STEPHANE YELLE	81	7	15	22	10-	48	93	231	29	46	75
JARI KURRI	70	5	17	22	6	12	61	1,241	601	797	1,398
TOM FITZGERALD	80	12	6	18	4-	79	119	569	81	112	193
SHEAN DONOVAN	67	8	10	18	6	70	81	228	30	24	54
ADAM FOOTE	77	3	14	17	3-	124	64	435	18	74	92
ERIC MESSIER	62	4	12	16	4	20	66	83	4	12	16
JON KLEMM	67	6	8	14	3-	30	60	218	19	36	55
ALEXEI GUSAROV	72	4	10	14	9	42	47	468	33	108	141
JEFF ODGERS	68	5	8	13	5	213	47	482	60	50	110
WARREN RYCHEL	71	5	6	11	11-	221	66	378	38	37	75
KEITH JONES	23	3	7	10	4-	22	31	348	88	92	180
S. LEFEBVRE	81	0	10	10	2	48	66	640	24	106	130
AARON MILLER	55	2	2	4	0	51	29	126	7	17	24
F. LEROUX	50	1	2	3	3-	140	14	249	3	20	23
PATRICK ROY	65	0	3	3	0	39	1	goalie			
WADE BELAK	8	1	1	2	3-	27	2	13	1	1	2
YVES SARAULT	2	1	0	1	1	0	1	63	5	3	8
P. TREPANIER	15	0	1	1	2-	18	9	15	0	1	1
BRAD LARSEN	1	0	0	0	0	0	0	1	0	0	0
C. MATTE	5	0	0	0	0	6	5	10	1	1	2
C. BILLINGTON	23	0	0	0	0	2	0	goalie			

* Team Rankings 1997-98 (previous year's ranking in parenthesis)

		Conference Rank	League Rank
Record	39-26-17	4 (1)	7 (1)
Home	21-10-10	4 (1)	7 (1)
Away	18-16-7	3 (2)	7 (3)
Versus Own Conference	28-18-10	3 (1)	6 (1)
Versus Other Conference	11-8-7	5 (3)	11 (5)
Team Plus\Minus	+5	7 (3)	12 (7)
Goals For	231	4 (1)	6 (2)
Goals Against	205	5 (3)	12 (5)
Average Shots For	27.9	3 (2)	6 (3)
Average Shots Against	29.5	10 (7)	22 (14)
Overtime	2-3-17	8 (7)	16 (12)
One Goal Games	16-9	2 (1)	3 (2)
Times outshooting opponent	35	9 (4)	17 (7)

Versus Teams Over .500	11-13-8	4 (3)	7 (4)
Versus Teams .500 or under	28-13-9	3 (3)	8 (4)
First Half Record	21-8-12	3 (1)	5 (1)
Second Half Record	18-18-5	7 (2)	13 (3)

PLAYOFFS

Results: lost 4-3 to Edmonton in conference quarter-finals
Record: 3-4
Home: 1-3
Away: 2-1
Goals For: 16 (2.3/game)
Goals Against: 19 (2.7/game)
Overtime: 1-0
Power play: 14.3% (9th)
Penalty Killing: 84.8% (8th)

	GP	G	A	PTS	+/-	PIM	PP	SH	GW	OT	S
PETER FORSBERG	7	6	5	11	3	12	2	0	0	0	18
SANDIS OZOLINSH	7	0	7	7	3-	14	0	0	0	0	19
CLAUDE LEMIEUX	7	3	3	6	2	8	1	0	1	0	29
JOE SAKIC	6	2	3	5	0	6	0	1	2	1	24
V. KAMENSKY	7	2	3	5	1	18	1	0	0	0	17
A. DEADMARSH	7	2	0	2	1-	4	1	0	0	0	14
STEPHANE YELLE	7	1	0	1	3-	12	0	0	0	0	7
TOM FITZGERALD	7	0	1	1	2-	20	0	0	0	0	8
ALEXEI GUSAROV	7	0	1	1	1	6	0	0	0	0	3
UWE KRUPP	7	0	1	1	2	4	0	0	0	0	18
PATRICK ROY	7	0	1	1	0	0	0	0	0	0	0

C. BILLINGTON	1	0	0	0	0	0	0	0	0	0	0
RENE CORBET	2	0	0	0	0	2	0	0	0	0	5
JARI KURRI	4	0	0	0	1-	0	0	0	0	0	2
JON KLEMM	4	0	0	0	1	0	0	0	0	0	1
WARREN RYCHEL	6	0	0	0	2-	24	0	0	0	0	4
JEFF ODGERS	6	0	0	0	1-	25	0	0	0	0	4
S. LEFEBVRE	7	0	0	0	1-	4	0	0	0	0	4
ADAM FOOTE	7	0	0	0	1-	23	0	0	0	0	12
KEITH JONES	7	0	0	0	1-	13	0	0	0	0	12
ERIC LACROIX	7	0	0	0	2-	6	0	0	0	0	5
AARON MILLER	7	0	0	0	0	8	0	0	0	0	6

GOALTENDER	GPI	MINS	AVG	W	L	EN	SO	GA	SA	SV %
C. BILLINGTON	1	1	.00	0	0	0	0	0	0	.000
PATRICK ROY	7	430	2.51	3	4	1	0	18	191	.906
COL TOTALS	7	435	2.62	3	4	1	0	19	192	.901

All-Time Leaders

Goals

Michel Goulet	456
Joe Sakic	387
Peter Stastny	380

Assists

Peter Stastny	668
Joe Sakic	548
Michel Goulet	489

Points

Peter Stastny	1,048
Michel Goulet	945
Joe Sakic	883

Best Individual Seasons

Goals

Michel Goulet	1982-83	57
Michel Goulet	1983-84	56
Michel Goulet	1984-85	55

Assists

Peter Stastny	1981-82	93
Peter Forsberg	1995-96	86
Peter Stastny	1985-86	81

Points

Peter Stastny	1981-82	139
Peter Stastny	1982-83	124
Peter Stastny	1985-86	122

TEAM

Last 3 years

	GP	W	L	T	Pts	%
1997-98	82	39	26	17	95	.579
1996-97	82	49	24	9	107	.652
1995-96	82	47	25	10	104	.634

Best 3 regular seasons

	GP	W	L	T	Pts	%
1994-95	48	30	13	5	65	.677
1996-97	82	49	24	9	107	.652
1995-96	82	47	25	10	104	.634

Worst 3 regular seasons

	GP	W	L	T	Pts	%
1989-90	80	12	61	7	31	.194
1990-91	80	16	50	14	46	.288
1991-92	80	20	48	12	52	.325

Most Goals (min. 70 game schedule)
1983-84   360
1981-82   356
1992-93   351

Fewest Goals (min. 70 game schedule)
1997-98   231
1990-91   236
1989-90   240

Most Goals Against (min. 70 game schedule)
1989-90   407
1990-91   354
1981-82   345

Fewest Goals Against (min. 70 game schedule)
1997-98   205
1996-97   205
1995-96   240

Dallas Stars

Would you like fries with your filet mignon?

Just what the Stars needed, something else to make them better. The free agent signing of Brett Hull pretty much ensures that Dallas can't lose this year.

Not that Hull is in his prime, but his contribution should just about do it.

The Stars aren't like other teams, such as those trying to be competitive or make the playoffs. No, they have to be better than Detroit. And now they are.

Don't think so? Let's compare.

Coaching: Ken Hitchcock is one of the best in the league. Scotty Bowman is one of the best of all-time. But, we still didn't know at press time if Bowman would be returning.
Edge: Hitchcock, if anyone but Bowman is coaching the Red Wings.

Defence: The Stars probably have the best defence in the league. The Wings have one of the best defencemen in Lidstrom and they've added Uwe Krupp. The Wings supporting cast is mediocre, but that's what it also was this year when they won the Stanley Cup.
Edge: Dallas.

Forwards: Let's narrow it down a bit. Detroit's top three is Brendan Shanahan, Sergei Fedorov, and Steve Yzerman. The top three on Dallas is Mike Modano, Joe Nieuwendyk and Brett Hull. Edge to Detroit. The next top three scorers on Detroit are Slava Kozlov, Igor Larionov and probably Darren McCarty. Dallas has Pat Verbeek, Jamie Langenbrunner and Jere Lehtinen, a big edge to Dallas. Detroit has a good cast of checkers and third or fourth liners, but they're no better than the likes of Carbonneau, Keane, and Skrudland.
Edge: Dallas

Goaltending: Ed Belfour versus Chris Osgood. Roman Turek versus Kevin Hodson
Edge: Dallas on both counts.

Intangibles: Detroit has won two Stanley Cups in a row, neither of them by accident. Dallas hasn't won anything except the President's Trophy for finishing first overall. But, the Stars are hungrier. Then again, they were hungrier last year, too. Okay, they're starving.
Edge: Detroit

Playoff Performers: Dallas has potentially

great playoff players, but Detriot has proven great performers. When it gets to the post-season tournament, the Red Wings know exactly what they have to do to win.

Edge: Detroit

STUFF

* The last two seasons have been the best two seasons in franchise history.
* The Stars led the league with a 54.87% face-off percentage.
* Jere Lehtinen won the Frank Selke Trophy as the league's best defensive forward.

TEAM PREVIEW

GOAL: Roman Turek would probably like to get some more playing time, but he'd be advised not to get in Ed Belfour's way. Just ask Jeff Hackett. Belfour will play as often as they let him, so a Turek trade isn't out of the question, as long as the Stars can figure out something they need.

With the lineup the Stars have, anyway, it doesn't matter that much who the goaltender is because he doesn't get many quality shots.

Hockey Annual Rating: 5 of 27

DEFENCE: The Stars have the best defence in the league, but they do have a few problems. Richard Matvichuk is out until December after surgery, and Sergei Zubov was arrested for assaulting his wife.

Once they're on the ice, however, the problems are few.

For defence, there's the shot-blocking Craig Ludwig, and defensive defenders Richard Matvichuk and Derien Hatcher, both of whom also know what to do with the puck when it's on their stick.

Zubov and Darryl Sydor are two of the best offensive defencemen in the league, with their scoring totals enhancing, or enhanced by, a superb group of scoring forwards.

Shawn Chambers is another all-round defenceman who missed a lot of time last year with injuries.

Roster fillers include Brad Lukowich, Sergei Gusev, and Petr Buzek. The prime prospect is Richard Jackman, who has an all-round game that suits the Stars perfectly. He will likely finish out his junior career in the OHL.

Hockey Annual Rating: 1 of 27

FORWARD: Where the heck are they going to put everybody. The Stars are going to have players in the pressbox that would be intregal parts of other teams.

The first two lines should be Lehtinen-Modano-Hull and Langenbrunner-Nieuwendyk-Verbeek.

The checking line should have Brian Skrudland between Guy Carbonneau and Mike Keane. The fourth line could be Juha Lind, with newcomers Tony Hrkac or Aaron Gavey at centre, and Grant Marshall on the right side. They

GOALTENDER	GPI	MINS	AVG	W	L	T	EN	SO	GA	SA	SV %
E. FERNANDE	2	69	1.74	1	0	0	0	0	2	35	.943
ED BELFOUR	61	3581	1.88	37	12	10	1	9	112	1335	.916
ROMAN TUREK	23	1324	2.22	11	10	1	3	1	49	496	.901
DAL TOTALS	82	4986	2.01	49	22	11	4	10	167	1870	.911

still have Dave Reid and Tyler Wright left over.

Joe Nieuwendyk is out until November after surgery, so some of the kids could get more playing time. Waiting for his chance, again, is Jason Botterill, but he may need another minor pro season after missing much of last year with injuries.

The only thing better than a top faceoff man is two top faceoff men, and the Stars had just that. Faceoff wins are an under-appreciated art that only gets the attention it deserves late in the game. Winning a faceoff in the attacking zone often means a shot on net and a possible goal. Losing it in the defensive end, of course, means the same thing. So many goals are the result of a clean faceoff win.

Guy Carbonneau and Joe Nieuwendyk proved to be two of the best. These are the top faceoff men in the NHL last year, using stats recorded by the league:

Eric Lindros	Phi	60.13%
JOE NIEUWENDYK	DAL	59.45%
GUY CARBONNEAU	DAL	59.35%
Mark Janssens	Pho	58.01%
Steve Yzerman	Det	57.88%
Bobby Holik	Det	57.68%

A couple years ago, before the NHL did it en masse, I used to record various statistics at Toronto Maple Leaf games for the Toronto Sun. At that time, Peter Zezel (16th last year) was arguably the best faceoff man in the league. But, Guy Carbonneau, who had a reputation as one of the great faceoff men, always did poorly in Toronto, and used to even wave off faceoffs in certain spots so a teammate could take it. I thought at the time that he had lost his faceoff

dominance because of age. Either he's got it back, or he never lost it. Another person on the above list, Steve Yzerman, also used to do poorly at this aspect of the game.

Hockey Annual Rating: 1 of 27

SPECIAL TEAMS: The Stars won't be able to improve on their first place power play ranking, but they might be able to score more goals with Brett Hull blasting away at the net.

The Stars are so well-equipped for the power play that their second unit could probably finish second in power play percentage.

Doug Jarvis, one of the best penalty-killers in the history of the NHL, handles the penalty killing coaching chores, and obviously is doing quite well.

Power Play	G	ATT	PCT
Overall	77	385	20.0% (1st NHL)
Home	37	200	18.5% (5th NHL)
Road	40	185	21.6% (1st NHL)

9 SHORT HANDED GOALS ALLOWED (T-9th NHL)

Penalty Killing	G	TSH	PCT
Overall	42	351	88.0% (2nd NHL)
Home	20	175	88.6% (5th NHL)
Road	22	176	87.5% (5th NHL)

11 SHORT HANDED GOALS SCORED (T-9th NHL)

STARS SPECIAL TEAMS SCORING

Power play	G	A	PTS
ZUBOV	5	29	34
NIEUWENDYK	14	15	29
SYDOR	4	24	28
LANGENBRUNNER	8	11	19
MODANO	7	12	19
VERBEEK	9	9	18

ADAMS	7	7	14
CHAMBERS	1	12	13
HATCHER	3	9	12
LEHTINEN	7	3	10
REID	3	3	6
MARSHALL	3	3	6
HOGUE	3	3	6
KEANE	2	2	4
MATVICHUK	0	2	2
HARVEY	0	2	2

Short handed	G	A	PTS
MODANO	5	2	7
LEHTINEN	2	3	5
ZUBOV	1	1	2
CHAMBERS	1	1	2
SYDOR	1	0	1
CARBONNEAU	1	0	1
LUDWIG	0	1	1

COACHING AND MANAGEMENT: Ken Hitchcock has proven himself to be one of the best coaches in the game. He took this team from nowhere and turned it around. Not only did he turn it around, but he kept it turned, something that new coaches often have trouble doing.

Bob Gainey has turned out to be a better GM that originally thought. He spares nothing in getting the best players to make this franchise successful.

When he's lacking in something small it doesn't matter. He goes and gets it anyway.
Hockey Annual Rating: 2 of 27

DRAFT

Round	Sel.	Player	Pos	Team
2	39	John Erskine	D	London (OHL)
2	57	Tyler Bouck	RW	Prince George (WHL)
3	86	Gabriel Karlsson	F	Sweden
6	173	Niko Kapanen	C	Finland
7	200	Scott Perry	C	Boston U. (HE)

The Stars didn't get a pick until the second round, and used it to pick up a big, scrappy defenceman in John Erskine. Playing with London in the OHL last season he had 205 PIM and nine points in 55 games.

PROGNOSIS: Guess what? The Stars are going all the way. That means finishing first in the Western Conference, first overall, beating Detroit and going all the way to the Stanley Cup finals. They may very well win it, too.

PREDICTION
Western Conference: 1st
Overall: 1st

STAT SECTION

Team Scoring Stats

	GP	G	A	PTS	+/-	PIM	SH	CAREER Gm	G	A	Pts
J. NIEUWENDYK	73	39	30	69	16	30	203	768	397	371	768
MIKE MODANO	52	21	38	59	25	32	191	633	277	377	654
PAT VERBEEK	82	31	26	57	15	170	190	1,147	461	470	931
SERGEI ZUBOV	73	10	47	57	16	16	148	380	64	258	322
J. LANGENBRUNNER	81	23	29	52	9	61	159	171	38	57	95
DARRYL SYDOR	79	11	35	46	17	51	166	475	41	166	207
JERE LEHTINEN	72	23	19	42	19	20	201	192	45	68	113
GREG ADAMS	49	14	18	32	11	20	75	852	306	325	631
DERIAN HATCHER	70	6	25	31	9	132	74	448	46	126	172
G. CARBONNEAU	77	7	17	24	3	40	81	1,175	246	385	631
S. CHAMBERS	57	2	22	24	11	26	73	560	48	176	224
MIKE KEANE	83	10	13	23	12-	52	128	725	120	219	339
BENOIT HOGUE	53	6	16	22	7	35	55	670	197	279	476
TODD HARVEY	59	9	10	19	5	104	88	239	38	61	99
GRANT MARSHALL	72	9	10	19	2-	96	91	200	24	34	58
DAVE REID	65	6	12	18	15-	14	90	750	147	177	324
R. MATVICHUK	74	3	15	18	7	63	71	296	16	46	62
B. SKRUDLAND	72	7	6	13	6-	49	55	819	119	216	335
BOB BASSEN	58	3	4	7	4-	57	40	697	86	139	225
CRAIG LUDWIG	80	0	7	7	21	131	46	1,176	36	178	214
JAMIE WRIGHT	21	4	2	6	8	2	15	21	4	2	6
JUHA LIND	39	2	3	5	4	6	27	39	2	3	5
DAN KECZMER	17	1	2	3	5	26	9	173	8	32	40
CRAIG MUNI	40	1	1	2	0	25	12	819	28	119	147
CHRIS TANCILL	2	0	1	1	1-	0	1	134	17	32	49
BRAD LUKOWICH	4	0	1	1	2-	2	2	4	0	1	1
MIKE KENNEDY	15	0	1	1	1-	16	12	144	16	36	52
PETER DOURIS	1	0	0	0	1-	0	3	321	54	67	121
E. FERNANDEZ	2	0	0	0	0	0	0	goalie			
PETR BUZEK	2	0	0	0	1	2	0	2	0	0	0
PATRICK COTE	3	0	0	0	1-	15	3	8	0	0	0
JASON BOTTERILL	4	0	0	0	1-	19	2	4	0	0	0
J. MITCHELL	7	0	0	0	0	7	3	7	0	0	0
SERGEY GUSEV	9	0	0	0	5-	2	5	9	0	0	0
ROMAN TUREK	23	0	0	0	0	2	0	goalie			
ED BELFOUR	61	0	0	0	0	18	0	goalie			

* Team Rankings 1997-98 (previous year's ranking in parenthesis)

		Conference Rank	League Rank
Record	49-22-11	1 (2)	1 (2)
Home	26-8-7	1 (2)	2 (5)
Away	23-14-4	1 (1)	1 (1)
Versus Own Conference	32-17-7	1 (2)	2 (2)
Versus Other Conference	17-5-4	1 (2)	1 (4)
Team Plus\Minus	+40	1 (1)	1 (1)
Goals For	242	3 (4)	3 (7)
Goals Against	167	1 (2)	2 (3)
Average Shots For	26.8	9 (7)	16 (12)
Average Shots Against	22.8	1 (2)	1 (2)
Overtime	5-1-11	1 (5)	1 (7)
One Goal Games	16-8	1 (2)	1 (4)
Times outshooting opponent	60	1 (2)	1 (4)
Versus Teams Over .500	19-10-7	1 (2)	2 (4)
Versus Teams .500 or under	30-12-4	1 (1)	2 (1)
First Half Record	25-9-7	1 (2)	1 (2)
Second Half Record	24-13-4	1 (1)	2 (2)

PLAYOFFS

Results: defeated San Jose 4-2 in conference quarter-finals

defeated Edmonton 4-2 in conference semi-finals

lost to Detroit 4-2 in conference finals

Record: 10-7

Home: 7-2

Away: 3-5

Goals For: 36 (2.1/game)

Goals Against: 32 (1.9/game)

Overtime: 3-0

Power play: 10.0% (15th)

Penalty Killing: 88.2% (5th)

	GP	G	A	PTS	+/-	PIM	PP	SH	GW	OT	S
MIKE MODANO	17	4	10	14	4	12	1	0	1	0	49
SERGEI ZUBOV	17	4	5	9	3	2	3	0	1	0	34
MIKE KEANE	17	4	4	8	7	0	0	1	1	1	23
JERE LEHTINEN	12	3	5	8	0	2	1	0	0	0	31
BENOIT HOGUE	17	4	2	6	0	16	1	0	2	1	23
DERIAN HATCHER	17	3	3	6	1-	39	2	0	0	0	22
PAT VERBEEK	17	3	2	5	3-	26	2	0	1	0	25
J.LANGENBRUNNER	16	1	4	5	5-	14	0	0	1	1	35
DARRYL SYDOR	17	0	5	5	5	14	0	0	0	0	38
G. CARBONNEAU	16	3	1	4	0	6	0	0	0	0	19
GREG ADAMS	12	2	2	4	4	0	0	0	2	0	14
JUHA LIND	15	2	2	4	4	8	0	0	1	0	15

DAVE REID	5	0	3	3	2-	2	0	0	0	0	8
S. CHAMBERS	14	0	3	3	5	20	0	0	0	0	16
R. MATVICHUK	16	1	1	2	2	14	0	0	0	0	20
G. MARSHALL	17	0	2	2	0	47	0	0	0	0	8
JOE NIEUWENDYK	1	1	0	1	1	0	0	0	0	0	1
BOB BASSEN	17	1	0	1	3-	12	0	0	0	0	13
CRAIG LUDWIG	17	0	1	1	0	22	0	0	0	0	10
B. SKRUDLAND	17	0	1	1	0	16	0	0	0	0	14
E. FERNANDEZ	1	0	0	0	0	0	0	0	0	0	0
DAN KECZMER	2	0	0	0	0	2	0	0	0	0	2
CRAIG MUNI	5	0	0	0	2-	4	0	0	0	0	1
JAMIE WRIGHT	5	0	0	0	3	0	0	0	0	0	6
ED BELFOUR	17	0	0	0	0	18	0	0	0	0	0

All-Time Leaders

Goals

Brian Bellows	342
Dino Ciccarelli	332
Mike Modano	277

Assists

Neal Broten	586
Brian Bellows	380
Mike Modano	377

Points

Neal Broten	852
Brian Bellows	722
Mike Modano	654

Best Individual Seasons

Goals

Brian Bellows	1989-90	55
Dino Ciccarelli	1981-82	55
Mike Modano	1993-94	50

Assists

Neal Broten	1985-86	76
Bobby Smith	1981-82	71
Tim Young	1976-77	66

Points

Bobby Smith	1981-82	114
Dino Ciccarelli	1981-82	106
Neal Broten	1985-86	105

TEAM

Last 3 years

	GP	W	L	T	Pts	%
1997-98	82	49	22	11	109	.665
1996-97	82	48	26	8	104	.634
1995-96	82	26	42	14	66	.402

Best 3 regular seasons

	GP	W	L	T	Pts	%
1997-98	82	49	22	11	109	.665
1996-97	82	48	26	8	104	.634
1982-83	80	40	24	16	96	.600

Worst 3 regular seasons

	GP	W	L	T	Pts	%
1977-78	80	18	53	9	45	.281
1975-76	80	20	53	7	47	.293
1987-88	80	19	48	13	51	.319

Most Goals (min. 70 game schedule)

1981-82	346
1983-84	345
1985-86	327

Fewest Goals (min. 70 game schedule)

1968-69	189
1970-71	191
1967-68	191

Most Goals Against (min. 70 game schedule)

1987-88	349
1983-84	344
1974-75	341

Fewest Goals Against (min. 70 game schedule)

1997-98	167
1971-72	191
1996-97	198

Detroit Red Wings

There were a ton of reasons why the Red Wings could not win the Stanley Cup last year:
* tough to be hungry again after winning the season before.
* tough to recover from the Vladimir Konstantinov tragedy.
* an old, slow defence.
* questionable goaltending.
* couldn't win without Mike Vernon.

The Wings dispelled every one of those reasons, of course, and won it all for the second year in a row. They even turned those negative factors into positive ones.

The Stanley Cup finals was a tribute to Konstantinov. Seeing him on the ice in his wheelchair with a big smile on his face while his teammates gave him the Stanley Cup was as touching and emotional as it gets.

Before we get to why Detroit won't win the Cup for the third time in a row, just one thing about the Stanley Cup finals. Why is it that the Stanley Cup finals so often is a sweep. Last year was the fourth time in a row. In the last 25 years, 10 final series were sweeps, while just two went to seven games.

One reason is emotion. Teams can win on emotion part of the time, but when two teams get to the finals, they're both as emotionally charged as they're going to get, so talent wins out and there's less chance of an upset. Another factor, with the same reason, is tiredness. Again, with two teams equally exhausted, both emotionally and physically, the one with more talent wins out.

For some teams, just getting to the finals is a victory in itself (such as Washington) and for others the only victory is winning the Stanley Cup (such as Detroit). Yet another possible reason is that winning the first game of the final series provides more momentum than winning the first game of an earlier series. Sort of like a top long-distance runner. When they can see the finish line, they pick up their speed even more.

Another possible reason is that often one team is just lucky to be there, and they know it. That could be a psychological downer.

Okay, so why can't the Red Wings win it all again?
* tough to be hungry again after winning two Cups in a row.
* old and slow defence.
* questionable goaltending
* a new one: Dallas has become a better team with off-season moves.

One thing the Red Wings have proven, though, is that the more reasons you give them for not being able to win, the more incentive it gives them to prove those reasons wrong.

STUFF
* Nicklas Lidstrom was second in voting for the Norris Trophy, behind Rob Blake.
* The Red Wings were the only team not to win or lose a regular season overtime game.

TEAM PREVIEW
GOAL: Chris Osgood is great for the highlight reels. It's not often you get to see opposing players score from centre ice, and it's even rarer when it happens twice in one playoff.

Those are just flukes, of course, and could happen to any goalie. Well, once or twice, anyway.

Speaking of any goalie, a pretty good case could be made that almost any NHL goalie could have won if they had been playing net for the Red Wings. That's why it made little difference when Mike Vernon departed and Osgood became number one for the Wings.

Except in Buffalo, and Philadelphia in the playoffs, the team makes the goalie, not the other way around. All you have to do is look around the league on teams that had two goalies playing equal amounts and it's amazing how close their statistics are.

But, you say, Osgood was sensational at times, and saved the Red Wings on more than one occasion. Here's a scoop for you, every single NHL goalie is sensational at times and every single one of them have saved their team's butts on occasion. A goalie for a team that goes further in the playoffs gets noticed more, and outstanding games are remembered.

Kevin Hodson will back up Osgood again this year, with Norm Maracle waiting in the wings for the Wings to notice him.

Hockey Annual Rating: 14 of 27

DEFENCE: The defence strategy is fairly simple in Detroit. Take players who weren't good enough to play for the Toronto Maple Leafs and make them their own. They had four of them last year: Larry Murphy, Bob Rouse, Jamie Macoun, and Dmitri Mironov. Except for Macoun, who worked hard last year in Toronto, none of them deserved to play for Toronto, yes, even for Toronto. Yet some of them seem to get such pleasure by, "Sticking it to their old team." As if it wasn't their own fault that they played lousy.

If Nicklas Lidstrom had been playing there, chances are all four of them could still be playing for the Maple Leafs. Get over it guys. The Detroit style of playing makes plodding, aging veterans look more effective.

GOALTENDER	GPI	MINS	AVG	W	L	T	EN	SO	GA	SA	SV %
NORM MARACLE	4	178	2.02	2	0	1	0	0	6	63	.905
CHRIS OSGOOD	64	3807	2.21	33	20	11	5	6	140	1605	.913
KEVIN HODSON	21	988	2.67	9	3	3	1	2	44	444	.901
DET TOTALS	82	4995	2.35	44	23	15	6	9	196	2118	.907

CHRIS OSGOOD and KEVIN HODSON shared a shutout vs COL on Apr 1, 1998

Uwe Krupp should be a good addition to the lineup, signed as a free agent away from arch-rival Colorado. Aaron Ward and Anders Erickson round out the roster, with Rouse, Mironov, and Viacheslav Fetisov all gone to free agency. Yan Golubovsky was protected in the expansion draft, so the Wings figure on him helping out, too.

Heaven help all of them if Lidstrom gets hurt, though, then they'll have to raid the Toronto defence again.

Hockey Annual Rating: 5 of 27

FORWARD: Not many individual Detroit forwards set the world on fire, with not even a 30-goal scorer among them, and only three players with at least 20 goals.

But, you figure Fedorov missed almost the whole season, and Shanahan had an off-year. Mostly, though, on the Wings, everybody shares in the fun. That's why somebody like Brent Gilchrist gets five power play goals, but wouldn't even see the ice with an extra man on a lot of teams. The same with Doug Brown.

Brown had a great season, but was taken by Nashville in the expansion draft. The Wings wisely traded back for him.

Is there anything to worry about on the Wings?

Not much, although Larionov and Yzerman are getting old enough to cause some fret, and have the team thinking in terms of replacements. That's about it.

It's the playoffs that count, though, and last year, Tomas Holmstrom broke free and was very impressive, finishing third on the team in scoring. Martin Lapointe is turning into another Claude Lapointe, following mediocre scoring regular seasons with outstanding playoffs.

Yes, everything is in order in the Wings forward units. And if somebody gets hurt, big deal. They already proved they could still win without Fedorov. No one player makes or breaks their chances.

Maybe that's called balance.

At centre, there's Fedorov, Yzerman, Larionov and Draper. On the left side, the Wings line up with Shanahan, Holmstrom, Gilchrist, Maltby and Kocur. Right wing has Slava Kozlov (also a left winger), Darren McCarty, Doug Brown, Mike Knuble and Mathieu Dandenault. On the wings, however, positions aren't so important because they all move around, sometimes from shift to shift. One thing you don't want to see too often though, is Fedorov on defence. We've seen that movie before and it was a horror show.

The Red Wing forward lines, however, are in for another award winning season.

Hockey Annual Rating: 3 of 27

SPECIAL TEAMS: Everybody plays the power play on Detroit, or pretty close. It's good strategy to let the third and fourth liners loose sometimes. Makes them feel more important and it kicks up their scoring stats. They're so happy to be out there that they're more intense and don't want to blow the opportunity. Every player, no matter how defensive he is, likes to get goals and assists. Mind you, a lot of teams can't or won't do that, but they probably should. Just another reason why Bowman is such a smart coach, and so successful.

Power Play	G	ATT	PCT
Overall	67	381	17.6% (6th NHL)

| Home | 35 | 195 | 17.9% (6th NHL) |
| Road | 32 | 186 | 17.2% (7th NHL) |

7 SHORT HANDED GOALS ALLOWED (7th NHL)

Penalty Killing	G	TSH	PCT
Overall	51	376	86.4% (T-8th NHL)
Home	21	194	89.2% (3rd NHL)
Road	30	182	83.5% (19th NHL)

8 SHORT HANDED GOALS SCORED (T-18th NHL)

RED WINGS SPECIAL TEAMS SCORING

Power play	G	A	PTS
LIDSTROM	7	26	33
YZERMAN	6	21	27
SHANAHAN	15	9	24
MIRONOV	3	19	22
KOZLOV	6	11	17
LARIONOV	3	13	16
MURPHY	2	12	14
BROWN	6	7	13
MCCARTY	5	8	13
LAPOINTE	4	4	8
GILCHRIST	5	1	6
ERIKSSON	1	4	5
FEDOROV	2	2	4
FETISOV	0	4	4
MALTBY	2	0	2
HOLMSTROM	1	1	2
DRAPER	1	1	2
KOCUR	0	1	1

Short handed	G	A	PTS
YZERMAN	2	1	3
MURPHY	1	2	3
LIDSTROM	1	2	3
SHANAHAN	1	0	1
MCCARTY	1	0	1
MALTBY	1	0	1
BROWN	1	0	1

| MIRONOV | 0 | 1 | 1 |
| LARIONOV | 0 | 1 | 1 |

COACHING AND MANAGEMENT: At press time it wasn't known whether Bowman would be back as coach this year, but he probably will. He takes his time to decide and then he says okay. He's not motivated by money at this stage of his career, and he's had more success than any coach in the history of the game, so he must just like coaching.

Ken Holland wasn't too busy in his first year as GM. And he shouldn't have been. Sometimes, you would think a new GM would like to get his hands in the mix and shuffle the ingredients. The less you tinker with this team, the better.

Hockey Annual Rating: 1 of 27

DRAFT

Round	Sel.	Player	Pos	Team
1	25	Jiri Fischer	D	Hull (QMJHL)
2	55	Ryan Barnes	LW	Sudbury (OHL)
2	56	Tomek Valtonen	W	Finland
3	83	Jake McCracken	G	S.S. Marie (OHL)
4	111	Brent Hobday	F	Moose Jaw (WHL)
5	142	Calle Steen	LW	Sweden
6	151	Adam Deleeuw	LW	Barrie (OHL)
6	171	Pavel Datsyuk	C	Russia
7	198	Jeremy Goetzinger	D	Prince Albert (WHL)
8	226	David Petrasek	D	Sweden
9	256	Petja Pietilainen	LW	Saskatoon (WHI)

Jiri Fischer dropped way off in value at the draft. Projected as a top 10 pick, he almost slid out of the first round. He's a big guy who can skate, but he doesn't use either of those attributes for physical or offensive play.

PROGNOSIS: Don't pay too much attention to what the Wings do during the regular season. They peak at the right time, the most impor-

tant time. They should be one of the top three teams in the Western Conference standings, and one of the top four teams in the Stanley Cup playoffs.

PREDICTION
Western Conference: 2nd
Overall: 3rd

STAT SECTION
Team Scoring Stats

	GP	G	A	PTS	+/-	PIM	SH	CAREER Gm	G	A	Pts
STEVE YZERMAN	75	24	45	69	3	46	188	1,098	563	846	1,409
N. LIDSTROM	80	17	42	59	22	18	205	831	87	279	366
B. SHANAHAN	75	28	29	57	6	154	266	788	363	380	743
V. KOZLOV	80	25	27	52	14	46	221	384	135	148	283
LARRY MURPHY	82	11	41	52	35	37	129	1,397	265	838	1,103
IGOR LARIONOV	69	8	39	47	14	40	93	509	115	282	397
DMITRI MIRONOV	77	8	35	43	7-	119	170	401	46	168	214
DOUG BROWN	80	19	23	42	17	12	145	663	132	174	306
D. MCCARTY	71	15	22	37	0	157	166	300	63	91	154
M. LAPOINTE	79	15	19	34	0	106	154	311	49	54	103
BRENT GILCHRIST	61	13	14	27	4	40	124	617	125	162	287
KIRK MALTBY	65	14	9	23	11	89	106	301	39	31	70
KRIS DRAPER	64	13	10	23	5	45	96	287	38	38	76
T. HOLMSTROM	57	5	17	22	6	44	48	104	11	20	31
ANDERS ERIKSSON	66	7	14	21	21	32	91	90	7	20	27
SERGEI FEDOROV	21	6	11	17	10	25	68	527	248	361	609
M.DANDENAULT	68	5	12	17	5	43	75	167	13	18	31
V. FETISOV	58	2	12	14	4	72	55	546	36	192	228
MICHAEL KNUBLE	53	7	6	13	2	16	54	62	8	6	14
BOB ROUSE	71	1	11	12	9-	57	54	965	37	169	206
JOEY KOCUR	63	6	5	11	7	92	53	781	78	77	165
AARON WARD	52	5	5	10	1-	47	47	107	8	11	19
JAMIE MACOUN	74	0	7	7	17-	65	78	1,059	75	272	347
YAN GOLUBOVSKY	12	0	2	2	1	6	9	12	0	2	2
D. LAPLANTE	2	0	0	0	0	0	2	2	0	0	0

NORM MARACLE	4	0	0	0	0	0	0	goalie
KEVIN HODSON	21	0	0	0	0	2	0	goalie
CHRIS OSGOOD	64	0	0	0	0	31	0	goalie

* Team Rankings 1997-98 (previous year's ranking in parenthesis)

		Conference Rank	League Rank
Record	44-23-15	2 (3)	4 (6)
Home	25-8-8	2 (4)	3 (10)
Away	19-15-7	2 (5)	6 (7)
Versus Own Conference	27-17-12	4 (6)	7 (12)
Versus Other Conference	17-6-3	2 (1)	2 (1)
Team Plus\Minus	+38	3 (2)	3 (5)
Goals For	250	2 (3)	2 (6)
Goals Against	196	2 (1)	7 (2)
Average Shots For	30.1	1 (1)	1 (1)
Average Shots Against	25.8	4 (1)	7 (1)
Overtime	0-0-15	7 (3)	15 (4)
One Goal Games	10-8	6 (8)	10 (16)
Times outshooting opponent	59	2 (1)	3 (1)

Versus Teams Over .500	18-12-6	3 (6)	4 (12)
Versus Teams .500 or under	26-11-9	2 (2)	7 (3)
First Half Record	24-9-8	2 (3)	2 (8)
Second Half Record	20-14-7	4 (4)	9 (6)

PLAYOFFS

Results: defeated Phoenix 4-2 in conference quarter-finals

defeated St. Louis 4-2 in conference semi-finals

defeated Dallas 4-2 in conference finals

defeated Washington 4-0 in finals

Record: 16-6

Home: 8-3

Away: 8-3

Goals For: 75 (3.4/game)

Goals Against: 49 (2.2/game)

Overtime: 2-1

Power play: 15.5% (7th)

Penalty Killing: 88.2% (5th)

	GP	G	A	PTS	+/-	PIM	PP	SH	GW	OT	S
STEVE YZERMAN	22	6	18	24	10	22	3	1	0	0	65
SERGEI FEDOROV	22	10	10	20	0	12	2	1	1	0	86
T. HOLMSTROM	22	7	12	19	9	16	2	0	0	0	27
N. LIDSTROM	22	6	13	19	12	8	2	0	2	0	59
M. LAPOINTE	21	9	6	15	6	20	2	1	1	0	55
LARRY MURPHY	22	3	12	15	12	2	1	2	1	0	36
V. KOZLOV	22	6	8	14	4	10	1	0	4	0	47

IGOR LARIONOV	22	3	10	13	5	12	0	0	0	0	27
D. MCCARTY	22	3	8	11	9	34	0	0	1	0	46
B. SHANAHAN	20	5	4	9	5	22	3	0	2	1	60
DOUG BROWN	9	4	2	6	1-	0	3	0	1	0	19
ANDERS ERIKSSON	18	0	5	5	7	16	0	0	0	0	17
JOEY KOCUR	18	4	0	4	3-	30	0	0	0	0	13
KIRK MALTBY	22	3	1	4	2	30	0	1	0	0	31
JAMIE MACOUN	22	2	2	4	3	18	0	0	2	0	21
KRIS DRAPER	19	1	3	4	4	12	0	0	1	1	20
BRENT GILCHRIST	15	2	1	3	2	12	0	0	0	0	17
DMITRI MIRONOV	7	0	3	3	1	14	0	0	0	0	15
V. FETISOV	21	0	3	3	4	10	0	0	0	0	14
BOB ROUSE	22	0	3	3	2	16	0	0	0	0	22
M.DANDENAULT	3	1	0	1	2-	0	1	0	0	0	4
MICHAEL KNUBLE	3	0	1	1	0	0	0	0	0	0	1
CHRIS OSGOOD	22	0	1	1	0	12	0	0	0	0	0
KEVIN HODSON	1	0	0	0	0	0	0	0	0	0	0

GOALTENDER	GPI	MINS	AVG	W	L	EN	SO	GA	SA	SV %
KEVIN HODSON	1	0	.00	0	0	0	0	0	0	.000
CHRIS OSGOOD	22	1361	2.12	16	6	1	2	48	588	.918
DET TOTALS	22	1367	2.15	16	6	1	2	49	589	.917

All-Time Leaders

Goals

Gordie Howe	786
Steve Yzerman	563
Alex Delvecchio	456

Assists

Gordie Howe	1,023
Steve Yzerman	846
Alex Delvecchio	825

Points

Gordie Howe	1,809
Steve Yzerman	1,408
Alex Delvecchio	1,281

BEST INDIVIDUAL SEASONS

Goals

Steve Yzerman	1988-89	65
Steve Yzerman	1989-90	62
Steve Yzerman	1992-93	58

Assists

Steve Yzerman	1988-89	90
Steve Yzerman	1992-93	79
Marcel Dionne	1974-75	74

Points

Steve Yzerman	1988-89	155
Steve Yzerman	1992-93	137
Steve Yzerman	1989-90	127

TEAM

Last 3 years

	GP	W	L	T	Pts	%
1997-98	82	44	23	15	103	.628
1996-97	82	38	26	18	94	.573
1995-96	82	62	13	7	131	.799

Best 3 regular seasons

	GP	W	L	T	Pts	%
1995-96	82	62	13	7	131	.799
1994-95	48	33	11	4	70	.729
1950-51	70	44	13	13	101	.721

Worst 3 regular seasons

	GP	W	L	T	Pts	%
1985-86	80	17	57	6	40	.250
1976-77	80	16	55	9	41	.256
1926-77	44	12	28	4	28	.318

Most Goals (min. 70 game schedule)

1992-83	369
1993-94	356
1995-96	325

Fewest Goals (min. 70 game schedule)

1958-59	167
1957-58	176
1976-77	183

Most Goals Against (min. 70 game schedule)

1985-86	415
1984-85	357
1981-82	351

Fewest Goals Against (min. 70 game schedule)

1953-54	132
1952-53	133
1951-52	133

Edmonton Oilers

There's good news and bad news in Edmonton. Same as always.

Good News: The Oilers have three of the best offensive defencemen in the NHL.
Bad News: They don't have three of the best defensive defencemen in the NHL, or the AHL, for that matter.

Good News: The Oilers have new owners.
Bad News: There's 36 of them.

Good News: Curtis Joseph played great for the Oilers last year.
Bad News: He's gone to free agency and the Oilers got nothing for him.

Good News: Doug Weight got 26 goals last year.
Bad News: He was their leading goal scorer, and nobody else got more than 20.

Good News: The Oilers won another first round playoff series in seven games, this time over Colorado.
Bad News: They can't win a second round series.

Good News: They cut their goals against down by 23.
Bad News: They scored 37 fewer goals.

Good News: The Oilers made the playoffs last year.
Bad News: They might not this year.

TEAM PREVIEW
GOAL: With Joseph gone to free agency and Toronto, the team's netminding duties are in the hands of Eric Fichaud. Not exactly a fair trade. Obviously, there is more to come, so stay tuned.
Hockey Annual Rating: 23 of 27

GOALTENDER	GPI	MINS	AVG	W	L	T	EN	SO	GA	SA	SV %
BOB ESSENSA	16	825	2.55	6	6	1	2	0	35	404	.913
CURTIS JOSEPH	71	4132	2.63	29	31	9	6	8	181	1901	.905
EDM TOTALS	82	4980	2.70	35	37	10	8	8	224	2313	.903

DEFENCE: The Oilers have almost two all-star teams on defence. The first features an all-star offensive team of Janne Niinimaa, Roman Hamrlik and Boris Mironov. The second is an AHL all-star team, of Drake Berehowsky and Greg deVries and whomever else they put in there.

The first all-star team here does not have any candidates for the all-star defensive defenceman all-star team. And there's one too many offensive stars anyway, which means one of them is trade bait.

Actually, they're all trade bait, because Glen Sather rarely keeps defencemen around for a whole season.

The Oilers have another wunderkind, who may move up to the big team. Tom Poti was an offensive wizard at Boston University and has been compared to Brian Leetch. Poti was 14-29-43 in 34 college games.

The Oilers have a few prospects, as well, such as Sean Brown, Chris Hajt, and Mathieu Descoteaux, but they'd probably like a tough dog or two to protect their pussycats.

But, same as last year and the year before and the year before that, the Oilers defence will look a lot different at the end of the year than it does at the start.

Hockey Annual Rating: 10 of 27

FORWARD: They can put together two-thirds of a top-notch scoring line. That's about the best you can say. Doug Weight and Bill Guerin are dependable scorers, but you have to look hard to find something else.

So, we will.

Take a look at the top Edmonton scorers in the second half of the season.

	G	A	P
McAmmond	14	22	36
Weight	13	21	34
Guerin	13	16	29

What name doesn't belong on the list? Especially at the top. Give up?

Dean McAmmond only had 14 points in the first half, so is his second half explosion is either a mirage or a sign of things to come?

Ryan Smyth can score better than the paltry 20-13-33 he put on the board, but don't expect anything else in the way of support.

The rest of the Oilers forwards all do something well, but for most of them it's not more than one thing. The exception is Andrei Kovalenko, who doesn't do anything well, unless you count six goals for an offensive forward as something. Sather was trying to trade him, and if he can pawn him off on someone he'll be the genius everyone thinks he is.

They have some speedy little skaters, some bruising wingers, and some other stuff, but it just doesn't add up.

Kelly Buchberger, Mike Grier, Mats Lindgren, Valeri Zelepukin (4 goals), Rem Murray and maybe Boyd Deveaux and Georges Laraque will help fill out the lineup. Most of the other prospects have been traded away or will be.

Sather will find replacement parts, like he did last year with Tony Hrkac, Ray Whitney (for a while) and Scott Fraser, who got a big free agent contract with the Rangers, after spending his career in the minors and 29 games in the NHL. Then, the Oilers will mush them all together and they won't fit, unless they make the playoffs, and then it will be for one round only.

Hockey Annual Rating: 18 of 27

SPECIAL TEAMS: The Oilers draw a lot of penalties because of their speed. That's why they were able to tie for the league lead with 77 power play goals. Check out the teams with the most power play opportunities last season. Nobody was even close to them. They were only plus 11 in special team goals, however, because their penalty killing was so weak.

Most Power Play Opportunities:

Edmonton	483
Colorado	425
Florida	409
Lge. Ave.	380

Power Play	G	ATT	PCT
Overall	77	483	15.9% (12th NHL)
Home	34	246	13.8% (T-17th NHL)
Road	43	237	18.1% (6th NHL)

11 SHORT HANDED GOALS ALLOWED (15th NHL)

Penalty Killing	G	TSH	PCT
Overall	66	406	83.7% (22nd NHL)
Home	34	205	83.4% (T-19th NHL)
Road	32	201	84.1% (17th NHL)

10 SHORT HANDED GOALS SCORED (T-13th NHL)

OILERS SPECIAL TEAMS SCORING

Power play	G	A	PTS
MIRONOV	10	19	29
WEIGHT	9	20	29
HAMRLIK	5	23	28
NIINIMAA	3	21	24
MCAMMOND	8	12	20
SMYTH	10	7	17
GUERIN	9	8	17
HRKAC	7	5	12
KOVALENKO	1	9	10
MARCHANT	2	4	6
MURRAY	2	3	5
ZELEPUKIN	0	5	5
LINDGREN	1	3	4
DOLLAS	0	3	3
BEREHOWSKY	1	1	2
MILLAR	1	0	1
GRIER	1	0	1
DE VRIES	1	0	1
BUCHBERGER	1	0	1
WATT	0	1	1
HULBIG	0	1	1

Short handed	G	A	PTS
LINDGREN	3	1	4
MARCHANT	1	3	4
MURRAY	2	0	2
MUSIL	1	0	1
MIRONOV	1	0	1
HAMRLIK	1	0	1
BUCHBERGER	1	0	1
FRASER	6	7	13
WEIGHT	0	1	1
NIINIMAA	0	1	1
DE VRIES	0	1	1

COACHING AND MANAGEMENT: Sather has his own way of doing things, as much by necessity as anything else. He tries to be fiscally responsible and in the meantime he has to bring in players who are cheap and ship out players who are not. That, of course, isn't conducive to winning hockey, but he doesn't have any other choice. Otherwise, the team goes out of business.

It's not just that he's fiscally responsible,

but also that he's sensible. He doesn't throw money away stupidly, as more than a few teams do. Actually, as most teams do.

As a general manager, his player selection isn't always great. He doesn't take character and winning attitude into the equation as much as he should. That's why he ends up with so many underachievers, such as Kovalenko most recently, and plenty of others through the years.

Coach Ron Low's biggest virtue is that he comes comparatively cheap. Actually, that's not true, but it helps when you coach Edmonton. He's a hard worker, who has the respect of the players and gets the most he can out of them.

Hockey Annual Rating: 8 of 27

DRAFT

Round	Sel.	Player	Pos	Team
1	13	Michael Henrich	RW	Barrie (OHL)
3	67	Alex Henry	D	London (OHL)
4	99	Shawn Horcoff	C	Michigan St. (CCHA)
4	113	Kristian Antila	G	Finland
5	128	Paul Elliot	D	Medicine Hat (WHL)
5	144	Oleg Smirnov	F	Russia
6	159	Trevor Ettinger	D	Cape Breton (QMJHL)
7	186	Michael Morrison	G	Exeter Acad. (USHS)
8	213	Christian Lefebvre	D	Did Not Play
9	241	Maxim Spirodonov	RW	London (OHL)

Being selected in the first round by the Oilers pretty much seals Michael Henrich's fate. You could count on a couple fingers the number of first round successes Edmonton has had in the last 15 years. Amazing, really.

Henrich is a goal scorer, who was supposed to be a top five pick. He was 41-22-63 with Barrie in the OHL last season. But, what was it that made other teams pass on him until he got to Edmonton?

PROGNOSIS: You'd like them to do better because of all they go through to get there. But, they won't this year, or any year in the near future.

This team has a character coach and a couple character wingers. You might argue that they must have character in order to knock off Dallas and Colorado in the playoffs the last two years, but they have to get into the playoffs this year and that isn't a sure thing.

They have a dynamite offensive trio of defensemen and a couple forwards of note. After that, they're taking away work for third and fourth liners from other teams.

It's not that they're a bad team, they can get by and even stray fairly close to .500, but it's that they're not a good team. They could finish anywhere from fifth to 10th.

PREDICTION
Western Conference: 5th
Overall: 12th

STAT SECTION

Team Scoring Stats

	GP	G	A	PTS	+/-	PIM	SH	CAREER Gm	G	A	Pts
DOUG WEIGHT	79	26	44	70	1	69	205	504	128	320	448
D. MCAMMOND	77	19	31	50	9	46	128	243	52	86	138
BORIS MIRONOV	81	16	30	46	8-	100	203	322	38	111	149
JANNE NIINIMAA	77	4	39	43	13	62	134	154	8	79	87
ROMAN HAMRLIK	78	9	32	41	15-	70	198	418	58	153	211
BILL GUERIN	59	18	21	39	1	93	178	420	121	122	243
TODD MARCHANT	76	14	21	35	9	71	194	285	60	74	134
RYAN SMYTH	65	20	13	33	24-	44	205	188	61	44	105
TONY HRKAC	49	13	14	27	3	10	57	382	75	148	223
MATS LINDGREN	82	13	13	26	0	42	131	151	24	27	51
SCOTT FRASER	29	12	11	23	6	6	61	44	14	11	25
A.KOVALENKO	59	6	17	23	14-	28	89	394	123	140	263
K.BUCHBERGER	82	6	17	23	10-	122	86	743	78	154	232
V.ZELEPUKIN	68	4	18	22	2-	89	101	408	87	143	230
REM MURRAY	61	9	9	18	9-	39	59	143	20	29	49
MIKE GRIER	66	9	6	15	3-	73	90	145	24	23	47
GREG DE VRIES	65	7	4	11	17-	80	53	115	8	9	17
BOBBY DOLLAS	52	2	6	8	6-	49	38	505	36	80	116
D.BEREHOWSKY	67	1	6	7	1	169	58	196	7	32	39
B.DEVEREAUX	38	1	4	5	5-	6	27	38	1	4	5
CRAIG MILLAR	11	4	0	4	3-	8	10	12	4	0	4
JOE HULBIG	17	2	2	4	1-	2	8	23	2	2	4
MIKE WATT	14	1	2	3	4-	4	14	14	1	2	3
FRANK MUSIL	17	1	2	3	1	8	8	745	34	101	135
CURTIS JOSEPH	71	0	2	2	0	4	0	goalie			
SEAN BROWN	18	0	1	1	1-	43	9	23	0	1	1
BILL HUARD	30	0	1	1	5-	72	12	219	16	18	34
SCOTT FERGUSON	1	0	0	0	1	0	0	1	0	0	0
L.BENYSEK	2	0	0	0	2-	0	0	2	0	0	0
JASON BOWEN	4	0	0	0	0	10	3	77	2	6	8
DENNIS BONVIE	4	0	0	0	0	27	0	14	0	0	0
KEVIN LOWE	7	0	0	0	3-	22	5	1,254	84	347	431
BRYAN MUIR	7	0	0	0	0	17	6	12	0	0	0
T. SANDWITH	8	0	0	0	4-	6	4	8	0	0	0
G. LARAQUE	11	0	0	0	4-	59	4	11	0	0	0

| BOB ESSENSA | 16 | 0 | 0 | 0 | 0 | 0 | 0 | goalie | | |
| DOUG FRIEDMAN | 16 | 0 | 0 | 0 | 0 | 20 | 8 | 16 | 0 | 0 | 0 |

* Team Rankings 1997-98 (previous year's ranking in parenthesis)

		Conference Rank	League Rank
Record	35-37-10	7 (7)	16 (13)
Home	20-16-5	6 (5)	11 (12)
Away	15-21-5	9 (7)	17 (15)
Versus Own Conference	27-25-4	7 (11)	13 (21)
Versus Other Conference	8-12-6	10 (4)	20 (6)
Team Plus\Minus	-20	10 (8)	18 (16)
Goals For	215	8 (4)	14 (7)
Goals Against	224	7 (9)	16 (16)
Average Shots For	28.7	2 (4)	4 (8)
Average Shots Against	28.2	8 (10)	17 (18)
Overtime	3-2-10	3 (13)	8 (26)
One Goal Games	15-12	5 (11)	9 (22)
Times outshooting opponent	39	8 (7)	13 (13)
Versus Teams Over .500	16-20-3	5 (11)	11 (22)
Versus Teams .500 or under	19-17-7	8 (4)	18 (6)
First Half Record	11-21-9	11 (6)	23 (13)
Second Half Record	24-16-1	2 (8)	4 (13)

PLAYOFFS

Results: defeated Colorado 4-3 in conference quarter-finals

lost 4-1 to Dallas in conference semi-finals

Record: 5-7

Home: 1-4

Away: 4-3

Goals For: 24 (2.0/game)

Goals Against: 25 (2.1/game)

Overtime: 0-2

Power play: 11.1% (13th)

Penalty Killing: 89.6% (3rd)

	GP	G	A	PTS	+/-	PIM	PP	SH	GW	OT	S
DOUG WEIGHT	12	2	7	9	4-	14	2	0	1	0	26
BILL GUERIN	12	7	1	8	6-	17	4	0	0	0	47
BORIS MIRONOV	12	3	3	6	3-	27	1	0	1	0	26
ROMAN HAMRLIK	12	0	6	6	4-	12	0	0	0	0	19
REM MURRAY	11	1	4	5	1-	2	0	0	0	0	15
D. MCAMMOND	12	1	4	5	0	12	0	0	0	0	22
MIKE GRIER	12	2	2	4	4	13	0	0	1	0	14
RYAN SMYTH	12	1	3	4	2-	16	1	0	0	0	24
V. ZELEPUKIN	8	1	2	3	3	2	0	0	0	0	8
D. BEREHOWSKY	12	1	2	3	1	14	0	0	1	0	4
K. BUCHBERGER	12	1	2	3	0	25	0	0	0	0	13
TONY HRKAC	12	0	3	3	2	2	0	0	0	0	11
SCOTT FRASER	11	1	1	2	0	0	0	0	0	0	17
JANNE NIINIMAA	11	1	1	2	3	12	0	0	1	0	20
MATS LINDGREN	12	1	1	2	0	10	0	0	0	0	16
TODD MARCHANT	12	1	1	2	0	10	0	0	0	0	17
BOB ESSENSA	1	0	0	0	0	0	0	0	0	0	0
KEVIN LOWE	1	0	0	0	0	4	0	0	0	0	0
A. KOVALENKO	1	0	0	0	0	2	0	0	0	0	2
BILL HUARD	4	0	0	0	0	2	0	0	0	0	3
FRANK MUSIL	7	0	0	0	1	6	0	0	0	0	0
GREG DE VRIES	7	0	0	0	4-	21	0	0	0	0	2
BOBBY DOLLAS	11	0	0	0	2	16	0	0	0	0	10
CURTIS JOSEPH	12	0	0	0	0	2	0	0	0	0	0

GOALTENDER	GPI	MINS	AVG	W	L	EN	SO	GA	SA	SV %
CURTIS JOSEPH	12	716	1.93	5	7	1	3	23	319	.928
BOB ESSENSA	1	27	2.22	0	0	0	0	1	11	.909
EDM TOTALS	12	749	2.00	5	7	1	3	25	331	.924

All-Time Leaders
Goals
Wayne Gretzky	583
Jari Kurri	474
Glenn Anderson	417

Assists
Wayne Gretzky	1,086
Mark Messier	642
Jari Kurri	569

Points
Wayne Gretzky	1,669
Jari Kurri	1,043
Mark Messier	1,034

Best Individual Seasons
Goals
Wayne Gretzky	1981-82	92
Wayne Gretzky	1983-84	87
Wayne Gretzky	1984-85	73

Assists
Wayne Gretzky	1985-86	163
Wayne Gretzky	1984-85	135
Wayne Gretzky	1982-83	125

Points
Wayne Gretzky	1985-86	215
Wayne Gretzky	1981-82	212
Wayne Gretzky	1984-85	208

TEAM
Last 3 years
	GP	W	L	T	Pts	%
1997-98	82	35	37	10	80	.488
1996-97	82	36	37	9	81	.494
1995-96	82	30	34	8	68	.415

Best 3 regular seasons
	GP	W	L	T	Pts	%
1983-84	80	57	18	5	119	.744
1985-86	80	56	17	7	119	.744
1981-82	80	48	17	15	111	.694

Worst 3 regular seasons
	GP	W	L	T	Pts	%
1992-93	84	26	50	8	60	.357
1993-94	84	25	45	14	64	.381
1995-96	48	17	27	4	38	.396

Most Goals (min. 70 game schedule)
1983-84	446
1985-86	426
1982-83	424

Fewest Goals (min. 70 game schedule)
1997-98	215
1995-95	240
1992-93	242

Most Goals Against (min. 70 game schedule)
1992-93	337
1980-81	327
1979-80	322

Fewest Goals Against (min. 70 game schedule)
1997-98	224
1996-97	242
1990-91	272

Los Angeles Kings

They had a party in Los Angeles last year. A surprise party. They jumped 20 points in the standings, second only to Boston as the most improved team.

Last year, *The Hockey Annual* suggested emphatically that "There is no hope for this team. None." *The Hockey Annual* went on to say that, "There isn't even a slight chance that they will make the playoffs."

Just goes to show you that miracles do happen.

The biggest surprise, of course, is that they won and made the playoffs. Here's some more.

* Rob Blake winning the Norris Trophy. It's not as if he wasn't capable of being the best defenceman in the league, but rather that he was capable of playing enough games to be considered.
* The breakout season of Glen Murray. Written off as a never-will-be after striking out with Boston and Pittsburgh, he hit a home run with the Kings, with 29 goals to lead the team.
* Yanic Perreault and Vladimir Tsyplakov. Neither of these two, along with Glen Murray, were expected to have such an impact. In fact, the three of them when they were together were one of the most productive lines of the season, on any team. Josef Stumpel replaced Perreault later in the season on the number one unit.

There were other reasons for the Kings' success, of course, but the performance of the above-mentioned four players is the key. None of them were expected to contribute as much as they did. In fact, if you take away Blake, they finish out of the playoffs, and closer to last overall, as predicted by *The Hockey Annual*.

The Kings were bombarded in the playoffs, four straight by St. Louis, but considering they weren't even supposed to be in the post-season, it was just a blip on the screen.

There are reasons to worry about their continued improvement. And there are reasons to be optimistic.

The Kings had a problem beating good teams last year. Their record against teams with records over .500 was just 9-18-6. They had Colorado's number, and were 4-1 against them. That means they were just 5-17-6 against the rest of the over .500 teams, and 5-21-6 if you count the playoffs.

The Kings were very good against under .500 teams, with a record of 27-15-5. Combined with their record against the good teams, that's both good and bad. It shows they play with intensity every game, because they didn't lose very often to weak teams, which is what happens to a lot of the good teams. If they're playing with that kind of intensity and still can't beat the better teams, however, it shows that they they're just not talented enough.

Another problem with the Kings was that they were outshot badly. Only Buffalo (31.2) and Anaheim (30.4) gave up more than the 30.3 shots the Kings averaged against every game. Sometimes that doesn't mean anything if they're limiting their opponents to poor percentage shots, but usually the better defensive teams just limit the shots on net, period.

Okay, one more worrisome area. Players who over-achieve one season, tend to fall back the next. The Kings have a lot of players in that category. And then Blake is one of the most injury prone players in the league, and if he's hurt, the Kings can forget it.

On the flip side, the Kings are a fairly young team, and success breeds confidence. They won't go into this season expecting to lose.

Larry Robinson is establishing himself as a good coach, who gets his players to play.

The Kings have a big, tough defence, which offsets their rather small forwards, and can allow the forwards to play bigger than their listed size.

The power play troubled them at times last year, and the Kings figure they've fixed that with the signing of free agent defenceman, Steve Duchesne.

But, considering they already had Garry Galley and Rob Blake minding the points with the man advantage, the law of diminishing returns suggest that Duchesne won't make that much of a difference.

The Kings also have some prospects coming through the system. Olli Jokinen had a great season in Finland, and is expected to crack the lineup this year.

The negatives outnumber the positives when considering the prospects of the Kings this year, but at least they "have a hope" of making the playoffs.

STUFF
* Including the playoffs, the Kings were 0-7-1 against St. Louis last year.
* The Kings scored a team record three shorthanded goals in one game, when
* Doug Bodger needs seven games for 1,000.

TEAM PREVIEW
GOAL: It's taken Jamie Storr a while, but he may have finally made it. The Kings selected him seventh overall in the 1994 draft. In each of the subsequent three seasons he had a five-game taste of the NHL and then spent the rest of his time in junior or the minors. Last year, he broke the five-game barrier and played in 17.

GOALTENDER	GPI	MINS	AVG	W	L	T	EN	SO	GA	SA	SV %
JAMIE STORR	17	920	2.22	9	5	1	0	2	34	482	.929
STEPHANE FISET	60	3497	2.71	26	25	8	4	2	158	1728	.909
FREDERIC CHABOT	12	554	3.14	3	3	2	0	0	29	267	.891
L.A TOTALS	82	4990	2.71	38	33	11	4	4	225	2481	.909

This year, he's likely to play in a lot more, maybe even more than the incumbent number one man, Stephane Fiset. Storr's GAA was a half a goal a game better than Fiset's and Storr was the goalie of choice in the playoffs.

If they play half the games each, it would be about right. Either way, the Kings aren't worrying about this position, and a draft choice from five years ago is about to pay off.

Goalies are different from other position players. It's not unusual for forwards to make the jump directly to the NHL, but guess how many goalies, of those who played in the league last season, did not play in the minors.

Give up? The answer is none. Every single one of them played some minor professional hockey. Patrick Roy only played one game in the AHL, but most played at least a season or two before making it to the NHL. Even Dominik Hasek played parts of two seasons in the minors before he was even able to obtain NHL backup status.

While it takes goalies longer to make it to the NHL, they tend to last longer as well, if they're good. Experience and knowledge that can only be picked up only by playing for so long is more valuable than that obtained by other position players.

Hockey Annual Rating: 18 of 27

DEFENCE: Years ago, people would say that Rob Blake was a future Norris Trophy winner. That was before he spent the better part of three years on the injury list playing just 92 of a possible 212 games.

Last year, Blake missed one game, and won one Norris Trophy as the league's best defense-man.

The Kings defence is tough and they hit. There were six Kings who recorded over 100 hits, according to the NHL's new stat system, and five of them were defencemen.

Top Hitters:

Player	Position	Hits
Ian Laperriere	centre	198
Rob Blake	defense	183
Mattias Norstrom	defense	147
Aki Berg	defense	138
Garry Galley	defense	102
Sean O'Donnell	defense	100

Part of the reason could be that opposing players spent a lot of time in their end, and another reason is that defencemen naturally hit more, but those numbers stack up pretty well against other teams in the league.

Just for interest sake, newcomer Steve Duchesne had a grand total of 16 hits, so don't expect him to play a physical game. Not that it's needed.

He contributes to their mobility, which will be very good. They need to get the puck out of their end and should be able to do it. They also traded for Doug Bodger, another offensive-type defenseman.

It's going to be hard getting everybody playing time. There's Blake, Duchesne and Galley, veterans who should play a lot. Then there's Berg, who needs to play to improve. Sean O'Donnell made a name for himself in the playoffs when he earned a five-minute penalty for protecting his goalie, and then the Blues scored four goals with the man-advantage. He should play, as should Norstrom, which leaves big-boy Sean McKenna, Doug Bodger, Philippe

Boucher and maybe Doug Zmolek fighting for ice-time.

If you go by the Kings expansion draft list, they only protected Blake, O'Donnell, Norstrom and Berg, but only lost goalie Frederic Chabot. They didn't have Duchesne at the time.

The Kings have the luxury of resting veterans Galley and Bodger, or they could trade one of the younger players for something else they need.

The Kings have most of the components of a good defence: an impact player in Blake, toughness, mobility, offensive-ability, experience, and youth.

That leaves the ability to stop opposing players from scoring, which is more important than the rest of the categories put together. And it's something they need to worry about.

Hockey Annual Rating: 14 of 27

FORWARD: The Kings went into last season with only one sure thing at forward. Josef Stumpel didn't disappoint until maybe later in the season when he slumped, but almost all the remaining scorers came as pleasant surprises.

Glen Murray had a breakout season with 29 goals and 31 assists. There were doubts that that would ever happen. He was a poster boy for disappointment in Boston and Pittsburgh before the Kings took him off the Penguins hands for aging veteran Ed Olczyk.

If you count Murray, with left winger Tsyplakov and centre Stumpel, as the first line, then the second line could be Perreault between Luc Robitaille and right winger Craig Johnson. But, then you have to fit centre Ray Ferraro and rookie Olli Jokkinen in there somewhere on scoring lines.

Defensively, Ian Laperriere and Dan Bylsma lead the pack, although Bylsma sits in the pressbox on occasion, on curious occasions considering he sat out some in the playoffs when penalty killing is what they needed most. Russ Courtnall isn't an offensive threat anymore so he must be contributing defensively. Add Sandy Moger and Nathan Lafayette to the mix, along with enforcer Matt Johnson, and it still doesn't add up to much.

If you go just by last year's numbers, the Kings should be decent at forward, but last year isn't this year and the scorers aren't sure bets to repeat. Look for one or two of them to falter and be replaced.

The Kings have a bunch of decent prospects who are close to making the team. Along with Jokinen there's Don MacLean, a big-time junior scorer who needs to regain his touch in the minors; Josh Green, a second round pick in 1996, is rounding out his game in the minors; Pavel Rosa is a scoring maching, but missed almost all of last year with injuries; and Eric Belanger is another prospect that the Kings like.

Hockey Annual Rating: 20 of 27

SPECIAL TEAMS: While the Kings power play was horrendous in the playoffs it was at least mediocre during the regular season. They're hoping Duchesne solves all their problems, but there's no guarantee in that because they weren't exactly lacking in point-producing defencemen. He and Blake on the points, however, make a formidable pair.

The Kings have some excellent defensive forwards and should be better at penalty killing.

Power Play	G	ATT	PCT
Overall	52	366	14.2% (15th NHL)
Home	29	210	13.8% (T-17th NHL)
Road	23	156	14.7% (14th NHL)

12 SHORT HANDED GOALS ALLOWED (T-16th NHL)

Penalty Killing	G	TSH	PCT
Overall	63	399	84.2% (19th NHL)
Home	34	206	83.5% (18th NHL)
Road	29	193	85.0% (T-13th NHL)

10 SHORT HANDED GOALS SCORED (T-13th NHL)

KINGS SPECIAL TEAMS SCORING

Power play	G	A	PTS
BLAKE	11	11	22
STUMPEL	4	17	21
GALLEY	7	13	20
ROBITAILLE	5	11	16
MURRAY	7	8	15
JOHNSON	6	3	9
PERREAULT	3	3	6
TSYPLAKOV	2	4	6
MOGER	1	3	4
COURTNALL	1	3	4
NORSTROM	0	4	4
BOUCHER	1	2	3
O'DONNELL	0	3	3
FERRARO	0	3	3
MACLEAN	2	0	2
LAPERRIERE	0	2	2
BERG	0	2	2
MCKENNA	1	0	1
LAFAYETTE	1	0	1
VOPAT	0	1	1

Short handed	G	A	PTS
COURTNALL	4	0	4
MURRAY	3	0	3
PERREAULT	2	0	2

LAPERRIERE	1	1	2
STUMPEL	0	2	2
O'DONNELL	0	2	2
ZMOLEK	0	1	1
BYLSMA	0	1	1
BLAKE	0	1	1

COACHING AND MANAGEMENT: Larry Robinson was a close second to Pat Burns in the Adams trophy voting for coach of the year. He was able to coerce a 20 point improvement out of the team. Often a coach has a lifespan of two or three years before his motivating techniques become old and don't work any more. Robinson seems to be getting more out of his team as he goes along.

At the end of last season, Robinson was the coach with the third longest tenure with his current team.

Most Consecutive Games as Current Team Coach:

Scotty Bowman	Detroit	378
Ron Low	Edmonton	259
Larry Robinson	Los Angeles	246

New GM Dave Taylor had a relatively easy season. Everything seemed to click and he didn't have to worry about making a lot of moves. It might be different this year, however.

Hockey Annual Rating: 19 of 27

DRAFT

Round	Sel.	Player	Pos	Team
1	21	Mathieu Biron	D	
				Shawinigan (QMJHL)
2	46	Justin Papineau	C	Belleville
				(OHL)

3	76	Alexie Volkov	G	Russia
4	103	Kip Brennan	D	Sudbury (OHL)
5	133	Joe Rullier	D	Rimouski (QMJHL)
6	163	Tomas Zizka	D	Czech
7	190	Tommi Hannu	C	Finland
8	217	Jim Henkel	C	New England Jr. (NAJHL)
9	248	Matthew Yeats	G	Olds (AJHL)

Mathieu Biron is a giant defenceman, at almost six feet seven inches. He was rated a lot higher than the Kings were able to choose him. He and Steve McKenna (6-8) would make an interesting defence pairing.

Second round pick Justin Papineau was supposed to be selected higher, as well. He's a little guy who reminds some of a Steve Yzerman or Doug Gilmour. He can score in junior (41-53-94) but will he be able to score in the NHL?

PROGNOSIS

It won't be easy this year to repeat last year's success. Often over-achieving teams fall back the following year.

As noted in the opening, there are lots of reasons for pessimism and a few for optimism. Take your pick.

Making the playoffs isn't something the Kings should count on for this season, but it should be only a babystep back before they take another step forward.

PREDICTION
Western Conference: 10th
Overall: 17th

STAT SECTION
Team Scoring Stats

	GP	G	A	PTS	+/-	PIM	SH	CAREER Gm	G	A	Pts
JOZEF STUMPEL	77	21	58	79	17	53	162	351	65	180	245
GLEN MURRAY	81	29	31	60	6	54	193	375	88	80	168
V. TSYPLAKOV	73	18	34	52	15	18	113	163	39	62	101
ROB BLAKE	81	23	27	50	3-	94	261	469	91	197	288
YANIC PERREAULT	79	28	20	48	6	32	206	237	69	66	135
LUC ROBITAILLE	57	16	24	40	5	66	130	889	478	524	1,002
CRAIG JOHNSON	74	17	21	38	9	42	125	180	37	38	65
GARRY GALLEY	74	9	28	37	5-	63	128	963	106	429	535
SANDY MOGER	62	11	13	24	4	70	89	194	38	36	74
IAN LAPERRIERE	77	6	15	21	0	131	74	248	33	55	88
RUSS COURTNALL	58	12	6	18	2-	27	97	972	291	434	725
SEAN O'DONNELL	80	2	15	17	7	179	71	221	9	34	43

P. BOUCHER	45	6	10	16	6	49	80	229	28	60	88
RAY FERRARO	40	6	9	15	10-	42	45	955	9	36	45
M. NORSTROM	73	1	12	13	14	90	61	207	4	40	44
DAN BYLSMA	65	3	9	12	9	33	57	148	6	15	21
N. LAFAYETTE	34	5	3	8	2	32	60	154	15	18	33
STEVE MCKENNA	62	4	4	8	9-	150	42	71	4	4	8
DOUG ZMOLEK	46	0	8	8	0	111	23	362	9	32	41
AKI BERG	72	0	8	8	3	61	58	164	3	21	24
D. MACLEAN	22	5	2	7	1-	4	25	22	5	2	7
MATT JOHNSON	66	2	4	6	8-	249	18	133	4	7	11
JAN VOPAT	21	1	5	6	8	10	13	65	6	14	20
ROMAN VOPAT	25	0	3	3	7-	55	36	69	6	11	17
JASON MORGAN	11	1	0	1	7-	4	5	14	1	0	1
V. YACHMENEV	4	0	1	1	1	4	4	149	29	57	86
STEPHANE FISET	60	0	1	1	0	8	0	goalie			
OLLI JOKINEN	8	0	0	0	5-	6	12	8	0	0	0
F. CHABOT	12	0	0	0	0	0	0	goalie			
JAMIE STORR	17	0	0	0	0	0	0	goalie			

* Team Rankings 1997-98 (previous year's ranking in parenthesis)

		Conference Rank	League Rank
Record	38-33-11	5 (12)	11 (24)
Home	22-16-3	5 (8)	10 (16)
Away	16-17-8	5 (13)	12 (26)
Versus Own Conference	29-22-5	5 (13)	9 (25)
Versus Other Conference	9-11-6	6 (11)	16 (20)
Team Plus\Minus	+13	4 (12)	9 (25)
Goals For	227	5 (11)	8 (23)
Goals Against	225	8 (11)	17 (20)
Average Shots For	26.8	9 (10)	16 (20)
Average Shots Against	30.3	12 (12)	24 (23)
Overtime	3-2-11	4 (12)	9 (24)
One Goal Games	14-13	10 (13)	16 (24)
Times outshooting opponent	26	12 (13)	24 (25)
Versus Teams Over .500	9-18-6	9 (13)	20 (26)
Versus Teams Under .500	27-15-5	4 (10)	10 (17)
First Half Record	17-17-7	6 (13)	12 (25)
Second Half Record	21-16-4	5 (11)	10 (22)

PLAYOFFS

Results: Lost 4-0 to St. Louis in conference quarter-finals

Record: 0-4

Home: 0-2

Away: 0-2

Goals For: 8 (2.0/gm)

Goals Against: 16 (4.0/gm)

Overtime: 0-0

Power play: 3.4% (16th)

Penalty Killing: 77.8% (15th)

	GP	G	A	PTS	+/-	PIM	PP	SH	GW	OT	S
LUC ROBITAILLE	4	1	2	3	1	6	0	0	0	0	13
JOZEF STUMPEL	4	1	2	3	2	2	0	0	0	0	7
YANIC PERREAULT	4	1	2	3	1-	6	1	0	0	0	7
AKI BERG	4	0	3	3	3	0	0	0	0	0	7
GLEN MURRAY	4	2	0	2	2	6	0	0	0	0	13
CRAIG JOHNSON	4	1	0	1	0	4	0	0	0	0	3
SEAN O'DONNELL	4	1	0	1	1	36	0	0	0	0	7
IAN LAPERRIERE	4	1	0	1	0	6	0	0	0	0	6
JAN VOPAT	2	0	1	1	1	2	0	0	0	0	1
RAY FERRARO	3	0	1	1	1	2	0	0	0	0	5
STEVE MCKENNA	3	0	1	1	1	8	0	0	0	0	3
GARRY GALLEY	4	0	1	1	2-	2	0	0	0	0	6
V. TSYPLAKOV	4	0	1	1	1-	8	0	0	0	0	4
STEPHANE FISET	2	0	0	0	0	0	0	0	0	0	0
DAN BYLSMA	2	0	0	0	3-	0	0	0	0	0	1
DOUG ZMOLEK	2	0	0	0	0	2	0	0	0	0	0
JAMIE STORR	3	0	0	0	0	0	0	0	0	0	0
ROB BLAKE	4	0	0	0	4-	6	0	0	0	0	15
RUSS COURTNALL	4	0	0	0	2-	2	0	0	0	0	7
N. LAFAYETTE	4	0	0	0	2-	2	0	0	0	0	4
M. NORSTROM	4	0	0	0	1-	2	0	0	0	0	3
MATT JOHNSON	4	0	0	0	1-	6	0	0	0	0	0

GOALTENDER	GPI	MINS	AVG	W	L	EN	SO	GA	SA	SV %
JAMIE STORR	3	145	3.72	0	2	0	0	9	77	.883
STEPHANE FISET	2	93	4.52	0	2	0	0	7	61	.885
L.A TOTALS	4	240	4.00	0	4	0	0	16	138	.884

All-Time Leaders
Goals
Marcel Dionne	550
Dave Taylor	431
Luc Robitaille	392

Assists
Marcel Dionne	757
Dave Taylor	638
Wayne Gretzky	619

Points
Marcel Dionne	1,307
Dave Taylor	1,069
Wayne Gretzky	858

Best Individual Seasons
Goals
Bernie Nicholls	1988-89	70
Luc Robitaille	1992-93	63
Marcel Dionne	1978-79	59

Assists
Wayne Gretzky	1990-91	122
Wayne Gretzky	1988-89	114
Wayne Gretzky	1989-90	102

Points
Wayne Gretzky	1988-89	168
Wayne Gretzky	1990-91	163
Bernie Nicholls	1988-89	150

TEAM
Last 3 years
	GP	W	L	T	Pts	%
1997-87	82	38	33	11	87	.530
1996-97	82	28	43	11	67	.409
1995-96	82	24	40	18	68	.415

Best 3 regular seasons
	GP	W	L	T	Pts	%
1974-75	80	47	17	21	105	.656
1990-91	80	46	24	10	102	.638
1980-81	80	43	24	13	99	.619

Worst 3 regular seasons
	GP	W	L	T	Pts	%
1969-70	76	14	52	10	38	.250
1971-72	78	20	49	9	49	.314
1985-86	80	23	49	8	54	.338

Most Goals (min. 70 game schedule)
1988-89	376
1990-91	340
1984-85	339

Fewest Goals (min. 70 game schedule)
1969-79	168
1968-69	185
1967-68	200

Most Goals Against (min. 70 game schedule)
1985-86	389
1983-84	376
1981-82	369

Fewest Goals Against (min. 70 game schedule)
1974-75	185
1967-68	224
1997-98	225

Nashville Predators

If nothing else, the management team of the Predators has done a remarkable job of sifting through the scrap heap. They didn't uncover any gems, but they made a lot of smart moves that will make them better than they might have been.

For one thing, they played the regulations to the maximum and made all kinds of helpful deals. A lot of teams wanted to give up a goalie in the draft so that they couldn't lose one the following year in the next expansion draft. Yeah, we can do that, said the Predators, but what will you give us in return. Some teams didn't want them to draft a certain player that they had to leave unprotected. Yeah, we can do that, said the Predators, what's in it for us.

Plenty, on both counts.

As well, the Predators drafted unrestricted free agents they knew they had no hope of signing, just so they could pick up a free draft pick as compensation next year.

Smart people, and it bodes well for the future of the franchise.

David Poile is the man in charge and he's no expansion rookie. He guided the Washington Capitals for 15 years and knows all the ins and outs of managing in the NHL.

For the sake of posterity, these are the Nashville expansion draft picks:

Goalie:

Mikhail Shtalenkov	Anaheim
Fredric Chabot	Los Angeles
Tomos Vokoun	Montreal
Mike Dunham	New Jersey
Mike Richter	NY Rangers

Defence:

Bob Boughner	Buffalo
Joel Bouchard	Calgary
Uwe Krupp	Colorado
Chris Armstrong	Florida
J.J. Daigneault	NY Islanders
John Slaney	Phoenix
Al Iafrate	San Jose
Rob Zettler	Toronto

Forward:

Mike Sullivan	Boston
Jeff Daniels	Carolina
Greg Johnson	Chicago
Patrick Cote	Dallas
Doug Brown	Detroit
Doug Friedman	Edmonton

Denny Lambert   Ottawa
Craig Darby   Philadelphia
Tony Hrkac   Pittsburgh
Blair Atcheynum   St. Louis
Paul Brosseau   Tampa Bay
Scott Walker   Vancouver
Andrew Brunette   Washington

So, how good can the Predators be this season? Consider some of the other expansion team records in their first season. These are true expansion teams, excluding the WHA entries and the 1967-68 expansion when six new teams were added.

The best two expansion records came with the last two expansion teams, which is cause for optimism in Nashville, but the worst expansion record came just one season before, in Ottawa.

Florida did it with a stifling defence, which may or may not work anymore, what with the expected opening up of the game. Besides that, when the Panthers did it, it was relatively new. Now, nobody's fooled by it.

We won't know what kind of team the Predator's will ice, of course, until they actually get on it, but chances are with this management team, they're not going to be the worst.

First Season Expansion Records

	Year	W	L	T	Pts	%
Florida	1993-94	33	34	17	83	.494
Anaheim	1993-94	33	46	5	71	.423
Atlanta (Cgy)	1972-73	25	38	15	65	.417
Buffalo	1970-71	24	39	15	63	.404
Vancouver	1970-71	24	46	8	56	.359
Tampa Bay	1992-93	23	54	7	53	.315
Kansas City (NJ)	1974-75	15	54	11	41	.256
San Jose	1991-92	17	58	5	39	.244

| NY Islanders | 1972-73 | 12 | 60 | 6 | 30 | .192 |
| Ottawa | 1992-93 | 10 | 70 | 4 | 24 | .143 |

TEAM PREVIEW

GOAL: Mike Dunham looks to be the number one man, after years of sitting on the bench watching Martin Brodeur. That's got to be worth something in itself.

Mikael Shtalenkov will battle it out for the backup job with probably Fredrik Chabot, but Dominic Roussel, who has NHL experience, might make a run for it, too.

As good as Dunham's numbers were in New Jersey, it's important not to forget that the Devils were one of the best defensive teams in the league. Nashville will be one of the worst.

Hockey Annual Rating: 27 of 27

DEFENCE: They're all fifth and sixth defencemen on most teams, but at least they're not all seventh or eighth defencemen. Each one of them can contribute in their own way, which would probably be valuable contributions to teams that didn't need them to do more.

Bob Boughner is an enforcer who played regularly for Buffalo; J.J. Daigneault is an offensive threat, who has played regularly for just about everyone; Rob Zettler, Jayson More, and Joel Bouchard are defensive defencemen; while Jan Vopat and Chris Armstrong give them some depth or some players to put on the minor league team for emergencies. And there should be a lot of those.

Hockey Annual Rating: 27 of 27

FORWARD: Let's play, make out the lineup for the first game.

Naturally, a lot depends on moves made after this publication date, and how things go in training camp, but we can do some guestimating.

The first line: Darren Turcotte-Greg Johnson-Blair Atcheynum. Turcotte is coming off a non-existent season, at least he hopes it was. He's shown he can score in the past, though, and with the added responsibility will do better than 12 goals and six assists. He's also a centre, but the Predators are loaded at that position. Greg Johnson had a decent season in Chicago, scoring 34 points on a team that hardly scored. Blair Atcheynum is a proven minor league scorer who got his first taste of a full season last year in St. Louis. Not so much because he's a first line winger, but more that he can score better than the other right wingers.

The Second Line: Andrew Brunette-David Legwand-Sergei Krivokrasov. Don't know if the second draft pick overall, Legwand, will be in the lineup, but if he is, there's no point wasting him. Brunette is a scorer who just exploded last season for the Capitals. He was 11-12-23 in an 18-game stretch. Then he didn't score for three games, and then he hardly played. Strange, but he's got something to prove, no doubt. Krivokrasov is a checker, but he might help out with two offensive-minded players.

The Third line: Denny Lambert-Tom Fitzgerald-and...?. This could be a legitimate third line. Tom Fitzgerald was named team captain immediately after signing with the Predators as a free agent. Lambert is a tough guy character player.

The Fourth Line. Choose one left winger: Ville Peltonen, Patrick Cote, or Doug Friedman. Cote is the toughest of the bunch, Friedman the most tenacious checker and Peltonen the most scoring promise. Choose one centre: Sebastien Bordeleau, Craig Darby, Jim Dowd and Scott Walker. Walker is a fan-

favorite type player which could be enough reason to give him the edge, Dowd is the biggest scoring threat. Choose one right winger: tough guy Jeff Daniels, Paul Brosseau or Vitali Yachmenev, who scored a whole bunch of points when he played on a line with Wayne Gretzky and scored almost nothing when he didn't.

The Predators have some bodies to choose from, so nobody needs to get their spot by default. It should be an exciting training camp seeing who gets the jobs.

There are a whole lot of hard-working character players in this lineup, more than some established teams. It doesn't appear they're going to lose because they don't give it a full effort. They'll lose more likely because goals aren't going to be easy to come by.

Hockey Annual Rating: 27 of 27

SPECIAL TEAMS: The power play doesn't look promising, even a little bit, their penalty killing does with all the defensive-type players they have. In fact, it should be better than average, which may be the only thing better than average on the Predators.

COACHING AND MANAGEMENT: David Poile gives the Predators a first rate NHL general manager. Before the season even started, he was their MVP. He may well be at the end of the season, as well.

Barry Trotz is the first coach of Nashville. He hasn't coached in the NHL before but he has an impressive minor league resume with a boatload of success, which should come in handy if you figure the Predators are going to be minor league for a while.

Trotz is young (36) and Poile knows him well from his days as coach in the Washington farm system.

Hockey Annual Rating: 11 of 27

DRAFT

Round	Sel.	Player	Pos	Team
1	2	David Legwand	C	Plymouth (OHL)
3	60	Denis Arhipov	W	Russia
3	85	Geoff Koch	LW	Michigan (CCHA)
4	88	Kent Sauer	D	North Iowa (USHL)
5	138	Martin Beauchesne	D	Sherbrooke (QMJHL)
6	147	Craig Brunel	RW	Prince Albert (WHL)
8	202	Martin Bartek	LW	Sherbrooke (QMJHL)
9	229	Karlis Skrastins	D	Finland

The Predators traded up because they wanted David Legwand so badly. There's no reason to think he won't be in the lineup this year. How well he'll do is another story.

PROGNOSIS: Of course they're going to finish in last place, both in the Western Conference and overall. That's what expansion teams are supposed to do.

PREDICTION
Western Conference: 13th
Overall: 27th

Phoenix Coyotes

Trying to find a team identity for the Coyotes is difficult. They don't stand out statistically in a positive or negative way from the rest of the league.

When you think Coyotes, the best you can do is think that they have a lot of individual stars: Keith Tkachuk, Nikolai Khabibulin, Oleg Tverdovsky and Jeremy Roenick. And older stars from another time, Rick Tocchet and Mike Gartner (last year).

You might also think of the Coyotes in terms of having more than their share of talkative gentlemen, namely Tkachuk and Roenick, but nothing really stands out on the ice.

It might be a team you'd want to go see, but it isn't a team that you would expect to lose or win a lot or a little.

In terms of stats, they've about average right across the board. In fact, they were the only team in the league that finished at exactly .500.

Nobody's saying it's important to have an identity, because what difference does it make as long as they win. It's just that most teams have one. Go on, pick a team.

Edmonton? A lot of speed and mobile defence.

Dallas? All-round team that plays outstanding defence, yet can score a lot of goals.

Buffalo? Everything dependant on Hasek.

And so on and so on.

But, guess what? The Coyotes may be a team about to establish their very own identity. Heck, they may even be modern-day hockey (as in the last 10 years) pioneers.

It looks as if the Coyotes are about to turn to a rather unique way of playing hockey in today's NHL. They're going to try scoring goals.

It starts with the defence, after the signing of free agent Jyrki Lumme. Consider the offensive output and potential of their top six defencemen.

Diduck is a defensive defenceman, but even 18 points was pretty good in the low-scoring NHL last season. With Tverdovsky back on track, and Quint pressured to show his offensive side, this should be one of the highest scoring defences in the league.

	1997-98	Career Best
Teppo Numminen	11-40-51	11-43-54
Oleg Tverdovsky	7-12-19 (47 gms.)	10-45-55
Jyrki Lumme	9-21-30	13-42-55
Deron Quint	4-7-11 (32 gms,)	5-13-18 (29-60-89 in jr.)

Keith Carney	3-19-22	3-19-22
Gerald Diduck	8-10-18	11-21-32

It doesn't stop there. At forward, the Coyotes are looking to put together three scoring lines and one checking line. If some teams could put out one scoring line last year they were doing well. The Coyotes don't have three scoring lines yet, mind you, but they have three scoring centres in Roenick, Cliff Ronning and rookie Daniel Briere. That would dictate the way they intend to play, because it wouldn't make much sense to have scorers doing the checking.

The Coyotes defence isn't going to win any defensive awards, although they have a number of defensive forwards, so it makes sense to go for the goals at the other end and try to outscore the opposition. With some of the players they have there, a disciplined defensive style doesn't make sense, just because it would require a total team committment. Why not just let 'em loose?

So many teams have turned to defence-first, that one team playing a different brand of hockey may just work. It may be shoot-the-lights out hockey in Phoenix this year.

STUFF

* The Coyotes scored six goals in a game six times last year, all for wins. In their next game, in each case, they scored exactly two goals, and lost them all.
* The Coyotes scored the second fewest goals

in team history and allowed the fewest, but that was more because of the style of play in the NHL last season.

* Teppo Numminen is the only NHL defenceman to play every single regular season game since the start of the 1996-97 season.

TEAM PREVIEW

GOAL: Nikolai Khabibulin wasn't up to miracles last season, in the regular season or playoffs. Instead, he was just adequate. In fact, he was outplayed by Jimmy Waite in the playoffs.

Waite became an unrestricted free agent, so it may be up to prospect Scott Langkow to back up Khabibulin.

Hockey Annual Rating: 15 of 27

DEFENCE: They may not be all that adept defensively, but there isn't a team in the league that can match this defence group offensively.

The big five is Numminen, Tverdovsky, newcomer free agent signee Lumme, Carney, and Diduck. Deron Quint has to step up and show he belongs in the NHL as an offensive source. And there's always Michel Petit, but he'll probably play with four or five teams this season before he's finished.

You can figure on Tverdovsky stepping back up to the forefront of offensive defencemen after a season of holdouts and injuries. In the playoffs, he had seven points in six games, which is more his style.

GOALTENDER	GPI	MINS	AVG	W	L	T	EN	SO	GA	SA	SV %
JIM WAITE	17	793	2.12	5	6	1	1	1	28	322	.913
N. KHABIBULIN	70	4026	2.74	30	28	10	4	4	184	1835	.900
SCOTT LANGKOW	3	137	4.38	0	1	1	0	0	10	60	.833
PHO TOTALS	82	4985	2.73	35	35	12	5	5	227	2222	.898

Gone from the team are Murray Baron (free agency) and Norm MacIver (free agency).

The major prospects are tough-guy Jason Doig (153 PIM in 46 games at Springfield) Dan Focht, another big tough guy, and yet another roughnik, Sean Gagnon (330 PIM in 54 games for Springfield).

There might be some grumbling about the defensive play of the Phoenix defence, but there will be less if they're scoring goals and winning.

Hockey Annual Rating: 13 of 27

FORWARD: Keith Tkachuk whines about pretty much everything, but he may have had a point when he expressed his displeasure at the trading of his centre, Craig Janney, to Tampa Bay for a bag of pucks and utility player Louie DeBrusk. Part of the reason was to lighten the payroll up so that they could pay Tkachuk. Do you think he understands that at all?

If he doesn't like it, maybe he could bust a bunch of chairs or something.

If not, he could go ask Jeremy Roenick, another outspoken whiner, who after years in hibernation, almost played as well as he talked last season.

But to be fair to both of them, some of the stuff they say gets blown way out of proportion and reaches the ridiculous stage. And because the media knows those guys will respond, they get asked a lot of stuff.

In any event, Tkachuk is one of the more valuable players in the league, so the Coyotes have to sign him.

Janney isn't a big loss because the Coyotes already have a playmaking centre in Ronning, and with Roenick there too, they have to make

room for possible rookie sensation Daniel Briere.

With Bob Corkum an excellent defensive centre, they're set at that position, but everywhere else they're awfully thin. Tkachuk and Rick Tocchet are the prime wingers and you can count on Jim Cummins taking the enforcer role.

It just leaves a whole pile of wingers who may or may not score, or have yet to prove themselves. Mike Gartner is gone to free agency and possible retirement, but he could still score on occasion. After the players already mentioned the top scorer was Dallas Drake and he had just 11 goals. After that, it goes down to single digits.

Youngsters Brad Isbister, Shane Doan, and Yuha Ylonen will have to step up a notch whether they're ready or not. Then, you have to choose among J.F. Jomphe, Louie DeBrusk, and defensive forwards Mike Sullivan, Jocelyn Lemieux and Mike Stapleton.

In order for the Coyotes forwards to be successful, there will have to be no surprises, and a lot of surprises. In other words, the veterans have to continue to do what they've been doing and the kids will have to do somthing they haven't.

Hockey Annual Rating: 15 of 27

SPECIAL TEAMS: The Coyotes are going to have to score a lot of goals on the power play this year to be successful because their offence is top-loaded, meaning they don't have good secondary scoring. They certainly have the potential to be good on the powerplay, as they showed in the playoffs when they were ranked first. They've got the snipers and they've got the point men.

Power Play	G	ATT	PCT
Overall	57	384	14.8% (14th NHL)
Home	28	197	14.2% (16th NHL)
Road	29	187	15.5% (T-9th NHL)

6 SHORT HANDED GOALS ALLOWED (6th NHL)

Penalty Killing	G	TSH	PCT
Overall	66	408	83.8% (21st NHL)
Home	33	199	83.4% (T-19th NHL)
Road	33	209	84.2% (16th NHL)

10 SHORT HANDED GOALS SCORED (T-13th NHL)

COYOTES SPECIAL TEAMS SCORING

Power play	G	A	PTS
NUMMINEN	6	16	22
RONNING	3	19	22
TKACHUK	11	10	21
ROENICK	6	14	20
TOCCHET	8	6	14
JANNEY	4	9	13
TVERDOVSKY	4	7	11
GARTNER	4	3	7
SLANEY	1	6	7
QUINT	1	5	6
DRAKE	3	1	4
STAPLETON	1	2	3
CARNEY	1	2	3
PETIT	1	1	2
ISBISTER	1	1	2
MACIVER	0	2	2
LEMIEUX	1	0	1
DIDUCK	1	0	1
DOAN	0	1	1

Short handed	G	A	PTS
CORKUM	5	1	6
ROENICK	1	2	3
CARNEY	1	2	3
YLONEN	1	1	2
NUMMINEN	0	2	2
STAPLETON	1	0	1
MACIVER	1	0	1
TKACHUK	0	1	1
DRAKE	0	1	1
DIDUCK	0	1	1

COACHING AND MANAGEMENT: Phoenix GM Bobby Smith is committed to winning, committed to fiscal responsibility and committed to doing things his way. So far, so good, and he's made some good deals.

Don't ask for a lot of loyalty from Smith. The first chance players get, they skip town for a better deal anyway, so Smith won't be dragged down by sentimental reasons. If a move helps the team he makes it.

Sometimes chemistry can be as important as anything for a hockey team, and it's not clear whether Smith recognizes that to the extent that he needs to.

Coach Jim Schoenfeld has his work cut out for him, because this doesn't appear to be a disciplined hockey team. He's certainly not intimidated by any star players and will do his best to get the best. Whether that's good enough or not remains to be seen.

Hockey Annual Rating: 18 of 27

DRAFT

Round	Sel.	Player	Pos	Team
1	14	Patrick DesRochers	G	Sarnia (OHL)
2	43	Ossi Vaananen	D	Finland
3	73	Pat O'Leary	C	Armstrong H.S. (USHS)
4	100	Ryan Vanbuskirk	D	Sarnia (OHL)

5	115	Jay Leach	C	Providence (HE)
5	116	Josh Blackburn	G	Lincoln (USHL)
5	129	Ryan Schnabel	D	Red Deer (WHL)
6	160	Rickard Wallin	C	Sweden
7	187	Erik Westrum	C	Minnesota (WCHA)
8	214	Justin Hansen	RW	Moose Jaw (WHL)

Patrick DesRochers was the top rated goalie in the draft and the first selected. The Coyotes need some depth at this position because they have none.

PROGNOSIS: You wouldn't want to be betting a lot of money on the Coyotes this year because too much has to go right for them to win. But, it was the same deal last year and they were a .500 club. If the power play works and the rest of the team piles in the goals, they could move up the ladder. It doesn't appear as if they'd move down the ladder, but they could stay in the middle of the ladder

PREDICTION
Western Conference: 7th
Overall: 16th

STAT SECTION
Team Scoring Stats

	GP	G	A	PTS	+/-	PIM	SH	CAREER Gm	G	A	Pts
KEITH TKACHUK	69	40	26	66	9	147	232	458	236	205	441
JEREMY ROENICK	79	24	32	56	5	103	182	675	330	401	731
CLIFF RONNING	80	11	44	55	5	36	197	695	196	363	559
CRAIG JANNEY	68	10	43	53	5	12	72	704	183	541	724
T. NUMMINEN	82	11	40	51	25	30	126	711	66	277	343
RICK TOCCHET	68	26	19	45	1	157	161	909	385	436	821
DALLAS DRAKE	60	11	29	40	17	71	112	369	86	139	225
MIKE GARTNER	60	12	15	27	4-	24	145	1,432	708	627	1,335
KEITH CARNEY	80	3	19	22	2-	91	71	342	18	62	80
BOB CORKUM	76	12	9	21	7-	28	105	448	73	75	148
O. TVERDOVSKY	46	7	12	19	1	12	83	248	27	89	116
GERALD DIDUCK	78	8	10	18	14	118	104	848	56	151	207
BRAD ISBISTER	66	9	8	17	4	102	115	66	9	8	17
JOHN SLANEY	55	3	14	17	3-	24	74	188	19	51	70
D. SHANNON	58	2	12	14	4	26	57	506	87	163	250
MARK JANSSENS	74	5	7	12	21-	154	53	587	39	67	106
JUHA YLONEN	55	1	11	12	3-	10	60	57	1	11	12

SHANE DOAN	33	5	6	11	3-	35	42	170	16	24	40
DERON QUINT	32	4	7	11	6-	16	61	110	12	31	43
MIKE STAPLETON	64	5	5	10	4-	36	69	507	50	84	134
NORM MACIVER	41	2	6	8	11-	38	37	500	55	230	285
JIM MCKENZIE	64	3	4	7	7-	146	35	489	29	25	54
MICHEL PETIT	32	4	2	6	4-	77	34	827	90	238	328
J. LEMIEUX	30	3	3	6	0	27	32	598	80	84	164
MURRAY BARON	45	1	5	6	10-	106	23	525	24	55	79
JIM JOHNSON	16	2	1	3	0	18	17	829	29	166	195
N. KHABIBULIN	70	0	2	2	0	22	0	goalie			
JIM CUMMINS	75	0	2	2	16-	225	43	263	14	16	30
DANIEL BRIERE	5	1	0	1	1	2	4	5	1	0	1
JASON DOIG	4	0	1	1	4-	12	1	19	1	2	3
SEAN GAGNON	5	0	1	1	1	14	3	5	0	1	1
JEFF CHRISTIAN	1	0	0	0	1-	0	0	18	2	2	4
BRAD TILEY	1	0	0	0	1	0	0	1	0	0	0
SCOTT LEVINS	2	0	0	0	1-	5	2	124	13	20	33
S. LANGKOW	3	0	0	0	0	0	0	goalie			
JIM WAITE	17	0	0	0	0	2	0	goalie			

* Team Rankings 1997-98 (previous year's ranking in parenthesis)

		Conference Rank	League Rank
Record	35-35-12	6 (5)	14 (11)
Home	19-16-6	7 (11)	12 (16)
Away	16-19-6	7 (3)	15 (5)
Versus Own Conference	28-22-6	6 (3)	11 (6)
Versus Other Conference	7-13-6	12 (9)	22 (17)
Team Plus\Minus	+6	5 (9)	11 (19)
Goals For	224	6 (9)	10 (11)
Goals Against	227	9 (8)	19 (15)
Average Shots For	27.7	6 (6)	11 (11)
Average Shots Against	27.1	6 (9)	12 (17)
Overtime	0-2-12	10 (6)	23 (8)
One Goal Games	13-12	9 (4)	15 (9)
Times outshooting opponent	41	7 (8)	12 (16)
Versus Teams Over .500	12-21-8	8 (8)	16 (18)
Versus Teams .500 or Under	23-14-4	5 (5)	11 (10)
First Half Record	18-16-7	5 (7)	10 (11)
Second Half Record	17-19-5	8 (7)	17 (11)

PLAYOFFS

Results: lost 4-2 to Detroit in Conference quarter-finals

Record: 2-4

Home: 1-2

Away: 1-2   Overtime: 0-0

Goals For: 18 (3.0/game)   Power play: 18.2% (1st)

Goals Against: 24 (4.0/game)   Penalty Killing: 83.3% (11th)

	GP	G	A	PTS	+/-	PIM	PP	SH	GW	OT	S
RICK TOCCHET	6	6	2	8	0	25	3	0	0	0	12
JEREMY ROENICK	6	5	3	8	1-	4	2	2	2	0	20
O. TVERDOVSKY	6	0	7	7	2-	0	0	0	0	0	7
KEITH TKACHUK	6	3	3	6	1-	10	0	0	0	0	24
CLIFF RONNING	6	1	3	4	1-	4	0	0	0	0	17
CRAIG JANNEY	6	0	3	3	2-	0	0	0	0	0	6
MURRAY BARON	6	0	2	2	2	6	0	0	0	0	4
GERALD DIDUCK	6	0	2	2	4-	20	0	0	0	0	14
MIKE GARTNER	5	1	0	1	2-	18	1	0	0	0	11
BOB CORKUM	6	1	0	1	3-	4	0	0	0	0	3
SHANE DOAN	6	1	0	1	2-	6	0	0	0	0	7
DALLAS DRAKE	4	0	1	1	4-	2	0	0	0	0	4
N. KHABIBULIN	4	0	1	1	0	0	0	0	0	0	0
DARRIN SHANNON	5	0	1	1	1-	4	0	0	0	0	2
NORM MACIVER	6	0	1	1	0	2	0	0	0	0	6
MARK JANSSENS	1	0	0	0	0	2	0	0	0	0	0
JIM MCKENZIE	1	0	0	0	0	0	0	0	0	0	0
T. NUMMINEN	1	0	0	0	0	0	0	0	0	0	0
JIM CUMMINS	3	0	0	0	0	4	0	0	0	0	2
JIM WAITE	4	0	0	0	0	0	0	0	0	0	0
MICHEL PETIT	5	0	0	0	1-	8	0	0	0	0	4
BRAD ISBISTER	5	0	0	0	1-	2	0	0	0	0	6
MIKE STAPLETON	6	0	0	0	0	2	0	0	0	0	5
KEITH CARNEY	6	0	0	0	3-	4	0	0	0	0	2

GOALTENDER	GPI	MINS	AVG	W	L	EN	SO	GA	SA	SV %
JIM WAITE	4	171	3.86	0	3	0	0	11	97	.887
N. KHABIBULIN	4	185	4.22	2	1	0	0	13	106	.877
PHO TOTALS	6	360	4.00	2	4	0	0	24	203	.882

All-Time Leaders
Goals
Dale Hawerchuk	379
Thomas Steen	259
Paul MacLean	248

Assists
Dale Hawerchuk	550
Thomas Steen	543
Teppo Numminen	277

Points
Dale Hawerchuk	929
Thomas Steen	802
Paul MacLean	518

Best Individual Seasons
Goals
Teemu Selanne	1992-93	76
Dale Hawerchuk	1984-85	53
Keith Tkachuk	1996-97	52

Assists
Phil Housley	1992-93	79
Dale Hawerchuk	1987-88	77
Dale Hawerchuk	1984-85	77

Points
Teemu Selanne	1992-93	132
Dale Hawerchuk	1984-85	130
Dale Hawerchuk	1987-88	121

TEAM
Last 3 years
	GP	W	L	T	Pts	%
1997-98	82	35	35	12	82	.500
1996-97	82	38	37	7	83	.506
1995-96	82	36	40	6	78	.476

Best 3 regular seasons
	GP	W	L	T	Pts	%
1984-85	80	43	27	10	96	.600
1986-87	80	40	32	8	88	.550
1989-90	80	37	32	11	85	.531

Worst 3 regular seasons
	GP	W	L	T	Pts	%
1980-81	80	9	57	14	32	.200
1979-89	80	20	49	11	51	.319
1993-94	84	24	51	9	57	.339

Most Goals (min. 70 game schedule)
1984-85	358
1983-84	340
1992-93	322

Fewest Goals (min. 70 game schedule)
1979-80	214
1988-89	224
1996-97	240

Most Goals Against (min. 70 game schedule)
1980-81	400
1983-84	374
1985-86	372

Fewest Goals Against (min. 70 game schedule)
1997-98	227
1996-97	243
1991-92	244

San Jose Sharks

Dean Lombardi doesn't get enough credit for the job he's done in San Jose. After the previous regime dragged the Sharks to the bottom, he's come on and made all the right moves to slowly transform this franchise from weakling losers to almost-winners.

The Sharks improved by seven wins for the second year in a row, all of it orchestrated from the top. Starting basically from scratch, Lombardi didn't use the common excuses that rebuilders use. He just did it.

He went about making the team a winner through brilliant manouvering and trading, and by making chemistry a priority. He acquired unselfish seasoned veterans with heart who were hungry for team success, and made it an atmosphere where his younger players could learn the game at the NHL level and still be successful.

He's got a team full of character and he's got four of the brightest young stars or prospects in the game: Jeff Friesen, Patrick Marleau, Andrei Zuyzin and Marco Sturm. All except Friesen were drafted by Lombardi, a marked improvement from the fruitless scouting missions of old.

Then Lombardi selected a coach in Darryl Sutter who could draw the most out of the players. There's some whining about the way Sutter treats them, but a lot of this team are Sutter-like in attitude, and it's unlikely they're the ones doing the most grumbling.

There were a lot of teams in the stretch run that had a chance to make the playoffs. They faltered. Some of them just collapsed. The Sharks rose to the occasion because of the type of players they had. In the playoffs they gave the Dallas Stars a darn good run for their money, losing in six games on an overtime goal.

Let's consider the stretch runs for those teams in the running in the Western Conference so we can see how much team character was responsible. On March 26, just after the trading deadline, the Sharks were three points out of a playoff spot and five points behind Chicago. They were also just four points ahead of Toronto, Calgary, and Anaheim, and just six ahead of Vancouver. The Sharks blew them all out of the water. It wasn't even close.

San Jose	7-2-3 in their last 12 games.
Calgary	2-6-2 in their last 10 games.
Chicago	2-9-1 in their last 12 games.

Toronto   6-10-1 in their last 17 games
Anaheim   2-7-2 in their last 11 games.
Vancouver   3-9-1 in their last 13 games.

STUFF

* 34 victories were one more than their previous team high of 33 in 1993-94.
* the penalty killing percentage of 85.3 was the best in team history.
* scored the fewest goals in team history by one (210) but allowed the fewest goals in team history (219) by 489.
* Jeff Friesen's 31 goals tied the team record, held by Owen Nolan.
* Friesen became the team's all-time leading goal scorer, passing Pat Falloon and Owen Nolan.
* were 17-19-5 at home and 17-19-5 on the road.

TEAM PREVIEW

GOAL: The Sharks will go into the season with Mike Vernon and backup Steve Shields, who was obtained from Buffalo, where he had a good view of the best goalie in the game from the end of the bench.

Even if the Sharks go with those two, it's likely that somebody else will play about 10 games. San Jose needs to expose someone in next year's expansion draft, who has played at least 10 games this season, and a couple seconds here and there doesn't count as a game.

That might make some sense in order to give the expansion team something to choose, but maybe it cuts into the integrity of the game if a club has to play a goalie for just that reason.

Kelly Hrudey became an unrestricted free agent at the end of the season. He had a terrible win-loss record, but it wasn't completely his fault. In 10 of his starts, the Sharks scored 0 or 1 goal.

Hockey Annual Rating: 19 of 27

DEFENCE: Only three teams allowed fewer shots on net per game than San Jose.

Fewest Shots Allowed:
Dallas   22.8
New Jersey   23.7
St. Louis   24.1
SAN JOSE   24.6
League Ave.   27.3

That's not just the result of the defencemen, it's the result of total team defence, which includes the forwards. Any defence is going to be better if the forwards do their job, and they did.

Bryan Marchment was a great late-season acquisition because the Sharks lacked that kind of toughness from their rearguards. Marty McSorley could give it to them, but he had been reduced to sitting out games and became

GOALTENDER	GPI	MINS	AVG	W	L	T	EN	SO	GA	SA	SV %
MIKE VERNON	62	3564	2.46	30	22	8	2	5	146	1401	.896
KELLY HRUDEY	28	1360	2.74	4	16	2	4	1	62	600	.897
JASON MUZZATTI	1	27	4.44	0	0	0	0	0	2	13	.846
S.J TOTALS	82	4973	2.61	34	38	10	6	7	216	2020	.893

KELLY HRUDEY and MIKE VERNON shared a shutout vs CGY on Apr 7, 1998

an unrestricted free agent after the season ended. Marchment recorded 27 hits in 12 games, which pro-rates to 185 in an 82-game schedule, or better yet, 128 more than any other Shark rearguard earned last year.

Free agent acquisition Gary Suter is going to be a help on the power play where he'll join offensive-minded Bill Houlder and Andrei Zyuzin. Zyuzin is a tremendous talent. Let's repeat that - absolutely tremendous.

Marcus Ragnarsson, Mike Rathje fill out the top six, so additions will be made, probably veterans while they wait for their prospects to develop further. They had Ken Sutton, who rarely played, and Al Iafrate who rarely wasn't injured. Iafrate was selected by Nashville in the expansion draft.

Hockey Annual Rating: 9 of 27

FORWARD: The Sharks are going to have to fill in some missing pieces on the forward line. John MacLean, Murray Craven, Bernie Nicholls, and Dave Lowry all became free agents at season end.

But, pieces they'll just be, because the Sharks have a great nucleus at forward, starting with Jeff Friesen. His 31 goals were equivalent to a 50-goal season when goals were easier to come by in the NHL. He's also darn close to being an all-star.

Owen Nolan only scored 14 goals last season, so there's room for him to improve, while Patrick Marleau and Marco Sturm are just getting started.

Mike Ricci, Stephane Matteau, Shawn Burr, Joe Murphy, Ron Sutter, Murray Craven and Tony Granato are all expected back.

The Sharks could use an enforcer, mostly

because they don't have one, unless you count Todd Ewen, who missed all last season with injuries.

Whatever players the Sharks pick up, you can bet they'll have heart, determination, and be willing to sacrifice for the team.

Hockey Annual Rating: 13 of 27

SPECIAL TEAMS: Friesen led the team with seven power play goals. So, guess who was second in special team goals. Well, uh, that's Friesen, too. He scored six shorthanded goals to tie John MacLean for second.

The Sharks signed free agent Gary Suter to help with their power play. A top point man will go a long way in making everyone else better. Suter had 23 power play points for Chicago, although their power play was even worse than the Sharks.

Last year, special teams didn't help San Jose and didn't hurt them. They were even with 49 net power play goals (54 power play goals less 5 shorthanded against) and 49 net power play goals against.

Power Play	G	ATT	PCT
Overall	54	400	13.5% (16th NHL)
Home	26	219	11.9% (22nd NHL)
Road	28	181	15.5% (T-9th NHL)

5 SHORT HANDED GOALS ALLOWED (T-4th NHL)

Penalty Killing	G	TSH	PCT
Overall	59	398	85.2% (T-12th NHL)
Home	32	191	83.2% (21st NHL)
Road	27	207	87.0% (6th NHL)

10 SHORT HANDED GOALS SCORED (T-13th NHL)

SHARKS SPECIAL TEAMS SCORING

Power play	G	A	PTS
FRIESEN	7	14	21
HOULDER	4	12	16
MACLEAN	6	9	15
NOLAN	3	10	13
RICCI	5	5	10
RAGNARSSON	3	7	10
NICHOLLS	3	6	9
MURPHY	4	3	7
MARLEAU	1	6	7
STURM	2	4	6
CRAVEN	2	3	5
GRANATO	3	1	4
ZYUZIN	2	2	4
IAFRATE	2	2	4
MARCHMENT	0	4	4
RATHJE	1	1	2
BRENNAN	1	1	2
MATTEAU	1	0	1
KOROLYUK	1	0	1
GUOLLA	0	1	1

Short handed	G	A	PTS
FRIESEN	6	1	7
NOLAN	1	4	5
CRAVEN	3	0	3
MARCHMENT	0	2	2
RAGNARSSON	0	1	1
MCSORLEY	0	1	1
MACLEAN	0	1	1
IAFRATE	0	1	1
HOULDER	0	1	1

COACHING AND MANAGEMENT: Not everybody likes coach Darryl Sutter. Todd Gill said he "treated us like dogs," after he was traded. He suggested Sutter verbally abused the players and was sarcastic in the way he talked to them.

Now, teams are fickle when it comes to coaches. If the coach is too tough, they think they need more of a player's coach. If the team is too soft, they need someone to crack the whip.

So, which is better? There seems to be a correlation between how poorly a coach treats the players and how much they win. In other words, the worse he treats them the better they play. But, there's always the danger of players rebelling and not playing well so that the coach gets fired.

Whatever works. In this case, Sutter's method worked, and he'll be back to make it work again. And there wasn't a lot of grumbling from the other players. In fact, it was the reverse.

GM Lombardi, whose virtues were praised in the opening, is close to being one of the best general managers in the game.

Hockey Annual Rating: 6 of 27

DRAFT

Round	Sel.	Player	Pos	Team
1	3	Brad Stuart	D	Regina (WHL)
2	29	Jonathan Cheechoo	RW	Belleville (OHL)
3	65	Eric LaPlante	LW	Halifax (QMJHL)
4	98	Rob Davison	D	North Bay (OHL)
4	104	Miroslav Zalesak	W	Slovakia
5	127	Brandon Coalter	LW	Oshawa (OHL)

The Sharks traded down one position to take Stuart, but you get the impression they were really trading up. He was the one they wanted, not David Legwand, who went number two.

Stuart is an all-round type defenceman, and it's amazing how rare those kind of players are. He's projected as a number one defenceman.

The Sharks second round pick has more than just a cool name. Jonathan Cheechoo, (Choo-choo Cheechoo?) seems to do everything well but skate. He only started playing hockey seriously at age 14, and last year scored 31-45-76 for Belleville in his rookie season in the OHL.

PROGNOSIS: The Sharks have some holes to fill, but they're not big ones. They should continue to improve, and it doesn't have to be by a whole lot. Slower but surer would be just fine, while the younger players and prospects continue to develop.

This team has a bright future, no matter what happens this season.

PREDICTION
Western Conference: 5th
Overall: 10th

STAT SECTION
Team Scoring Stats

	GP	G	A	PTS	+/-	PIM	SH	CAREER Gm	G	A	Pts
JEFF FRIESEN	79	31	32	63	8	40	186	288	89	107	196
JOHN MACLEAN	77	16	27	43	6-	42	213	985	360	373	733
OWEN NOLAN	75	14	27	41	2-	144	192	487	191	198	389
P. MARLEAU	74	13	19	32	5	14	90	74	13	19	32
BILL HOULDER	82	7	25	32	13	48	102	454	41	130	171
MARCO STURM	74	10	20	30	2-	40	118	74	10	20	30
S. MATTEAU	73	15	14	29	4	60	79	524	100	118	218
MURRAY CRAVEN	67	12	17	29	4	25	107	1,009	262	281	543
BERNIE NICHOLLS	60	6	22	28	4-	26	81	1,117	475	732	1,207
MIKE RICCI	65	9	18	27	4-	32	91	544	141	207	348
TONY GRANATO	59	16	9	25	3	70	119	630	232	226	458
M. RAGNARSSON	79	5	20	25	11-	65	91	219	16	65	81
JOE MURPHY	37	9	13	22	9	36	81	634	195	252	447
MIKE RATHJE	81	3	12	15	4-	59	61	228	6	43	49
ANDREI ZYUZIN	56	6	7	13	8	66	72	56	6	7	13
B. MARCHMENT	61	2	11	13	3-	144	56	478	25	84	109
SHAWN BURR	42	6	6	12	2	50	63	856	181	256	437
M. MCSORLEY	56	2	10	12	10	140	46	888	104	245	349
AL IAFRATE	21	2	7	9	1-	28	37	799	152	311	463
RON SUTTER	57	2	7	9	2-	22	57	935	196	314	510
DAVE LOWRY	57	4	4	8	1-	53	51	798	126	136	262

A. KOROLYUK	19	2	3	5	5-	6	23	19	2	3	5
R. BRENNAN	11	1	2	3	4-	2	24	13	1	2	3
S. GUOLLA	7	1	1	2	2-	0	9	50	14	9	23
MIKE VERNON	62	0	2	2	0	24	0	goalie			
BARRY POTOMSKI	9	0	1	1	1	30	4	68	6	5	11
N. ANDERSSON	5	0	0	0	1-	2	6	129	26	44	70
JASON MUZZATTI	7	0	0	0	0	10	0	goalie			
DODY WOOD	8	0	0	0	3-	40	4	106	8	10	18
KEN SUTTON	21	0	0	0	3-	21	12	303	21	69	90
KELLY HRUDEY	28	0	0	0	0	2	0	goalie			

* Team Rankings 1997-98 (previous year's ranking in parenthesis)

		Conference Rank	League Rank
Record	34-38-10	8 (13)	17 (25)
Home	17-19-5	9 (13)	16 (26)
Away	17-19-5	6 (10)	14 (23)
Versus Own Conference	25-26-5	8 (12)	15 (23)
Versus Other Conference	9-12-5	9 (13)	19 (26)
Team Plus\Minus	-1	8 (13)	15 (25)
Goals For	210	10 (13)	15 (26)
Goals Against	216	6 (13)	14 (24)
Average Shots For	26.5	12 (11)	19 (22)
Average Shots Against	24.6	3 (5)	4 (11)
Overtime	0-2-10	12 (3)	24 (5)
One Goal Games	12-10	8 (5)	12 (10)

Times outshooting opponent	47	3 (9)	7 (18)
Versus Teams Over .500	14-19-4	7 (10)	14 (21)
Versus Teams Under .500	20-19-6	10 (13)	20 (26)
First Half Record	15-21-5	8 (11)	18 (22)
Second Half Record	19-17-5	6 (13)	11 (25

PLAYOFFS

Results: lost 4-2 to Dallas

Record: 2-4

Home: 2-1

Away: 0-3

Goals For: 12 (2.0/game)

Goals Against: 16 (2.7/game)

Overtime: 1-1

Power play: 16.7% (4th)

Penalty Killing: 81.6% (13th)

	GP	G	A	PTS	+/-	PIM	PP	SH	GW	OT	S
JOHN MACLEAN	6	2	3	5	1	4	1	0	0	0	18
B. NICHOLLS	6	0	5	5	2-	8	0	0	0	0	6
OWEN NOLAN	6	2	2	4	1-	26	2	0	1	0	16
MIKE RICCI	6	1	3	4	0	6	0	0	0	0	8
BILL HOULDER	6	1	2	3	0	2	0	0	0	0	8
MURRAY CRAVEN	6	1	1	2	2-	0	0	0	0	0	6
JOE MURPHY	6	1	1	2	1-	20	1	0	0	0	10
AL IAFRATE	6	1	0	1	4-	10	1	0	0	0	10
RON SUTTER	6	1	0	1	1-	14	0	0	0	0	7
MIKE RATHJE	6	1	0	1	3-	6	1	0	0	0	2
ANDREI ZYUZIN	6	1	0	1	2-	14	0	0	1	1	6
S. MATTEAU	4	0	1	1	1	0	0	0	0	0	2
P. MARLEAU	5	0	1	1	1-	0	0	0	0	0	2
JEFF FRIESEN	6	0	1	1	1-	2	0	0	0	0	9
TONY GRANATO	1	0	0	0	0	0	0	0	0	0	2
KELLY HRUDEY	1	0	0	0	0	0	0	0	0	0	0
MARCO STURM	2	0	0	0	2-	0	0	0	0	0	3
SHAWN BURR	6	0	0	0	1-	8	0	0	0	0	4
DAVE LOWRY	6	0	0	0	0	18	0	0	0	0	3
B. MARCHMENT	6	0	0	0	1	10	0	0	0	0	5
MIKE VERNON	6	0	0	0	0	0	0	0	0	0	0
M. RAGNARSSON	6	0	0	0	2	4	0	0	0	0	4

GOALTENDER	GPI	MINS	AVG	W	L	EN	SO	GA	SA	SV %
MIKE VERNON	6	348	2.41	2	4	1	1	14	138	.899
KELLY HRUDEY	1	20	3.00	0	0	0	0	1	6	.833
S.J TOTALS	6	370	2.59	2	4	1	1	16	145	.890

All-Time Leaders
Goals
Jeff Friesen 89
Pat Falloon 76
Owen Nolan 74

Assists
Jeff Friesen 107
Owen Nolan 91
Pat Falloon 86

Points
Jeff Friesen 196
Owen Nolan 165
Pat Falloon 162

Best Individual Seasons
Goals
Jeff Friesen 1997-98 31
Owen Nolan 1996-97 31
Sergei Makarov 1993-94 30

Assists
Kelly Kisio 1992-93 52
Johan Garpenlov 1992-93 44
Todd Elik 1993-94 41

Points
Kelly Kisio 1992-93 78
Sergei Makarov 1993-94 68
Todd Elik 1993-94 66
Johan Garpenlov 1992-93 66

TEAM
Last 3 years

	GP	W	L	T	Pts	%
1997-98	82	34	38	10	78	.476
1996-97	82	27	48	8	62	.378
1995-96	82	20	55	7	47	.287

Best 3 regular seasons

	GP	W	L	T	Pts	%
1993-94	84	33	35	16	82	.488
1997-98	82	34	38	10	78	.476
1994-95	48	19	25	4	42	.438

Worst 3 regular seasons

	GP	W	L	T	Pts	%
1992-93	84	11	71	2	24	.143
1991-92	80	17	58	5	39	.244
1995-96	82	20	55	7	47	.287

Most Goals (min. 70 game schedule)
1995-96 252
1993-94 252
1991-92 219

Fewest Goals (min. 70 game schedule)
1997-98 210
1996-97 211
1992-93 218

Most Goals Against (min. 70 game schedule)
1992-93 414
1991-92 359
1995-96 357

Fewest Goals Against (min. 70 game schedule)
1997-98 216
1993-94 265
1996-97 278

St. Louis Blues

The Blues were one of the most improved teams in the NHL last season. They surprised everyone by going one game over .500 to two games under 100 points.

And they did it with smoke and mirrors. They were a poor team on paper, with only a few sure things. Players came out of nowhere to make major contributions. Pavol Demitra, Craig Conroy, Jim Campbell, Scott Pellerin and Blair Atcheynum all achieved more than the team could have even imagined.

The defence was dynamite, with two offensive stars, and another who emerged as one of the best defencemen in the league. With Joel Quenneville at the helm, they were able to come together as a team and as individual contributors.

There is a problem, though. It's not going to happen again this year. In fact, making the playoffs is not a certainty.

Hogwash you say? Consider.

* Brett Hull was lost to free agency. He may have slowed down (only 27 goals) but he was still their leading scorer. When the top scorer is eliminated from the mix, other ingredients tend to suffer as well.

* Coaches are usually most effective in their first full season. After that, unless they're Scotty Bowman, motivation tends to become repetitive and less effective, fewer players have something to prove (i.e. they've already shown the coach what they can do), and coaches themselves have less to prove.

* Steve Duchesne was lost to free agency and Los Angeles. Duchesne was only three points away from being the top scoring defenceman in the league, and led the Blues in power play points.

* Overachievers, and the Blues had a number of them, tend to underachieve the next season.

* Key players are getting older. That includes Geoff Courtnall (36), Al MacInnis (35) and Grant Fuhr (36). Despite what contracts may say, nobody can play forever and these three are already past the danger point.

* Goals will be harder to come by. Pierre Turgeon is mainly a playmaker, but who is he going to make the plays to? No Hull. No MacInnis.

* The Blues only have two-thirds of a first line. That's Turgeon and Courtnall. Most of the rest of the team are good third-liners.

* The Blues have some high-salaried players, which means it's difficult financially to get more high-salaried players. They didn't sign Hull or Duchesne, which would have sky-rock-

eted their budget, and they missed out on all the top free agents who were left.

* The power play is unlikely to be as good as last year, with two major members of that unit — Hull and Duchesne — no longer on the team.

* The Blues are going to need new players that come from nowhere. They managed to do that last year, but they may not be so lucky this time around.

* The plan is to build up the organization with good players that can move up to the NHL eventually. They're not at that stage yet.

STUFF

* Craig Conway was third in Selke Trophy voting for the league's best defensive forwards, behind Mike Peca and the winner, Jere Lehtinen.

* Joel Quenneville was named NHL Coach of the Year, by The Hockey News.

* Chris Pronger was named The Hockey News Defenseman of the Year.

* Pronger led the league with a +47. That was 12 better than the runner-up, Larry Murphy.

* a seven-game winning streak tied the team record.

TEAM PREVIEW

GOAL: Jamie McLelland proved to be quite a find. Signed as a free agent after bouncing around the minors for years and playing a few games here and there for the Islanders, he came up big for the Blues last season. Although he usually just spelled Fuhr, he did start nine games in a row when Fuhr was out, and the Blues won the first six of them.

Grant Fuhr once played 79 games in one season, an NHL record. With McLennan playing so well, he's going to have to be content with considerably less.

Hockey Annual Rating: 9 of 26

DEFENCE: This is a strength position for the Blues. Chris Pronger is one of the best overall in the league. Al Macinnis is still one of the best on the power play. Todd Gill and Marc Bergevin are experienced veterans, and Chris McAlpine is one of the top four defencemen on the Blues.

So, who's going to pick up the offensive slack provided by Duchesne? Don't look to Todd Gill, who exploded with 13 goals last year, a fluke. It's worth noting that the season before he had exactly zero goals. Pronger could spend more time on the power play without hurting the team much.

Maybe, it's time for Jamie Rivers to get it done. He's shown outstanding offensive ability everywhere but the NHL. In junior, he once had 89 assists and 121 points. In 77 NHL games, however, he is just 4-9-13. In the NHL getting

GOALTENDER	GPI	MINS	AVG	W	L	T	EN	SO	GA	SA	SV %
RICH PARENT	1	12	.00	0	0	0	0	0	0	1	1.000
JAMIE MCLENNAN	30	1658	2.17	16	8	2	1	2	60	618	.903
GRANT FUHR	58	3274	2.53	29	21	6	5	3	138	1354	.898
STL TOTALS	82	4970	2.46	45	29	8	6	5	204	1979	.897

points is a simple matter of getting on the power play and staying there for a while. If he gets that opportunity, his point totals will reflect it.

Even without Duchesne, the Blues have a good starting six.

After that, Rudy Poeschek can come out of the press box, or Rory Fitzpatrick.

Hockey Annual Rating: 7 of 27

FORWARD: Assuming the Blues will need to score goals after checking opposing teams to death, there could be a problem. An aging Courtnall and Turgeon are the only proven offensive players of note. Demitra has to prove he can do it for another year and then they'll have three offensive players of note. With the possible exception of Jim Campbell, the rest could play on a lot of teams third and fourth lines.

That's not to say they wouldn't be good in those roles. Craig Conroy established himself as a premier defensive forward; Kelly Chase and Tony Twist can dance with the best of them; and Scott Pellerin, Terry Yake, Pascal Rheaume and Mike Eastwood make contributions that aren't found on the scoreboard.

Others who could get work include proven minor league scorer, Michel Picard, and Chris Kenady. Michal Handzus could also get a look.

Let's look at where some of last year's key Blues forwards came from, besides nowhere.

Craig Conroy - a virtual throw-in in the big deal that brought the Blues Pierre Turgeon and Rory Fitzpatrick for Shayne Corson and Murray Baron. He's spent a lot of time in the minors, where he even did some scoring, before playing his first full season in the NHL.

Blair Atcheynum - a career minor-leaguer if there ever was one. Before last season, he had played 549 minor league games for nine different teams. His only NHL experience was four games for Ottawa in the 1992-93 season. Nashville picked him up in the expansion draft.

Pavol Demitra - an annual candidate for the Bruce Boudreau award, after some great minor league scoring and failed NHL attempts with Ottawa. You may not remember Boudreau. He was a guy for Toronto could shoot the lights out in the minors but couldn't get it done at the NHL level, despite a number of opportunities. Just when they were going to change the name to the Pavol Demitra Award, he came through with an excellent offensive season

Scott Pellerin - was gearing up for a run at the Pavol Demitra Award both with New Jersey and St. Louis farm teams. In his sixth pro season he finally got to spend the whole year in the NHL.

Hockey Annual Rating: 19 of 27

SPECIAL TEAMS: With MacInnis and Duchesne on the points and Hull and Turgeon up front, you would have thought the Blues power play would burn up the league. They have to find replacements for Duchesne and Hull, and they're not easily replaced.

Power Play	G	ATT	PCT
Overall	62	368	16.8% (T-9th NHL)
Home	38	201	18.9% (T-3rd NHL)
Road	24	167	14.4% (15th NHL)

4 SHORT HANDED GOALS ALLOWED (T-2nd NHL)

Penalty Killing	G	TSH	PCT
Overall	49	367	86.6% (T-5th NHL)
Home	25	189	86.8% (8th NHL)
Road	24	178	86.5% (8th NHL)

12 SHORT HANDED GOALS SCORED (T-7th NHL)

BLUES CURRENT SCORING STREAKS

Power play	G	A	PTS
DUCHESNE	5	24	29
MACINNIS	9	17	26
TURGEON	6	17	23
HULL	10	12	22
GILL	7	9	16
CAMPBELL	7	8	15
COURTNALL	6	8	14
DEMITRA	4	7	11
PRONGER	1	8	9
YAKE	3	3	6
TURCOTTE	3	1	4
RHEAUME	1	2	3
RIVERS	1	1	2
PELLERIN	1	0	1
ZABRANSKY	0	1	1
CONROY	0	1	1

Short handed	G	A	PTS
DEMITRA	4	0	4
CONROY	3	1	4
PELLERIN	1	2	3
MACINNIS	1	1	2
DUCHESNE	1	1	2
ATCHEYNUM	1	1	2
PRONGER	0	2	2
YAKE	1	0	1
TURGEON	0	1	1
TURCOTTE	0	1	1
HULL	0	1	1
BERGEVIN	0	1	1

COACHING AND MANAGEMENT: Joel Quenneville did a great job as coach, coaxing far more out of this team than he should have with a collection of mostly third and fourth liners. A bigger test will be this season when he has to coax more out of more third and fourth liners.

Larry Pleau has a plan to build the team all the way through the organization. That's a good plan, and the opposite of what the old St. Louis regime used to do. Those plans don't come together overnight, however, despite what the Blues accomplished last season. It's still a good plan, though.

Hockey Annual Rating: 10 of 27

DRAFT

Round	Sel.	Player	Pos	Team
1	24	Christian Backman	D	Sweden
2	41	Maxim Linnik	D	St. Thomas (WOJHL)
3	83	Matt Walker	D	Portland (WHL)
6	157	Brad Voth	RW	Medicine Hat (WHL)
6	170	Andrei Trachinsky	C	Kazakhstan
7	197	Brad Twordik	C	Brandon (WHL)
8	225	Yevgeny Pastukh	F	Russia
9	255	John Pohl	C	Minnesota (USHS)

Christian Backman is an offensive defenceman who can one day run the power play. He was projected to go as high as tenth in the draft, so the Blues got a bargain, or a bust.

PROGNOSIS: The Blues are a good bet to be the most disappointing team in the league. Read the opening to see all the reasons why.

The only hope is that Quenneville can continue his magic act. If he can make the bunnies keep jumping out of a hat, the Blues could slide into the playoffs.

Last year, they were fairly close to pulling off an upset, losing to Detroit in the conference semi-finals. They're not any closer this year, however.

PREDICTION
Western Conference: 8th
Overall: 19th

STAT SECTION
Team Scoring Stats

	GP	G	A	PTS	+/-	PIM	SH	CAREER Gm	G	A	Pts
BRETT HULL	66	27	45	72	1-	26	211	801	554	433	987
PIERRE TURGEON	60	22	46	68	13	24	140	810	291	566	857
G. COURTNALL	79	31	31	62	12	94	189	1,018	360	423	783
STEVE DUCHESNE	80	14	42	56	9	32	153	845	202	436	638
PAVOL DEMITRA	61	22	30	52	11	22	147	128	38	44	82
AL MACINNIS	71	19	30	49	6	80	227	1,060	270	733	1,003
CRAIG CONROY	81	14	29	43	20	46	118	155	21	40	61
JIM CAMPBELL	76	22	19	41	0	55	147	144	47	42	89
CHRIS PRONGER	81	9	27	36	47	180	145	362	37	103	140
TODD GILL	75	13	17	30	11-	41	122	793	72	248	320
SCOTT PELLERIN	80	8	21	29	14	62	96	186	28	43	71
B. ATCHEYNUM	61	11	15	26	5	10	103	65	11	16	27
TERRY YAKE	65	10	15	25	1	38	60	270	58	85	143
D. TURCOTTE	62	12	6	18	6	26	75	586	191	210	401
PASCAL RHEAUME	48	6	9	15	4	35	45	50	7	9	16
MIKE EASTWOOD	58	6	5	11	2-	22	38	322	39	58	97
CHRIS MCALPINE	54	3	7	10	14	36	35	93	3	10	13
MARC BERGEVIN	81	3	7	10	2-	90	40	859	30	114	144
MICHEL PICARD	16	1	8	9	3	29	19	112	16	27	43
RUDY POESCHEK	50	1	7	8	5-	64	29	336	6	25	31
KELLY CHASE	67	4	3	7	10	231	29	388	14	28	42
JAMIE RIVERS	59	2	4	6	5	36	53	77	4	9	13
TONY TWIST	60	1	1	2	4-	105	17	382	8	12	20
C. KENADY	5	0	2	2	1	0	3	5	0	2	2
GRANT FUHR	58	0	2	2	0	6	0	goalie			
LIBOR ZABRANSKY	6	0	1	1	3-	6	2	6	0	1	1
RICARD PERSSON	1	0	0	0	0	0	0	67	6	9	15
RICH PARENT	1	0	0	0	0	0	0	goalie			
JAMIE MCLENNAN	30	0	0	0	0	4	0	goalie			

* Team Rankings 1997-98 (previous year's ranking in parenthesis)

		Conference Rank	League Rank
Record	45-29-8	3 (6)	4 (12)
Home	26-10-5	3 (10)	4 (21)
Away	19-19-3	4 (4)	8 (6)
Versus Own Conference	32-20-4	2 (4)	3 (10)
Versus Other Conference	13-9-4	4 (8)	5 (16)
Team Plus\Minus	+39	2 (6)	2 (11)
Goals For	256	1 (8)	1 (14)
Goals Against	204	4 (6)	11 (13)
Average Shots For	26.9	8 (8)	15 (15)
Average Shots Against	24.1	2 (3)	3 (7)
Overtime	2-2-8	7 (7)	14 (13)
One Goal Games	15-11	3 (3)	7 (7)
Times outshooting opponent	47	3 (5)	7 (9)

Versus Teams Over .500	19-12-5	2 (7)	3 (13)
Versus Teams .500 or under	26-17-3	6 (7)	12 (13)
First Half Record	22-13-6	4 (7)	6 (14)
Second Half Record	23-16-2	4 (5)	6 (8)

PLAYOFFS

Results: defeated Los Angeles 4-0 in conference quarter-finals
lost to Detroit in conference semi-finals
Record: 6-4
Home: 2-3
Away: 4-1
Goals For: 29 (2.9/game)
Goals Against: 31 (3.1/game)
Overtime: 0-1
Power play: 17.3% (3rd)
Penalty Killing: 89.9% (2nd)

	GP	G	A	PTS	+/-	PIM	PP	SH	GW	OT	S
JIM CAMPBELL	10	7	3	10	1-	12	4	0	2	0	23
G. COURTNALL	10	2	8	10	2-	18	1	0	0	0	24
CHRIS PRONGER	10	1	9	10	2-	26	0	0	0	0	24
PIERRE TURGEON	10	4	4	8	5-	2	2	0	0	0	27
AL MACINNIS	8	2	6	8	1	12	1	0	0	0	27
BRETT HULL	10	3	3	6	3-	2	1	0	1	0	32
PAVOL DEMITRA	10	3	3	6	3-	2	0	0	0	0	32
TODD GILL	10	2	2	4	3-	10	1	1	0	0	16
PASCAL RHEAUME	10	1	3	4	0	8	1	0	0	0	10
STEVE DUCHESNE	10	0	4	4	8-	6	0	0	0	0	28
TERRY YAKE	10	2	1	3	3-	6	2	0	1	0	6
CRAIG CONROY	10	1	2	3	1-	8	0	0	1	0	17

SCOTT PELLERIN	10	0	2	2	1	10	0	0	0	0	10
MIKE EASTWOOD	3	1	0	1	1-	0	0	0	1	0	4
MARC BERGEVIN	10	0	1	1	1-	8	0	0	0	0	6
GRANT FUHR	10	0	1	1	0	2	0	0	0	0	0
JAMIE MCLENNAN	1	0	0	0	0	0	0	0	0	0	0
RUDY POESCHEK	2	0	0	0	2-	6	0	0	0	0	0
KELLY CHASE	7	0	0	0	2-	23	0	0	0	0	0
D. TURCOTTE	10	0	0	0	4-	2	0	0	0	0	5
B. ATCHEYNUM	10	0	0	0	2-	2	0	0	0	0	13
CHRIS MCALPINE	10	0	0	0	1-	16	0	0	0	0	5

GOALTENDER	GPI	MINS	AVG	W	L	EN	SO	GA	SA	SV %
GRANT FUHR	10	616	2.73	6	4	2	0	28	297	.906
JAMIE MCLENNAN	1	14	4.29	0	0	0	0	1	4	.750
STL TOTALS	10	631	2.95	6	4	2	0	31	303	.898

All-Time Leaders
Goals

Brett Hull	527
Bernie Federko	352
Brian Sutter	303

Assists

Bernie Federko	721
Brett Hull	409
Brian Sutter	334

Points

Bernie Federko	1,073
Brett Hull	936
Brian Sutter	636

Best Individual Seasons
Goals

Brett Hull	1990-91	86
Brett Hull	1989-90	72
Brett Hull	1991-92	70

Assists

Adam Oates	1990-91	90
Craig Janney	1992-93	82
Adam Oates	1989-90	79

Points

Brett Hull	1990-91	131
Adam Oates	1990-91	115
Brett Hull	1989-90	113

TEAM
Last 3 years

	GP	W	L	T	Pts	%
1997-98	82	45	29	8	98	.598
1996-97	82	36	35	11	82	.506
1995-96	82	32	34	16	80	.488

Best 3 regular seasons

	GP	W	L	T	Pts	%
1980-81	80	45	18	17	107	.669
1990-91	80	47	22	11	105	.656
1994-95	48	28	15	5	61	.635

Worst 3 regular seasons

	GP	W	L	T	Pts	%
1978-79	80	18	50	12	48	.300
1977-78	80	20	47	13	53	.331
1982-83	80	25	40	15	65	.406

Most Goals (min. 70 game schedule)

1980-81	352
1981-82	315
1990-91	310

Fewest Goals (min. 70 game schedule)

1967-68	177
1968-69	204
1973-74	206

Most Goals Against (min. 70 game schedule)

1981-82	349
1978-79	348
1982-83	316
1983-84	316

Fewest Goals Against (min. 70 game schedule)

1968-69	157
1969-70	179
1967-68	191

Vancouver Canucks

The 1997-98 award for underachieving goes to...(drum roll) the Vancouver Canucks, for the second year in a row.

They coulda, shoulda, woulda, been better.

They even made all the right moves to ensure they would be better, and they still weren't.

The Canucks should have been better because:

* Pavel Bure is one of the premier scorers in the game.

* Alexander Mogilny is one of the premier scorers in the game, when he feels like it.

* Mark Messier is one of the all-time best leaders in hockey.

* Mike Keenan has a proven track record as a great coach.

* They made excellent trades.

* They had one of the best rookies of the year in Mattias Ohlund.

* They had probably the toughest team in the league
.

The Canucks weren't better because:

* too many changes in too short a time.

* whiners like Bure and floaters like Mogilny detract from the team concept.

* resentment of some players that the Canucks were trading away the core of the team.

* resentment that Messier had a hand in the trading away of core players and the firing of Tom Renney.

* they didn't have a number one goalie.

* they were too tough, as in too many penalties. They were the most penalized team in the league, with almost twice as many minutes as Ottawa.

* losing attitude hard to shake.

* couldn't win at home.

* special teams were lousy.

They will be better this year because:

* more stability with player movement lessened.

* Mike Keenan always coaches better when he gets the players he likes, although Stephane Matteau has yet to join the team.

* new general manager Brian Burke

* have some explosive scorers if they feel like playing.

* might trade Bure and Mogilny and get a lot for them.

* young defencemen will gain more experience.

* the old group of losers is almost completely moved out.

* can't possibly start the season without a new number one goalie.

They won't be better this year because:
* free agents may not want to play for Keenan because of his coaching style, especially goalies.
* they don't have a number one goalie.
* thin at centre, left wing, right wing, defence and goalie.
* Keenan doesn't practise special teams because he thinks other teams can just pick up on their system and knock it down.

STUFF
* a 10-game losing streak was a team record
* 22 home losses were the most in team history, one more than in the 1976-77 season.
* Mattias Ohlund was second in Calder Trophy voting, behind Sergi Samsonov.

TEAM PREVIEW
GOAL: As of this writing, the Canuck goalies were Garth Snow and Corey Hirsch. As of this reading (by you) they've probably rectified the situation and come up with a number one man.

Last year, Vancouver served as a goaltender clearing house, with five experienced goalies seeing action. Arturs Irbe was the best of the bunch, while Sean Burke was the most disappointing.

Hockey Annual Rating: 24 of 27

DEFENCE: Let's see now, Bryan McCabe is one of the best young defencemen in the game, a player with leadership ability (was captain of the Islanders) hitting and fighting ability and offensive ability.

Mattias Ohlund is another of the best young defensemen, and Jason Strudwick is a stay-at-home type who is tough. Bret Hedican is one of the fastest skaters in the game. Free agent signee Murray Baron is a dependable stay-at-home type.

That's pretty good for a top five, and the Canucks won't miss Jyrki Lumme at all. He's a soft player who got benched for it. The only thing he led the Canucks in last year was the minus stat, where his -25 was more than twice as bad as anybody else who played on the team all season. He signed a five year deal with Phoenix for big bucks. Incredible.

Others who expect to see playing time include Jamie Huscroft, Chris McAllister, Adrian Aucoin, Bert Robertsson and Steve Staios. Robertsson and Staois were also wingers last year. Of this group, only Huscroft and McAllister were protected in the expansion draft.

This group needs time to play together. They could be pretty good, and for sure they're better than the defence in recent years.

Hockey Annual Rating: 18 of 27

FORWARD: The Canucks didn't have a hard time scoring goals, they just had a hard time scoring more than their opponents.

GOALTENDER	GPI	MINS	AVG	W	L	T	EN	SO	GA	SA	SV %
ARTURS IRBE	41	1999	2.73	14	11	6	3	2	91	982	.907
GARTH SNOW	12	504	3.10	3	6	0	0	0	26	262	.901
SEAN BURKE	16	838	3.51	2	9	4	1	0	49	396	.876
KIRK MCLEAN	29	1583	3.68	6	17	4	1	1	97	800	.879
COREY HIRSCH	1	50	6.00	0	0	0	0	0	5	34	.853
VAN TOTALS	82	4996	3.28	25	43	14	5	3	273	2479	.890

Pavel Bure said he'd let the Canucks know whether he was interested in playing there again next year or if he wanted to be traded. For 10 million bucks a year, he should play goalie if the team wants him to. If it's my money, he doesn't get a cent of it, he gets traded for players who want to commit to the team and not be a whiner. Never mind the 51 goals.

Hold on, okay, for 51 goals he can be a nuisance, because he's also an electrifying player and a favorite of the fans.

Not Mogilny though, no way. The Canucks might not want to trade him because his value is so low after scoring a crummy 18 goals, although in just 51 games. The Canucks would have to wait for his value to go up, otherwise they look dumb when Mogilny scores 50 goals, like he can when the mood strikes him.

Mark Messier is the opposite of both of the above, but he's just getting too old. He had a slow start last year, but then came on big-time. He's the number one centre over retread Peter Zezel, Dave Scatchard and maybe junior Josh Holden.

At left wing, the Canucks have Brad May and Todd Bertuzzi. May won't score a lot of goals, but will contribute with toughness and character, while Bertuzzi is expected to move up a level or two. Naslund has a scoring history, but he's clearly not Keenan's type of player and found himself watching games from the pressbox. The Canucks drafted Jarko Ruuttu in the third round last year. He's been given a good chance of stepping right into the lineup this year. Donald Brashear can handle the enforcer duties.

The Canucks have some dynamite forwards, but they don't have a lot of depth. Count on some changes, maybe big ones.

Hockey Annual Rating: 14 of 27

SPECIAL TEAMS: The Canucks led in one special team category, shorthanded goal scoring. That was also the reason they were ranked 24th in penalty killing. Bure and Mogilny would never see the ice ten years ago when down a man, but times have changed. Teams use their offensive stars in penalty-killing roles, but with Bure and Mogilny more worried about scoring than stopping the other team, it makes them weaker defensively.

Power Play	G	ATT	PCT
Overall	48	373	12.9% (T-19th NHL)
Home	21	198	10.6% (T-23rd NHL)
Road	27	175	15.4% (T-11th NHL)

12 SHORT HANDED GOALS ALLOWED (T-16th NHL)

Penalty Killing	G	TSH	PCT
Overall	77	432	82.2% (24th NHL)
Home	40	216	81.5% (23rd NHL)
Road	37	216	82.9% (T-20th NHL)

19 SHORT HANDED GOALS SCORED (1st NHL)

CANUCKS SPECIAL TEAMS SCORING

Power play	G	A	PTS
BURE	13	12	25
MESSIER	8	17	25
MOGILNY	5	12	17
LUMME	4	8	12
OHLUND	1	8	9
MCCABE	1	8	9
BERTUZZI	2	6	8
HEDICAN	1	5	6
MAY	4	1	5
NASLUND	2	3	5
ZEZEL	2	1	3
NOONAN	1	0	1
AUCOIN	1	0	1

SCATCHARD	0	1	1
CONVERY	0	1	1

Short handed	G	A	PTS
BURE	6	3	9
HEDICAN	0	7	7
MOGILNY	4	2	6
MESSIER	2	2	4
OHLUND	0	4	4
MCCABE	1	1	2
BERTUZZI	1	1	2
WALKER	1	0	1
NASLUND	1	0	1
ZEZEL	0	1	1

COACHING AND MANAGEMENT: Brian Burke will go from handing out suspensions in the league office this season to appealing them. And with the Canucks that could happen fairly frequently.

He got the job once the Canucks were sure they couldn't get Glen Sather, which isn't exactly a ringing endorsement for Burke, but he doesn't care. Don't ask him about it though, or he's likely to snap at you.

He has a temper which was most evident in last year's playoffs when replies to simple questions by interviewers were coated with salt an vinegar.

Burke should have an interesting viewpoint of the game, however, from his years in the league office, and his temper is likely to keep Keenan from bugging him too much.

Keenan is Keenan is Keenan. Except for his last two ventures, into Vancouver and St. Louis, he's been one of the most successful coaches in the game. As long as he's not in charge of making the personnel moves, there's no reason he

can't make this team more successful.

Hockey Annual Rating: 15 of 27

DRAFT

Round	Sel.	Player	Pos	Team
1	4	Bryan Allen	D	Oshawa (OHL)
2	31	Artem Chubarov	D	Russia
3	68	Jarko Ruutu	LW	Finland
3	81	Justin Morrison	RW	Colorado Col. (WCHA)
4	90	Regan Darby	D	Tri-City (WHL)
5	136	David Jonsson	D	Sweden
5	140	Rick Bertran	D	Kitchener (OHL)
6	149	Paul Cabana	W	Fort McMurray (AJHL)
7	177	Vincent Malts	RW	Hull (QMJHL)
8	204	Graig Mischler	C	Northeastern (HE)
8	219	Curtis Valentine	LW	Bowling Green (CCHA)
9	232	Jason Metcalfe	D	London

Bryan Allen is a big, bruising defenceman. Those type of players seem to be in short supply these days for some reason, with teams worried about mobility from their blue-liners. There's room for both kinds, though, and Allen will eventually make room for himself.

PROGNOSIS: The Canucks should have made the playoffs last year, and the year before.

You may have heard this before, but the Canucks will make the playoffs this year. They have a lot of talent that can play or be traded, and they don't seem like the type of management team to let holes go unfilled.

It might help the Canucks that the league should be more offensive-minded, since they have a head start. Also, their defence is solid on paper and should improve with more time together on the ice.

PREDICTION
Western Conference: 6th
Overall: 14th

STAT SECTION
Team Scoring Stats

	GP	G	A	PTS	+/-	PIM	SH	CAREER Gm	G	A	Pts
PAVEL BURE	82	51	39	90	5	48	329	428	254	224	479
MARK MESSIER	82	22	38	60	10-	58	139	1,354	597	1,015	1,612
A. MOGILNY	51	18	27	45	6-	36	118	587	315	354	669
M. NASLUND	76	14	20	34	5	56	106	315	63	82	145
TODD BERTUZZI	74	13	20	33	17-	121	102	214	41	54	95
JYRKI LUMME	74	9	21	30	25-	34	117	654	85	260	345
MATTIAS OHLUND	77	7	23	30	3	76	172	77	7	23	30
BRET HEDICAN	71	3	24	27	3	79	84	375	16	93	109
BRIAN NOONAN	82	10	15	25	19-	62	87	622	116	159	275
DAVE SCATCHARD	76	13	11	24	4-	165	85	76	13	11	24
BRYAN MCCABE	82	4	20	24	19	209	123	246	19	56	75
BRAD MAY	63	13	10	23	2	154	97	452	76	92	168
PETER ZEZEL	30	5	15	20	15	2	40	832	213	381	594
D. BRASHEAR	77	9	9	18	9-	372	64	247	20	21	41
SCOTT WALKER	59	3	10	13	8-	164	40	197	10	34	44
DANA MURZYN	31	5	2	7	3-	42	29	826	52	150	202
STEVE STAIOS	77	3	4	7	3-	134	45	152	6	18	24
ADRIAN AUCOIN	35	3	3	6	4-	21	44	155	13	33	46
BERT ROBERTSSON	30	2	4	6	2	24	19	30	2	4	6
JAMIE HUSCROFT	51	0	4	4	2-	177	26	308	5	31	36
C. MCALLISTER	36	1	2	3	12-	106	15	36	1	2	3
LUBOMIR VAIC	5	1	1	2	2-	2	8	5	1	1	2
DAVID ROBERTS	13	1	1	2	1-	4	14	125	20	33	53
B. CONVERY	7	0	2	2	0	0	2	57	7	12	19
J. STRUDWICK	28	0	2	2	2-	65	8	29	0	2	2
COREY HIRSCH	1	0	0	0	0	0	0	goalie			
MARK WOTTON	5	0	0	0	2-	6	3	42	3	6	9

LARRY COURVILLE	11	0	0	0	7-	5	3	33	1	2	3
ARTURS IRBE	41	0	0	0	0	2	0	goalie			
GARTH SNOW	41	0	0	0	0	22	0	goalie			

* Team Rankings 1997-98 (previous year's ranking in parenthesis)

		Conference Rank	League Rank
Record	25-43-14	13 (9)	24 (15)
Home	15-22-4	12 (7)	23 (14)
Away	10-21-10	12 (7)	24 (16)
Versus Own Conference	16-29-11	11 (7)	22 (13)
Versus Other Conference	9-14-3	11 (10)	21 (18)
Team Plus\Minus	-20	9 (7)	19 (12)
Goals For	224	6 (2)	10 (5)
Goals Against	273	13 (11)	26 (23)
Average Shots For	25.5	13 (13)	25 (24)
Average Shots Against	30.2	11 (7)	23 (14)
Overtime	0-3-14	13 (1)	25 (2)
One Goal Games	4-14	13 (7)	26 (15)
Times outshooting opponent	20	13 (10)	26 (19)
Versus Teams Over .500	7-26-7	12 (5)	24 (11)
Versus Teams Under .500	18-17-7	9 (11)	20 (20)
First Half Record	11-24-6	13 (4)	25 (10)
Second Half Record	14-19-8	11 (10)	21 (21)

All-Time Leaders
Goals
Stan Smyl 262
Pavel Bure 254
Tony Tanti 250

Assists
Stan Smyl 411
Thomas Gradin 353
Trevor Linden 322

Points
Stan Smyl 673
Trevor Linden 569
Thomas Gradin 550

Best Individual Seasons
Goals
Pavel Bure 1993-94 60
Pavel Bure 1992-93 60
Alexander Mogilny 1995-96 55

Assists
Andre Boudrias 1974-75 62
Andre Boudrias 1973-74 59
Thomas Gradin 1983-84 57

Points
Pavel Bure 1992-93 110
Alexander Mogilny 1995-96 107
Pavel Bure 1993-94 107

PLAYOFF
- did not make the playoffs

TEAM

Last 3 years

	GP	W	L	T	Pts	%
1997-98	82	25	43	14	64	.390
1996-97	82	35	40	7	77	.470
1995-96	82	32	35	15	79	.482

Best 3 regular seasons

	GP	W	L	T	Pts	%
1992-93	84	46	29	9	101	.601
1991-92	80	42	27	12	96	.600
1974-75	80	38	32	10	86	.538

Worst 3 regular seasons

	GP	W	L	T	Pts	%
1971-72	78	20	50	8	48	.308
1972-73	78	22	47	9	53	.340
1977-78	80	27	43	17	57	.359

Most Goals (min. 70 game schedule)

1992-93	346
1983-84	306
1982-83	303

Fewest Goals (min. 70 game schedule)

1971-72	203
1978-79	217
1973-74	224
1997-98	224

Most Goals Against (min. 70 game schedule)

1984-85	401
1972-73	339
1985-86	333

Fewest Goals Against (min. 70 game schedule)

1991-92	250
1988-89	253
1974-75	254

Townsend's Ultimate Pool Picks

Usually, you buy a book, and that's it. You read it, and put it somewhere. Hey, not this one. It just keeps giving and giving and giving....

A book that never ends, how do you like that?

Need help with your hockey pool? Wondering if you should trade so and so for so and so? Draft coming up and you have some questions? Anything, anytime, all year long.

My e-mail address is:

mtownsend@mailserv.interhop.net

and if you're not hooked up to the internet you can write me at 625 Joyce Blvd., Milton, Ontario, L9T 3E3. I try to reply the same day, although last year I received a ton of e-mail, both from this book and from my online hockey pool column with *The Hockey News* at www.thn.com, so sometimes it was a day or two before I could research and write back.

I keep all my own stats, including some you've never even heard of, so don't hesitate to contact me.

The pool section is broken down into a couple different categories. There is the player ratings, with some statistics and a one line comment for each player. I find the comments can be helpful when selecting between a couple different players. If you're using the list at your draft, after the first 30 or so players, don't think of them as being in exact order. Look above and below each player, maybe five or so places, to see who best suits your own needs or wants.

Also, included is a team-by-team pool recap section with a number of different categories in each, including probable top line and power play lineup, emerging players, who's going up and who's going down.

This year, we've also added goaltender ratings, thanks to the suggestion of loyal readers, Gord Gent and Bryan Gent.

Good luck, and let me know how you do.

Player	Team	1997-98 Rank	GP	Pts	1st Hlf	2nd Hlf	Comment
90 points plus							
Kariya	Ana	22	31	182	11	20	health shouldn't be concern
Jagr	Pit	77	102	1	47	55	didn't need Lemieux, doesn't need Francis
Selanne	Ana	73	86	8	45	41	comes through no matter what
Lindros	Phi	63	71	20	51	20	back up to the top
Forsberg	Col	72	91	2	51	40	100 point season again
LeClair	Phi	82	87	5	51	36	50 goals guaranteed
Sakic	Col	64	63	33	43	20	too good not to rebound from last year
Modano	Dal	52	59	41	38	21	missed 30 games last season
Palffy	NYI	82	87	6	37	50	proven consistency
Bure	Van	82	90	3	47	43	could be traded
60-89 points							
Gretzky	NYR	82	90	4	36	54	amazing
Tkachuk	Pho	69	66	25	42	24	big jump in points
Bondra	Wsh	76	78	11	38	40	one of most consistent goal scorers
Stumpel	LA	77	79	10	40	39	reliable top scorer
Allison	Bos	81	83	9	39	44	last year's most improved player
Francis	Car	81	87	7	44	43	1st line centre
Recchi	Mtl	82	74	16	39	25	never misses a game
Khristich	Bos	82	66	26	29	37	works well with Allison and Samsonov
Brind'Amour	Phi	82	74	14	36	38	great power play mates
Friesen	SJ	79	63	32	27	36	moving up to all-star status
Nieuwendyk	Dal	73	69	22	32	37	could have Hull as winger
Yashin	Ott	82	72	18	36	36	good scorer on non-scoring team
Sundin	Tor	82	74	15	37	37	can't do it all himself
Koivu	Mtl	59	57	46	35	22	could make big jump after injuries

Fedorov	Det	21	17	332	0	17	out most of last season, contract dispute
Fleury	Cgy	82	78	12	38	40	could have change of scenery
Kapanen	Car	81	63	35	31	32	coming off breakout season
Amonte	Chi	82	73	17	38	35	has Gilmour as new centre
Hull	Dal	66	72	19	36	36	slowing down, but revitalized in new city
Kamensky	Col	75	66	27	29	37	can't beat his linemates
Alfredsson	Ott	55	45	93	17	28	big jump if healthy
Yzerman	Det	75	69	23	34	35	has to slow down sooner or later
Shanahan	Det	75	57	45	35	22	coming off sub-par season
Leetch	NYR	76	50	68	21	29	just had an off year, will be back
Gratton	Phi	82	62	38	31	31	consistent
Weight	Edm	79	70	21	36	34	no competition for top Oiler
Roenick	Pho	79	56	49	31	25	coming off comeback year of sorts
Turgeon	StL	60	68	24	23	45	will miss Hull
Holik	NJ	82	65	30	38	27	competition for no.1 centre job
Gilmour	Chi	63	53	57	32	25	takes over top centre role
Oates	Wsh	82	76	13	39	37	still can set em up
Niedermaye	NJ	81	57	47	32	25	should score even more with looser reins
Lidstrom	Det	80	59	43	31	28	top scoring defenceman last year
Samsonov	Bos	81	47	80	13	34	sophomore jinx?
Ozolinsh	Col	66	51	64	18	33	quarterback for best power play
Daigle	Phi	75	42	113	14	28	came on big when joined Flyers
Morrison	NJ	11	9	443	1	8	rookie of year candidate
Arnott	NJ	70	33	171	18	15	major comeback a possibility
Mogilny	Van	51	45	92	16	29	could be big scorer, if feels like it

40-59 points

Kovalev	NYR	73	53	54	20	33	slow start, but came on big
Peca	Buf	61	40	122	15	25	all-round player
Gelinas	Car	64	34	158	8	26	proven 30-goal scorer
Primeau	Car	81	63	34	28	35	primeau centre
Daze	Chi	80	42	108	22	20	has real number one centre now
Nolan	SJ	75	41	119	23	18	can make a big jump in points
Smyth	Edm	65	33	166	22	11	hampered by injuries; big comeback?
Berard	NYI	75	46	88	25	21	consistency will come
Reichel	NYI	83	65	31	40	25	slowed down when Linden came on board
Zubov	Dal	73	57	48	34	23	point man on potent power play
Lemieux	Col	78	53	53	31	22	sometimes saves his best for playoffs
Green	Ana	76	42	111	22	20	should rebound from weak season
Heinze	Bos	61	46	84	14	32	sleeper pick if he can stay healthy
Damphousse	Mtl	76	59	42	25	34	could improve over bad season
Juneau	Wsh	56	31	187	17	14	off poor regular season; great playoff
Whitney	Fla	77	65	28	32	33	was last season a mirage or for real?
Kozlov	Det	80	52	59	26	26	always on top two lines
MacInnis	StL	71	49	72	22	27	will miss Hull
Sundstrom	NYR	70	47	81	22	25	on number one line
Courtnall	StL	79	62	36	33	29	will miss Hull
Barnes	Pit	78	65	29	19	37	points should drop
Linden	NYI	67	38	135	17	21	new life in New York
Marleau	SJ	74	32	178	13	19	should improve off rookie year
Savage	Mtl	64	43	99	14	29	can't stay healthy
Rucchin	Ana	72	53	56	20	33	Kariya and Selanne center?

Langen.	Dal	81	52	60	33	19	slowed down in second half
Messier	Van	82	60	40	35	25	slowing down considerably
Niedermy.	Fla	33	15	357	9	6	missed most of last season with injuries
Audette	Buf	75	44	95	16	28	sniper scores if healthy
Deadmarsh	Col	73	43	100	23	20	can be 30-goal scorer again
Guerin	Edm	59	39	131	10	29	top-line power forward
Blake	LA	81	50	66	20	30	has to stay injury free
Sykora	NJ	58	36	145	20	16	could be breakout season
Ronning	Pho	80	55	52	22	33	more playmaking with Janney gone
Kozlov	Fla	64	30	191	8	22	maybe he's ready to break out
Verbeek	Dal	82	57	44	32	25	good linemates
Janney	TB	68	53	58	36	17	great playmaker
Rolston	NJ	76	30	192	12	18	breakout season possibility
Carter	Bos	78	43	102	18	25	only one season under belt
Sanderson	Buf	75	29	202	17	11	one bad year - has talent to rebound
Langkow	TB	68	22	273	14	8	breakout possibility
Roberts	Car	61	49	71	28	21	injury problems a concern
Cassels	Cgy	81	44	97	17	27	comback season?
Smolinski	NYI	81	43	104	24	19	coming off poor season
Sydor	Dal	79	46	89	23	23	point man on great power play
Rucinsky	Mtl	78	53	55	27	26	on one of top two lines
Cullen	Ana	61	27	220	8	19	could play between Kariya and Selanne
Holzinger	Buf	69	35	153	17	18	ready to step up a level
Murray	LA	81	60	39	29	31	coming off breakout season
Iginla	Cgy	70	32	177	22	10	coming off poor season
Bertuzzi	Van	74	33	170	16	17	showing improvement
Duchesne	LA	80	56	50	30	26	him and Blake should make good duo
Svelha	Fla	79	43	105	24	19	power play point
Graves	NYR	72	35	150	17	18	look for big comeback season

Campbell	StL	76	41	117	21	20	not much help
Satan	Buf	79	46	85	27	19	45-point range is max
O'Neill	Car	74	39	130	18	21	still getting better
McInnis	Cgy	75	44	96	21	23	always in the 40's
Corson	Mtl	62	55	51	39	16	such high scoring uncharacteristic
Bourque	Bos	82	48	79	24	24	look for point production to slow down
Jones	Col	23	10	431	0	10	coming off injury-plagued season
Dawe	NYI	81	39	128	25	14	can score, but not consistent
Pederson	NJ	80	28	209	14	14	could add more scoring to defensive play
Mellanby	Fla	79	39	134	22	17	slowing down with age
Stillman	Cgy	72	49	69	26	23	coming off breakout year
Zhamnov	Chi	70	49	70	21	28	moves down to second line centre
Tsyplakov	LA	73	52	62	25	27	first-liner in LA
McEachern	Ott	81	48	75	26	22	on top Senators line
Hatcher	Pit	74	48	77	11	26	power play not as explosive
Numminen	Pho	82	51	65	19	32	one of top offensive defencemen
Tverdovsky	Pho	46	19	304	0	19	should make a huge point leap
Brunette	Nsh	28	23	256	2	21	had one of league's hottest streaks
Lehtinen	Dal	72	42	109	23	19	top two scoring lines
Harvey	NYR	59	19	301	9	10	breakout possibility
Malakhov	Mtl	74	44	98	20	24	attitude could mean trade
Dumont	Chi	-	-	-	-	-	rookie has a chance to do damage
Barnaby	Buf	72	25	240	7	18	led Sabres in playoff scoring
Chelios	Chi	81	42	116	22	20	team should score more, so should he
Plante	Buf	72	34	161	21	13	usually has good season after bad one
Johnson	Tor	82	47	82	28	19	slowed down later in season

Murphy	SJ	37	22	271	7	15	could make point jump
McCarty notches	Det	71	37	141	24	13	could move up a couple
Nikolishin	Wsh	38	16	344	0	16	coming into his own
Domenich. score	Cgy	41	16	342	0	16	if he gets the chance, will
Renberg on Lightning	TB	68	38	137	16	22	still no Lindros or LeClair
Banham junior	Ana	21	11	409	5	11	was an 83-goal scorer in
Morris time	Cgy	82	29	204	16	13	good potential if gets pp
Demitra could go down	StL	61	52	61	24	28	overachieved last year;
Coffey ly motivated	Chi	57	29	207	18	11	getting too old, but fresh-
Ferraro injuries	LA	40	15	358	2	13	comeback season after
Wiemer year	Cgy	79	22	269	9	13	last chance for breakout
Moreau	Chi	54	18	313	10	8	look for big improvement
Lecavalier	TB	-	-	-	-	-	top draft choice this year
Pronger	StL	81	36	149	15	21	one of league's best
Niinimaa	Edm	77	43	107	17	26	reliable point producer
McAmmond scoring	Edm	77	50	67	14	36	led Oilers in second-half
Gagner	Fla	78	48	76	28	20	slowing down
Dackell	Ott	82	33	168	16	17	decent rookie season
Titov failed to deliver	Pit	68	40	123	22	18	power play sniper, who
Naslund	Van	76	34	160	17	17	can do better

20-39 points

Nedved greeditis	Pit	-	-	-	-	-	sat out last season with
Schneider threat	Tor	76	37	142	19	18	top offensive defenceman
Suter	SJ	73	42	114	17	25	power play quarterback

Ohlund	Van	77	30	197	16	14	great rookie season
Simon	Wsh	28	17	331	17	9	good sleeper pick
Modin	Tor	74	32	175	8	24	had explosive stretch
Richer	TB	40	29	199	6	23	never healthy for long
Zhitnik	Buf	78	45	94	16	29	consistent around 40 points
Klatt	Phi	82	42	115	18	24	played some on top line
Konowalchuk	Wsh	80	34	163	13	21	should score more
McCauley	Tor	60	16	346	11	5	steady improvement
Perreault	LA	79	48	73	29	19	slowed down when taken off top line
Wilkie	TB	34	7	494	1	6	has to step up and show offence
Sturm	SJ	74	30	195	20	10	good rookie season
Sillinger	Phi	75	41	118	12	29	22 points in 27 Flyers games
McLean	NYR	77	43	101	17	25	past the age danger zone
Desjardins	Phi	77	33	174	15	18	solid and dependable
Mironov	Wsh	77	43	106	24	19	free agent gets power play point
Zyuzin	SJ	56	13	382	2	11	explosive offensive talent
Tocchet	Pho	68	45	90	42	24	injuries always a concern
Kilger	Chi	32	12	399	1	11	hasn't shown all he can do yet
Murphy	Det	82	52	63	31	21	can't play forever, time to slow down
Conroy	StL	81	43	103	18	25	great find, but points should decrease
Straka	Pit	75	42	110	18	25	is a magician; could disappear anytime
Zamuner	TB	77	26	224	17	9	defensive forward
Johansson	Wsh	73	35	152	21	14	role could be reduced
Morozov	Pit	76	26	225	11	15	will build on rookie season
Thomas	Tor	55	24	243	9	15	glory days just an old song
Arvedsson	Ott	61	26	227	8	18	room to move up
Sullivan	Tor	63	28	211	20	8	doesn't get quality time
Hamrlik	Edm	78	41	121	16	25	can shut down at any time
Nylander	Cgy	65	36	147	19	17	unreliable, let someone else take chance

Holmstrom	Det	57	22	277	10	12	outstanding playoff moves him up ladder
Legwand	Nsh	-	-	-	-	-	second draft pick overall
Jonsson	NYI	81	40	126	20	20	still improving
Briere	Pho	5	1	-	0	1	could have super rookie season
Robitaille	LA	57	40	124	29	11	can't have too much left
Zednik	Wsh	65	26	223	18	8	could be surprisingly good scorer
Mironov	Edm	81	46	87	18	28	gets a power play point
Elias	NJ	74	37	140	21	16	faded in second half
Drake	Pho	60	40	128	23	17	consistent scorer when in lineup
Johnson	LA	74	38	136	22	16	speedy, and should benefit from new rules
Ysebeart	TB	82	40	127	18	22	shouldn't be top scoring forward in TB
Bulis	Wsh	48	16	349	12	4	might get regular time
Primeau	Buf	69	12	393	3	10	could be breakout season
Ricci	SJ	65	27	218	12	15	contributes more than points
Matteau	SJ	73	29	198	12	17	poor man's power forward
McGillis	Phi	80	31	186	15	16	decent offensive threat
Fraser	NYR	29	23	255	2	21	big numbers in short time in Edmonton
McKay	NJ	74	48	74	31	17	great scoring out of character
Quint	Pho	32	11	419	9	2	offensive defenceman needs playing time
Donato	Bos	79	39	133	28	11	slumped big-time late in season
Wooley	Buf	71	35	156	17	18	power play specialist
Brown	Det	80	42	112	19	23	valuable performer overachieved last year
Selivanov	TB	70	35	151	19	16	could make big jump in points
Bure	Cgy	66	38	138	24	14	inconsistent, scores in bunches

Emerson	Car	81	45	91	25	20	coming off comeback season
Krupp	Det	78	31	188	17	14	good fit on Detroit for former Avalanche
Chorske	NYI	82	35	155	17	18	not supposed to be a scorer
Washburn	Fla	58	19	300	14	5	could jump in points
Brunet	Mtl	68	32	179	9	23	amazing scoring leap in second half
Lapointe	Det	79	34	159	16	18	saves his best for playoffs
Shantz	Chi	61	31	185	17	14	decent scorer for third or fourth line
Grosek	Buf	67	30	194	14	15	was a good scorer in playoffs
Redden	Ott	80	22	274	8	14	could get more offensive
Marchant	Edm	76	35	154	14	21	speedy but not much else
Brisebois	Mtl	79	37	143	17	20	coming off best season
Galley	LA	74	37	144	19	18	could be odd-man with Duchesne on board
Cote	Tor	71	25	242	11	14	should man the power play point
Nemirovsky	Fla	41	21	283	13	8	showed something when given chance
Hatcher	Dal	70	31	190	16	15	will get points, forwards will score
McCabe	Van	82	24	250	3	21	point explosion in second half
Mann	Bos	9	1	-	0	1	could do damage if makes team
Johnson	Nsh	74	34	162	15	19	could be top centre on Predators
Iafrate	Car	21	9	452	3	6	injuries are major worry
Sheppard	Car	71	37	139	19	18	scoring less and less regularly
Kron	Car	81	36	146	17	19	third or fourth liner now
Larionov	Det	59	47	83	27	20	won't play every game
May	Van	63	23	253	9	14	can score with right linemates

Bordeleau	Nsh	53	14	369	8	6	gets a chance to play
Lacroix	Col	82	31	184	20	11	scored less when Jones returned from inj.
Stevens	NYR	80	41	120	23	18	on his last legs
Grier	Edm	66	15	356	8	7	contributes off scoreboard
Lindren	Edm	82	26	226	16	10	hasn't shown much
Thornton	Bos	55	7	485	1	6	will improve over rookie season
Gilchrist	Det	61	27	215	20	7	not counted on to score too much
Leroux	Chi	66	13	383	3	10	should step up scoring
Housley	Wsh	64	31	189	23	8	could be just about done
Dvorak	Fla	64	36	148	14	22	good second half
Taylor	Bos	79	31	181	16	15	slowed down after good start
Brown	Buf	63	24	245	8	16	time to step up a level
Ciccarelli	Fla	62	33	167	14	19	down for the count?
Varada	Buf	27	11	414	1	10	could be a regular this year
Chambers	Dal	57	24	251	8	16	will get points, forwards will score
Chiasson	Car	66	34	164	19	15	all-round player
Tkachuk	Cgy	-	-	-			rookie could make grade
Marha	Ana	23	18	312	2	16	has a chance to stick around
Corbet	Col	68	28	208	15	13	potential to score more if on right line
Lindsay	Fla	82	28	210	14	14	not a scorer
Axelsson	Bos	82	27	219	11	16	hard to get time on top lines
Sweeney,D	Bos	59	16	354	8	8	scoring has slowed in recent years
Marshall	Dal	72	19	302	9	10	ready to move up a notch
Yelle	Col	81	22	275	13	9	possibility of big point increase
Wesley	Car	82	25	238	16	9	not as much offence as previously
Messier	Col	62	16	351	10	6	gets more offensive time with Krupp gone

Keane	Dal	83	23	260	15	8	not counted on for scoring
Lind	Dal	39	5	-	0	5	likely to get lots of playing time
Lumme	Pho	74	30	196	15	15	coming off poor season
Turcotte	Nsh	62	18	310	8	10	gets chance to renew career
Battaglia	Car	33	6	-	0	5	played regularly late in season
Slaney	Nsh	55	17	339	13	3	power play spot on Predators
Eriksson	Det	66	21	284	13	8	some veteran defencemen no longer around
Bonk	Ott	65	16	343	13	3	one last time
Murray	Edm	61	18	314	11	7	better produce early or else
Jovanovski	Fla	81	23	261	9	14	can contribute more offensively
Podein	Phi	82	24	247	11	13	defensive player
Smehlik	Buf	72	20	296	11	9	doesn't get power play time
Daigneault	Nsh	71	23	267	14	9	power play spot on Predators
Andreychuk	NJ	75	48	78	23	25	fading fast
Karpovtsev	NYR	47	10	432	10	0	injured much of last year
King,D	Tor	77	46	86	21	25	should go down
Muller	Fla	70	29	205	13	16	going, going....
Hulse	Cgy	79	27	221	17	10	added surprising offence last year
Buchberger	Edm	82	23	264	14	9	role player
Murphy	Fla	79	17	335	9	8	not an offensive threat anymore
Laperriere	LA	77	21	286	13	8	good defensive forward
Reid	Dal	65	18	322	16	2	has been counted out before and rebounded
Jokkinen	LA	8	0	-	0	0	should be full-time King this year
Czercawski	NYI	68	25	232	11	14	consistently inconsistent
Kravchuk	Ott	81	35	157	20	15	top offensive defenceman on Senators
Zubrus	Phi	69	33	172	22	11	disappointing progress

Krivokrasov	Nsh	58	23	257	17	6	somebody has to score on Predators
Gardiner	Ott	55	18	321	10	8	defensive forward
Manson	Mtl	81	34	165	14	20	contributes in all different ways
Berezin	Tor	68	31	183	19	12	out to lunch
Maltby	Det	65	23	252	11	12	role player
Hoglund	Mtl	78	25	233	10	15	not worth wasting a pick
Moger	LA	62	24	246	14	10	missed 20 games last year
Ward	Buf	71	23	258	6	16	role player
Leach	Car	45	9	447	8	1	injury champion
Weinrich	Chi	82	23	268	11	12	second unit power play
Svejkovsky	Wsh	17	5	-	4	1	could score big, or could score none
Dandenault	Det	68	17	336	12	5	could score if gets chance
Savard	NYR	28	6	-	2	4	rookie could get shot
Probert	Chi	14	3	-	1	2	yet another comeback
Laukkanen	Ott	60	21	288	14	7	more points if stays healthy
Gonchar	Wsh	72	21	287	8	13	inconsistent offensively
Isbister	Pho	66	17	328	13	4	should increase points
Sacco	NYI	80	25	234	11	14	not a scorer
Dineen	Car	54	23	262	15	8	hangin on, but barely
Houlder	SJ	82	32	180	17	15	Suter on board to help out
Atcheynum	Nsh	61	26	228	14	12	chance to play on scoring line
Nemchinov	NYI	74	29	203	21	8	defensive player
Stevens	NJ	80	26	230	12	14	not counted on for big point production
Wells	Fla	61	15	363	11	4	maybe he can improve scoring
Forbes	Phi	63	19	299	8	11	surprise scorer last year
Pellerin	StL	80	29	206	15	14	defensive forward
Scatchard	Van	76	24	244	11	13	defensive forward
Hedican	Van	71	27	222	19	8	speedy defenceman inconsistent scorer
Craven	SJ	67	29	200	15	14	slowing down to a stop
Draper	Det	64	23	254	15	8	role player
Clark	TB	47	19	298	16	3	shadow of former self

Lapointe	NYI	78	20	290	11	9	defensive player
Van Allen	Ott	80	19	306	11	8	defensive forward
Thornton	Mtl	67	15	360	8	7	defensive forward
Quintal	Mtl	71	16	347	8	8	can contribute a little offensively
Zelepukin	Edm	68	22	279	10	12	not much left
Gill	StL	75	30	193	13	17	all those goals last year were a fluke
Burr	SJ	42	12	392	3	9	not counted on much for points
Walker	Nsh	59	13	386	9	4	should be fan fave, so could be incentive
Zezel	Van	30	20	294	1	19	late season scoring just a mirage
Hossa	Ott	7	1	-	1	0	could be hotshot rookie
Ragnarsson	SJ	79	25	241	11	14	moves down a notch with Suter signed
Markov	Tor	25	7	493	0	6	looked good in late season audition
Stevenson	Mtl	63	10	430	4	6	could score more
Prospal	Ott	56	25	237	18	7	didn't show much in Ottawa
Malhotra	NYR	-	-	-	-	-	rookie could make team
Therien	Phi	78	19	307	9	10	not counted on for offence
Hunter	Wsh	82	26	229	12	14	not counted on for points
Tucker	TB	74	20	293	5	15	scoring came on in second half
Noonan	F/A	82	25	236	14	11	defensive forward
Doan	Pho	33	11	415	5	6	will get more playing time
Lang	Pit	54	22	272	6	16	bit player with good stretches
Odelein	NJ	79	23	265	17	6	won't score a lot
McCarthy	TB	66	18	318	5	13	can be force if on top two lines
Bureau	Mtl	74	19	297	6	13	surprise offence last season
Pronger	Pit	67	21	285	9	12	played poorly with Penguins
Korolev	Tor	78	39	132	25	14	disappeared after fast start

Courtnall	LA	58	18	309	4	14	can't be relied on for much scoring
Poulin	Mtl	78	19	305	9	10	all hope just about lost
Cullen	TB	-	-	-	-	-	return isn't guaranteed
LaFontaine	NYR	67	62	37	42	20	don't know if he will even play
Bradley	TB	14	7	492	7	0	return isn't guaranteed

GOALTENDER RATINGS

Player	Team	1997-98 Gms	Record	Shutouts	Comment
Brodeur	NJ	70	43-17-8	10	will play almost every game
Belfour	Dal	61	37-12-1	9	is on a can't-lose team
Hasek	Buf	72	33-23-4	13	no comment needed
Roy	Col	65	31-19-13	4	still has good years left
Vanbies.	Phi	60	18-29-11	4	best days behind him
Osgood	Det	64	33-20-11	8	teams wins, so he does too
Kidd	Car	47	21-21-3	3	number one with a bullet
Dafoe	Bos	65	30-25-9	6	established himself number one
Richter	NYR	72	21-31-15	0	can't win unless team solid
Hackett	Chi	58	21-25-11	8	good backup behind him, could play less
Barrasso	Pit	63	31-14-13	7	Repeat of last year too iffy
Vernon	SJ	62	30-22-8	5	Sharks could be winning more
Joseph	Tor	71	29-31-9	8	can only do so much for sadsack Leafs
Fuhr	StL	58	29-21-6	3	Blues are in trouble
Potvin	Tor	67	26-33-7	5	see which team he's traded to
Thibault	Mtl	47	19-15-8	2	another goalie may be on way to Montreal
Hebert	Ana	46	13-24-6	3	troubled by injuries last year
Tugnutt	Ott	42	15-14-8	3	shares time with Rhodes
Rhodes	Ott	50	19-19-7	5	shares time with Tugnutt
Storr	LA	17	9-5-1	2	more playing time, but not all
Wregget	Cgy	15	3-6-2	0	new start, but maybe too late
Ranford	TB	22	7-12-2	0	gets number one job again
McLean	Fla	51	14-21-5	1	majority of games not guaranteed

Salo	NYI	62	23-29-5	4	number one, but NYI looking elsewhere
Fiset	LA	60	26-25-8	2	will share more with Storr
Hextall	Phi	46	21-17-7	4	no room with Vanbiesbrouck signed
Snow	Van	41	17-15-4	0	has a chance for backup role in Vancouver
Tabaracci	Cgy	42	13-22-6	0	maybe has run out of chances
Fichaud	Edm	17	3-8-3	0	Oiler No.1 goalie at press time
Dunham	Nsh	15	5-5-3	1	Brodeur understudy in NJ

Pool Teams

ANAHEIM

Top Scoring Line: Paul Kariya-Steve Rucchin-Teemu Selanne, with the possibility that Matt Cullen or Travis Green could get some time in the middle instead of Rucchin.

Top Power Play Unit: Kariya-Green-Selanne, with point men still to be determined. As of this writing, the Ducks would need two forwards on the points.

Rookie Scoring Candidates: Mike Crowley is an offensive defenceman on a team desperate for one. Johan Davidson was signed during the summer and could make the team at centre.

Possible Breakout Players: Frank Banham was a big-time scorer in junior and did well in a late-season callup by the Ducks.

Sleeper: Green had scored 70 and 64 points prior to last season. If Crowley gets a spot on the power play point, look for his points to balloon.

Going Up: Kariya only played 22 games, so he's going up. In fact, he's going all the way to the top.

Going Down: Tomas Sandstrom is down for the count.

Goalie: Guy Herbert will play the majority of the games, 60 plus, but he gets injured a lot. Patrick Lalime is the backup.

Top 5 Scorers: Kariya, Selanne, Green, Rucchin, Cullen

Notes: The Ducks didn't have anyone for the points on the power play when this was done. Obviously, a defenceman or two will have to be added. If they don't, look for Crowley to get a lot of points.

BOSTON

Top Scoring Line: Sergei Samsonov, Jason Allison, Dimitri Khristich

Top Power Play Unit: Samsonov, Allison, Khristich, Ray Bourque, and the closest defenceman. Steve Heinze is somewhat of a sniper on the power play, as well.

Rookie Scoring Candidates: Cameron Mann, Randy Robitaille, Shawn Bates

Possible Breakout Players: Landon Wilson

Sleeper: Steve Heinze. He's been hampered by injuries in recent years, but does great job when he's in the lineup.

Going Up: Joe Thornton has to get more quality playing time.

Going Down: Tim Taylor and Ted Donato. Taylor tailed off later in the year. Donato scored well last season, but that's not his role.

Goalies: Byron Dafoe good for 60 plus games. Don't count out Jim Carey making something of a comeback.

Top 5 scorers: Allison, Khristich, Samsonov, Heinze, Bourque

BUFFALO

Top Scoring Line: They don't have one.

Top Power Play Unit: Jason Wooley and Alexei Zhitnik man the points, and usually Donald Audette is one of the forwards. Derek Plante could get more time there this year.

Rookie Scoring Candidates: Eric Rasmussen

Possible Breakout Players: Wayne Primeau, Curtis Brown.

Sleeper: Derek Plante follows bad years with good ones. Geoff Sanderson's bad year may have been just a blip.

Going Up: Matthew Barnaby, Geoff Sanderson.

Going Down: Miroslav Satan

Goalies: Dominik Hasek

Top 5 Scorers: Peca, Plante, Sanderson, Audette, Holzinger

CALGARY

Top Scoring Line: Theoren Fleury is only undisputed first liner.

Top Power Play Unit: Fleury and whomever is hot, with Derek Morris and Cale Hulse on the points.

Rookie Scoring Candidates: Daniel Tkachuk

Possible Breakout Players: Jason Wiemer, for the third year in a row. Hnat Domenichelli if the Flames give him regular duty on a scoring line.

Sleeper: Andrew Cassels was a proven playmaking centre, until last year. Could rebound.

Going Up: Cassels, Wiemer, Jarome Iginla.

Going Down: Nobody scored enough to score less.

Top 5 Scorers: Fleury, Cassels, Iginla, Stillman, McInnis

Goalies: Ken Wregget is the top man now, but didn't play much last year. Rick Tabaracci could do the job if he teammates scored any goals for him.

Notes: The Flames are probably going to make

some trades before the season starts. They're looking for a number one centre and a power play quarterback. Fleury is the most rumored trade bait.

CAROLINA
Top Scoring Line: Ron Francis between Gary Roberts or Martin Gelinas, and Sami Kapanan.

Top Power Play Unit: Francis, Keith Primeau and probably Kapanan, Roberts and Gelinas on the wings. Al Iafrate gets a point spot if he's not injured, with Steve Chiasson and Glen Wesley also getting time on the blueline.

Rookie Scoring Candidates: None

Possible Breakout Players: Jeff O'Neill would have been one, but now he's knocked down to third-line centre with the addition of Francis.

Sleeper: Martin Gelinas has a bad injury-plagued season. Look for him to flourish with two top centres on the Hurricanes.

Going Up: Iafrate, but this is a recording: "ONLY IF HE STAYS HEALTHY."

Going Down: One of Chiasson or Wesley, with the addition of Iafrate. Kron may move too low on the depth chart.

Goalies: Trevor Kidd is free and clear as the number one man. He should play 65 plus games.

Top 5 Scorers: Francis, Kapanan, Primeau, Gelinas, Roberts

Notes: The Hurricanes are an up-and-coming team this year, and are going to be a higher scoring team. With Carolina not normally associated with being a winning team, you should be able to get some of their better players. You don't want to take Roberts or Iafrate too high, however, due to injury concerns.

CHICAGO
Top Scoring Line: Eric Daze-Doug Gilmour-Tony Amonte

Top Power Play Unit: First Line with Paul Coffey and Chris Chelios on the points

Rookie Scoring Candidates: J-P Dumont is a big-time junior scorer who shold get a shot on a Blackhawk scoring line.

Possible Breakout Players: Ethan Moreau

Sleeper: Chad Kilger would have had a better shot at number two centre, but he knows he has to start scoring or else.

Going Up: Paul Coffey could be revitalized on a team that could appreciate him still. At least on the power play.

Going Down: Alexei Zhamnov couldn't score on the first line, so the second line doesn't look too promising.

Goalies: Jeff Hackett is clearly number one, but at this writing the Blackhawks had both Mark Fitzpatrick and Chris Terreri in the wings. Hackett could play less often.

Top Five Scorers: Amonte, Gilmour, Daze, Dumont, Zhamnov

Notes: The Blackhawks look ripe for some deals, with excess goaltending and maybe Zhamnov as trade bait. Watch Dumont carefully in the pre-season before you pick him and make sure he's on a top line and is scoring.

COLORADO

Top Scoring Line: Valeri Kamensky-Peter Forsberg-Claude Lemieux and their second top scoring line of Joe Sakic, Keith Jones and Adam Deadmarsh

Top Power Play Unit: Forsberg, Kamensky, Lemieux, Sakic and Ozolinsh.

Rookie Scoring Candidates: None

Possible Breakout Players: Little opportunity to play on top two scoring lines.

Sleeper: Keith Jones missed most of last year with injuries.

Going Up: Sakic had an injury-plagued off season.

Going Down: None

Goalies: Patrick Roy will get the huge bulk of the playing time, with Craig Billington spelling him on occasion.

Top Five Scorers: Forsberg, Sakic, Kamensky, Ozololinsh, Lemieux

DALLAS

Top Scoring Line: have two top scoring lines. Langenbrunner-Modano-Lehtinen, Verbeek-Nieuwendyk-Hull, or you can mix-and-match.

Top Power Play Unit: Modano, Nieuwendyk and Hull figure to get the most time up front, with Sergei Zubov and Darryl Sydor handling the points.

Rookie Scoring Candidates: None

Possible Breakout Players: None

Sleeper: None

Going Up: Most players can expect to be up some in their points because if opposing teams key on one line, the other top scoring line is just as good.

Going Down: Pat Verbeek will have a reduced role with Hull in town.

Goalies: Ed Belfour doesn't like to share. Roman Turek may need a trade to get playing time.

Top Five Scorers: Modano, Hull, Nieuwendyk, Langenbrunner, Zubov

DETROIT

Top Scoring Line: Brendan Shanahan, Sergei Fedorov, Slava Kozlov, Steve Yzerman, Tomas Holmstrom, and Darren McCarty to choose from.

Top Power Play Unit: Yzerman, Shanahan, and Fedorov figure to get the most work up front, with Nicklas Lidstrom full-time on one point, and Larry Murphy getting the most playing time on the other.

Rookie Scoring Candidates: None

Possible Breakout Players: None

Sleeper: Holmstrom was a big factor in the playoffs after a poor regular season.

Going Up: Holmstrom, and Anders Ericksson will get more time with veterans moved out.

Going Down: Doug Brown overachieved and should come down slightly; Larry Murphy has passed the danger zone age-wise. Igor Larionov in the same boat.

Goalies: Chris Osgood will play at least two-thirds of the games. Kevin Hodson is the backup.

Top Five Scorers: Fedorov, Shanahan, Yzerman, Lidstrom, Kozlov

EDMONTON
Top Scoring Line: Ryan Smyth-Doug Weight-Bill Guerin

Top Power Play Unit: Three offensive defencemen to choose from in Roman Hamrlik, Janne Niinimaa and Boris Mironov. Maybe one too many. Up front, look for the top scoring line.

Rookie Scoring Candidates: Boyd Devereaux, but not likely to score too much right away.

Possible Breakout Players: Mats Lindgren a longshot possibility.

Sleeper: Smyth was plagued by injuries last season. He and Guerin have less games played so they'll be down scoring lists. Josef Berenak is back from Europe, but didn't score much the last time he was in North America

Going Up: Smyth and Guerin.

Going Down: Dean McAmmond has to show last year's second half uprising wasn't just a mirage.

Goalies: Eric Fichaud was the only goalie on board at press time. Count on changes there.

FLORIDA
Top Scoring Line: have mostly third lines.

Top Power Play Unit: Ray Whitney, Dino Cicarelli, Rob Niedermayer, Robert Svehla on one point, maybe Ed Jovanovski on the other.

Rookie Scoring Candidates: Jaroslav Spacek could see time on the power play. He is a 24-year-old drafted this year.

Possible Breakout Players: Take your pick — Radek Dvorak, Viktor Kozlov, David Nemirovsky, Ed Jovanovski, Steve Washburn, Chris Wells.

Sleeper: Niedermayer missed most of last season, so he won't be high on many lists.

Going Up: all the possible breakout players listed above. Possibly.

Going Down: Age is catching up with

Ciccarelli. Can Whitney repeat last year's offensive explosion?

Goalies: Kirk McLean and Kevin Weekes were on board at press time, but don't be surprised if a change is made there.

Top 5 Scorers: Niedermayer, Whitney, Kozlov, Mellanby, Svehla

LOS ANGELES
Top Scoring Line: Vladimir Tsyplakov-Josef Stumpel-Glen Murray

Top Power Play Unit: top line plus Steve Duchesne and Rob Blake.

Rookie Scoring Candidates: Olli Jokkinen

Possible Breakout Players: None

Sleeper: Ray Ferraro, if he can make a successful return after injuries.

Going Up: None

Going Down: Garry Galley is a third wheel with Duchesne signed as a free agent. Yanic Perreault slowed down when taken off top line.

Goalies: Jamie Storr may be ready to challenge Stephane Fiset for the number one job. Or more likely, they may just share it.

Top 5 Scorers: Stumpel, Duchesne, Murray, Tsyplakov, Blake

MONTREAL
Top Scoring Line: Shayne Corson-Saku Koivu-Mark Recchi, but second number one line could be Martin Rucinsky-Vincent Damphousse-Brian Savage.

Top Power Play Unit: Vladimir Malakhov and Patrice Brisebois on the points with Corson, Koivu and Recchi most often among the forwards.

Rookie Scoring Candidates: None

Possible Breakout Players: None likely

Sleeper: Benoit Brunet caught fire in second half, but isn't expected to be a big scorer.

Going Up: Koivu, Savage and Corson all missed significant time with injuries.

Going Down: Corson may have problems maintaining the same pace he had last year, because it was out of character with recent performance.

Goalies: Jocelyn Thibault and Jose Theodore, but Felix Potvin may have been on the way there after press deadline.

Top 5 Scorers: Recchi, Koivu, Damphousse, Savage, Rucinsky

NASHVILLE
Top Scoring Line: Wait until training camp

Top Power Play Unit: Wait until training camp

Rookie Scoring Candidates: David Legwand

Possible Breakout Players: Anybody who gets to play

Sleeper: Just about every player

Going Up: Most of them because they're getting a chance to play regularly, some on scoring line. And no matter what team it is, somebody has to score.

Going Down: Almost impossible

Goalies: Mike Dunham looks to have the inside track for number one, with Mikael Shtalenkov for the backup. It won't matter anyway, because you don't want any of these guys in your pool, they're going to lose a lot of games.

Top Five Scorers: Brunette, Legwand, Bordeleau, Johnson, Turcotte

NEW JERSEY
Top Scoring Line: could have three evenly matched lines.

Top Power Play Unit: Could be Brendan Morrison, Bobby Holik, Dave Andreychuk and Rob Niedermayer on the point with the closest defenceman.

Rookie Scoring Candidates: Brendan Morrison could be rookie of the year.

Possible Breakout Players: The Devils often have two or three in that category. This year, there's Brian Rolston and Denis Pederson.

Sleeper: Jason Arnott is still young

Going Up: Arnott, Rolston, Pederson.

Going Down: Randy McKay isn't like to repeat career season.

Goalies: Martin Brodeur is all we need to know

Top Five Scorers: Holik, Niedermayer, Morrison, Arnott, Rolston

NY ISLANDERS
Top Scoring Line: Trevor Linden and Ziggy Palffy, with Mariusz Czercawski sometimes.

Top Power Play Unit: Linden, Palffy, Robert Reichel up front, with Bryan Berard and Kenny Jonsson on the points.

Rookie Scoring Candidates: Dmitri Nabokov

Possible Breakout Players: None

Sleeper: Bryan Smolinski is coming off a terrible year

Going Up: Smolinski and Jason Dawe if he gets time on the number one line.

Going Down: Reichel moves down a notch with Linden on board.

Goalies: Tommy Salo is the incumbent number one, but the Islanders are looking for someone else.

Top Five Scorers: Palffy, Berard, Reichel, Linden, Smolinski

NY RANGERS

Top Scoring Line: Niklas Sundstrom-Wayne Gretzky-Alexei Kovalev

Top Power Play Unit: Top Line with Adam Graves frequently up front, and Brian Leetch and possibly Alexander Karpovtsev on the points.

Rookie Scoring Candidates: Marc Savard and Manny Maholtra

Possible Breakout Players: Todd Harvey

Sleeper: Adam Graves was plagued by injuries last season and could rebound in a big way.

Going Up: Graves, Harvey.

Going Down: Kevin Stevens and John McLean are both getting too old, and neither are Wayne Gretzky.

Goalies: Mike Richter re-signed with the Rangers. Dan Cloutier should get more playing time.

Top Five Scorers: Gretzky, Leetch, Kovalev, Sundstrom, Graves

Notes: Pat LaFontaine still hadn't been cleared to play at press time. Even if he his, however, there's no guarantee of how much or how long he'll be able to play.

OTTAWA

Top Scoring Line: Shawn McEachern-Alexei Yashin-Daniel Alfredsson

Top Power Play Unit: Top line with Igor Kravchuk, Janne Laukkanen, or Wade Redden.

Rookie Scoring Candidates: None

Possible Breakout Players: Radek Bonk for about the 10th year in a row.

Sleeper: Alfredsson missed 28 games with injuries, so he's down on the scoring lists.

Going Up: Alfredsson

Going Down: Vaclav Prospal could go down further, like to the minors.

Goalies: Tugnutt and Rhodes have a fairly even split of games played.

Top Five Scorers: Yashin, Alfredsson, McEachern, Dackell, Arvedsson

Notes: The Senators need a power play quarterback. If they get one he should score well because the team only has one scoring line.

PHILADELPHIA

Top Scoring Line: Eric Lindros-John LeClair-a lucky right winger.

Top Power Play Unit: Lindros, LeClair, Rod Brind'Amour, and Eric Desjardins and Dan McGillis on the points.

Rookie Scoring Candidates: None

Possible Breakout Players: Danius Zubrus, but it's a longshot

Sleeper: Alexandre Daigle might click on first line and pile in points.

Going Up: Daigle, Mike Sillinger, Lindros.

Going Down: Trent Klatt got a lot of points last year on top line, but that isn't the place for him.

Goalies: John Vanbiesbrouck takes over as the number one goalie. That means Ron Hextall is on way out.

Top Five Scorers: Lindros, LeClair, Brind'Amour, Gratton, Daigle

PHOENIX
Top Scoring Line: Keith Tkachuk-Jeremy Roenick-Rick Tocchet

Top Power Play Unit: top line with a bunch of possible pointmen including Teppo Numminen, Jrkyi Lumme, Oleg Tverdovsky and Deron Quint

Rookie Scoring Candidates: Daniel Briere is a rookie-of-the-year candidate

Possible Breakout Players: Quint if he gets the necessary power play time.

Sleeper: Nobody stands out.

Going Up: None

Going Down: None

Goalies: Nikolai Khabibulin

Top Five Scorers: Tocchet, Roenick, Ronning,

Tverdovsky, Numminen

PITTSBURGH
Top Scoring Line: German Titov-Stu Barnes-Jaromir Jagr

Top Power Play Unit: Titov, Barnes, Jagr, Kevin Hatcher and a player to be named later.

Rookie Scoring Candidates: None

Possible Breakout Players: None

Sleeper: Petr Nedved still hadn't been signed as of press time.

Going Up: Titov has better linemates than in Calgary

Going Down: Many should suffer with the loss of Francis.

Goalies: Tom Barrasso, but continued good health a major concern.

Top Five Scorers: Jagr, Barnes, Hatcher, Titov, Morozov

Notes: If the Penguins trade Nedved it will probably be for someone who can play with Jagr. Whoever it is will jump in point value.

SAN JOSE
Top Scoring Line: Jeff Friesen-Patrick Marleau-Owen Nolan

Top Power Play Unit: Top line with newcomer Gary Suter on one point and Bill Houlder,

Marcus Ragnarsson, and Andrei Zyuzin sharing the other.

Rookie Scoring Candidates: None

Possible Breakout Players: Zyuzin has great offensive potential, but needs time on the power play

Sleeper: Joe Murphy could make comeback from injuries

Going Up: Murphy, Mike Ricci

Going Down: None

Goalies: Mike Vernon, with backup from Steve Shields

Top Five Scorers: Friesen, Nolan, Marleau, Murphy, Suter

Notes: A number of free agents who were with the Sharks last year had not signed, but were expected to, including Tony Granato and Bernie Nicholls.

ST.LOUIS
Top Scoring Line: Pierre Turgeon and Geoff Courtnall are looking for a new right winger with departure of Brett Hull

Top Power Play Unit: Turgeon, Courtnall, Al MacInnis, and open auditions.

Rookie Scoring Candidates: None

Possible Breakout Players: depends on latest

career minor league signed by Blues.

Sleeper: None

Going Up: None

Going Down: Just about everyone

Goalies: Grant Fuhr will probably share more time with Jamie McLellan, who earned it last year.

Top Five Scorers: Turgeon, Courtnall, MacInnis, Campbell, Demitra

Notes: The Blues look like a team capable of taking a big nosedive in the standings.

TAMPA BAY

Top Scoring Line: Stephane Richer-Craig Janney-Mikael Renberg

Top Power Play Unit: Top Line with rookie Vincent Lecavalier probably getting time. David Wilkie should assert himself as one of the pointmen.

Rookie Scoring Candidates: Top draft pick, Vincent Lecavalier

Possible Breakout Players: Daymond Langkow, Darcy Tucker

Sleeper: Brian Bradley if he plays.

Going Up: Langkow

Going Down: Paul Ysebeart

Goalies: Bill Ranford has something to prove after being pushed aside in Washington.

Top Five Scorers: Janney, Renberg, Langkow, Lecavalier, Richer

Notes: The status of Brian Bradley and John Cullen was unknown at press time. Watch training camp to see what happens with them.

TORONTO
Top Scoring Line: Steve Thomas-Mats Sundin-Mike Johnson, although both spots beside Sundin could be filled via trade.

Top Power Play Unit: Sundin with Mathieu Schneider and Sylvain Cote on the points. Take your pick of available forwards for the leftovers.

Rookie Scoring Candidates: None

Possible Breakout Players: Fredrik Modin had a wild scoring stretch for about a month last season.

Sleeper: If anybody other than Sundin scores a lot it will be a surprise, so theoretically the whole team could be sleepers.

Going Up: Thomas, Modin, Alyn McCauley

Going Down: Derek King moves down a notch on left wing with addition of Thomas. Igor Korolev all but invisible after fast start.

Goalies: As of this writing, the Leafs had Curtis Joseph and Felix Potvin, which would give them the best goaltending duo in the league. Obviously, they will trade Potvin.

Notes: Whomever the Leafs get for Potvin is likely to be an impact player on the Leafs. If they're a scorer they have a good shot at playing on the top line, so their point value should be increased.

VANCOUVER
Top Scoring Line: Pavel Bure, with Mark Messier and maybe Alexander Mogilny.

Top Power Play Unit: Bure, Messier, Mogilny, and Scott McCabe and Mattias Ohlund on the points.

Rookie Scoring Candidates: Josh Holden

Possible Breakout Players: Todd Bertuzzi

Sleeper: Alexander Mogilny can shoot up the point ladder if he feels like it.

Going Up: Mogilny, but maybe not with Canucks.

Going Down: Peter Zezel scored late in the season, but that's not his game anymore.

Goalies: Were still looking for one, but had two backups in Garth Snow and Corey Hirsch.

Notes: This is one team that will probably make some changes close to the start of the season.

WASHINGTON
Top Scoring Line: Joe Juneau-Adam Oates-Peter Bondra

Top Power Play Unit: Oates, Juneau, Bondra, and lots of other forward possibilities, with Dmitri Mironov and Calle Johansson minding the points.

Rookie Scoring Candidates: Yogi Svejkovsky

Possible Breakout Players: None

Sleeper: Andrei Nikolishin may be back in form

Going Up: Jan Bulis, Richard Zednik, Steve Konowalchuk

Going Down: None

Goalies: Olaf Kolzig

Top Five Scorers: Bondra, Oates, Juneau, Nikolishin, Mironov

Stat Section

EASTERN CONFERENCE (X-qualified for Stanley Cup playoffs)
Northeast Division

	GP	W	L	T	GF	GA	PTS	PCT
X-PITTSBURGH (2)	82	40	24	18	228	188	98	.598
X-BOSTON (5)	82	39	30	13	221	194	91	.555
X-BUFFALO (6)	82	36	29	17	211	187	89	.543
X-MONTREAL (7)	82	37	32	13	235	208	87	.530
X-OTTAWA (8)	82	34	33	15	193	200	83	.506
CAROLINA (9)	82	33	41	8	200	219	74	.451

Atlantic Division

	GP	W	L	T	GF	GA	PTS	PCT
X-NEW JERSEY (1)	82	48	23	11	225	166	107	.652
X-PHILADELPHIA (3)	82	42	29	11	242	193	95	.579
X-WASHINGTON (4)	82	40	30	12	219	202	92	.561
NY ISLANDERS (10)	82	30	41	11	212	225	71	.433
NY RANGERS (11)	82	25	39	18	197	231	68	.415
FLORIDA (12)	82	24	43	15	203	256	63	.384
TAMPA BAY (13)	82	17	55	10	151	269	44	.268

WESTERN CONFERENCE
Central Division

	GP	W	L	T	GF	GA	PTS	PCT
X-DALLAS (1)	82	49	22	11	242	167	109	.665

	GP	W	L	T	GF	GA	PTS	PCT
X-DETROIT (3)	82	44	23	15	250	196	103	.628
X-ST LOUIS (4)	82	45	29	8	256	204	98	.598
X-PHOENIX (6)	82	35	35	12	224	227	82	.500
CHICAGO (9)	82	30	39	13	192	199	73	.445
TORONTO (10)	82	30	43	9	194	237	69	.421

Pacific Division

	GP	W	L	T	GF	GA	PTS	PCT
X-COLORADO(2)	82	39	26	17	231	205	95	.579
X-LOS ANGELES (5)	82	38	33	11	227	225	87	.530
X-EDMONTON(7)	82	35	37	10	215	224	80	.488
X-SAN JOSE (8)	82	34	38	10	210	216	78	.476
CALGARY (11)	82	26	41	15	217	252	67	.409
ANAHEIM (12)	82	26	43	13	205	261	65	.396
VANCOUVER (13)	82	25	43	14	224	273	64	.390

TEAM STANDINGS (by conference)

Eastern Conference

	GP	W	L	T	GF	GA	PTS	PCT
NEW JERSEY	82	48	23	11	225	166	107	.652
PITTSBURGH	82	40	24	18	228	188	98	.598
PHILADELPHIA	82	42	29	11	242	193	95	.579
WASHINGTON	82	40	30	12	219	202	92	.561
BOSTON	82	39	30	13	221	194	91	.555
BUFFALO	82	36	29	17	211	187	89	.543
MONTREAL	82	37	32	13	235	208	87	.530
OTTAWA	82	34	33	15	193	200	83	.506
CAROLINA	82	33	41	8	200	219	74	.451
NY ISLANDERS	82	30	41	11	212	225	71	.433
NY RANGERS	82	25	39	18	197	231	68	.415
FLORIDA	82	24	43	15	203	256	63	.384
TAMPA BAY	82	17	55	10	151	269	44	.268

Western Conference

	GP	W	L	T	GF	GA	PTS	PCT
DALLAS	82	49	22	11	242	167	109	.665
DETROIT	82	44	23	15	250	196	103	.628
ST LOUIS	82	45	29	8	256	204	98	.598
COLORADO	82	39	26	17	231	205	95	.579
LOS ANGELES	82	38	33	11	227	225	87	.530
PHOENIX	82	35	35	12	224	227	82	.500
EDMONTON	82	35	37	10	215	224	80	.488
SAN JOSE	82	34	38	10	210	216	78	.476
CHICAGO	82	30	39	13	192	199	73	.445
TORONTO	82	30	43	9	194	237	69	.421
CALGARY	82	26	41	15	217	252	67	.409
ANAHEIM	82	26	43	13	205	261	65	.396
VANCOUVER	82	25	43	14	224	273	64	.390

OVERALL STANDINGS

	GP	W	L	T	GF	GA	PTS	PCT
DALLAS	82	49	22	11	242	167	109	.665
NEW JERSEY	82	48	23	11	225	166	107	.652
DETROIT	82	44	23	15	250	196	103	.628
ST LOUIS	82	45	29	8	256	204	98	.598
PITTSBURGH	82	40	24	18	228	188	98	.598
PHILADELPHIA	82	42	29	11	242	193	95	.579
COLORADO	82	39	26	17	231	205	95	.579
WASHINGTON	82	40	30	12	219	202	92	.561
BOSTON	82	39	30	13	221	194	91	.555
BUFFALO	82	36	29	17	211	187	89	.543
LOS ANGELES	82	38	33	11	227	225	87	.530
MONTREAL	82	37	32	13	235	208	87	.530
OTTAWA	82	34	33	15	193	200	83	.506
PHOENIX	82	35	35	12	224	227	82	.500
EDMONTON	82	35	37	10	215	224	80	.488
SAN JOSE	82	34	38	10	210	216	78	.476
CAROLINA	82	33	41	8	200	219	74	.451
CHICAGO	82	30	39	13	192	199	73	.445

NY ISLANDERS	82	30	41	11	212	225	71	.433
TORONTO	82	30	43	9	194	237	69	.421
NY RANGERS	82	25	39	18	197	231	68	.415
CALGARY	82	26	41	15	217	252	67	.409
ANAHEIM	82	26	43	13	205	261	65	.396
VANCOUVER	82	25	43	14	224	273	64	.390
FLORIDA	82	24	43	15	203	256	63	.384
TAMPA BAY	82	17	55	10	151	269	44	.268

TEAMS' HOME-AND-ROAD RECORD (by conference)

HOME

Eastern Conference

	GP	W	L	T	GF	GA	PTS	PCT
NEW JERSEY (1)	41	29	10	2	131	86	60	.732
PITTSBURGH (4)	41	21	10	10	125	98	52	.634
PHILADELPHIA (2)	41	24	11	6	116	86	54	.659
WASHINGTON (3)	41	23	12	6	116	94	52	.634
BOSTON (6)	41	19	16	6	108	94	44	.537
BUFFALO (5)	41	20	13	8	113	82	48	.585
MONTREAL 9)	41	15	17	9	117	109	39	.476
OTTAWA (7)	41	18	16	7	102	98	43	.524
CAROLINA (8)	41	16	18	7	106	109	39	.476
NY ISLANDERS (10)	41	17	20	4	106	104	38	.463
NY RANGERS (11)	41	14	18	9	102	103	37	.451
FLORIDA (13)	41	11	24	6	102	135	28	.341
TAMPA BAY (12)	41	11	23	7	88	127	29	.354
CONFERENCE TOTAL	533	238	208	87	1,432	1,325	563	.528

Western Conference

	GP	W	L	T	GF	GA	PTS	PCTG
DALLAS (1)	41	26	8	7	123	73	59	.720
DETROIT (2)	41	25	8	8	130	92	58	.707
ST LOUIS (3)	41	26	10	5	131	94	57	.695
COLORADO (4)	41	21	10	10	119	95	52	.634
LOS ANGELES (5)	41	22	16	3	128	115	47	.573

PHOENIX (7)	41	19	16	6	123	115	44	.537
EDMONTON (6)	41	20	16	5	103	103	45	.549
SAN JOSE (9)	41	17	19	5	106	102	39	.476
CHICAGO (11)	41	14	19	8	82	90	36	.439
TORONTO (10)	41	16	20	5	110	128	37	.451
CALGARY (8)	41	18	17	6	118	118	42	.512
ANAHEIM (13)	41	12	23	6	94	134	30	.366
VANCOUVER (12)	41	15	22	4	110	131	34	.415
CONFERENCE TOTAL	533	251	204	78	1,477	1,390	580	.544
HOME TOTAL	1,066	489	412	165	2,909	2,715	1,143	.536

ROAD

Eastern Conference

	GP	W	L	T	GF	GA	PTS	PCT
NEW JERSEY (3)	41	19	13	9	94	80	47	.573
PITTSBURGH (4)	41	19	14	8	103	90	46	.561
PHILADELPHIA (5)	41	18	18	5	126	107	41	.500
WASHINGTON (7)	41	17	18	6	103	108	40	.488
BOSTON (2)	41	20	14	7	113	100	47	.573
BUFFALO (6)	41	16	16	9	98	105	41	.500
MONTREAL (1)	41	22	15	4	118	99	48	.585
OTTAWA (8)	41	16	17	8	91	102	40	.488
CAROLINA (9)	41	17	23	1	94	110	35	.427
NY ISLANDERS (11)	41	13	21	7	106	121	33	.402
NY RANGERS (12)	41	11	21	9	95	128	31	.378
FLORIDA (10)	41	13	19	9	101	121	35	.427
TAMPA BAY (13)	41	6	32	3	63	142	15	.183
CONFERENCE TOTAL	533	207	241	85	1,305	1,413	499	.468

Western Conference

	GP	W	L	T	GF	GA	PTS	PCT
DALLAS (1)	41	23	14	4	119	94	50	.610
DETROIT (2)	41	19	15	7	120	104	45	.549
ST LOUIS (4)	41	19	19	3	125	110	41	.500
COLORADO (3)	41	18	16	7	112	110	43	.524

LOS ANGELES (5)	41	16	17	8	99	110	40	.488
PHOENIX (7)	41	16	19	6	101	112	38	.463
EDMONTON 9)	41	15	21	5	112	121	35	.427
SAN JOSE 6)	41	17	19	5	104	114	39	.476
CHICAGO (8)	41	16	20	5	110	109	37	.451
TORONTO (11)	41	14	23	4	84	109	32	.390
CALGARY (13)	41	8	24	9	99	134	25	.305
ANAHEIM (10)	41	14	20	7	111	127	35	.427
VANCOUVER (12)	41	10	21	10	114	142	30	.366
CONFERENCE TOTAL	533	205	248	80	1,410	1,496	490	.460
ROAD TOTAL	1,066	412	489	165	2,715	2,909	989	.464

TEAMS' INTER-CONFERENCE RECORD

AGAINST OWN CONFERENCE
Eastern Conference

	GP	W	L	T	GF	GA	PTS	PCT
NEW JERSEY (1)	56	36	13	7	158	109	79	.705
PITTSBURGH (2)	56	28	16	12	151	124	68	.607
PHILADELPHIA (3)	56	29	19	8	167	138	66	.589
WASHINGTON (4)	56	28	20	8	146	130	64	.571
BOSTON (5)	56	26	19	11	153	134	63	.563
BUFFALO (6)	56	25	20	11	137	118	61	.545
MONTREAL (8)	56	22	26	8	157	145	52	.464
OTTAWA (7)	56	24	22	10	130	135	58	.518
CAROLINA (11)	56	20	32	4	129	145	44	.393
NY ISLANDERS (9)	56	22	26	8	148	152	52	.464
NY RANGERS (12)	56	15	30	11	129	167	41	.366
FLORIDA (10)	56	22	26	8	153	175	52	.464
TAMPA BAY (13)	56	10	38	8	102	188	28	.250
CONF. TOTAL	728	307	307	114	1,860	1,860	728	.500

Western Conference

	GP	W	L	T	GF	GA	PTS	PCT
DALLAS (1)	56	32	17	7	160	119	71	.634
DETROIT (4)	56	27	17	12	175	140	66	.589
ST LOUIS (2)	56	32	20	4	181	137	68	.607
COLORADO (3)	56	28	18	10	164	134	66	.589
LOS ANGELES (5)	56	29	22	5	160	160	63	.563
PHOENIX (6)	56	28	22	6	166	153	62	.554
EDMONTON (7)	56	27	25	4	152	153	58	.518
SAN JOSE (8)	56	25	26	5	148	150	55	.491
CHICAGO (10)	56	16	29	11	127	146	43	.384
TORONTO (9)	56	22	27	7	138	155	51	.455
CALGARY (12)	56	16	30	10	153	188	42	.375
ANAHEIM (13)	56	16	32	8	135	191	40	.357
VANCOUVER (11)	56	16	29	11	150	183	43	.384
CONF. TOTAL	728	314	314	100	2,009	2,009	728	.500

VS. OWN CONF.   1,456 621   621   214   3,869   3,869   1,456 .500

AGAINST OTHER CONFERENCE
Eastern Conference

	GP	W	L	T	GF	GA	PTS	PCT
NEW JERSEY (6)	26	12	10	4	67	57	28	.538
PITTSBURGH (3)	26	12	8	6	77	64	30	.577
PHILADELPHIA (4)	26	13	10	3	75	55	29	.558
WASHINGTON (7)	26	12	10	4	73	72	28	.538
BOSTON (5)	26	13	11	2	68	60	28	.538
BUFFALO (8)	26	11	9	6	74	69	28	.538
MONTREAL (1)	26	15	6	5	78	63	35	.673
OTTAWA (10)	26	10	11	5	63	65	25	.481
CAROLINA (2)	26	13	9	4	71	74	30	.577
NY ISLANDERS (11)	26	8	15	3	64	73	19	.365
NY RANGERS (9)	26	10	9	7	68	64	27	.519
FLORIDA (13)	26	2	17	7	50	81	11	.212
TAMPA BAY (12)	26	7	17	2	49	81	16	.308
CONF. TOTAL	338	138	142	58	877	878	334	.494

Western Conference

	GP	W	L	T	GF	GA	PTS	PCT
DALLAS (1)	26	17	5	4	82	48	38	.731
DETROIT (2)	26	17	6	3	75	56	37	.712
ST LOUIS (4)	26	13	9	4	75	67	30	.577
COLORADO (5)	26	11	8	7	67	71	29	.558
LOS ANGELES (8)	26	9	11	6	67	65	24	.462
PHOENIX (12)	26	7	13	6	58	74	20	.385
EDMONTON (10)	26	8	12	6	63	71	22	.423
SAN JOSE (9)	26	9	12	5	62	66	23	.442
CHICAGO (3)	26	14	10	2	65	53	30	.577
TORONTO (13)	26	8	16	2	56	82	18	.346
CALGARY (6)	26	10	11	5	64	64	25	.481
ANAHEIM (7)	26	10	11	5	70	70	25	.481
VANCOUVER (11)	26	9	14	3	74	90	21	.404
CONF. TOTAL	338	142	138	58	878	877	342	.506

VS. OTHER CONF.	676	280	280	116	1,755	1,755	676	.500

DURACELL POWER PLAY REPORT

(ADV) TOTAL ADVANTAGES (PPGF) POWER-PLAY GOALS FOR
(PCTG) ARRIVED BY DIVIDING NUMBER OF POWER-PLAY GOALS BY TOTAL ADVANTAGES

	HOME					ROAD					OVER ALL				
	TEAM	GP	ADV	PPGF	PCT	TEAM	GP	ADV	PPGF	PCT	TEAM	GP	ADV	PPGF	PCT
1	N.J	41	158	38	24.1	DAL	41	185	40	21.6	DAL	82	385	77	20.0
2	NYI	41	197	38	19.3	PHI	41	190	38	20.0	N.J	82	333	63	18.9
3	STL	41	201	38	18.9	MTL	41	186	37	19.9	MTL	82	372	68	18.3
4	NYR	41	175	33	18.9	BOS	41	162	31	19.1	PHI	82	399	71	17.8
5	DAL	41	200	37	18.5	COL	41	207	38	18.4	NYR	82	351	62	17.7
6	DET	41	195	35	17.9	EDM	41	237	43	18.1	DET	82	381	67	17.6
7	WSH	41	174	31	17.8	DET	41	186	32	17.2	COL	82	425	74	17.4
8	PIT	41	209	37	17.7	NYR	41	176	29	16.5	BOS	82	359	62	17.3
9	MTL	41	186	31	16.7	PHO	41	187	29	15.5	STL	82	368	62	16.8
10	COL	41	218	36	16.5	S.J	41	181	28	15.5	NYI	82	364	61	16.8
11	PHI	41	209	33	15.8	CHI	41	175	27	15.4	PIT	82	407	67	16.5

#	TEAM	GP				TEAM	GP				TEAM	GP			
12	BOS	41	197	31	15.7	VAN	41	175	27	15.4	EDM	82	483	77	15.9
13	BUF	41	197	30	15.2	PIT	41	198	30	15.2	WSH	82	350	55	15.7
14	OTT	41	199	30	15.1	L.A	41	156	23	14.7	PHO	82	384	57	14.8
15	TOR	41	186	27	14.5	STL	41	167	24	14.4	L.A	82	366	52	14.2
16	PHO	41	197	28	14.2	N.J	41	175	25	14.3	S.J	82	400	54	13.5
17	EDM	41	246	34	13.8	ANA	41	202	28	13.9	FLA	82	409	55	13.4
18	L.A	41	210	29	13.8	NYI	41	167	23	13.8	CAR	82	378	50	13.2
19	FLA	41	207	28	13.5	WSH	41	176	24	13.6	BUF	82	396	51	12.9
20	CAR	41	195	26	13.3	FLA	41	202	27	13.4	CHI	82	364	47	12.9
21	CGY	41	180	22	12.2	CAR	41	183	24	13.1	VAN	82	373	48	12.9
22	S.J	41	219	26	11.9	CGY	41	176	21	11.9	OTT	82	375	48	12.8
23	VAN	41	198	21	10.6	BUF	41	199	21	10.6	CGY	82	356	43	12.1
24	CHI	41	189	20	10.6	OTT	41	176	18	10.2	ANA	82	392	46	11.7
25	T.B	41	182	19	10.4	T.B	41	171	14	8.2	TOR	82	359	41	11.4
26	ANA	41	190	18	9.5	TOR	41	173	14	8.1	T.B	82	353	33	9.3
		1,066	5,114	776	15.2		1,066	4,768	715	15.0		1,066	9,882	1,491	15.1

TEAMS' PENALTY KILLING RECORD

(TSH) TOTAL TIMES SHORT-HANDED (PPGA) POWER-PLAY GOALS AGAINST
(PCTG) ARRIVED BY DIVIDING -TIMES SHORT MINUS POWER-PLAY GOALS AGAINST-
BY TIMES SHORT

	HOME					ROAD					OVER ALL				
	TEAM	GP	TSH	PPGA	PCT	TEAM	GP	TSH	PPGA	PCT	TEAM	GP	TSH	PPGA	PCT
1	PHI	41	171	15	91.2	WSH	41	192	21	89.1	WSH	82	361	39	89.2
2	WSH	41	169	18	89.3	TOR	41	191	21	89.0	DAL	82	351	42	88.0
3	DET	41	194	21	89.2	PIT	41	173	21	87.9	COL	82	410	53	87.1
4	BUF	41	187	21	88.8	COL	41	209	26	87.6	N.J	82	309	41	86.7
5	DAL	41	175	20	88.6	DAL	41	176	22	87.5	PHI	82	382	51	86.6
6	MTL	41	194	25	87.1	S.J	41	207	27	87.0	TOR	82	372	50	86.6
7	NYI	41	186	24	87.1	N.J	41	167	22	86.8	STL	82	367	49	86.6
8	STL	41	189	25	86.8	STL	41	178	24	86.5	PIT	82	338	46	86.4
9	COL	41	201	27	86.6	BOS	41	147	20	86.4	DET	82	376	51	86.4
10	N.J	41	142	19	86.6	CHI	41	197	28	85.8	NYI	82	384	54	85.9
11	CGY	41	201	28	86.1	T.B	41	198	29	85.4	NYR	82	376	55	85.4
12	NYR	41	170	24	85.9	CAR	41	197	29	85.3	CAR	82	391	58	85.2
13	CAR	41	194	29	85.1	L.A	41	193	29	85.0	S.J	82	398	59	85.2
14	OTT	41	141	21	85.1	NYR	41	206	31	85.0	CHI	82	381	58	84.8

15	PIT	41	165	25	84.8		NYI	41	198	30	84.8		BOS	82	285	44	84.6
16	TOR	41	181	29	84.0		PHO	41	209	33	84.2		MTL	82	401	62	84.5
17	CHI	41	184	30	83.7		EDM	41	201	32	84.1		OTT	82	303	47	84.5
18	L.A	41	206	34	83.5		OTT	41	162	26	84.0		BUF	82	413	65	84.3
19	PHO	41	199	33	83.4		DET	41	182	30	83.5		L.A	82	399	63	84.2
20	EDM	41	205	34	83.4		VAN	41	216	37	82.9		CGY	82	430	69	84.0
21	S.J	41	191	32	83.2		PHI	41	211	36	82.9		PHO	82	408	66	83.8
22	BOS	41	138	24	82.6		ANA	41	220	39	82.3		EDM	82	406	66	83.7
23	VAN	41	216	40	81.5		MTL	41	207	37	82.1		T.B	82	410	72	82.4
24	ANA	41	176	33	81.3		CGY	41	229	41	82.1		VAN	82	432	77	82.2
25	T.B	41	212	43	79.7		FLA	41	222	41	81.5		ANA	82	396	72	81.8
26	FLA	41	181	41	77.3		BUF	41	226	44	80.5		FLA	82	403	82	79.7
		1,066	4,768	715	85.0			1,066	5,114	776	84.8			1,066	9,882	1491	84.9

SHORT HAND GOALS FOR

	HOME				ROAD				OVER ALL		
	TEAM	GP	SHGF		TEAM	GP	SHGF		TEAM	GP	SHGF
1	CGY	41	11		VAN	41	13		VAN	82	19
2	MTL	41	10		CHI	41	10		CGY	82	18
3	BUF	41	9		FLA	41	9		BUF	82	15
4	EDM	41	8		DAL	41	9		WSH	82	14
5	T.B	41	7		WSH	41	7		MTL	82	13
6	COL	41	7		STL	41	7		CHI	82	13
7	WSH	41	7		CGY	41	7		FLA	82	12
8	NYI	41	7		BUF	41	6		STL	82	12
9	L.A	41	7		PHO	41	6		PIT	82	11
10	PIT	41	6		ANA	41	6		T.B	82	11
11	VAN	41	6		PIT	41	5		DAL	82	11
12	STL	41	5		S.J	41	5		NYI	82	11
13	S.J	41	5		OTT	41	4		L.A	82	10
14	DET	41	5		CAR	41	4		PHO	82	10
15	PHI	41	4		NYI	41	4		S.J	82	10
16	TOR	41	4		T.B	41	4		EDM	82	10
17	PHO	41	4		L.A	41	3		ANA	82	9
18	BOS	41	4		DET	41	3		CAR	82	8
19	CAR	41	4		MTL	41	3		COL	82	8
20	ANA	41	3		PHI	41	3		DET	82	8
21	CHI	41	3		EDM	41	2		PHI	82	7

22	FLA	41	3		N.J	41	2		OTT	82	6
23	OTT	41	2		COL	41	1		TOR	82	5
24	DAL	41	2		TOR	41	1		BOS	82	5
25	N.J	41	2		BOS	41	1		N.J	82	4
26	NYR	41	0		NYR	41	0		NYR	82	0
		1066	135			1066	125			1066	260

SHORT HAND GOALS AGAINST

	HOME			ROAD			OVER ALL		
	TEAM	GP	SHGA	TEAM	GP	SHGA	TEAM	GP	SHGA
1	STL	41	1	L.A	41	1	BOS	82	3
2	WSH	41	1	BOS	41	1	WSH	82	4
3	CHI	41	1	PHO	41	2	STL	82	4
4	PHI	41	2	MTL	41	2	CHI	82	5
5	COL	41	2	S.J	41	2	S.J	82	5
6	BOS	41	2	WSH	41	3	PHO	82	6
7	S.J	41	3	STL	41	3	DET	82	7
8	OTT	41	3	CHI	41	4	MTL	82	8
9	DAL	41	3	DET	41	4	OTT	82	9
10	DET	41	3	N.J	41	4	PHI	82	9
11	PHO	41	4	ANA	41	4	DAL	82	9
12	CAR	41	4	CGY	41	4	N.J	82	9
13	NYR	41	4	EDM	41	5	CAR	82	10
14	T.B	41	5	PIT	41	5	ANA	82	10
15	BUF	41	5	TOR	41	5	EDM	82	11
16	N.J	41	5	OTT	41	6	L.A	82	12
17	FLA	41	5	CAR	41	6	BUF	82	12
18	MTL	41	6	DAL	41	6	COL	82	12
19	EDM	41	6	VAN	41	6	VAN	82	12
20	VAN	41	6	BUF	41	7	TOR	82	13
21	ANA	41	6	NYI	41	7	CGY	82	13
22	TOR	41	8	PHI	41	7	NYR	82	13
23	CGY	41	9	NYR	41	9	PIT	82	16
24	NYI	41	9	COL	41	10	FLA	82	16
25	PIT	41	11	FLA	41	11	T.B	82	16
26	L.A	41	11	T.B	41	11	NYI	82	16
		1,066	125		1,066	135		1,066	260

INDIVIDUAL SCORING LEADERS

PLAYER	TEAM	GP	G	A	PTS	+/-	PIM	PP	SH	GW	GT	S	PCT
JAROMIR JAGR	PITTSBURGH	77	35	67	102	17	64	7	0	8	2	262	13.4
P. FORSBERG	COLORADO	72	25	66	91	6	94	7	3	7	1	202	12.4
PAVEL BURE	VANCOUVER	82	51	39	90	5	48	13	6	4	1	329	15.5
W. GRETZKY	NY RANGERS	82	23	67	90	11-	28	6	0	4	2	201	11.4
JOHN LECLAIR	PHILADELPHIA	82	51	36	87	30	32	16	0	9	1	303	16.8
Z. PALFFY	NY ISLANDERS	82	45	42	87	2-	34	17	2	5	1	277	16.2
RON FRANCIS	PITTSBURGH	81	25	62	87	12	20	7	0	5	2	189	13.2
T. SELANNE	ANAHEIM	73	52	34	86	12	30	10	1	10	3	268	19.4
JASON ALLISON	BOSTON	81	33	50	83	33	60	5	0	8	2	158	20.9
JOZEF STUMPEL	LOS ANGELES	77	21	58	79	17	53	4	0	2	1	162	13.0
PETER BONDRA	WASHINGTON	76	52	26	78	14	44	11	5	13	2	284	18.3
T. FLEURY	CALGARY	82	27	51	78	0	197	3	2	4	1	282	9.6
ADAM OATES	WASHINGTON	82	18	58	76	6	36	3	2	3	0	121	14.9
R. BRIND'AMOUR	PHILADELPHIA	82	36	38	74	2-	54	10	2	8	0	205	17.6
MATS SUNDIN	TORONTO	82	33	41	74	3-	49	9	1	5	1	219	15.1
MARK RECCHI	MONTREAL	82	32	42	74	11	51	9	1	6	0	216	14.8
TONY AMONTE	CHICAGO	82	31	42	73	21	66	7	3	5	0	296	10.5
ALEXEI YASHIN	OTTAWA	82	33	39	72	6	24	5	0	6	0	291	11.3
BRETT HULL	ST LOUIS	66	27	45	72	1-	26	10	0	6	0	211	12.8
ERIC LINDROS	PHILADELPHIA	63	30	41	71	14	134	10	1	4	0	202	14.9
DOUG WEIGHT	EDMONTON	79	26	44	70	1	69	9	0	4	0	205	12.7
J. NIEUWENDYK	DALLAS	73	39	30	69	16	30	14	0	11	0	203	19.2
S. YZERMAN	DETROIT	75	24	45	69	3	46	6	2	0	2	188	12.8
P. TURGEON	ST LOUIS	60	22	46	68	13	24	6	0	4	0	140	15.7
K. TKACHUK	PHOENIX	69	40	26	66	9	147	11	0	8	1	232	17.2
D. KHRISTICH	BOSTON	82	29	37	66	25	42	13	2	1	0	144	20.1

DEFENCEMEN SCORING LEADERS

PLAYER	TEAM	GP	G	A	PTS	+/-	PIM	PP	SH	GW	GT	S	PCT
N. LIDSTROM	DETROIT	80	17	42	59	22	18	7	1	1	1	205	8.3
S. NIEDERMAYER	NEW JERSEY	81	14	43	57	5	27	11	0	1	0	175	8.0
SERGEI ZUBOV	DALLAS	73	10	47	57	16	16	5	1	2	1	148	6.8
S. DUCHESNE	ST LOUIS	80	14	42	56	9	32	5	1	1	0	153	9.2
LARRY MURPHY	DETROIT	82	11	41	52	35	37	2	1	2	0	129	8.5

S. OZOLINSH	COLORADO	66	13	38	51	12-	65	9	0	2	1	135	9.6
T. NUMMINEN	PHOENIX	82	11	40	51	25	30	6	0	2	0	126	8.7
ROB BLAKE	LOS ANGELES	81	23	27	50	3-	94	11	0	4	0	261	8.8
BRIAN LEETCH	NY RANGERS	76	17	33	50	36-	32	11	0	2	2	230	7.4
AL MACINNIS	ST LOUIS	71	19	30	49	6	80	9	1	2	0	227	8.4
KEVIN HATCHER	PITTSBURGH	74	19	29	48	3-	66	13	1	3	1	169	11.2
RAY BOURQUE	BOSTON	82	13	35	48	2	80	9	0	3	1	264	4.9

INDIVIDUAL ROOKIE SCORING LEADERS

PLAYER	TEAM	GP	G	A	PTS	+/-	PIM	PP	SH	GW	GT	S	PCT
S. SAMSONOV	BOSTON	81	22	25	47	9	8	7	0	3	0	159	13.8
MIKE JOHNSON	TORONTO	82	15	32	47	4-	24	5	0	0	1	143	10.5
PATRIK ELIAS	NEW JERSEY	74	18	19	37	18	28	5	0	6	1	147	12.2
P. MARLEAU	SAN JOSE	74	13	19	32	5	14	1	0	2	0	90	14.4
MARCO STURM	SAN JOSE	74	10	20	30	2-	40	2	0	3	0	118	8.5
M. OHLUND	VANCOUVER	77	7	23	30	3	76	1	0	0	0	172	4.1
DEREK MORRIS	CALGARY	82	9	20	29	1	88	5	1	1	1	120	7.5
PER AXELSSON	BOSTON	82	8	19	27	14-	38	2	0	1	0	144	5.6
MATT CULLEN	ANAHEIM	61	6	21	27	4-	23	2	0	0	0	75	8.0
R. ZEDNIK	WASHINGTON	65	17	9	26	2-	28	2	0	2	0	148	11.5
A. MOROZOV	PITTSBURGH	76	13	13	26	4-	8	2	0	3	0	80	16.3
M. ARVEDSON	OTTAWA	61	11	15	26	2	36	0	1	0	1	90	12.2

INDIVIDUAL LEADERS

GOAL SCORING

NAME	TEAM	GP	G
T. SELANNE	ANAHEIM	73	52
PETER BONDRA	WASHINGTON	76	52
JOHN LECLAIR	PHILADELPHIA	82	51
PAVEL BURE	VANCOUVER	82	51
Z. PALFFY	NY ISLANDERS	82	45
K. TKACHUK	PHOENIX	69	40
J. NIEUWENDYK	DALLAS	73	39
R. BRIND'AMOUR	PHILADELPHIA	82	36
JAROMIR JAGR	PITTSBURGH	77	35
RAY WHITNEY	EDM-FLA	77	33

ASSISTS

NAME	TEAM	GP	A
JAROMIR JAGR	PITTSBURGH	77	67
W. GRETZKY	NY RANGERS	82	67
P. FORSBERG	COLORADO	72	66
RON FRANCIS	PITTSBURGH	81	62
JOZEF STUMPEL	LOS ANGELES	77	58
ADAM OATES	WASHINGTON	82	58
T. FLEURY	CALGARY	82	51
JASON ALLISON	BOSTON	81	50
SERGEI ZUBOV	DALLAS	73	47
P. TURGEON	ST LOUIS	60	46

JASON ALLISON	BOSTON	81	33		BRETT HULL	ST LOUIS	66	45
MATS SUNDIN	TORONTO	82	33		S. YZERMAN	DETROIT	75	45
ALEXEI YASHIN	OTTAWA	82	33		DOUG WEIGHT	EDMONTON	79	44
MARK RECCHI	MONTREAL	82	32		CLIFF RONNING	PHOENIX	80	44
G. COURTNALL	ST LOUIS	79	31		CRAIG JANNEY	PHOENIX	68	43
JEFF FRIESEN	SAN JOSE	79	31		SAKU KOIVU	MONTREAL	69	43
ERIC DAZE	CHICAGO	80	31		S. NIEDERMAYER	NEW JERSEY	81	43
PAT VERBEEK	DALLAS	82	31					
TONY AMONTE	CHICAGO	82	31					

POWER PLAY GOALS

NAME	TEAM	GP	PP
Z. PALFFY	NY ISLANDERS	82	17
JOHN LECLAIR	PHILADELPHIA	82	16
B. SHANAHAN	DETROIT	75	15
STU BARNES	PITTSBURGH	78	15
S. CORSON	MONTREAL	62	14
J. NIEUWENDYK	DALLAS	73	14
KEVIN HATCHER	PITTSBURGH	74	13
D. KHRISTICH	BOSTON	82	13
PAVEL BURE	VANCOUVER	82	13
JOE SAKIC	COLORADO	64	12
RAY WHITNEY	EDM-FLA	77	12

SHORT HAND GOALS

NAME	TEAM	GP	SH
JEFF FRIESEN	SAN JOSE	79	6
PAVEL BURE	VANCOUVER	82	6
MIKE MODANO	DALLAS	52	5
MICHAEL PECA	BUFFALO	61	5
PETER BONDRA	WASHINGTON	76	5
BOB CORKUM	PHOENIX	76	5
A. MOGILNY	VANCOUVER	51	4
R.COURTNALL	LOS ANGELES	58	4
PAVOL DEMITRA	ST LOUIS	61	4
CORY STILLMAN	CALGARY	72	4
MIKE SILLINGER	VAN-PHI	75	4
MARTY MCINNIS	CALGARY	75	4
TOM CHORSKE	NY ISLANDERS	82	4

POWER PLAY ASSISTS

NAME	TEAM	GP	PPA
JAROMIR JAGR	PITTSBURGH	77	31
P. FORSBERG	COLORADO	72	30
SERGEI ZUBOV	DALLAS	73	29
S. OZOLINSH	COLORADO	66	26
N. LIDSTROM	DETROIT	80	26
RON FRANCIS	PITTSBURGH	81	25
DARRYL SYDOR	DALLAS	79	24
S. DUCHESNE	ST LOUIS	80	24
W. GRETZKY	NY RANGERS	82	24
R. REICHEL	NY ISLANDERS	82	24

SHORT HAND ASSISTS

NAME	TEAM	GP	SHA
BRET HEDICAN	VANCOUVER	71	7
T. FLEURY	CALGARY	82	5
MICHAEL PECA	BUFFALO	61	4
STEVE RUCCHIN	ANAHEIM	72	4
OWEN NOLAN	SAN JOSE	75	4
*M. OHLUND	VANCOUVER	77	4
A. CASSELS	CALGARY	81	4
DALE HUNTER	WASHINGTON	82	4
ADAM OATES	WASHINGTON	82	4

POWER PLAY POINTS

NAME	TEAM	GP	PPP
JAROMIR JAGR	PITTSBURGH	77	38
P. FORSBERG	COLORADO	72	37
S. OZOLINSH	COLORADO	66	35
Z. PALFFY	NY ISLANDERS	82	35
S. ZUBOV	DALLAS	73	34
B. LEETCH	NY RANGERS	76	34
N. LIDSTROM	DETROIT	80	33
RON FRANCIS	PITTSBURGH	81	32
R. REICHEL	NY ISLANDERS	82	32
RAY BOURQUE	BOSTON	82	30
W. GRETZKY	NY RANGERS	82	30

SHORT HAND POINTS

NAME	TEAM	GP	SHP
MICHAEL PECA	BUFFALO	61	9
PAVEL BURE	VANCOUVER	82	9
MIKE MODANO	DALLAS	52	7
BRET HEDICAN	VANCOUVER	71	7
JEFF FRIESEN	SAN JOSE	79	7
T. FLEURY	CALGARY	82	7
A. MOGILNY	VANCOUVER	51	6
MARTIN STRAKA	PITTSBURGH	75	6
BOB CORKUM	PHOENIX	76	6
ADAM OATES	WASHINGTON	82	6
TONY AMONTE	CHICAGO	82	6

GAME WINNING GOALS

NAME	TEAM	GP	GW
PETER BONDRA	WASHINGTON	76	13
J. NIEUWENDYK	DALLAS	73	11
T. SELANNE	ANAHEIM	73	10
B. SHANAHAN	DETROIT	75	9
JOHN LECLAIR	PHILADELPHIA	82	9

GAME TYING GOALS

NAME	TEAM	GP	GT
P. LAFONTAINE	NY RANGERS	67	3
TEEMU SELANNE	ANAHEIM	73	3
A. DEADMARSH	COLORADO	73	3
23 PLAYERS WITH TWO			

SHOTS

NAME	TEAM	GP	S
PAVEL BURE	VANCOUVER	82	329
JOHN LECLAIR	PHILADELPHIA	82	303
TONY AMONTE	CHICAGO	82	296
ALEXEI YASHIN	OTTAWA	82	291
PETER BONDRA	WASHINGTON	76	284
T. FLEURY	CALGARY	82	282
Z. PALFFY	NY ISLANDERS	82	277

SHOOTING PERCENTAGE (MIN 82 SHOTS)

NAME	TEAM	GP	G	S	PCTG
MIKE SILLINGER	VAN-PHI	75	21	96	21.9
JASON ALLISON	BOSTON	81	33	158	20.9
D. KHRISTICH	BOSTON	82	29	144	20.1
T. SELANNE	ANAHEIM	73	52	268	19.4

J. NIEUWENDYK	DALLAS	73	39	203	19.2
RAY WHITNEY	EDM-FLA	77	33	175	18.9
GARY ROBERTS	CAROLINA	61	20	106	18.9

PLUS/MINUS

NAME	TEAM	GP	+/-
CHRIS PRONGER	ST LOUIS	81	47
LARRY MURPHY	DETROIT	82	35
JASON ALLISON	BOSTON	81	33
RANDY MCKAY	NEW JERSEY	74	30
JOHN LECLAIR	PHILADELPHIA	82	30
D. ZUBRUS	PHILADELPHIA	69	29
D. SHANNON	BUFFALO	76	26

RECORD OF GOALTENDERS

ALL GOALS AGAINST A TEAM IN ANY GAME ARE CHARGED TO THE GOALTENDER OF THAT GAME FOR PURPOSES OF AWARDING THE BILL JENNINGS TROPHY

WON-LOST-TIED RECORD IS BASED UPON WHICH GOALTENDER WAS PLAYING WHEN THE WINNING OR TYING GOAL WAS SCORED

OVERALL RANKING IS BASED ON GOALS AGAINST AVERAGE, (MINIMUM OF 1360 MINUTES PLAYED)

EMPTY-NET GOALS ARE NOT COUNTED IN PERSONAL AVERAGES BUT ARE INCLUDED IN THE TEAM TOTAL

(GPI) GAMES PLAYED IN, (MINS) MINUTES PLAYED, (AVG) 60 MINUTE AVERAGE
(ENG) EMPTY-NET GOALS AGAINST, (SO) SHUTOUTS, (GA) GOALS AGAINST
(SA) SHOTS AGAINST, (SV %) SAVE PERCENTAGE, (RNK) OVERALL RANKING

RNK	SW#	GOALTENDER	GPI	MINS	AVG	W	L	T	EN	SO	GA	SA	SV %	G	A	PIM
2	30	M. BRODEUR	70	4,128	1.89	43	17	8	4	10	130	1,569	.917	0	3	10
	35	R. SHULMISTRA	1	62	1.94	0	1	0	0	0	2	30	.933	0	0	0
	1	MIKE DUNHAM	15	773	2.25	5	5	3	0	1	29	332	.913	0	1	0
	31	P. SIDORKIEWIC	1	20	3.00	0	0	0	0	0	1	8	.875	0	0	0
N.J TOTALS			82	4,991	2.00	48	23	11	4	11	166	1,943	.915			

	No	Name	GP	Min	GAA	W	L	T			GA		SV%			
	30	*E. FERNANDE	2	69	1.74	1	0	0	0	0	2	35	.943	0	0	0
1	20	ED BELFOUR	61	3,581	1.88	37	12	10	1	9	112	1,335	.916	0	0	18
1		ROMAN TUREK	23	1,324	2.22	11	10	1	3	1	49	496	.901	0	0	2
DAL TOTALS			82	4,986	2.01	49	22	11	4	10	167	1,870	.911			
4	39	DOMINIK HASEK	72	4,220	2.09	33	23	13	3	13	147	2,149	.932	0	2	12
	31	*STEVE SHIELDS	16	785	2.83	3	6	4	0	0	37	408	.909	0	0	17
BUF TOTALS			82	5,019	2.24	36	29	17	3	13	187	2,560	.927			
1		*PETER SKUDRA	17	851	1.83	6	4	3	2	0	26	341	.924	0	1	2
3	35	TOM BARRASSO	63	3542	2.07	31	14	13	8	7	122	1,556	.922	0	2	14
	31	KEN WREGGET	15	611	2.75	3	6	2	2	0	28	293	.904	0	0	6
PIT TOTALS			82	5,022	2.25	40	24	18	12	7	188	2,202	.915			
5	27	RON HEXTALL	46	2,688	2.17	21	17	7	2	4	97	1,089	.911	0	0	10
19	30	GARTH SNOW	29	1,651	2.43	14	9	4	0	1	67	682	.902	0	0	18
32	33	SEAN BURKE	11	632	2.56	7	3	0	0	1	27	311	.913	0	0	0
PHI TOTALS			82	4,988	2.32	42	29	11	2	6	193	2,084	.907			
	35	ROBBIE TALLAS	14	788	1.83	6	3	3	0	1	24	326	.926	0	0	0
11	34	BYRON DAFOE	65	3693	2.24	30	25	9	8	6	138	1602	.914	0	3	2
	30	JIM CAREY	10	496	2.90	3	2	1	0	2	24	225	.893	0	0	0
BOS TOTALS			82	4995	2.33	39	30	13	8	9	194	2161	.910			
	34	*NORM MARACLE	4	178	2.02	2	0	1	0	0	6	63	.905	0	0	0
10	30	CHRIS OSGOOD	64	3807	2.21	33	20	11	5	6	140	1,605	.913	0	0	31
	31	*KEVIN HODSON	21	988	2.67	9	3	3	1	2	44	444	.901	0	0	2
DET TOTALS			82	4,995	2.35	44	23	15	6	9	196	2,118	.907			

CHRIS OSGOOD and KEVIN HODSON shared a shutout vs COL on Apr 1, 1998

	No	Name	GP	Min	GAA	W	L	T			GA		SV%			
9	31	JEFF HACKETT	58	3,441	2.20	21	25	11	3	8	126	1,520	.917	0	0	8
	40	CHRIS TERRERI	21	1,222	2.41	8	10	2	4	2	49	519	.906	0	1	2
	29	ANDREI TREFILOV	6	299	3.41	1	4	0	0	0	17	145	.883	0	0	0
CHI TOTALS			82	4,999	2.39	30	39	13	7	10	199	2,191	.909			
12	31	RON TUGNUTT	42	2,236	2.25	15	14	8	6	3	84	882	.905	0	0	0
13	1	DAMIAN RHODES	50	2,743	2.34	19	19	7	3	5	107	1,148	.907	0	1	0
OTT TOTALS			82	5,002	2.40	34	33	15	9	8	200	2,039	.902			

8	37	OLAF KOLZIG	64	3788	2.20	33	18	10	5	5	139	1729	.920	0	1	12
	30	BILL RANFORD	22	1183	2.79	7	12	2	3	0	55	555	.901	0	1	0
WSH TOTALS			82	4997	2.43	40	30	12	8	5	202	2292	.912			
	1	C. BILLINGTON	23	1,162	2.32	8	7	4	2	1	45	588	.923	0	0	2
14	33	PATRICK ROY	65	3,835	2.39	31	19	13	5	4	153	1,825	.916	0	3	39
COL TOTALS			82	5,017	2.45	39	26	17	7	5	205	2,420	.915			
	30	*RICH PARENT	1	12	.00	0	0	0	0	0	0	1	1.000	0	0	0
7	29	JAMIE MCLENNAN	30	1658	2.17	16	8	2	1	2	60	618	.903	0	0	4
18	31	GRANT FUHR	58	3274	2.53	29	21	6	5	3	138	1354	.898	0	2	6
STL TOTALS			82	4970	2.46	45	29	8	6	5	204	1979	.897			
16	41	J. THIBAULT	47	2,652	2.47	19	15	8	1	2	109	1,109	.902	0	2	0
17	35	ANDY MOOG	42	2,337	2.49	18	17	5	1	3	97	1,024	.905	0	0	4
MTL TOTALS			82	5,009	2.49	37	32	13	2	5	208	2,135	.903			
15	29	MIKE VERNON	62	3,564	2.46	30	22	8	2	5	146	1,401	.896	0	2	24
28	32	KELLY HRUDEY	28	1,360	2.74	4	16	2	4	1	62	600	.897	0	0	2
	30	JASON MUZZATTI	1	27	4.44	0	0	0	0	0	2	13	.846	0	0	0
S.J TOTALS			82	4,973	2.61	34	38	10	6	7	216	2,020	.893			

KELLY HRUDEY and MIKE VERNON shared a shutout vs CGY on Apr 7, 1998

6	37	TREVOR KIDD	47	2,685	2.17	21	21	3	6	3	97	1,238	.922	0	0	2
32	33	SEAN BURKE	25	1,415	2.80	7	11	5	2	1	66	655	.899	0	1	6
	39	PAT JABLONSKI	5	279	3.01	1	4	0	1	0	14	115	.878	0	0	0
36	1	KIRK MCLEAN	8	401	3.29	4	2	0	1	0	22	180	.878	0	1	0
	30	*MICHAEL FOUNTAIN	3	163	3.68	0	3	0	0	0	10	68	.853	0	0	2
CAR TOTALS			82	4,973	2.64	33	41	8	10	4	219	2,266	.903			
	30	BOB ESSENSA	16	825	2.55	6	6	1	2	0	35	404	.913	0	0	0
20	31	CURTIS JOSEPH	71	4,132	2.63	29	31	9	6	8	181	1,901	.905	0	2	4
EDM TOTALS			82	4,980	2.70	35	37	10	8	8	224	2,313	.903			
	1	*JAMIE STORR	17	920	2.22	9	5	1	0	2	34	482	.929	0	0	0
23	35	STEPHANE FISET	60	3,497	2.71	26	25	8	4	2	158	1,728	.909	0	1	8
	31	F. CHABOT	12	554	3.14	3	3	2	0	0	29	267	.891	0	0	0
L.A TOTALS			82	4,990	2.71	38	33	11	4	4	225	2,481	.909			

	#	Player	GP	MINS	GAA	W	L	T	EN	SO	GA	SA	SV%			
	30	WADE FLAHERTY	16	694	1.99	4	4	3	0	3	23	309	.926	0	1	0
21	35	TOMMY SALO	62	3461	2.64	23	29	5	9	4	152	1617	.906	0	1	31
	1	ERIC FICHAUD	17	807	2.97	3	8	3	1	0	40	422	.905	0	0	0
NYI TOTALS			82	4982	2.71	30	41	11	10	8	225	2358	.905			

WADE FLAHERTY and TOMMY SALO shared a shutout vs NYR on Apr 4, 1998

	28	JIM WAITE	17	793	2.12	5	6	1	1	1	28	322	.913	0	0	2
27	35	N. KHABIBULIN	70	4026	2.74	30	28	10	4	4	184	1835	.900	0	2	22
	31	*SCOTT LANGKOW	3	137	4.38	0	1	1	0	0	10	60	.833	0	0	0
PHO TOTALS			82	4985	2.73	35	35	12	5	5	227	2222	.898			

	34	*DAN CLOUTIER	12	551	2.50	4	5	1	0	0	23	248	.907	0	0	19
22	35	MIKE RICHTER	72	4143	2.66	21	31	15	6	0	184	1,888	.903	0	1	2
	30	JASON MUZZATTI	6	313	3.26	0	3	2	1	0	17	156	.891	0	0	10
NYR TOTALS			82	5,028	2.76	25	39	18	7	0	231	2,299	.900			

	31	*M. COUSINEAU	2	17	.00	0	0	0	0	0	0	9	1.000	0	0	0
25	29	FELIX POTVIN	67	3864	2.73	26	33	7	4	5	176	1882	.906	0	0	8
	30	GLENN HEALY	21	1068	2.98	4	10	2	4	0	53	453	.883	0	0	0
TOR TOTALS			82	4970	2.86	30	43	9	8	6	237	2352	.899			

GLENN HEALY and MARCEL COUSINEAU shared a shutout vs S.J on Nov 4, 1997

30	31	RICK TABARACCI	42	2,419	2.88	13	22	6	2	0	116	1,087	.893	0	1	14
33	30	D. ROLOSON	39	2,205	2.99	11	16	8	4	0	110	997	.890	0	4	10
	1	*TYLER MOSS	6	367	3.27	2	3	1	0	0	20	186	.892	0	0	0
CGY TOTALS			82	5,016	3.01	26	41	15	6	0	252	2,276	.889			

29	34	J. VANBIESBROUCK	60	3,451	2.87	18	29	11	4	4	165	1,638	.899	0	3	6
34	30	M. FITZPATRICK	12	640	3.00	2	7	2	0	1	32	265	.879	0	0	2
36	1	KIRK MCLEAN	7	406	3.25	4	2	1	0	0	22	207	.894	0	0	0
	1	*KEVIN WEEKES	11	485	3.96	0	5	1	1	0	32	247	.870	0	0	0
FLA TOTALS			82	5,009	3.07	24	43	15	5	5	256	2,362	.892			

	67	*TOM ASKEY	7	273	2.64	0	1	2	2	0	12	113	.894	0	0	0
31	31	GUY HEBERT	46	2,660	2.93	13	24	6	4	3	130	1,339	.903	0	1	4
35	35	M. SHTALENKOV	40	2,049	3.22	13	18	5	3	1	110	1,031	.893	0	1	0
ANA TOTALS			82	5,007	3.13	26	43	13	9	4	261	2,492	.895			

24	93	DAREN PUPPA	26	1,456	2.72	5	14	6	6	0	66	660	.900	0	0	6
	32	COREY SCHWAB	16	821	2.92	2	9	1	2	1	40	370	.892	0	0	2
34	30	M. FITZPATRICK	34	1,938	3.16	7	24	1	5	1	102	975	.895	0	1	14
	35	*D. WILKINSON	8	311	3.28	2	4	1	1	0	17	148	.885	0	0	0
	1	*ZAC BIERK	13	433	4.16	1	4	1	0	0	30	210	.857	0	0	0
T.B TOTALS			82	4,978	3.24	17	55	10	14	3	269	2,377	.887			

COREY SCHWAB and DEREK WILKINSON shared a shutout vs NYR on Dec 31, 1997

26	32	ARTURS IRBE	41	1,999	2.73	14	11	6	3	2	91	982	.907	0	0	2
19	30	GARTH SNOW	12	504	3.10	3	6	0	0	0	26	262	.901	0	0	4
32	33	SEAN BURKE	16	838	3.51	2	9	4	1	0	49	396	.876	0	1	14
36	1	KIRK MCLEAN	29	1,583	3.68	6	17	4	1	1	97	800	.879	0	0	0
	31	COREY HIRSCH	1	50	6.00	0	0	0	0	0	5	34	.853	0	0	0
VAN TOTALS			82	4,996	3.28	25	43	14	5	3	273	2,479	.890			

GOALTENDING LEADERS (MIN. 26 GPI)

GOALS AGAINST AVERAGE

GOALTENDER	TEAM	GPI	MINS	GA	AVG
ED BELFOUR	DALLAS	61	3581	112	1.88
MARTIN BRODEUR	NEW JERSEY	70	4128	130	1.89
TOM BARRASSO	PITTSBURGH	63	3542	122	2.07
DOMINIK HASEK	BUFFALO	72	4220	147	2.09
RON HEXTALL	PHILADELPHIA	46	2688	97	2.17
TREVOR KIDD	CAROLINA	47	2685	97	2.17
JAMIE MCLENNAN	ST LOUIS	30	1658	60	2.17

WINS

GOALTENDER	TEAM	GPI	MINS	W	L	T
MARTIN BRODEUR	NEW JERSEY	70	4128	43	17	8
ED BELFOUR	DALLAS	61	3581	37	12	10
OLAF KOLZIG	WASHINGTON	64	3788	33	18	10
CHRIS OSGOOD	DETROIT	64	3807	33	20	11
DOMINIK HASEK	BUFFALO	72	4220	33	23	13
TOM BARRASSO	PITTSBURGH	63	3542	31	14	13
PATRICK ROY	COLORADO	65	3835	31	19	13
MIKE VERNON	SAN JOSE	62	3564	30	22	8
BYRON DAFOE	BOSTON	65	3693	30	25	9
N. KHABIBULIN	PHOENIX	70	4026	30	28	10

SAVE PERCENTAGE

GOALTENDER	TEAM	GPI	MINS	GA	SA	SPCT	W	L	T
DOMINIK HASEK	BUFFALO	72	4220	147	2149	.932	33	23	13
TOM BARRASSO	PITTSBURGH	63	3542	122	1556	.922	31	14	13
TREVOR KIDD	CAROLINA	47	2685	97	1238	.922	21	21	3
OLAF KOLZIG	WASHINGTON	64	3788	139	1729	.920	33	18	10
MARTIN BRODEUR	NEW JERSEY	70	4128	130	1569	.917	43	17	8
JEFF HACKETT	CHICAGO	58	3441	126	1520	.917	21	25	11
PATRICK ROY	COLORADO	65	3835	153	1825	.916	31	19	13
ED BELFOUR	DALLAS	61	3581	112	1335	.916	37	12	10

SHUTOUTS

GOALTENDER	TEAM	GPI	MINS	SO	W	L	T
DOMINIK HASEK	BUFFALO	72	4220	13	33	23	13
MARTIN BRODEUR	NEW JERSEY	70	4128	10	43	17	8
ED BELFOUR	DALLAS	61	3581	9	37	12	10
JEFF HACKETT	CHICAGO	58	3441	8	21	25	11
CURTIS JOSEPH	EDMONTON	71	4132	8	29	31	9
TOM BARRASSO	PITTSBURGH	63	3542	7	31	14	13
BYRON DAFOE	BOSTON	65	3693	6	30	25	9
CHRIS OSGOOD	DETROIT	64	3807	6	33	20	11

CONSECUTIVE SCORING STREAKS

GOALS SCORED IN 5 OR MORE CONSECUTIVE GAMES

GM	PLAYER	TEAM	FROM	TO	G
11	TEEMU SELANNE	ANAHEIM	Oct 21	Nov 10	17
7	JOE SAKIC	COLORADO	Oct 07	Oct 22	7
6	JOHN LECLAIR	PHILADELPHIA	Oct 11	Oct 23	8
6	JOHN LECLAIR	PHILADELPHIA	Oct 29	Nov 08	7
6	PETER FORSBERG	COLORADO	Dec 13	Dec 27	7
6	ED OLCZYK	PITTSBURGH	Oct 19	Nov 01	6
6	KEITH PRIMEAU	CAROLINA	Dec 30	Jan 08	6
6	ANDREW BRUNETTE	WASHINGTON	Dec 29	Jan 09	6
5	PETER BONDRA	WASHINGTON	Nov 09	Nov 18	7
5	JOHN LECLAIR	PHILADELPHIA	Dec 27	Jan 08	7
5	PAVEL BURE	VANCOUVER	Nov 22	Dec 01	7
5	PETER BONDRA	WASHINGTON	Jan 21	Jan 31	6
5	RANDY MCKAY	NEW JERSEY	Dec 18	Dec 29	6

5	VALERI KAMENSKY	COLORADO	Mar 11	Mar 21	6
5	KEITH TKACHUK	PHOENIX	Jan 09	Jan 21	6
5	DEREK KING	TORONTO	Jan 01	Jan 10	5
5	JOHN MACLEAN	N.J-S.J	Apr 01	Apr 09	5
5	PAVEL BURE	VANCOUVER	Jan 24	Jan 31	5
5	STEVE HEINZE	BOSTON	Apr 11	Apr 19	5
5	ALEXEI ZHAMNOV	CHICAGO	Dec 28	Jan 05	5
5	*SCOTT FRASER	EDMONTON	Apr 06	Apr 15	5

ASSISTS AWARDED IN 6 OR MORE CONSECUTIVE GAMES

GM	PLAYER	TEAM	FROM	TO	A
8	ADAM OATES	WASHINGTON	Nov 08	Nov 23	10
8	WAYNE GRETZKY	NY RANGERS	Jan 20	Feb 04	9
7	SHAYNE CORSON	MONTREAL	Oct 25	Nov 07	9
7	ROBERT REICHEL	NY ISLANDERS	Oct 03	Oct 19	8
7	JOE SAKIC	COLORADO	Oct 09	Oct 24	8
7	VALERI KAMENSKY	COLORADO	Apr 02	Apr 18	8
7	MIKE MODANO	DALLAS	Oct 25	Nov 07	7
7	KEITH PRIMEAU	CAROLINA	Feb 01	Mar 06	7
6	WAYNE GRETZKY	NY RANGERS	Mar 14	Mar 25	11
6	JAROMIR JAGR	PITTSBURGH	Mar 02	Mar 14	11
6	BRETT HULL	ST LOUIS	Apr 07	Apr 18	9
6	ANDREW BRUNETTE	WASHINGTON	Jan 21	Feb 01	9
6	BRETT HULL	ST LOUIS	Mar 01	Mar 11	8
6	ANSON CARTER	BOSTON	Oct 13	Oct 23	8
6	GREG JOHNSON	PIT-CHI	Mar 15	Mar 25	7
6	CRAIG JANNEY	PHOENIX	Jan 30	Feb 25	6
6	CLAUDE LEMIEUX	COLORADO	Dec 15	Dec 29	6
6	DALLAS DRAKE	PHOENIX	Jan 09	Jan 24	6

POINTS GAINED IN 8 OR MORE CONSECUTIVE GAMES

GM	PLAYER	TEAM	FROM	TO	G	A	PTS
13	ZIGMUND PALFFY	NY ISLANDERS	Feb 01	Mar 18	10	8	18
12	PIERRE TURGEON	ST LOUIS	Mar 26	Apr 19	7	11	18 #
11	TEEMU SELANNE	ANAHEIM	Oct 21	Nov 10	17	2	19
11	PETER BONDRA	WASHINGTON	Nov 08	Nov 29	12	6	18
10	PAVEL BURE	VANCOUVER	Nov 11	Dec 01	8	8	16
10	ANDREW BRUNETTE	WASHINGTON	Jan 13	Feb 07	5	10	15

10	MARK MESSIER	VANCOUVER	Oct 30	Nov 20	5	9	14
9	ZIGMUND PALFFY	NY ISLANDERS	Oct 29	Nov 14	6	7	13
9	CLAUDE LEMIEUX	COLORADO	Dec 15	Jan 03	4	7	11
9	GERMAN TITOV	CALGARY	Dec 01	Dec 18	6	3	9
8	TEEMU SELANNE	ANAHEIM	Jan 21	Feb 07	8	11	19
8	JAROMIR JAGR	PITTSBURGH	Dec 06	Dec 26	7	8	15
8	JOE SAKIC	COLORADO	Oct 07	Oct 24	7	8	15
8	SHAYNE CORSON	MONTREAL	Oct 23	Nov 07	5	9	14
8	ADAM OATES	WASHINGTON	Nov 08	Nov 23	3	10	13
8	JOZEF STUMPEL	LOS ANGELES	Oct 01	Oct 17	5	8	13
8	KEITH PRIMEAU	CAROLINA	Feb 01	Mar 08	5	7	12
8	JOZEF STUMPEL	LOS ANGELES	Jan 10	Jan 31	2	10	12
8	WAYNE GRETZKY	NY RANGERS	Oct 24	Nov 12	3	8	11
8	WAYNE GRETZKY	NY RANGERS	Jan 20	Feb 04	1	9	10

TEAM STREAKS

CONSECUTIVE WINS

GM	TEAM	FROM	TO
8	NEW JERSEY	NOV. 5	NOV. 20
7	ST LOUIS	OCT. 3	OCT. 18
7	MONTREAL	NOV. 1	NOV. 13
7	DALLAS	NOV. 22	DEC. 5
7	NEW JERSEY	FEB. 2	MAR. 2
6	PITTSBURGH	NOV. 20	DEC. 1
6	NEW JERSEY	DEC. 4	DEC. 16
6	EDMONTON	JAN. 7	JAN. 20
6	ST LOUIS	FEB. 28	MAR. 9
6	DETROIT	MAR. 29	APR. 11
5	BOSTON	OCT. 13	OCT. 21
5	CHICAGO	OCT. 29	NOV. 8
5	COLORADO	NOV. 28	DEC. 6
5	BOSTON	DEC. 3	DEC. 15
5	DETROIT	DEC. 19	DEC. 27
5	PHOENIX	DEC. 26	JAN. 3
5	DALLAS	JAN. 12	JAN. 26
5	COLORADO	FEB. 2	FEB. 26
5	DALLAS	FEB. 2	FEB. 28

| 5 | ST LOUIS | MAR. 26 | APR.   4 |
| 5 | DALLAS | APR. 6 | APR. 15 |

CONSECUTIVE UNDEFEATED

GM	TEAM	W	T	FROM	TO
13	BUFFALO	7	6	JAN. 21	MAR. 2
13	NEW JERSEY	9	4	JAN. 31	MAR. 12
10	COLORADO	6	4	DEC. 13	JAN. 3
10	DALLAS	7	3	DEC. 15	JAN. 5
8	ST LOUIS	7	1	OCT. 3	OCT. 20
8	NEW JERSEY	8	0	NOV. 5	NOV. 20
8	PITTSBURGH	7	1	NOV. 15	DEC. 1
8	PHILADELPHIA	6	2	DEC. 5	DEC. 23
8	DETROIT	6	2	DEC. 17	DEC. 31
7	COLORADO	5	2	OCT. 1	OCT. 15
7	MONTREAL	7	0	NOV. 1	NOV. 13
7	DALLAS	7	0	NOV. 22	DEC. 5
7	NEW JERSEY	6	1	DEC. 4	DEC. 18
7	SAN JOSE	5	2	DEC. 4	DEC. 21
7	BOSTON	4	3	DEC. 31	JAN. 14
7	LOS ANGELES	6	1	JAN. 12	JAN. 31
7	WASHINGTON	5	2	JAN. 13	JAN. 31
7	PITTSBURGH	5	2	JAN. 20	JAN. 31
7	SAN JOSE	4	3	APR. 1	APR. 15

CONSECUTIVE HOME WINS

GM	TEAM	FROM	TO
8	WASHINGTON	MAR. 7	APR. 4
7	ST LOUIS	OCT. 3	OCT. 25
7	DALLAS	NOV. 19	DEC. 10
6	LOS ANGELES	JAN. 12	FEB. 5
6	ST LOUIS	JAN. 29	MAR. 7
6	DALLAS	MAR. 29	APR. 18
5	NEW JERSEY	DEC. 6	DEC. 26
5	WASHINGTON	JAN. 6	JAN. 25
5	DALLAS	JAN. 21	FEB. 28
5	COLORADO	JAN. 26	FEB. 26
5	PITTSBURGH	MAR. 7	MAR. 21

5	ST LOUIS	MAR. 26	APR. 9
5	DETROIT	MAR. 29	APR. 11
5	EDMONTON	MAR. 30	APR. 18

CONSECUTIVE HOME TIES - MINIMUM 3 GAMES

GM	TEAM	FROM	TO
5	BUFFALO	JAN. 27	FEB. 25

CONSECUTIVE HOME UNDEFEATED - MINIMUM 5 GAMES

GM	TEAM	W	T	FROM	TO
11	WASHINGTON	10	1	MAR. 7	APR. 19 #
10	BUFFALO	4	6	DEC. 31	FEB. 25
10	PITTSBURGH	6	4	FEB. 4	MAR. 29
9	ST LOUIS	8	1	OCT. 3	NOV. 1
9	DETROIT	7	2	MAR. 12	APR. 11 #
8	COLORADO	4	4	OCT. 1	NOV. 1
8	DALLAS	7	1	NOV. 12	DEC. 10
8	TAMPA BAY	4	4	NOV. 19	DEC. 22
8	COLORADO	5	3	DEC. 2	DEC. 31
8	PHILADELPHIA	6	2	DEC. 11	JAN. 26
8	NEW JERSEY	7	1	FEB. 4	MAR. 24
8	OTTAWA	5	3	FEB. 5	MAR. 20
8	PHILADELPHIA	6	2	MAR. 5	MAR. 22
7	ST LOUIS	6	1	JAN. 22	MAR. 7
7	CALGARY	6	1	FEB. 5	MAR. 22

CONSECUTIVE ROAD WINS - MINIMUM 3 GAMES

GM	TEAM	FROM	TO
6	DETROIT	OCT. 1	OCT. 26
6	BOSTON	OCT. 13	NOV. 2
5	MONTREAL	OCT. 25	NOV. 13
5	NEW JERSEY	OCT. 27	NOV. 15
5	PITTSBURGH	NOV. 15	DEC. 10
5	CHICAGO	DEC. 20	JAN. 14
5	MONTREAL	DEC. 31	JAN. 12
5	CAROLINA	MAR. 23	APR. 6
5	OTTAWA	APR. 3	APR. 19 #

CONSECUTIVE ROAD UNDEFEATED - MINIMUM 5 GAMES

GM	TEAM	W	T	FROM	TO
10	MONTREAL	8	2	DEC. 27	FEB. 1
8	NEW JERSEY	5	3	JAN. 31	MAR. 12
8	BUFFALO	6	2	FEB. 1	MAR. 10
7	PITTSBURGH	5	2	NOV. 15	DEC. 19
7	BOSTON	4	3	FEB. 1	MAR. 21
6	DETROIT	6	0	OCT. 1	OCT. 26
6	BOSTON	6	0	OCT. 13	NOV. 2
6	FLORIDA	4	2	OCT. 23	NOV. 30
6	CHICAGO	5	1	DEC. 17	JAN. 14
6	DALLAS	5	1	DEC. 18	JAN. 5
6	PITTSBURGH	3	3	JAN. 22	FEB. 25
6	FLORIDA	3	3	MAR. 28	APR. 18 #
6	OTTAWA	5	1	MAR. 29	APR. 19 #